Guru Guru Pon-Chan

6

Satomi Ikezawa

Translated by Doug Varenas

Adapted by Nunzio DeFilippis and Christina Weir

Lettering and touchup by Steve Palmer

Published in the United Kingdom by Tanoshimi in 2006

1 3 5 7 9 10 8 6 4 2

First published in 1999 Japan by Kodansha Ltd., Tokyo

Published by arrangement with Kodansha Ltd., Tokyo and with Del Rey,
an imprint of Random House Inc., New York

Tanoshimi
The Random House Group Limited
20 Vauxhall Bridge Road, London, SW1V 2SA

www.tanoshimi.tv
www.randomhouse.co.uk

Addresses for companies within The Random House Group Limited can be found at:
www.randomhouse.co.uk

Random House Group Limited Reg. No. 954009

A CIP catalogue record for this book is available from the British Library

ISBN 9780099504825 (from Jan 2007)
ISBN 0 09 950482 5

Papers used by Random House
are natural, recyclable products made from wood grown in sustainable forests.
The manufacturing processes conform to the environmental regulations of the country of origin

Printed and bound in Germany by GGP Media GmbH, Pößneck

Translated by Doug Varenas
Adapted by Nunzio DeFilippis and Christina Weir
Lettering and touchup by Steve Palmer

A Word from the Author

♡ I went to the beach with my Pon-Chan and Guts-Chan. There weren't many people, and I let them loose to play. When I'd throw a ball into the ocean, they boldly splashed in to get it. Their faces covered with sand, they were cheerful and having fun. Early the next day after we came back, they pooped out a sand dookie that was something to behold (ha ha!).

Satomi Ikezawa

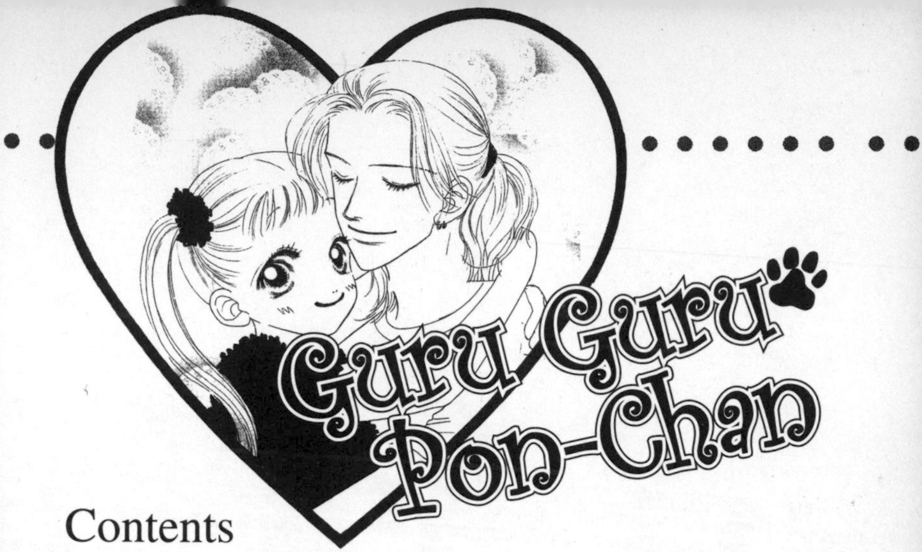
Guru Guru Pon-Chan

Contents

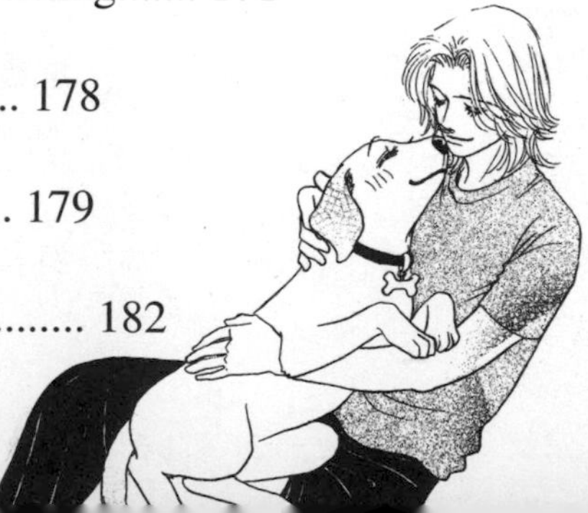

Honorifics

Throughout the Tanoshimi Manga books, you will find Japanese honorifics left intact in the translations. For those not familiar with how the Japanese use honorifics, and more important, how they differ from English honorifics, we present this brief overview.

Politeness has always been a critical facet of Japanese culture. Ever since the feudal era, when Japan was a highly stratified society, use of honorifics—which can be defined as polite speech that indicates relationship or status—has played an essential role in the Japanese language. When addressing someone in Japanese, an honorific usually takes the form of a suffix attached to one's name (example: "Asuna-san"), or as a title at the end of one's name or in place of the name itself (example: "Negi-sensei," or simply "Sensei!").

Honorifics can be expressions of respect or endearment. In the context of manga and anime, honorifics give insight into the nature of the relationship between characters. Many English translations leave out these important honorifics, and therefore distort the feel of the original Japanese. Because Japanese honorifics contain nuances that English honorifics lack, it is our policy at Tanoshimi not to translate them. Here, instead, is a guide to some of the honorifics you may encounter in Tanoshimi Manga.

-san: This is the most common honorific, and is equivalent to Mr., Miss, Ms., Mrs. It is the all-purpose honorific and can be used in any situation where politeness is required.

-sama: This is one level higher than "-san." It is used to confer great respect.

-dono: This comes from the word "tono," which means "lord." It is an even higher level than "-sama," and confers utmost respect.

-kun: This suffix is used at the end of boys' names to express familiarity or endearment. It is also sometimes used by men amongst friends, or when addressing someone younger or of a lower station.

-chan: This is used to express endearment, mostly towards girls. It is also used for little boys, pets, and even among lovers. It gives a sense of childish cuteness.

Bozu: This is an informal way to refer to a boy, similar to the English term "kid".

Sempai/Senpai: This title suggests that the addressee is one's "senior" in a group or organization. It is most often used in a school setting, where underclassmen refer to their upperclassmen as "sempai." It can also be used in the workplace, such as when a newer employee addresses an employee who has seniority in the company.

Kohai: This is the opposite of "sempai," and is used towards underclassmen in school or newcomers in the workplace. It connotes that the addressee is of a lower station.

Sensei: Literally meaning "one who has come before," this title is used for teachers, doctors, or masters of any profession or art.

[blank]: This is usually forgotten in these lists, but it is perhaps the most significant difference between Japanese and English. The lack of honorific means that the speaker has permission to address the person in a very intimate way. Usually, only family, spouses, or very close friends have this kind of permission. Known as *yobisute*, it can be gratifying when someone who has earned the intimacy starts to call one by one's name without an honorific. But when that intimacy hasn't been earned, it can be very insulting.

Guru Guru Pon-Chan

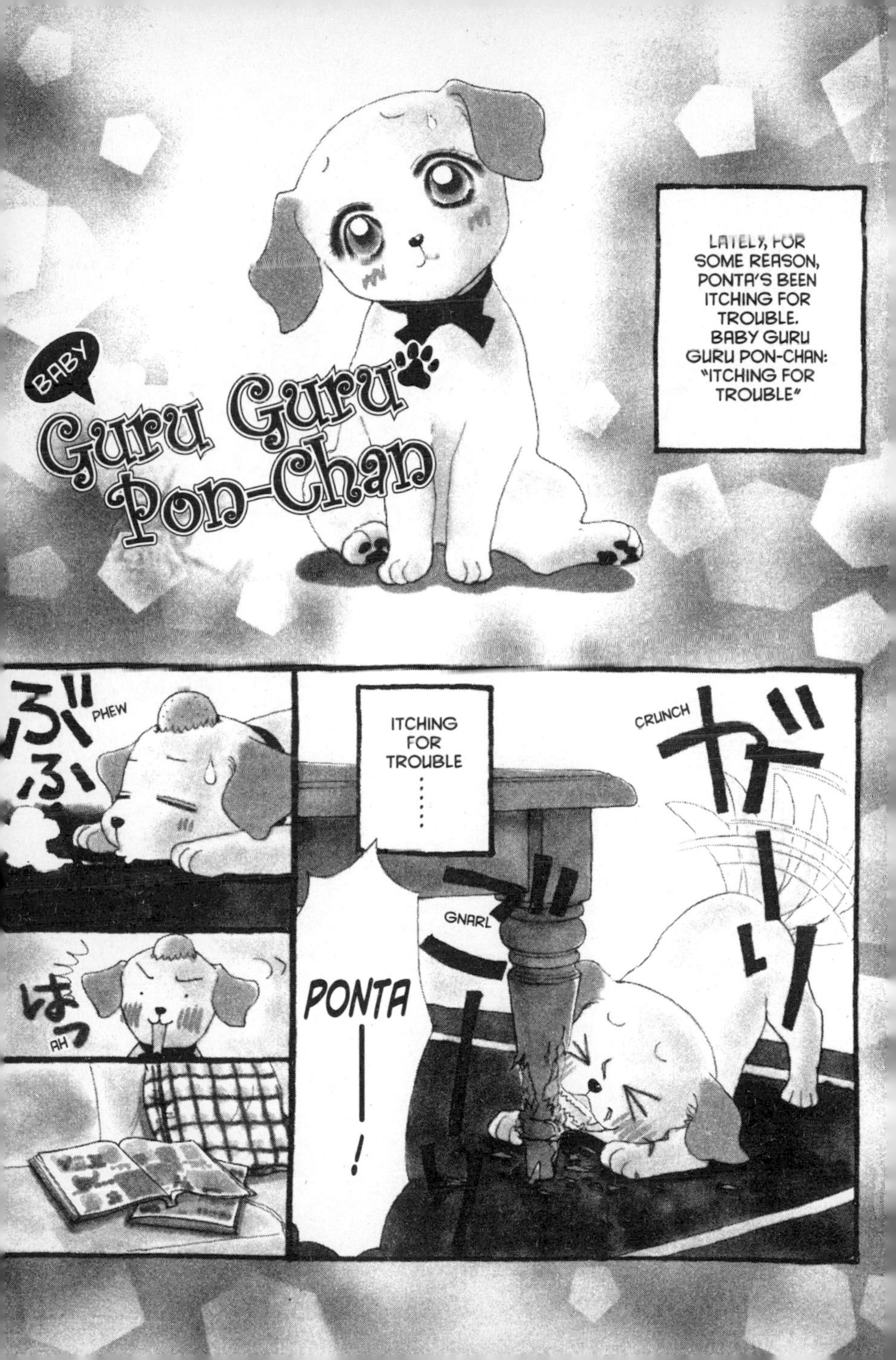
BABY
Guru Guru Pon-Chan
LATELY, FOR SOME REASON, PONTA'S BEEN ITCHING FOR TROUBLE. BABY GURU GURU PON-CHAN: "ITCHING FOR TROUBLE"
CRUNCH
ITCHING FOR TROUBLE ......
GNARL
PONTA ——!
PHEW
AH

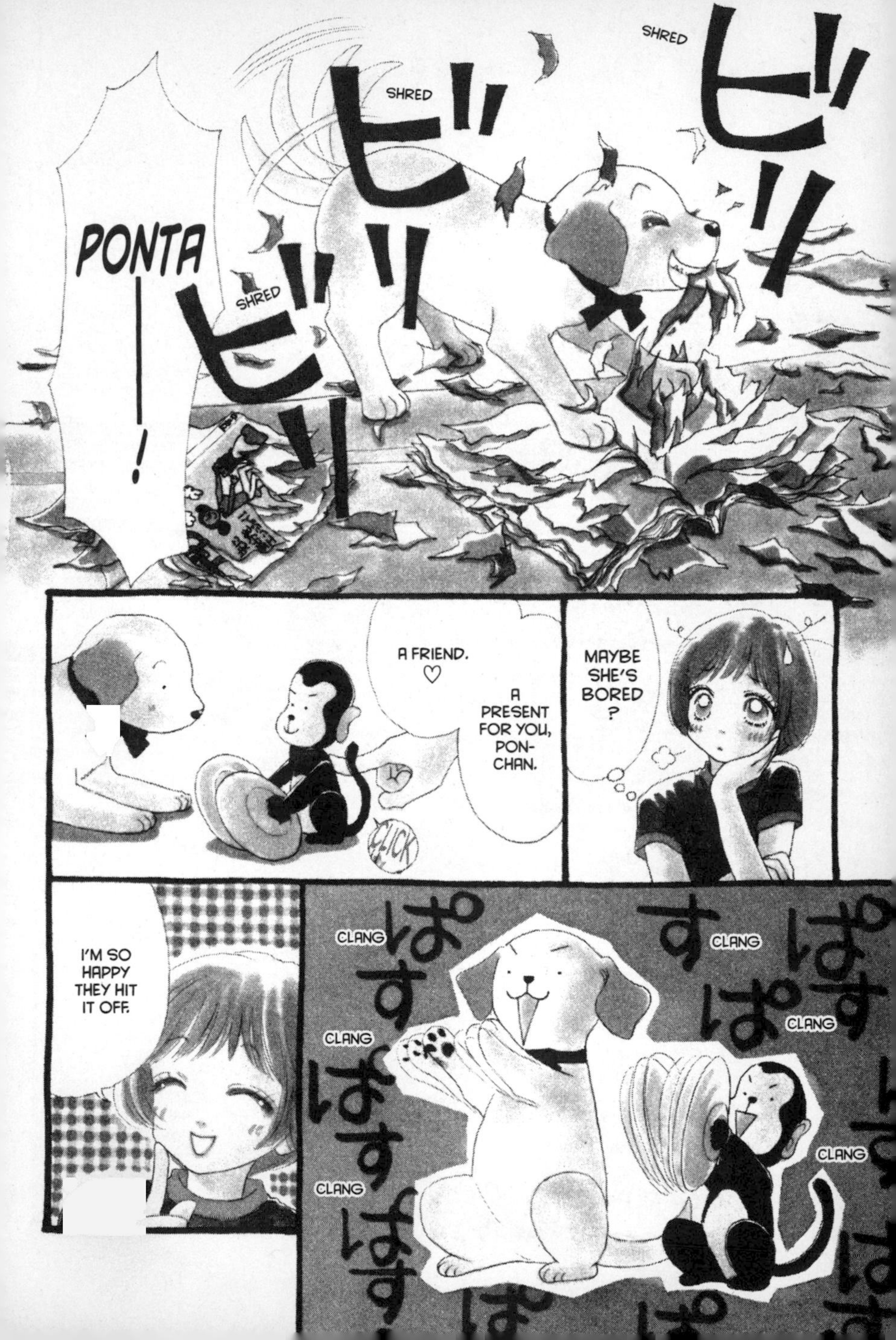
SHRED
ビリ
SHRED
ビリ
SHRED
ビリ
PONTA—!
MAYBE SHE'S BORED?
A FRIEND. ♡
A PRESENT FOR YOU, PON-CHAN.
CLICK
CLANG
CLANG
CLANG
CLANG
CLANG
CLANG
I'M SO HAPPY THEY HIT IT OFF.

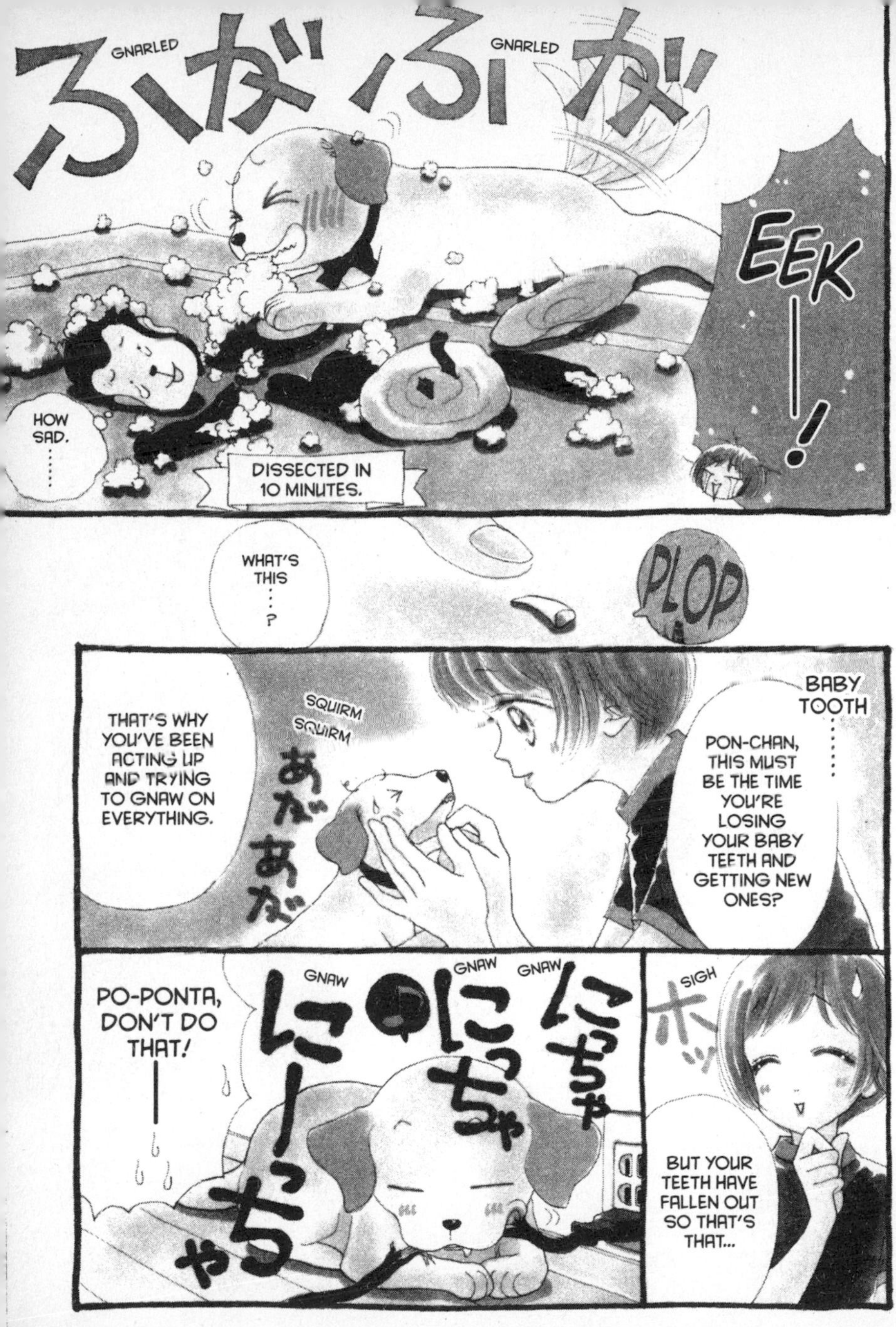
GNARLED
GNARLED
ふがふが
EEK——!
DISSECTED IN 10 MINUTES.
HOW SAD. ......
PLOP
WHAT'S THIS ....?
BABY TOOTH ......
PON-CHAN, THIS MUST BE THE TIME YOU'RE LOSING YOUR BABY TEETH AND GETTING NEW ONES?
SQUIRM SQUIRM
THAT'S WHY YOU'VE BEEN ACTING UP AND TRYING TO GNAW ON EVERYTHING.
SIGH
BUT YOUR TEETH HAVE FALLEN OUT SO THAT'S THAT...
GNAW GNAW GNAW
PO-PONTA, DON'T DO THAT!——

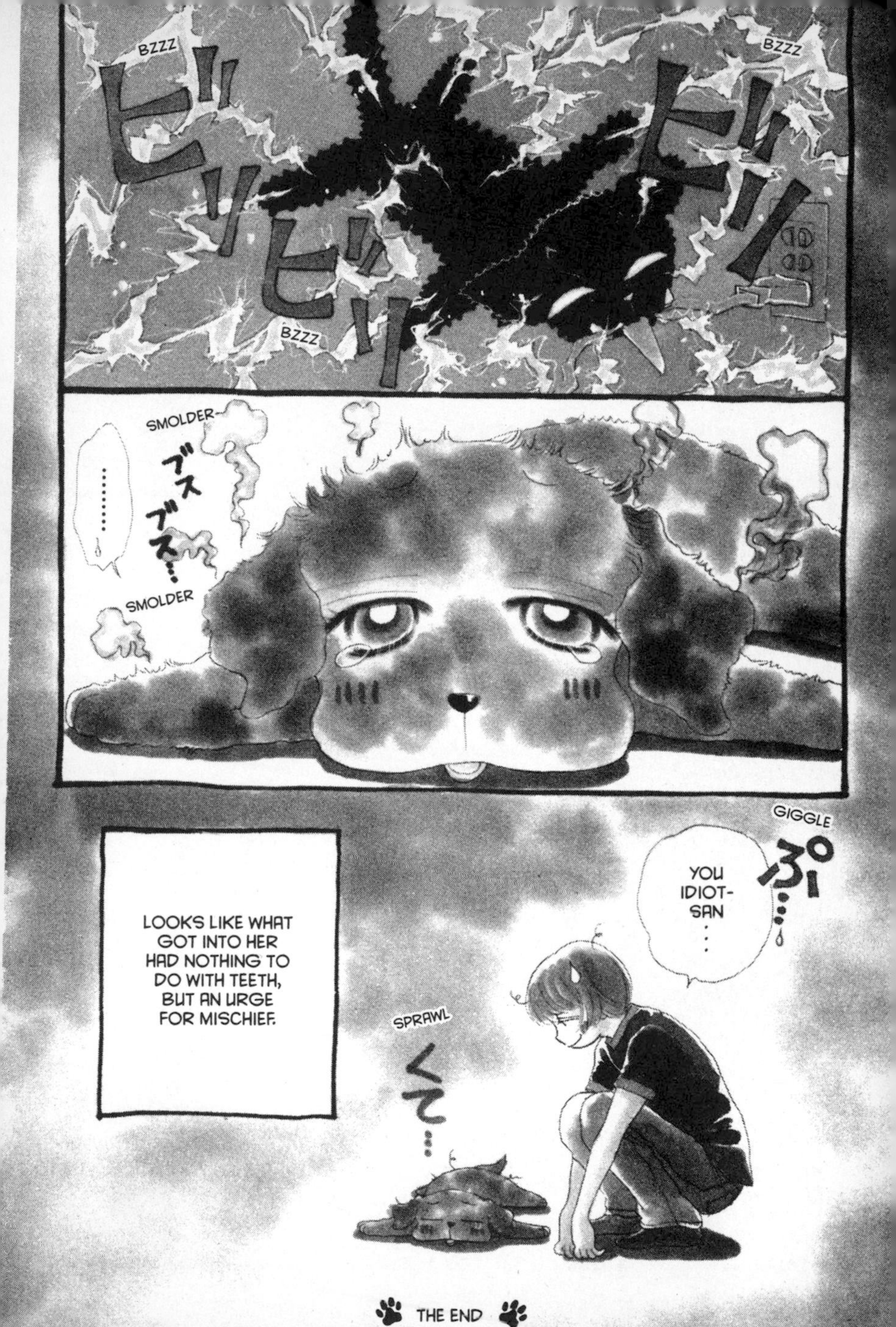
BZZZ
BZZZ
BZZZ
SMOLDER-
ブスブス…
SMOLDER
……
GIGGLE
ぷ…
YOU IDIOT-SAN . . .
SPRAWL
くて…
LOOKS LIKE WHAT GOT INTO HER HAD NOTHING TO DO WITH TEETH, BUT AN URGE FOR MISCHIEF.

THE END

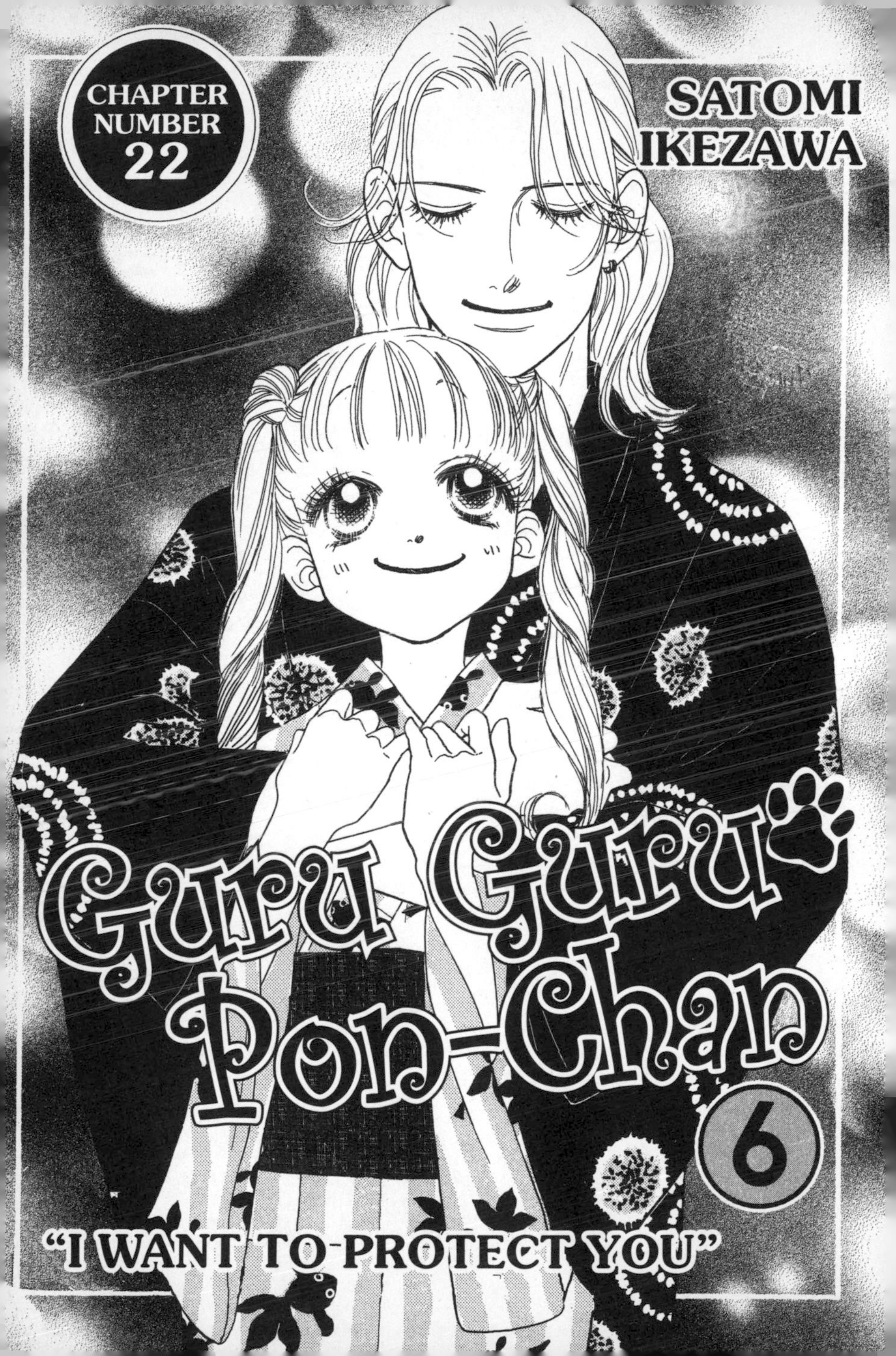
CHAPTER NUMBER 22
SATOMI IKEZAWA
Guru Guru Pon-Chan
6
"I WANT TO PROTECT YOU"

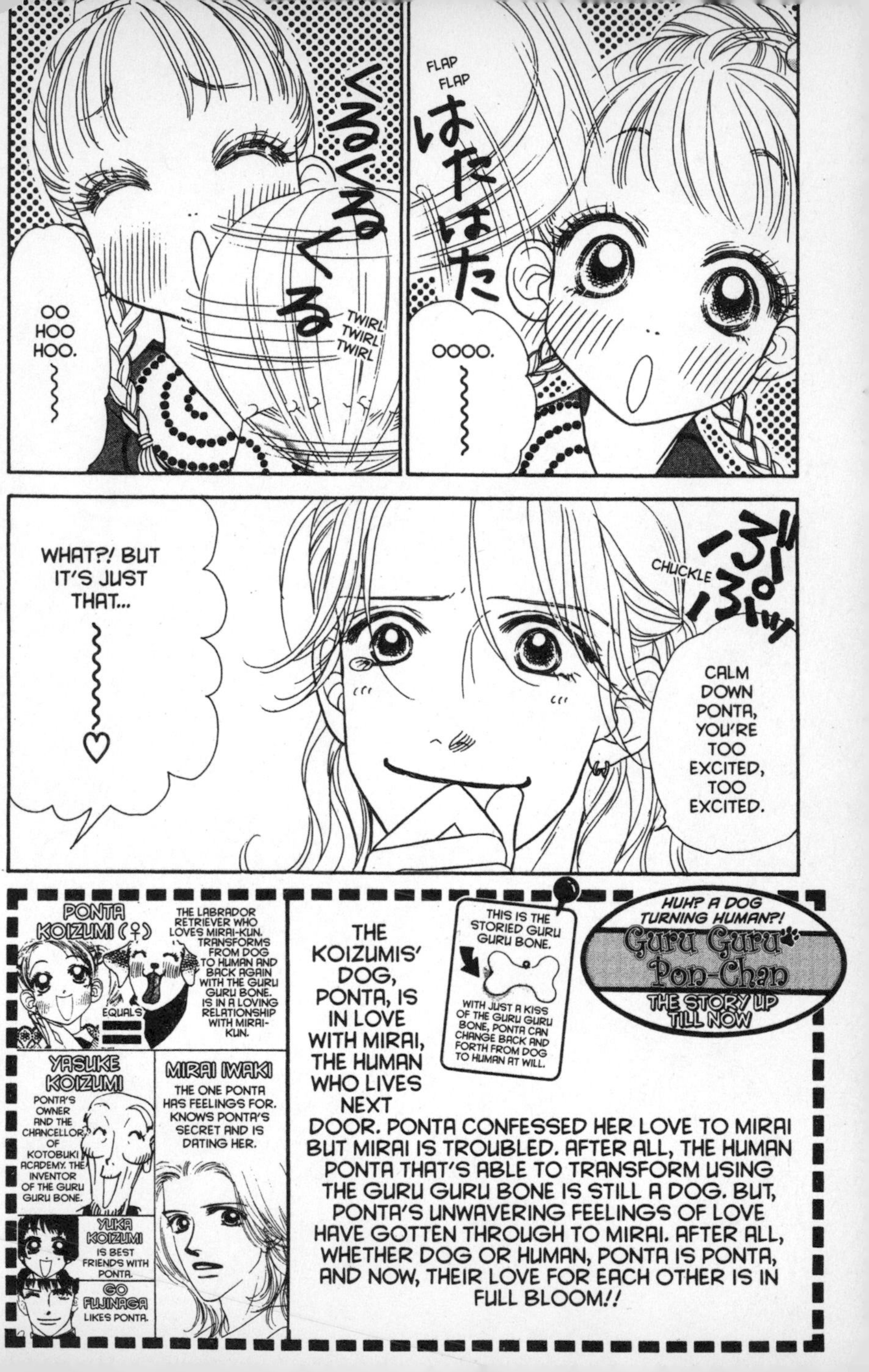
FLAP FLAP
はたはた
OOOO.
~
くるくるくる
TWIRL TWIRL TWIRL
OO HOO HOO.
~
ぷぷっ
CHUCKLE
CALM DOWN PONTA, YOU'RE TOO EXCITED, TOO EXCITED.
WHAT?! BUT IT'S JUST THAT...
~♡

HUH? A DOG TURNING HUMAN?!

Guru Guru Pon-Chan

THE STORY UP TILL NOW

THE KOIZUMIS' DOG, PONTA, IS IN LOVE WITH MIRAI, THE HUMAN WHO LIVES NEXT DOOR. PONTA CONFESSED HER LOVE TO MIRAI BUT MIRAI IS TROUBLED. AFTER ALL, THE HUMAN PONTA THAT'S ABLE TO TRANSFORM USING THE GURU GURU BONE IS STILL A DOG. BUT, PONTA'S UNWAVERING FEELINGS OF LOVE HAVE GOTTEN THROUGH TO MIRAI. AFTER ALL, WHETHER DOG OR HUMAN, PONTA IS PONTA, AND NOW, THEIR LOVE FOR EACH OTHER IS IN FULL BLOOM!!

THIS IS THE STORIED GURU GURU BONE.

WITH JUST A KISS OF THE GURU GURU BONE, PONTA CAN CHANGE BACK AND FORTH FROM DOG TO HUMAN AT WILL.

PONTA KOIZUMI (♀) THE LABRADOR RETRIEVER WHO LOVES MIRAI-KUN. TRANSFORMS FROM DOG TO HUMAN AND BACK AGAIN WITH THE GURU GURU BONE. IS IN A LOVING RELATIONSHIP WITH MIRAI-KUN.

EQUALS

MIRAI IWAKI THE ONE PONTA HAS FEELINGS FOR. KNOWS PONTA'S SECRET AND IS DATING HER.

YASUKE KOIZUMI PONTA'S OWNER AND THE CHANCELLOR OF KOTOBUKI ACADEMY. THE INVENTOR OF THE GURU GURU BONE.

YUKA KOIZUMI IS BEST FRIENDS WITH PONTA.

GO FUJINAGA LIKES PONTA.

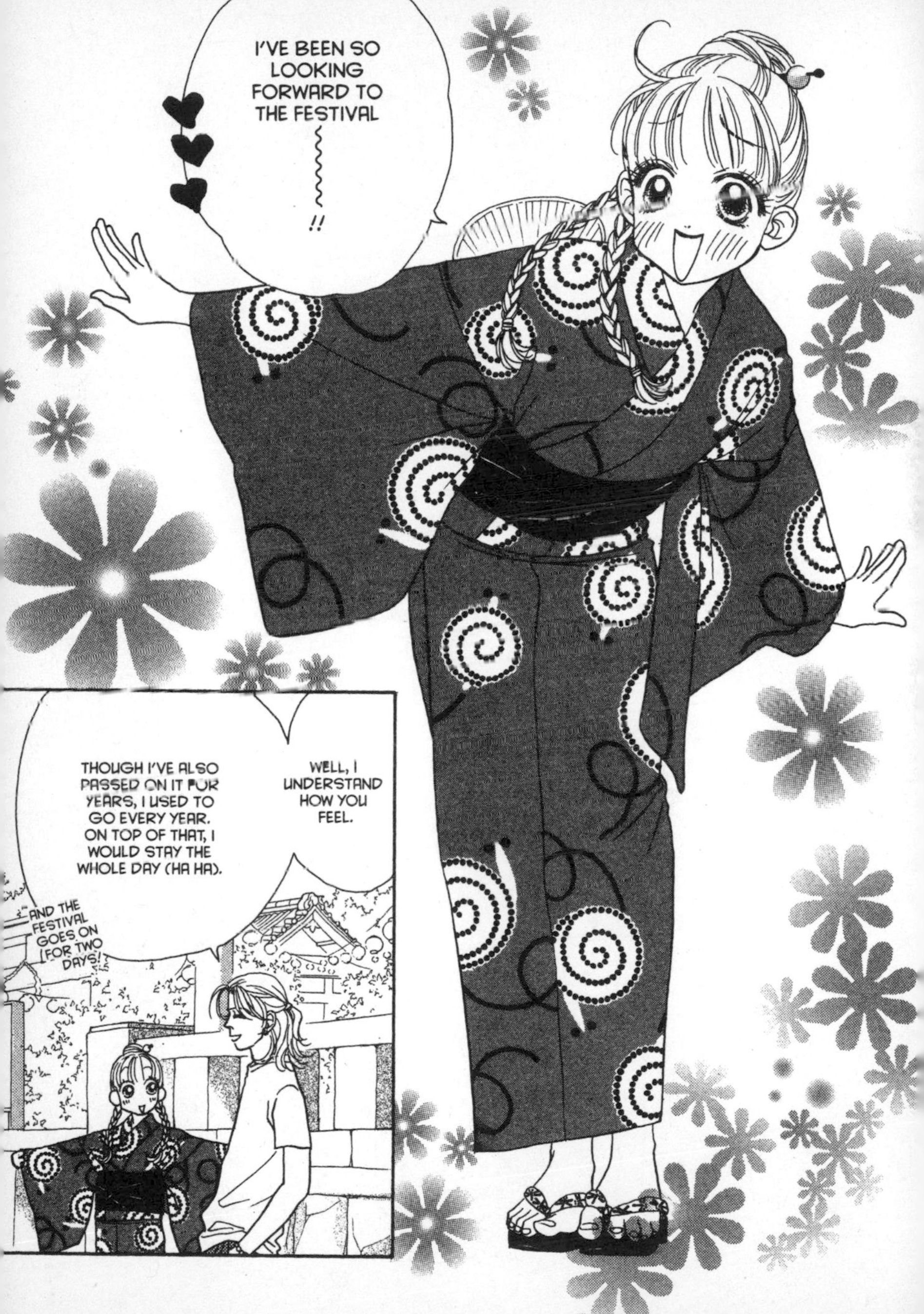
I'VE BEEN SO LOOKING FORWARD TO THE FESTIVAL ~~~~~~!!
WELL, I UNDERSTAND HOW YOU FEEL.
THOUGH I'VE ALSO PASSED ON IT FOR YEARS, I USED TO GO EVERY YEAR. ON TOP OF THAT, I WOULD STAY THE WHOLE DAY (HA HA).
AND THE FESTIVAL GOES ON FOR TWO DAYS!

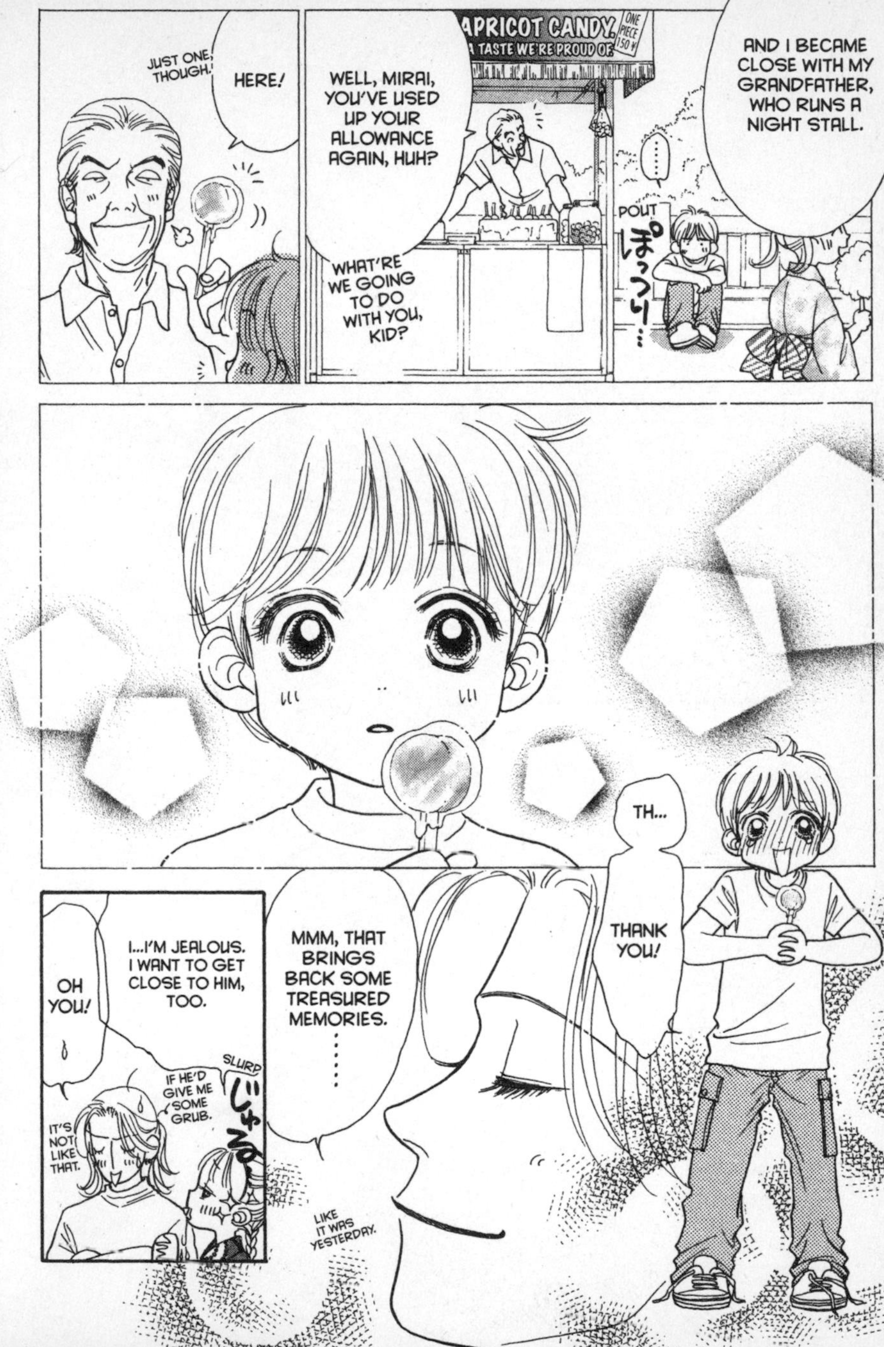
AND I BECAME CLOSE WITH MY GRANDFATHER, WHO RUNS A NIGHT STALL.
......
POUT
ぽっつり…
APRICOT CANDY.
A TASTE WE'RE PROUD OF.
ONE PIECE 150¥
WELL, MIRAI, YOU'VE USED UP YOUR ALLOWANCE AGAIN, HUH?
WHAT'RE WE GOING TO DO WITH YOU, KID?
HERE!
JUST ONE, THOUGH!
TH...
THANK YOU!
MMM, THAT BRINGS BACK SOME TREASURED MEMORIES.
......
LIKE IT WAS YESTERDAY.
I...I'M JEALOUS. I WANT TO GET CLOSE TO HIM, TOO.
OH YOU!
SLURP
じゅるっ
IF HE'D GIVE ME SOME GRUB.
IT'S NOT LIKE THAT.

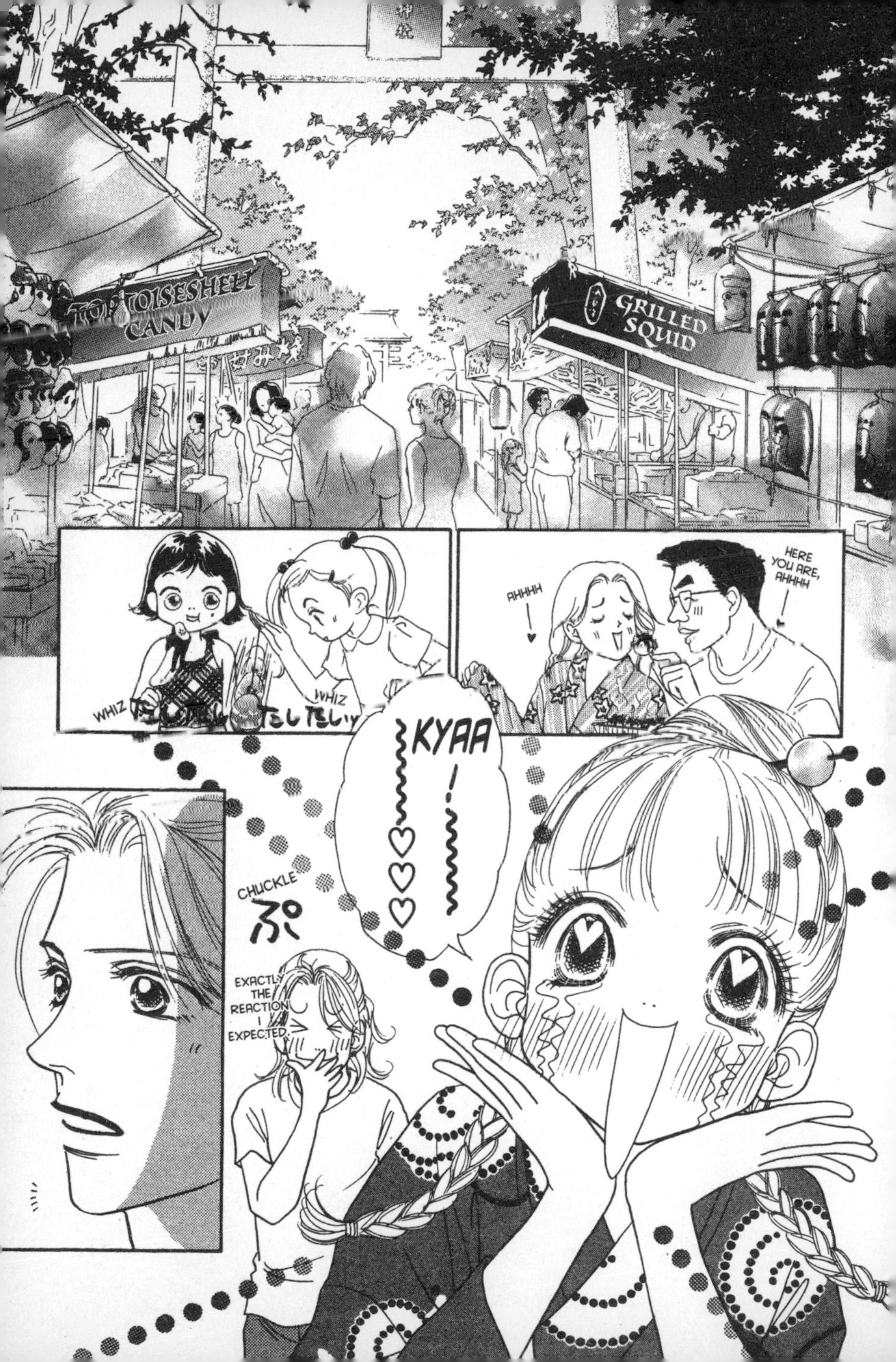
GRILLED SQUID
TORTOISESHELL CANDY
HERE YOU ARE, AHHHH
AHHHH
WHIZ
WHIZ
KYAA!
CHUCKLE
ぷ
EXACTLY THE REACTION I EXPECTED.

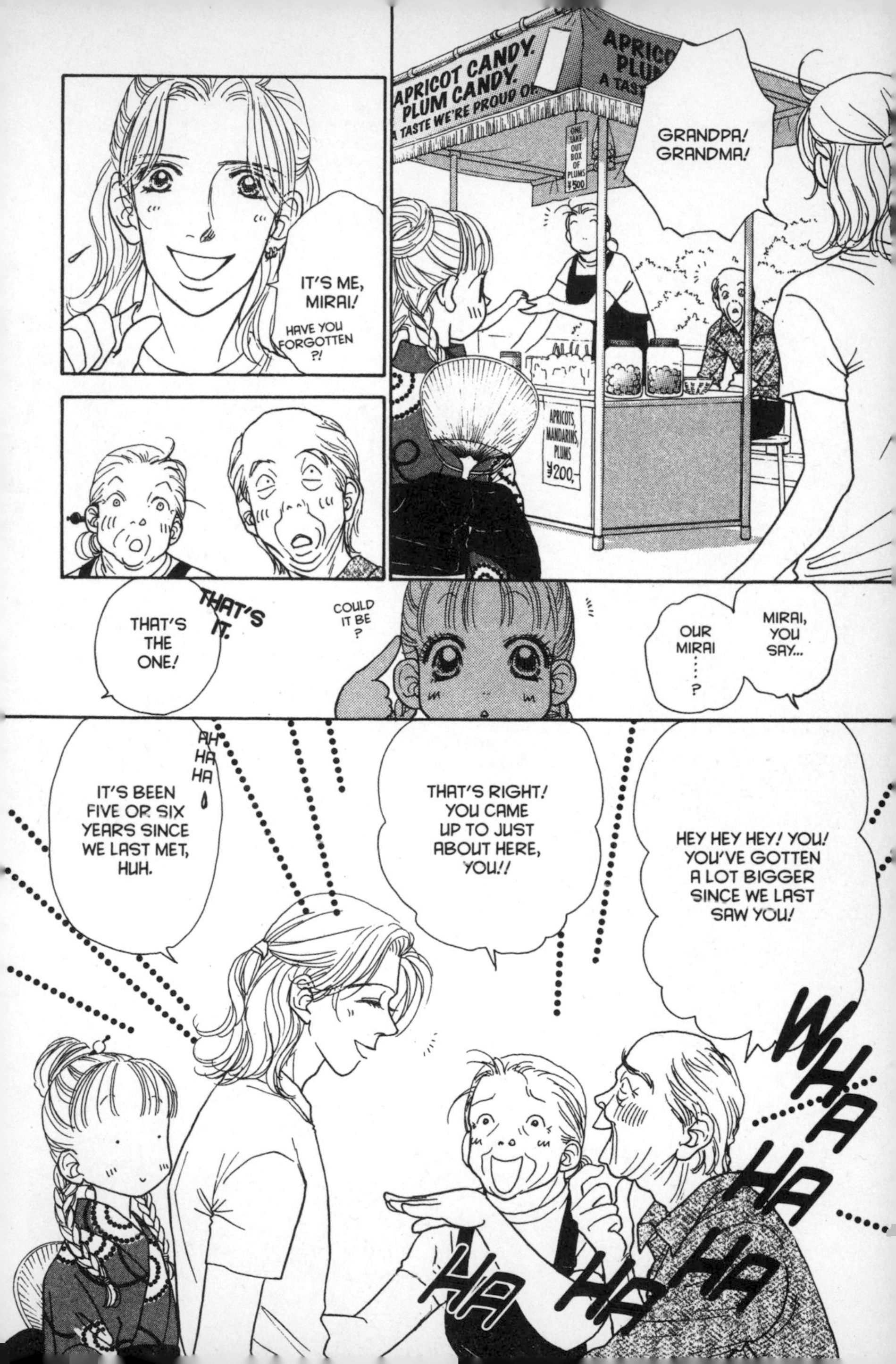
APRICOT CANDY. PLUM CANDY. A TASTE WE'RE PROUD OF.
ONE TAKE-OUT BOX OF PLUMS ¥500
APRICOTS, MANDARINS, PLUMS ¥200,-
GRANDPA! GRANDMA!
IT'S ME, MIRAI!
HAVE YOU FORGOTTEN ?!
MIRAI, YOU SAY...
OUR MIRAI .....?
COULD IT BE ?
THAT'S IT.
THAT'S THE ONE!
HEY HEY HEY! YOU! YOU'VE GOTTEN A LOT BIGGER SINCE WE LAST SAW YOU!
WHA HA HA HA
THAT'S RIGHT! YOU CAME UP TO JUST ABOUT HERE, YOU!!
AH HA HA
IT'S BEEN FIVE OR SIX YEARS SINCE WE LAST MET, HUH.
HA HA HA

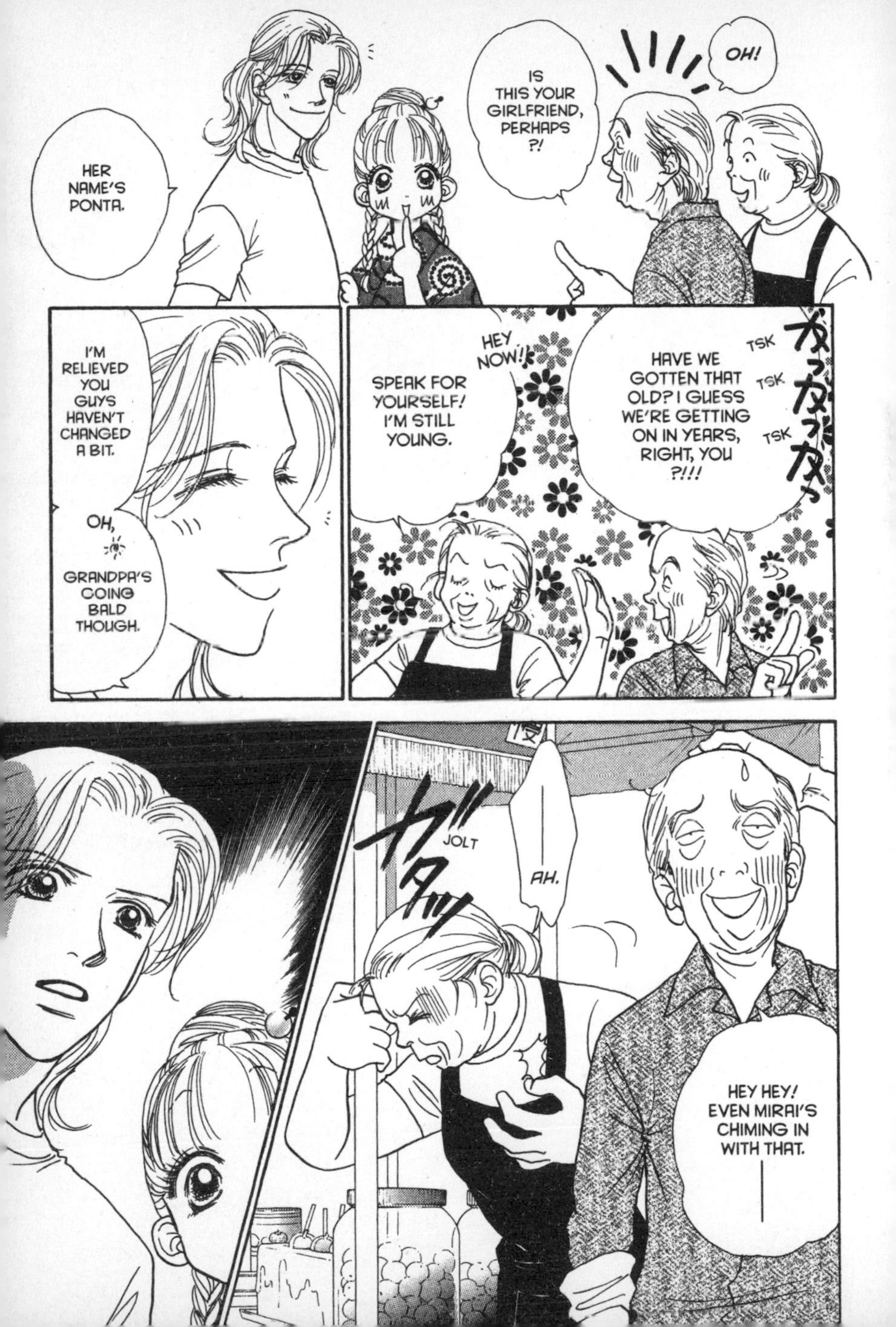
OH!
IS THIS YOUR GIRLFRIEND, PERHAPS?!
HER NAME'S PONTA.
TSK TSK TSK
HAVE WE GOTTEN THAT OLD? I GUESS WE'RE GETTING ON IN YEARS, RIGHT, YOU?!!!
HEY NOW!!
SPEAK FOR YOURSELF! I'M STILL YOUNG.
I'M RELIEVED YOU GUYS HAVEN'T CHANGED A BIT.
OH, GRANDPA'S GOING BALD THOUGH.
HEY HEY! EVEN MIRAI'S CHIMING IN WITH THAT.
AH.
JOLT

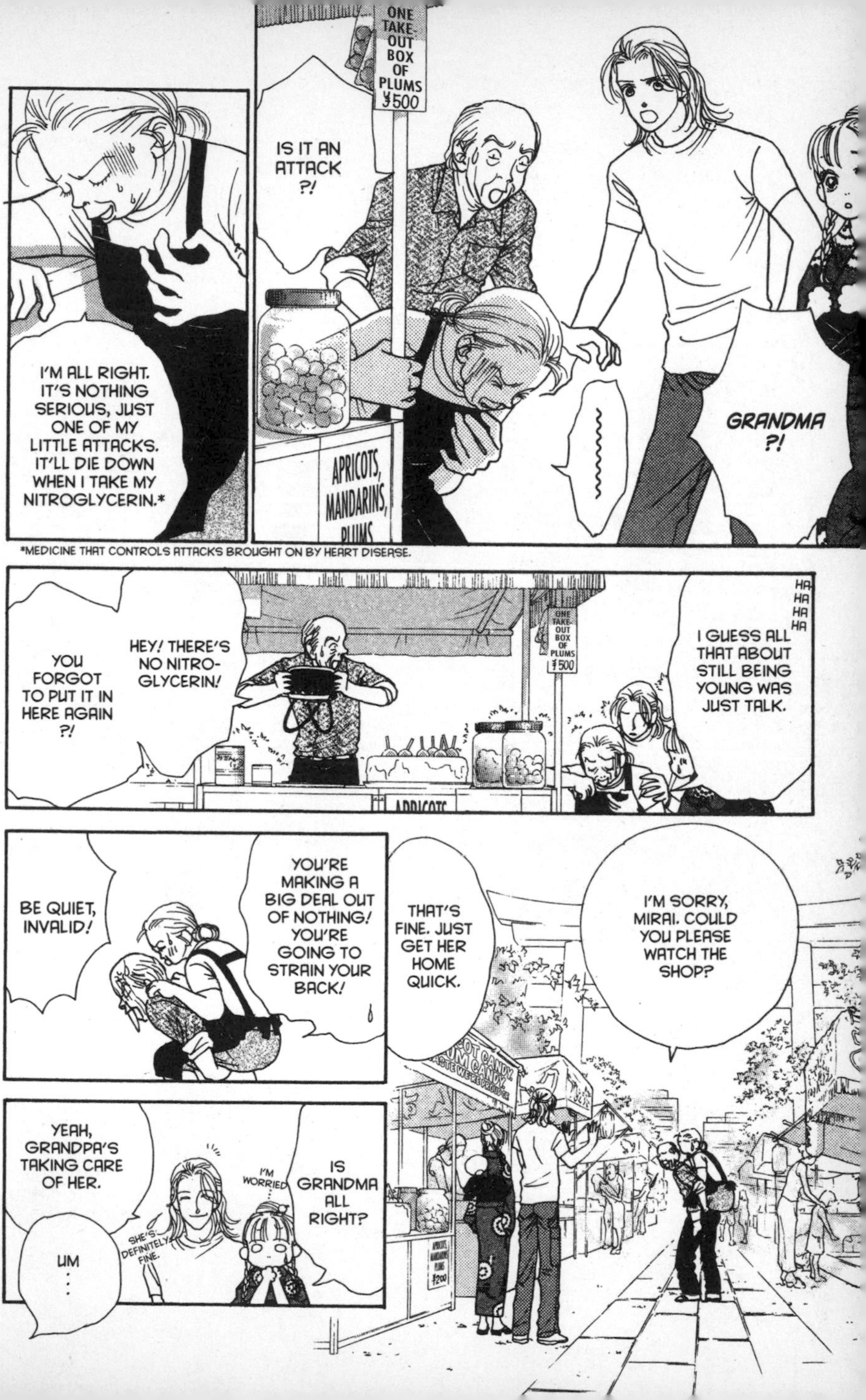
GRANDMA ?!
ONE TAKE-OUT BOX OF PLUMS ¥500
IS IT AN ATTACK ?!
APRICOTS, MANDARINS, PLUMS
I'M ALL RIGHT. IT'S NOTHING SERIOUS, JUST ONE OF MY LITTLE ATTACKS. IT'LL DIE DOWN WHEN I TAKE MY NITROGLYCERIN.*
HA HA HA HA
I GUESS ALL THAT ABOUT STILL BEING YOUNG WAS JUST TALK.
ONE TAKE-OUT BOX OF PLUMS ¥500
HEY! THERE'S NO NITRO-GLYCERIN!
YOU FORGOT TO PUT IT IN HERE AGAIN ?!
I'M SORRY, MIRAI. COULD YOU PLEASE WATCH THE SHOP?
THAT'S FINE. JUST GET HER HOME QUICK.
YOU'RE MAKING A BIG DEAL OUT OF NOTHING! YOU'RE GOING TO STRAIN YOUR BACK!
BE QUIET, INVALID!
IS GRANDMA ALL RIGHT?
I'M WORRIED...
YEAH, GRANDPA'S TAKING CARE OF HER.
SHE'S DEFINITELY FINE.
UM...

*MEDICINE THAT CONTROLS ATTACKS BROUGHT ON BY HEART DISEASE.

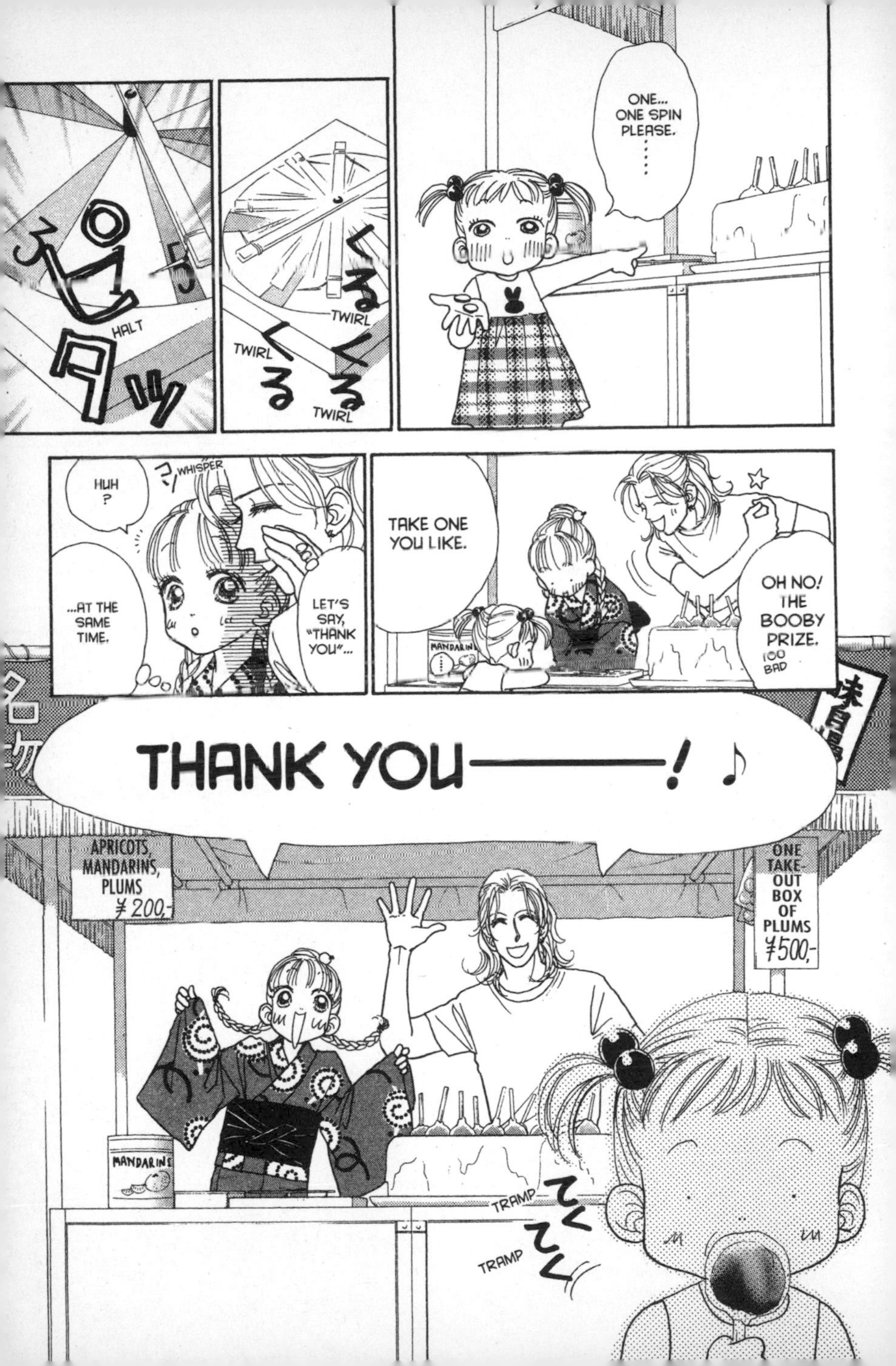

ONE... ONE SPIN PLEASE. ......
くるくるくる
TWIRL TWIRL TWIRL
ピタッ
HALT
OH NO! THE BOOBY PRIZE.
TOO BAD
TAKE ONE YOU LIKE.
WHISPER
HUH?
LET'S SAY, "THANK YOU"...
...AT THE SAME TIME.
THANK YOU———! ♪
ONE TAKE-OUT BOX OF PLUMS ¥500,-
APRICOTS, MANDARINS, PLUMS ¥200,-
MANDARINS
てくてく
TRAMP TRAMP

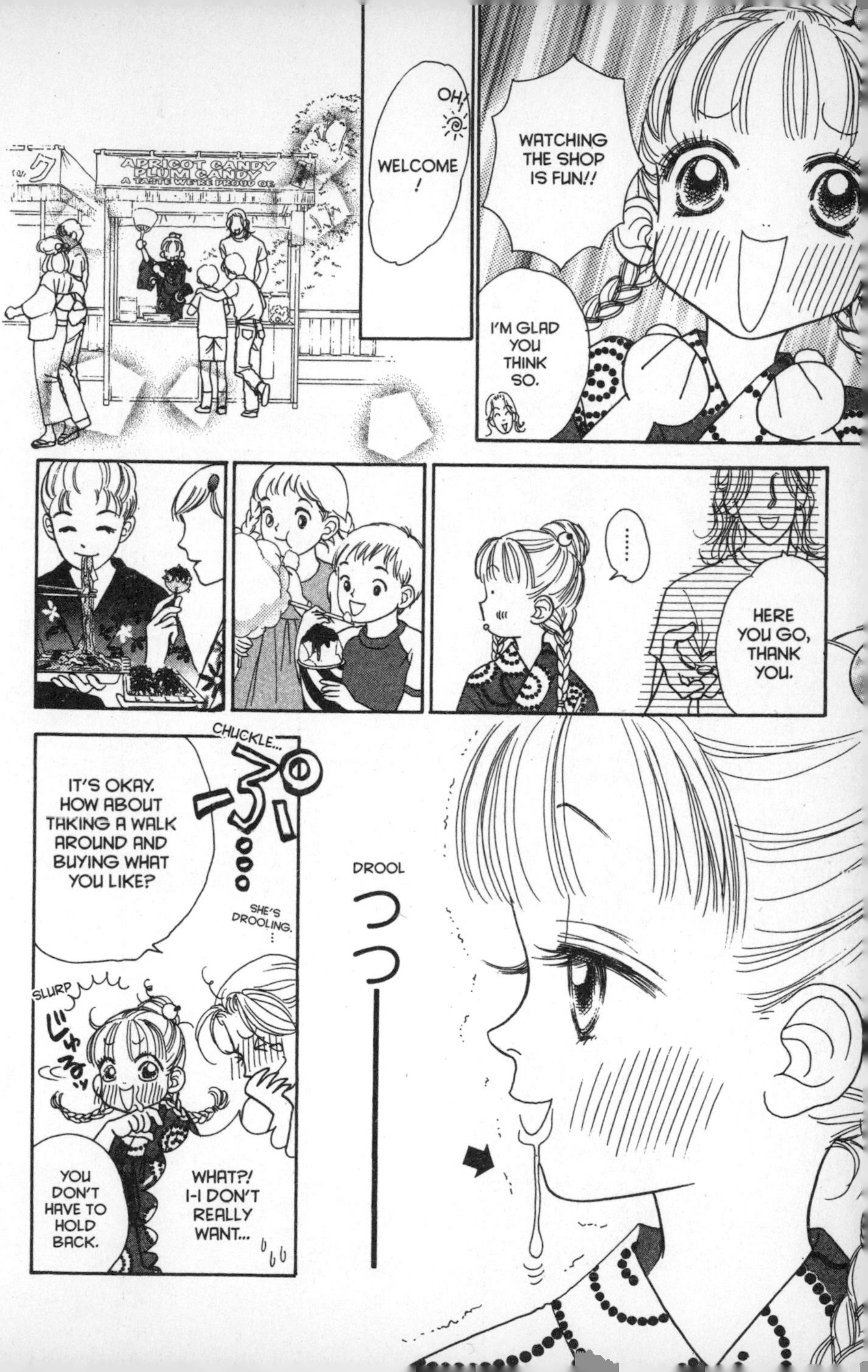
WATCHING THE SHOP IS FUN!!
I'M GLAD YOU THINK SO.
OH!
WELCOME!
APRICOT CANDY PLUM CANDY A TASTE WE'RE PROUD OF.
HERE YOU GO, THANK YOU.
......
DROOL
CHUCKLE...
IT'S OKAY. HOW ABOUT TAKING A WALK AROUND AND BUYING WHAT YOU LIKE?
SHE'S DROOLING...
SLURP
WHAT?! I-I DON'T REALLY WANT...
YOU DON'T HAVE TO HOLD BACK.

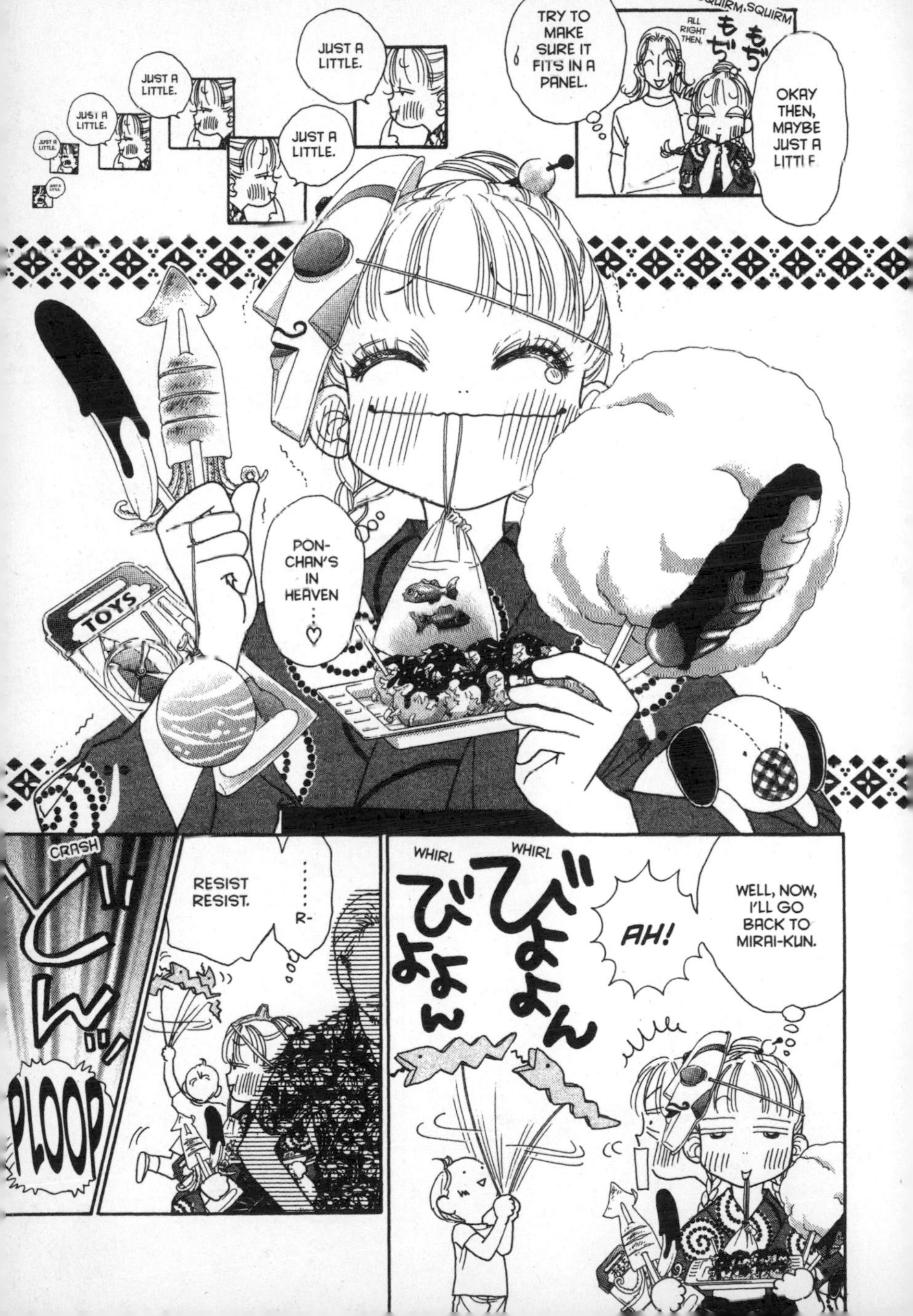
SQUIRM SQUIRM
もぢもぢ
OKAY THEN, MAYBE JUST A LITTLE.
TRY TO MAKE SURE IT FITS IN A PANEL.
ALL RIGHT THEN.
JUST A LITTLE.
JUST A LITTLE.
JUST A LITTLE.
JUST A LITTLE.
JUST A LITTLE.
JUST A LITTLE.
PON-CHAN'S IN HEAVEN ...♡
WHIRL WHIRL
びよん びよん
WELL, NOW, I'LL GO BACK TO MIRAI-KUN.
AH!
RESIST RESIST.
......R-
CRASH
PLOOP

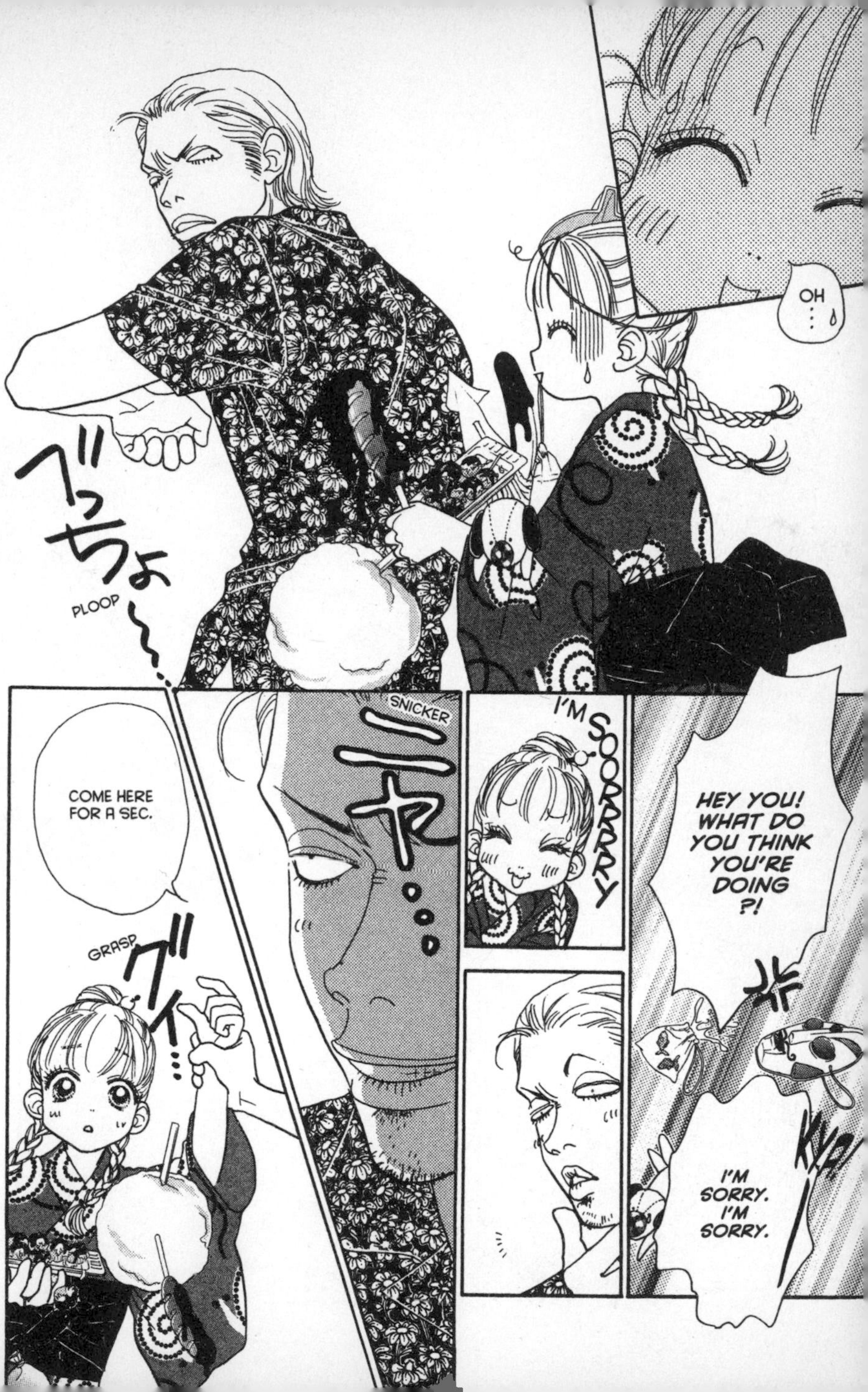
OH...
べっちょ～
PLOOP
HEY YOU! WHAT DO YOU THINK YOU'RE DOING ?!
KYA!
I'M SORRY. I'M SORRY.
I'M SOORRRRY
ニヤ…
SNICKER
COME HERE FOR A SEC.
グイ…
GRASP

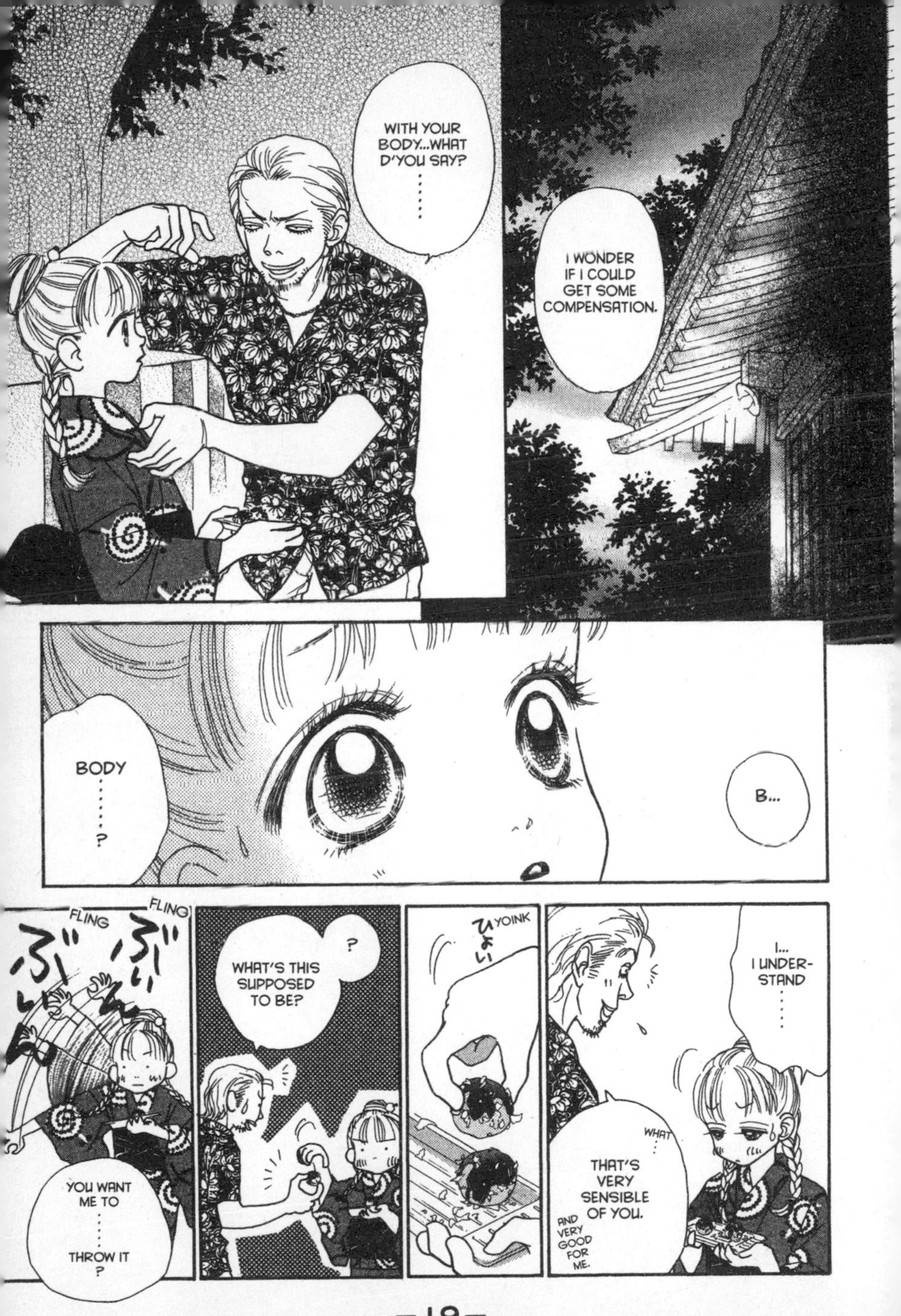
I WONDER IF I COULD GET SOME COMPENSATION.
WITH YOUR BODY...WHAT D'YOU SAY? ......
B...
BODY ......?
I... I UNDERSTAND ......
WHAT ...
THAT'S VERY SENSIBLE OF YOU.
AND VERY GOOD FOR ME.
ひょい YOINK
?
WHAT'S THIS SUPPOSED TO BE?
FLING
FLING
YOU WANT ME TO ...... THROW IT ?

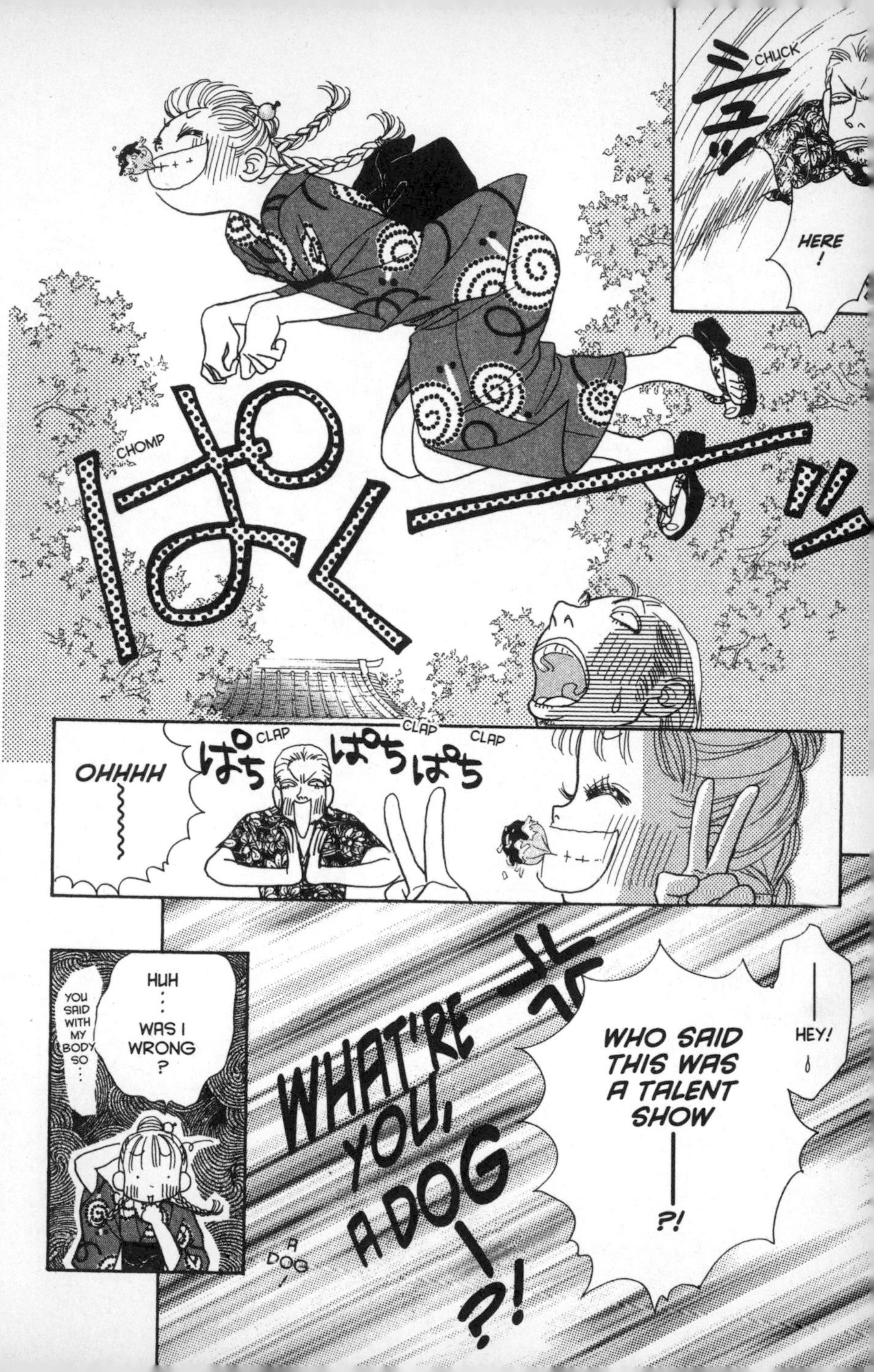

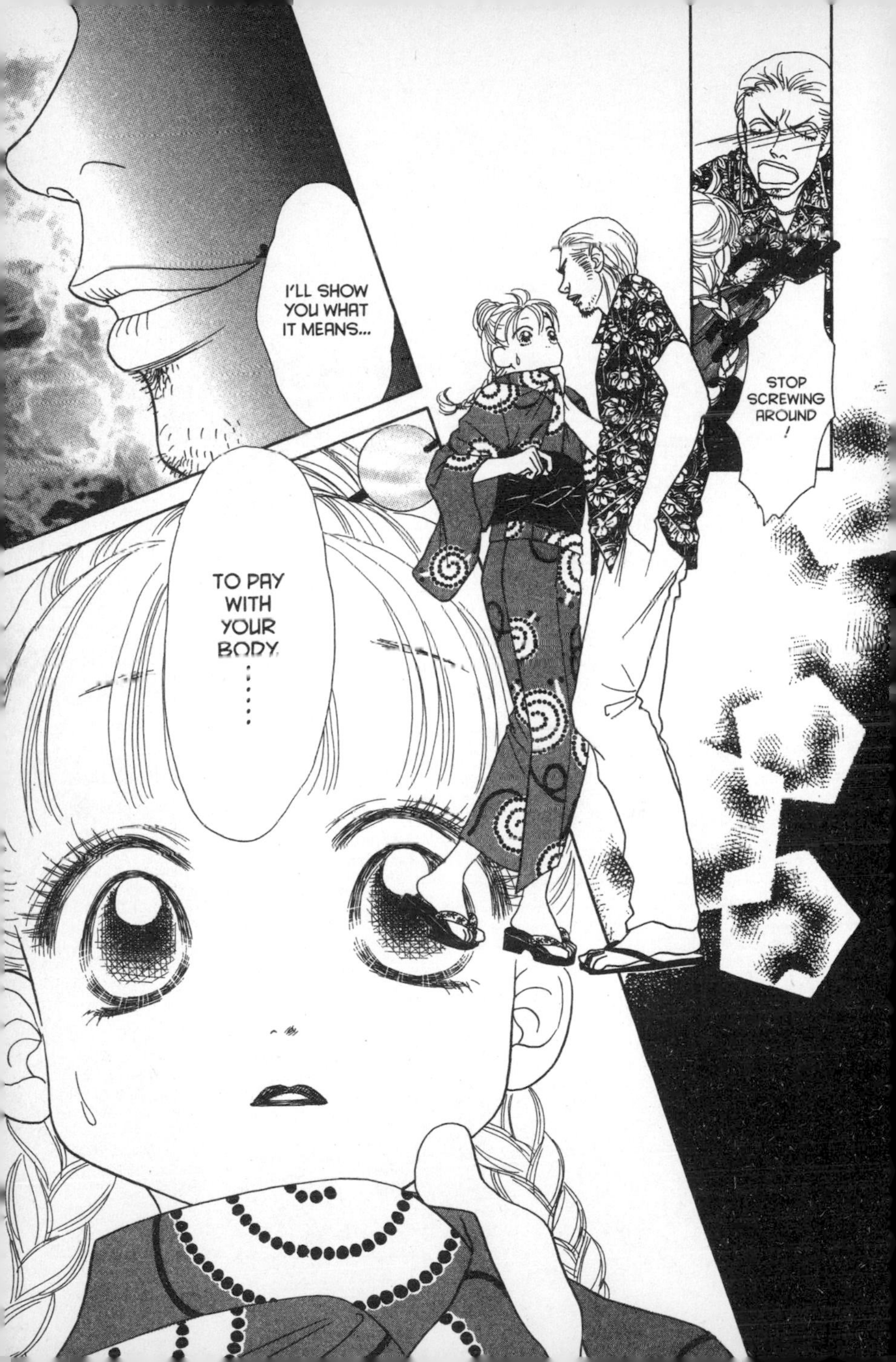
STOP SCREWING AROUND!
I'LL SHOW YOU WHAT IT MEANS...
TO PAY WITH YOUR BODY......

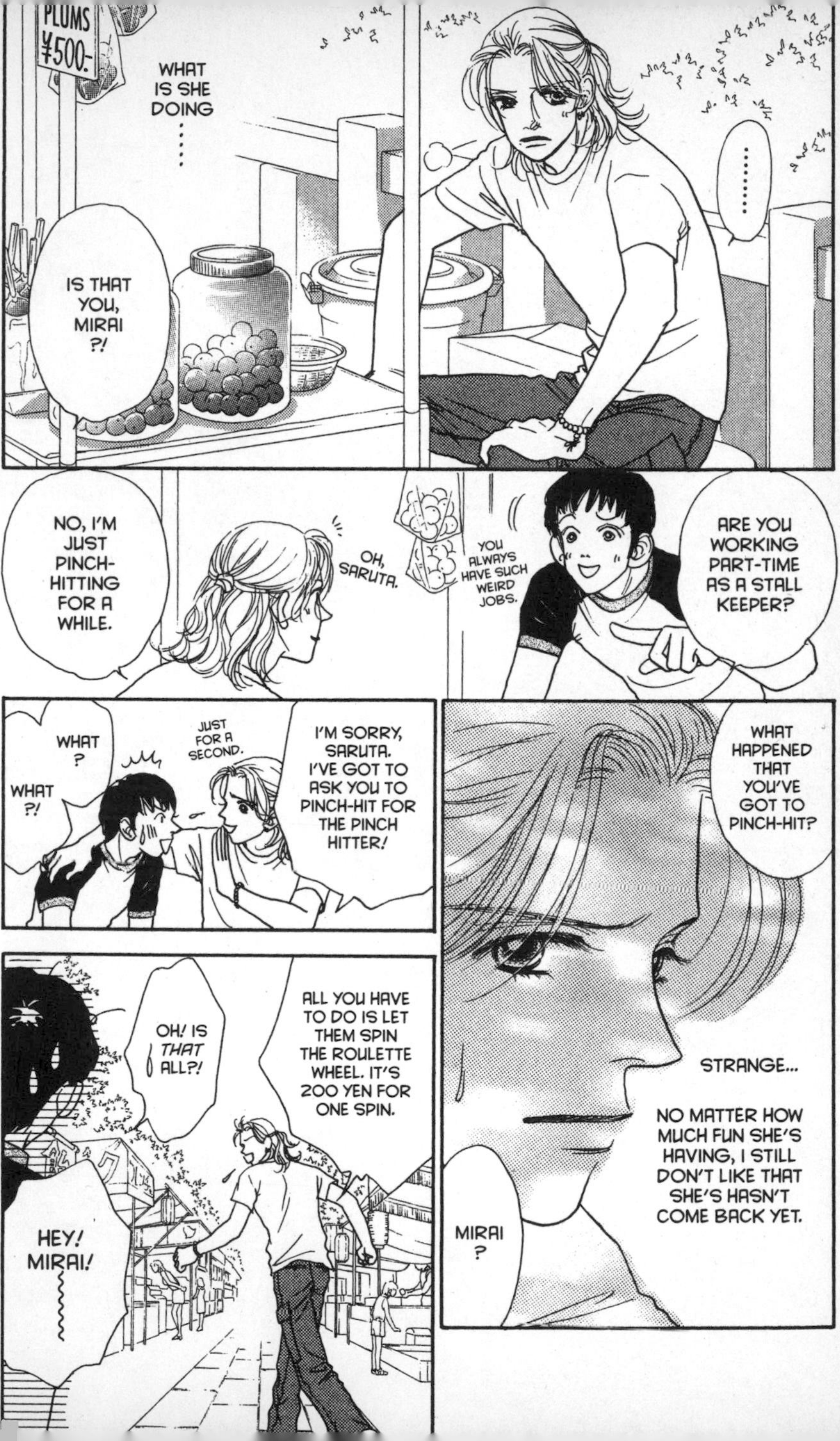
PLUMS ¥500-
......
WHAT IS SHE DOING ......
IS THAT YOU, MIRAI ?!
ARE YOU WORKING PART-TIME AS A STALL KEEPER?
YOU ALWAYS HAVE SUCH WEIRD JOBS.
OH, SARUTA.
NO, I'M JUST PINCH-HITTING FOR A WHILE.
WHAT HAPPENED THAT YOU'VE GOT TO PINCH-HIT?
STRANGE...
NO MATTER HOW MUCH FUN SHE'S HAVING, I STILL DON'T LIKE THAT SHE'S HASN'T COME BACK YET.
MIRAI ?
I'M SORRY, SARUTA. I'VE GOT TO ASK YOU TO PINCH-HIT FOR THE PINCH HITTER!
JUST FOR A SECOND.
WHAT ?
WHAT ?!
ALL YOU HAVE TO DO IS LET THEM SPIN THE ROULETTE WHEEL. IT'S 200 YEN FOR ONE SPIN.
OH! IS *THAT* ALL?!
HEY! MIRAI!

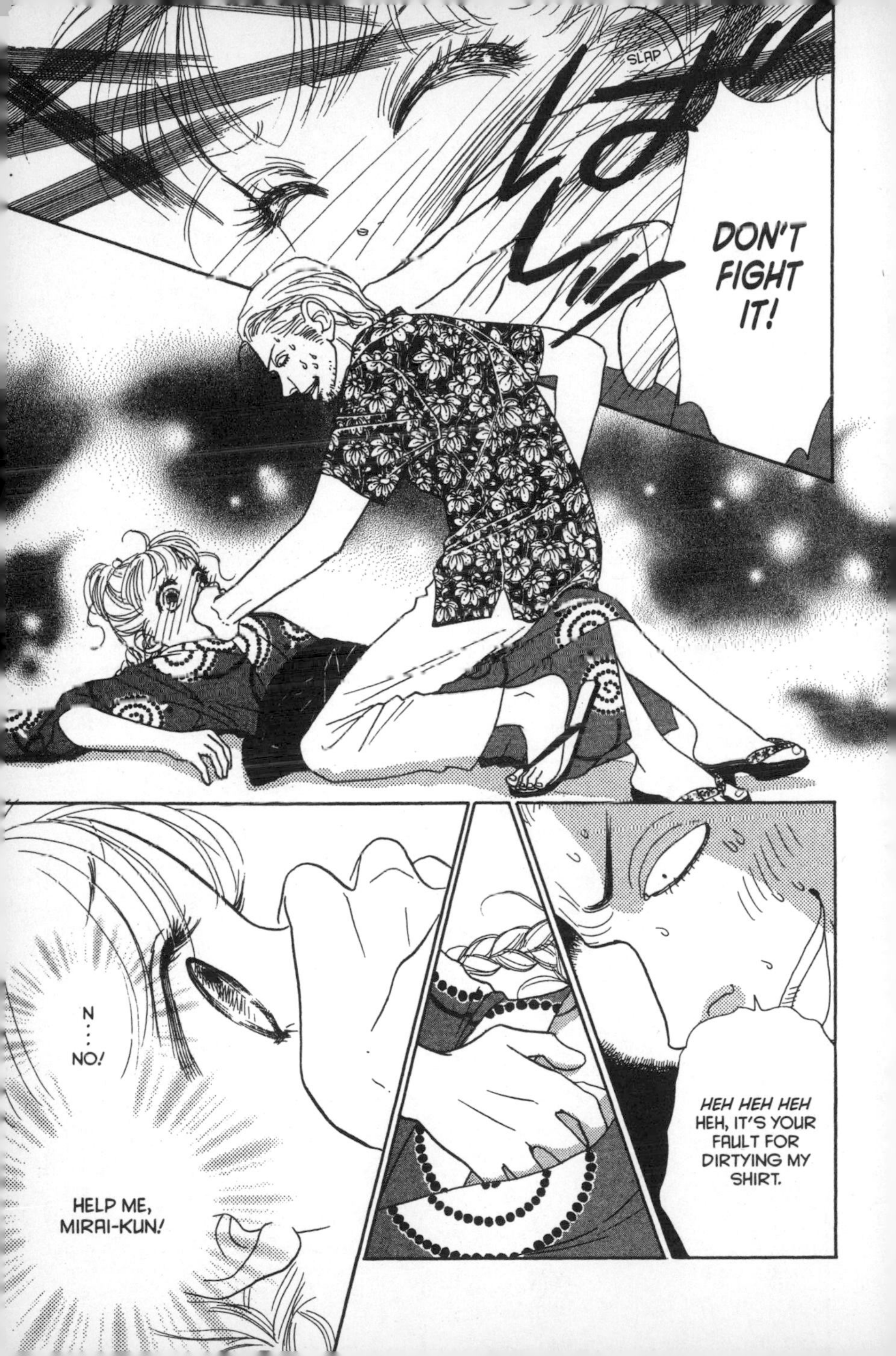
SLAP
DON'T FIGHT IT!
HEH HEH HEH HEH, IT'S YOUR FAULT FOR DIRTYING MY SHIRT.
N... NO!
HELP ME, MIRAI-KUN!

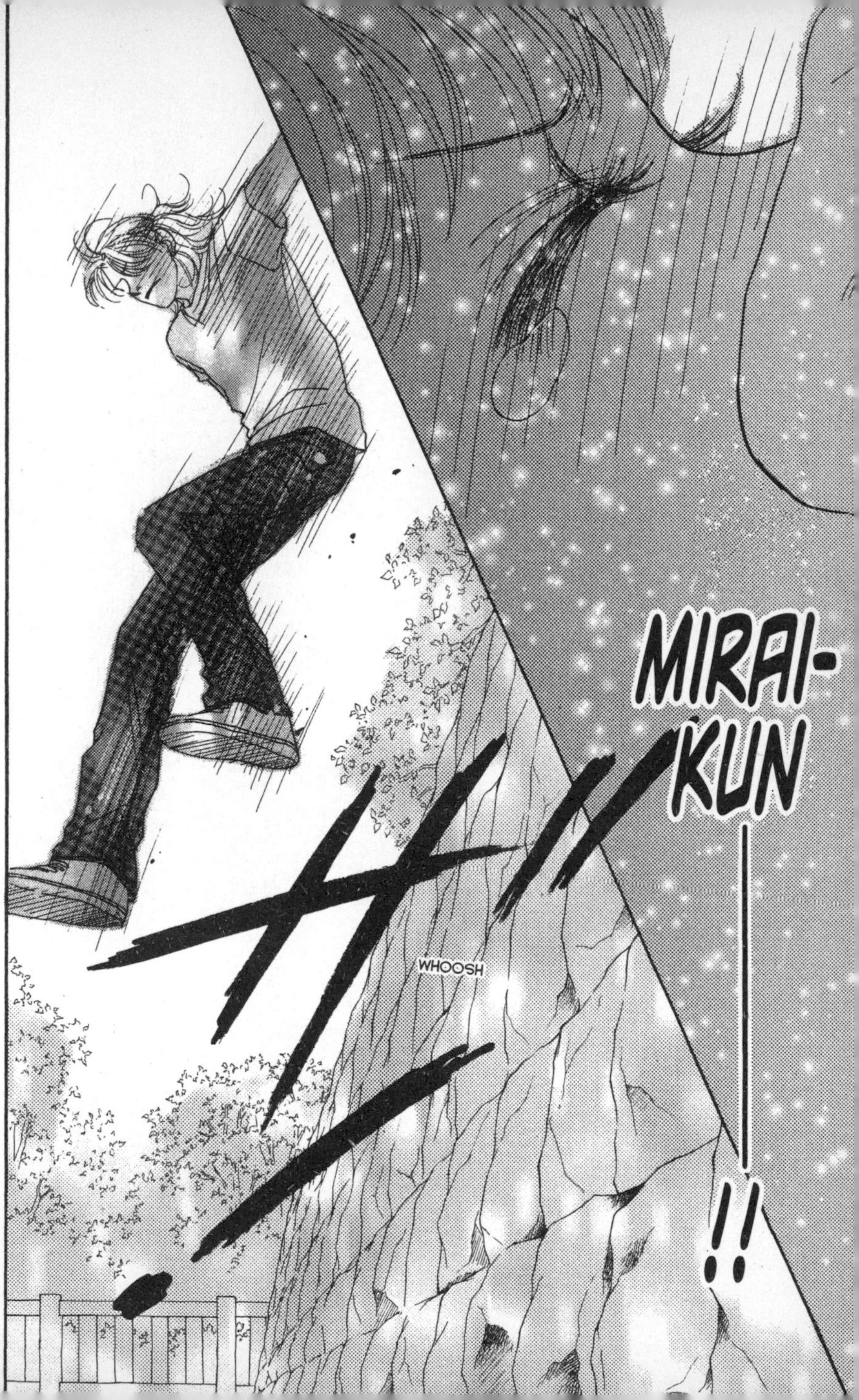
MIRAI-KUN——!!
WHOOSH

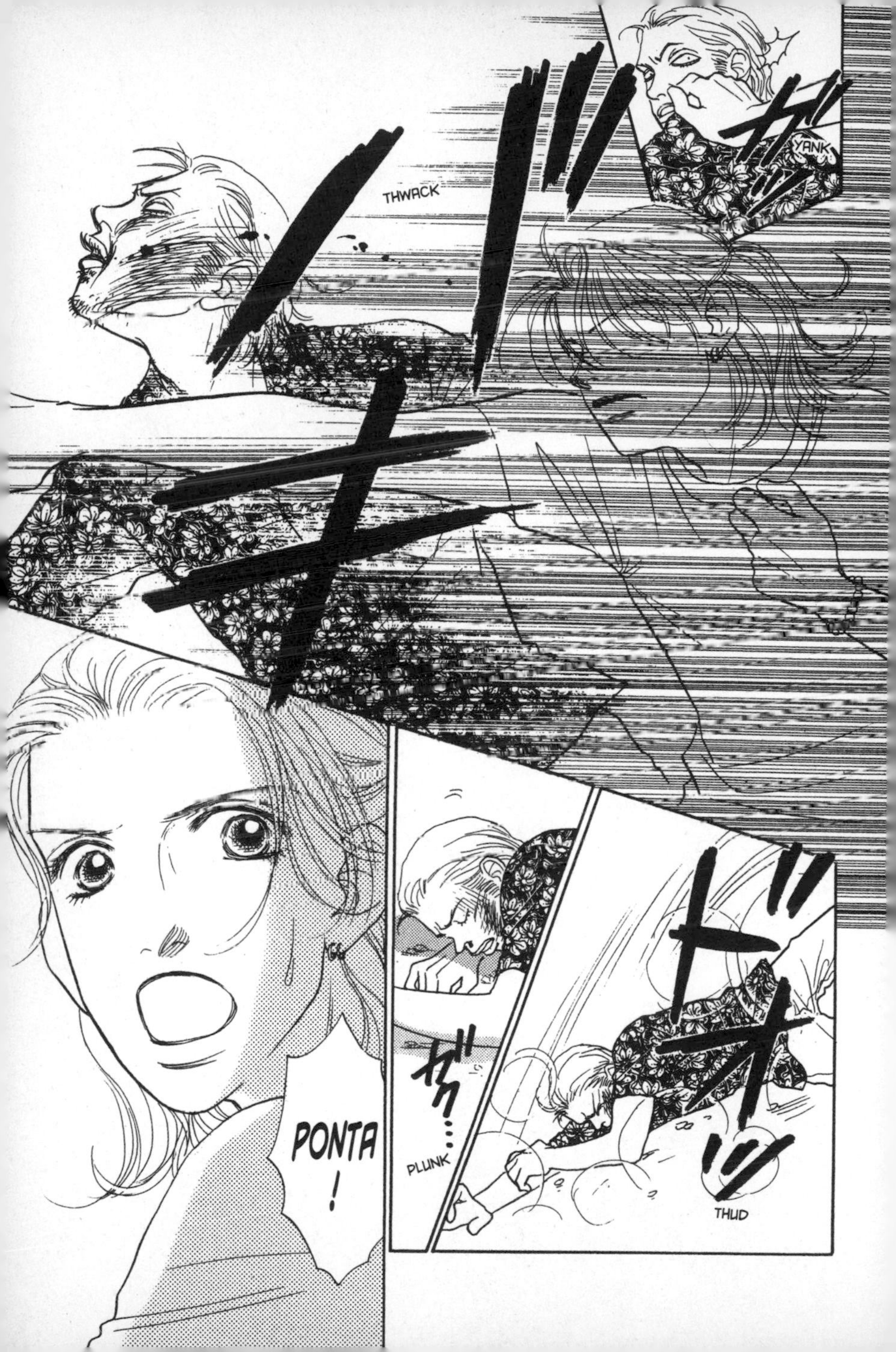
YANK
THWACK
THUD
PLUNK
PONTA
!

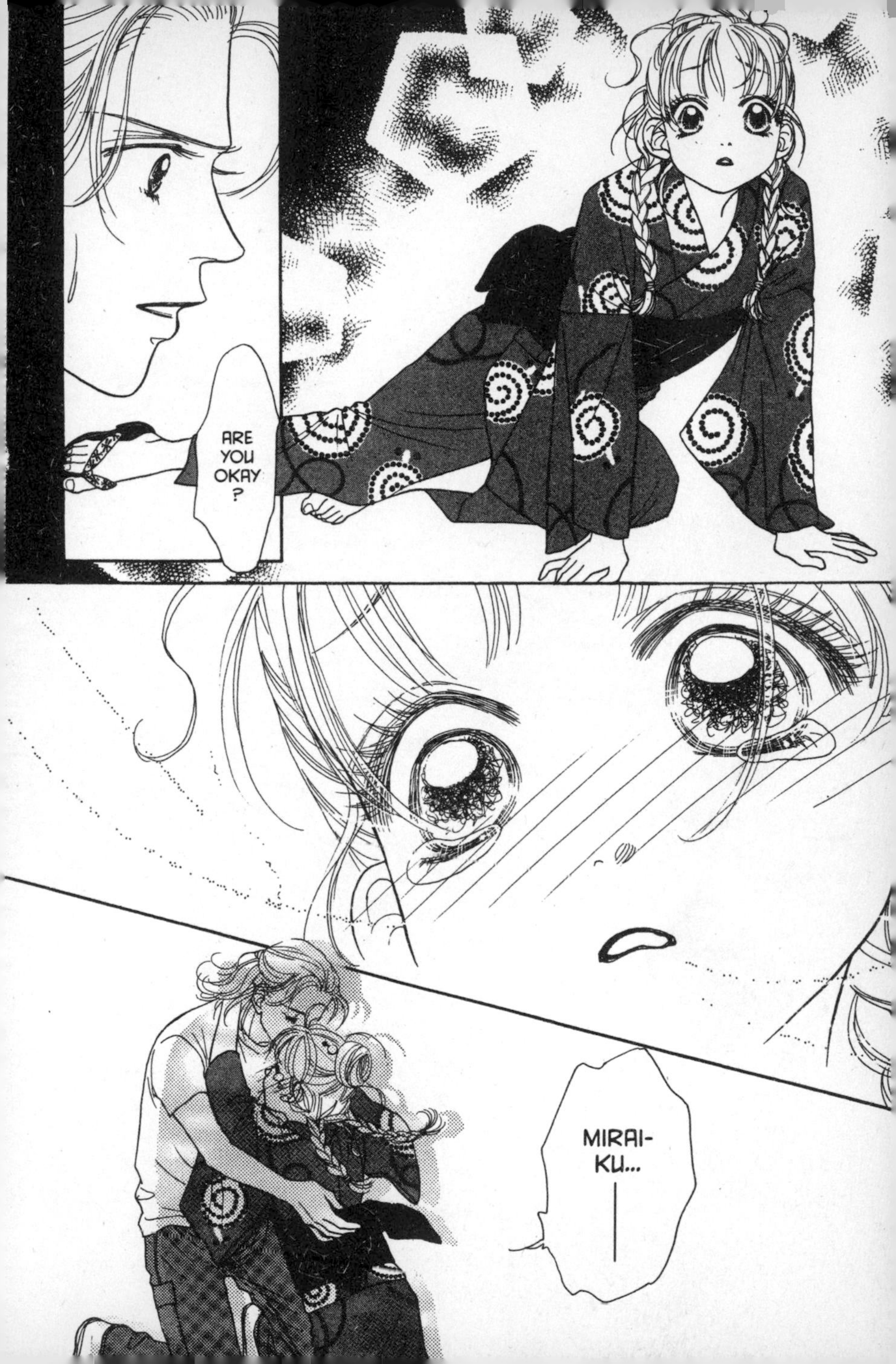
ARE YOU OKAY?
MIRAI-KU... —

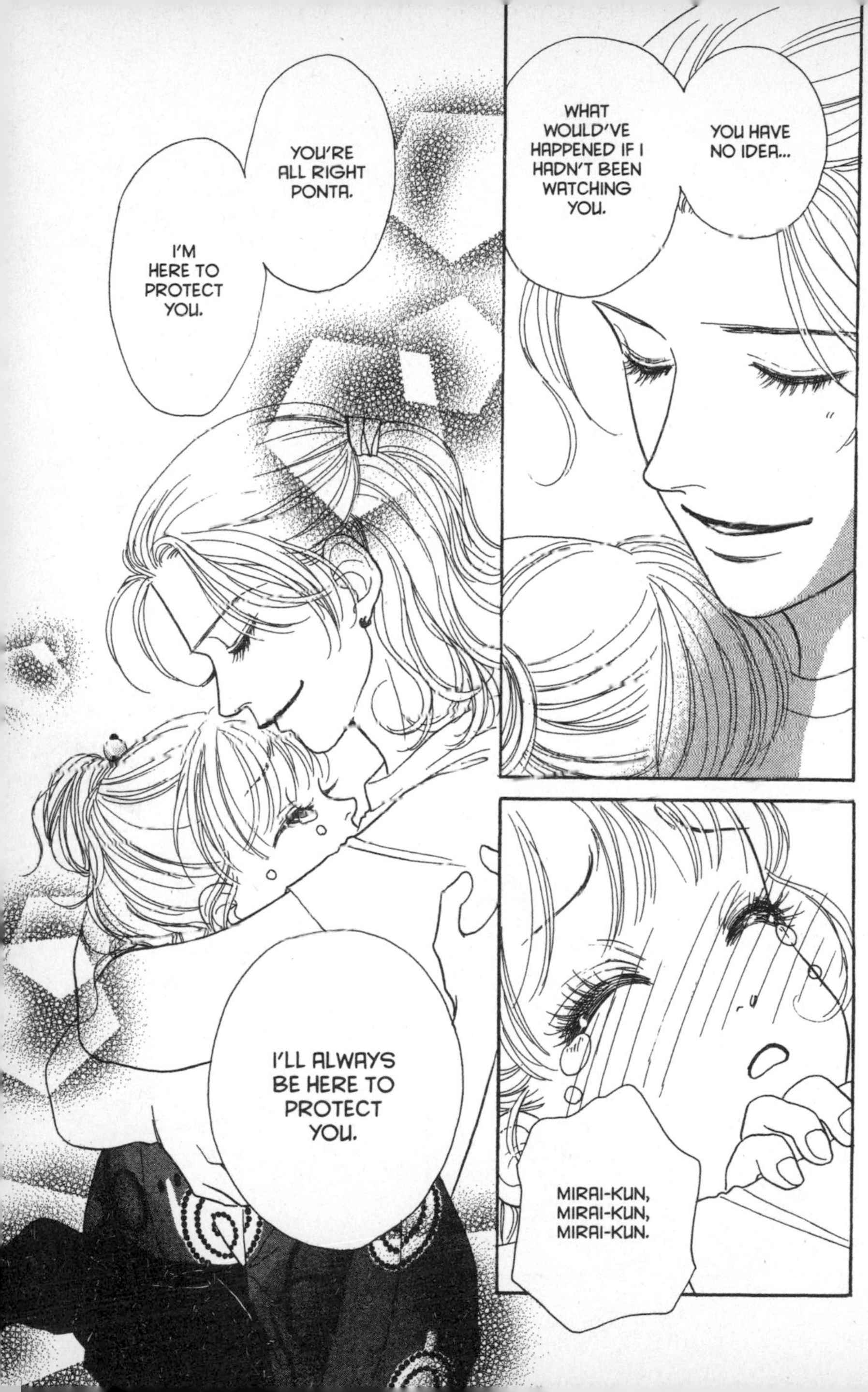
YOU HAVE NO IDEA...
WHAT WOULD'VE HAPPENED IF I HADN'T BEEN WATCHING YOU.
MIRAI-KUN, MIRAI-KUN, MIRAI-KUN.
YOU'RE ALL RIGHT PONTA.
I'M HERE TO PROTECT YOU.
I'LL ALWAYS BE HERE TO PROTECT YOU.

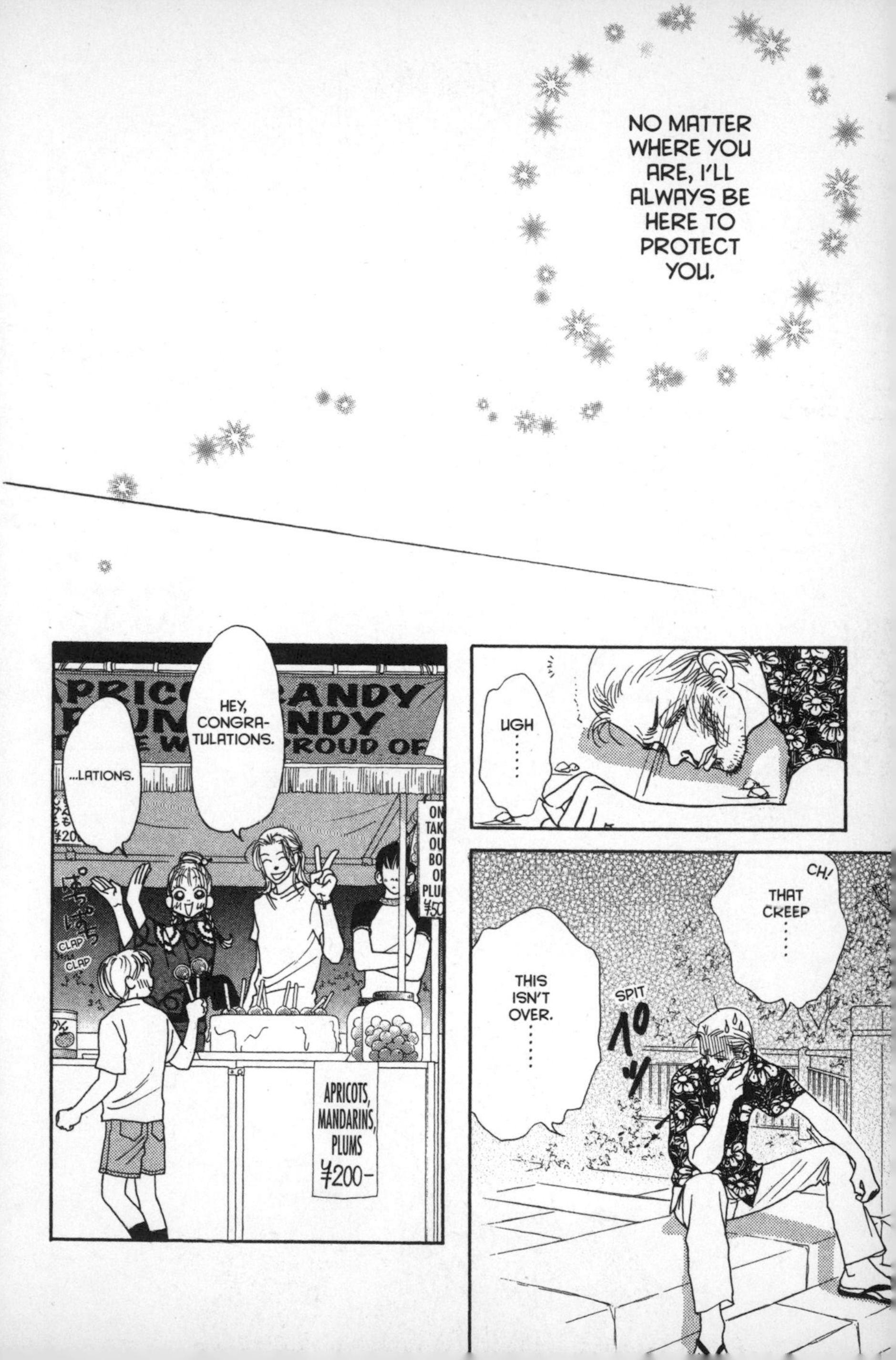
NO MATTER WHERE YOU ARE, I'LL ALWAYS BE HERE TO PROTECT YOU.
UGH ......
CH!
THAT CREEP ......
SPIT
THIS ISN'T OVER. ......
HEY, CONGRA-TULATIONS.
...LATIONS.
CLAP CLAP
APRICOTS, MANDARINS, PLUMS ¥200-

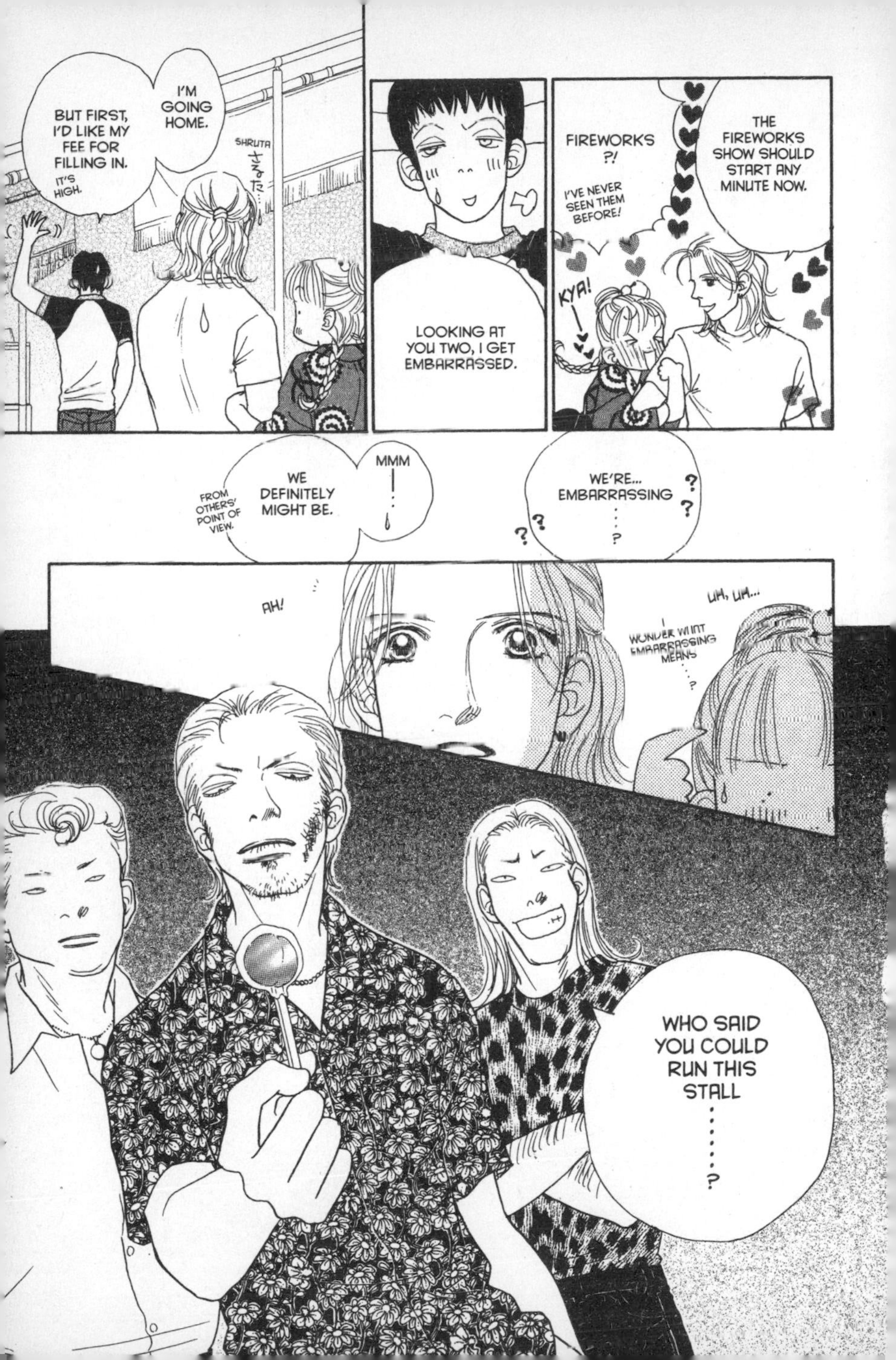

THE FIREWORKS SHOW SHOULD START ANY MINUTE NOW.
FIREWORKS?!
I'VE NEVER SEEN THEM BEFORE!
KYA!
LOOKING AT YOU TWO, I GET EMBARRASSED.
I'M GOING HOME.
SHRUTA
BUT FIRST, I'D LIKE MY FEE FOR FILLING IN.
IT'S HIGH.
WE'RE... EMBARRASSING...?
MMM!...
WE DEFINITELY MIGHT BE.
FROM OTHERS' POINT OF VIEW.
UH, UH...
I WONDER WHAT EMBARRASSING MEANS...?
AH!
WHO SAID YOU COULD RUN THIS STALL......?

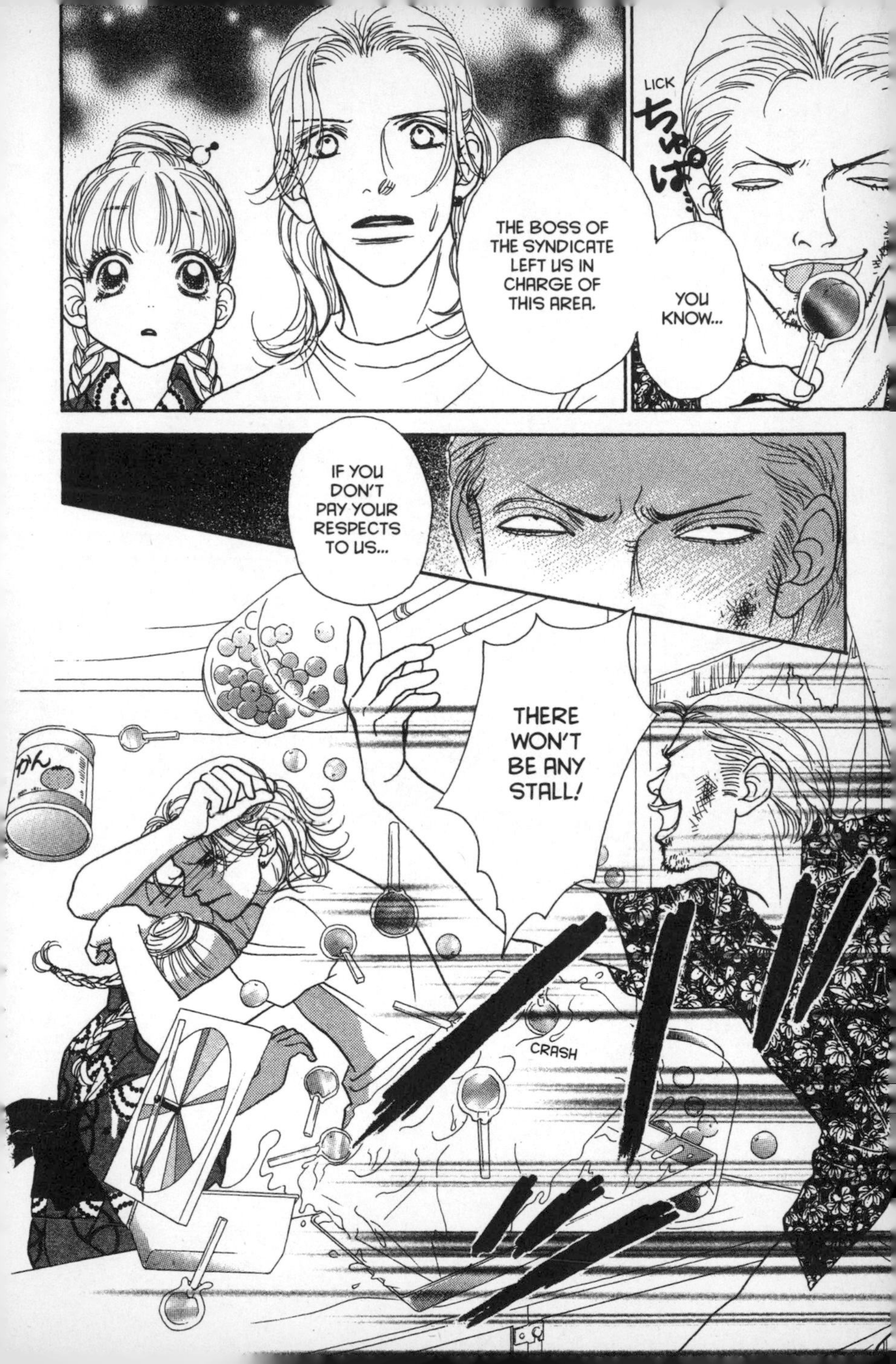

LICK
ちゅぱ
YOU KNOW...
THE BOSS OF THE SYNDICATE LEFT US IN CHARGE OF THIS AREA.
IF YOU DON'T PAY YOUR RESPECTS TO US...
THERE WON'T BE ANY STALL!
CRASH

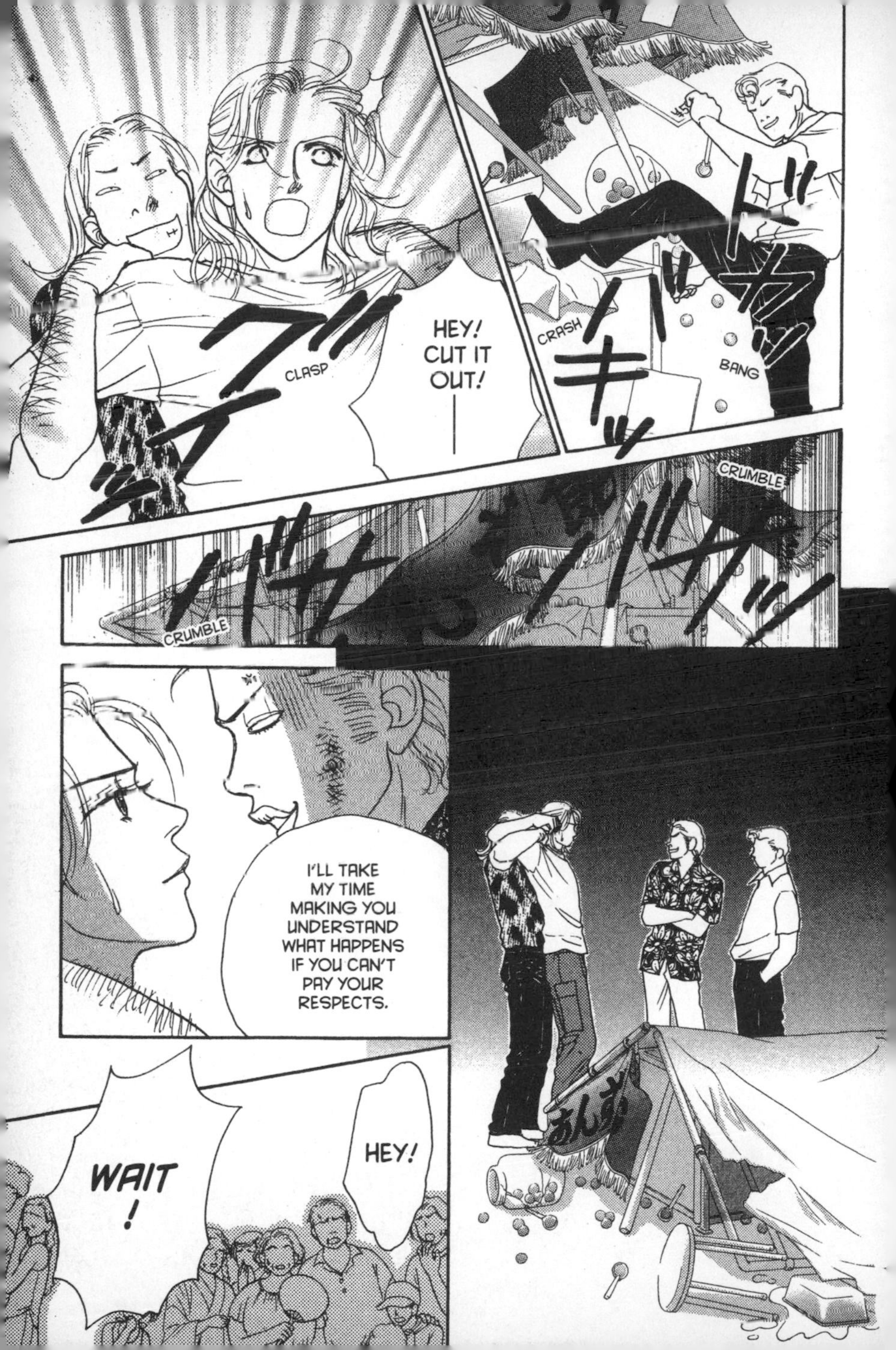
CRASH
BANG
CLASP
HEY! CUT IT OUT!
CRUMBLE
CRUMBLE
I'LL TAKE MY TIME MAKING YOU UNDERSTAND WHAT HAPPENS IF YOU CAN'T PAY YOUR RESPECTS.
HEY!
WAIT!

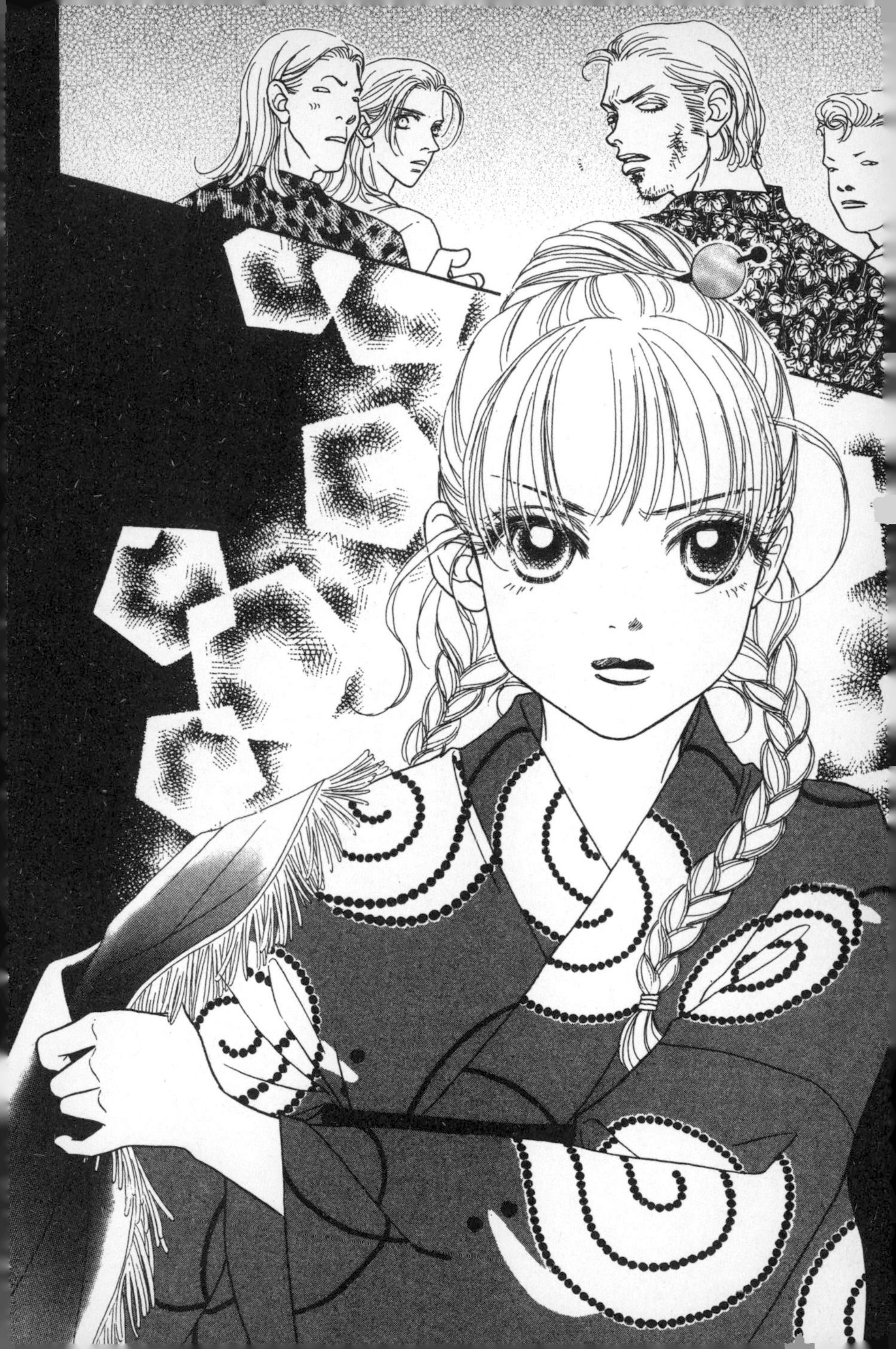

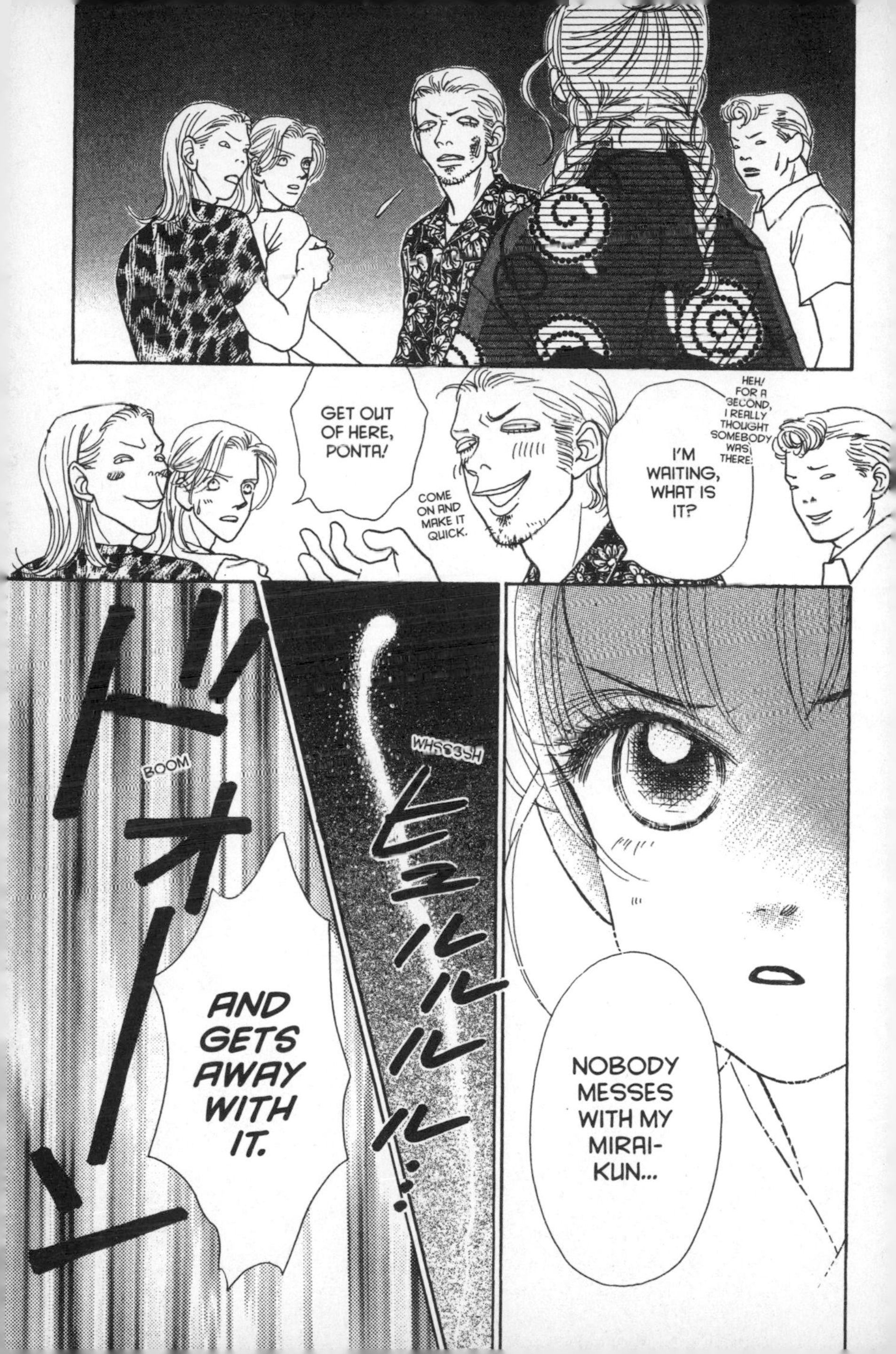
HEH! FOR A SECOND, I REALLY THOUGHT SOMEBODY WAS THERE!
I'M WAITING, WHAT IS IT?
COME ON AND MAKE IT QUICK.
GET OUT OF HERE, PONTA!
NOBODY MESSES WITH MY MIRAI-KUN...
WHSSSSH
ヒュルルルル…
BOOM
ドオーン
AND GETS AWAY WITH IT.

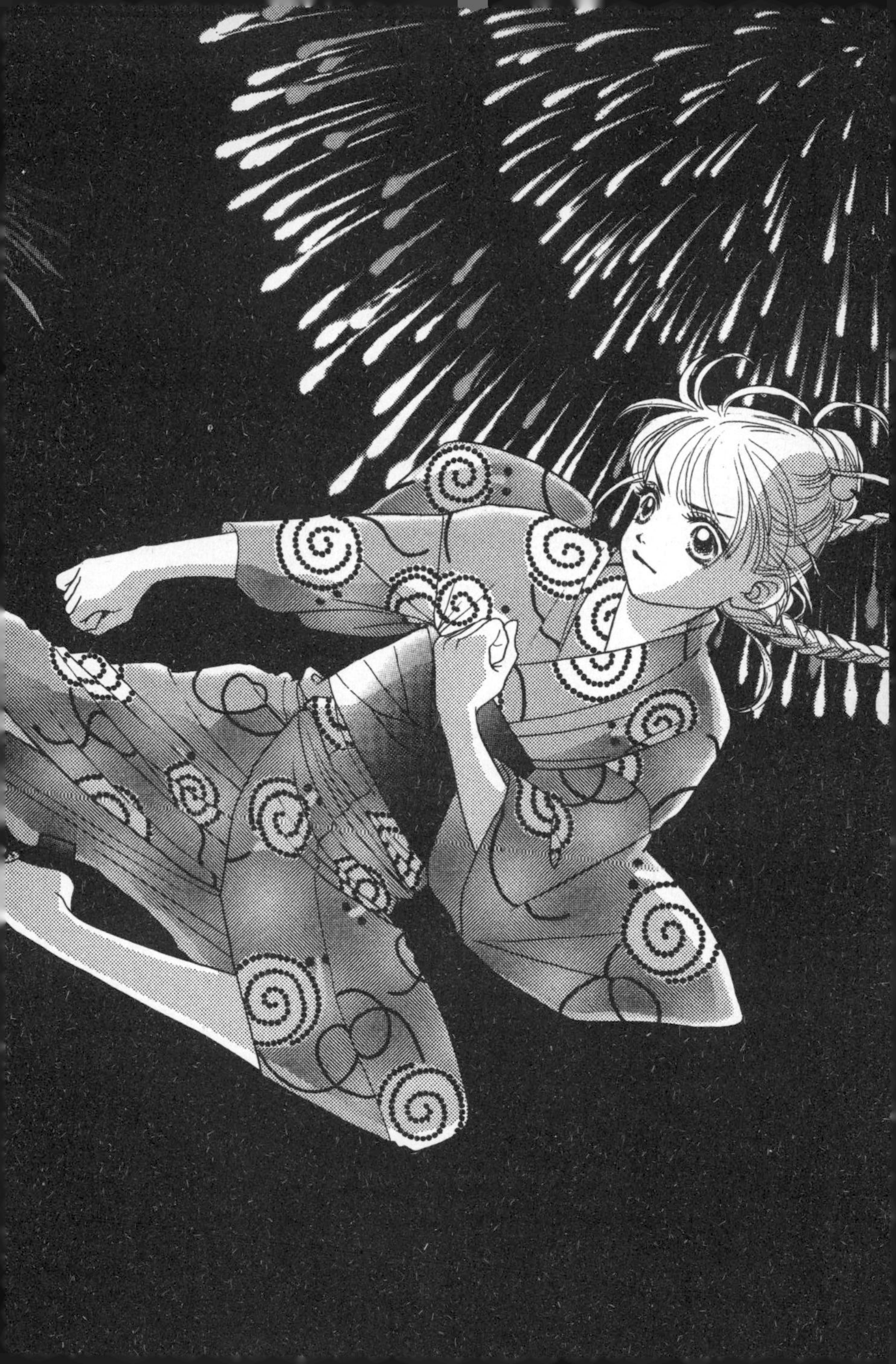

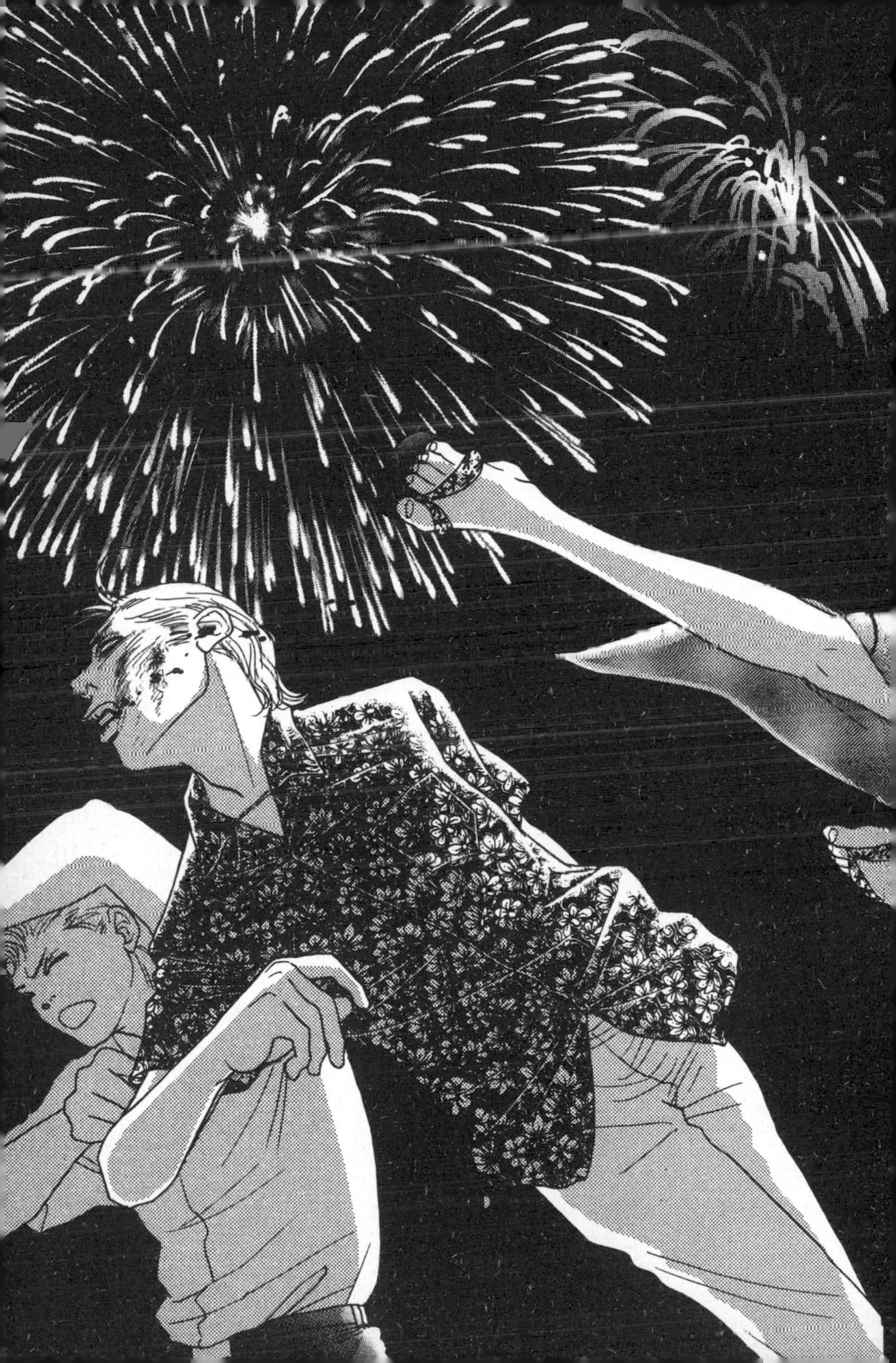

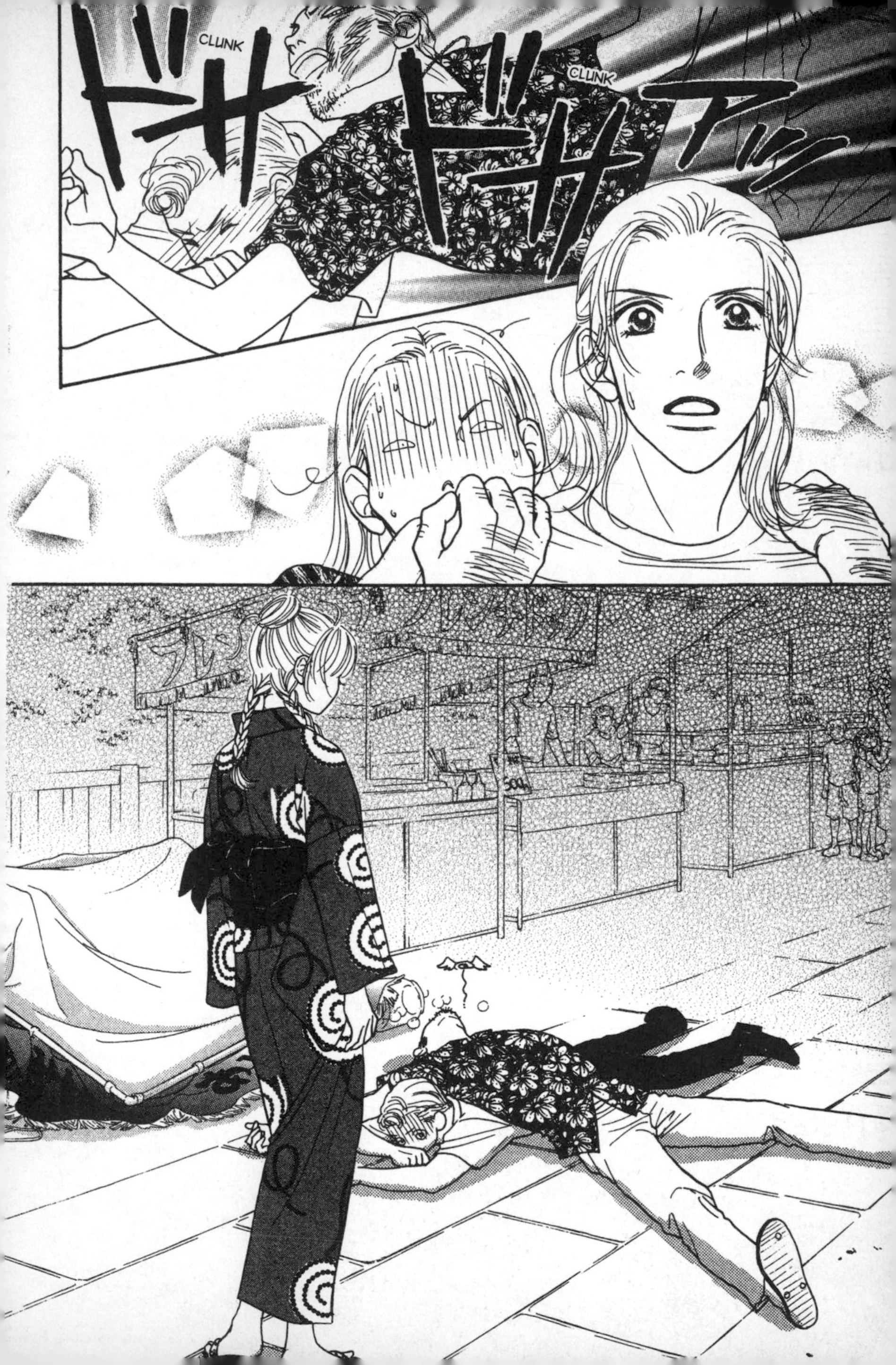
CLUNK
CLUNK

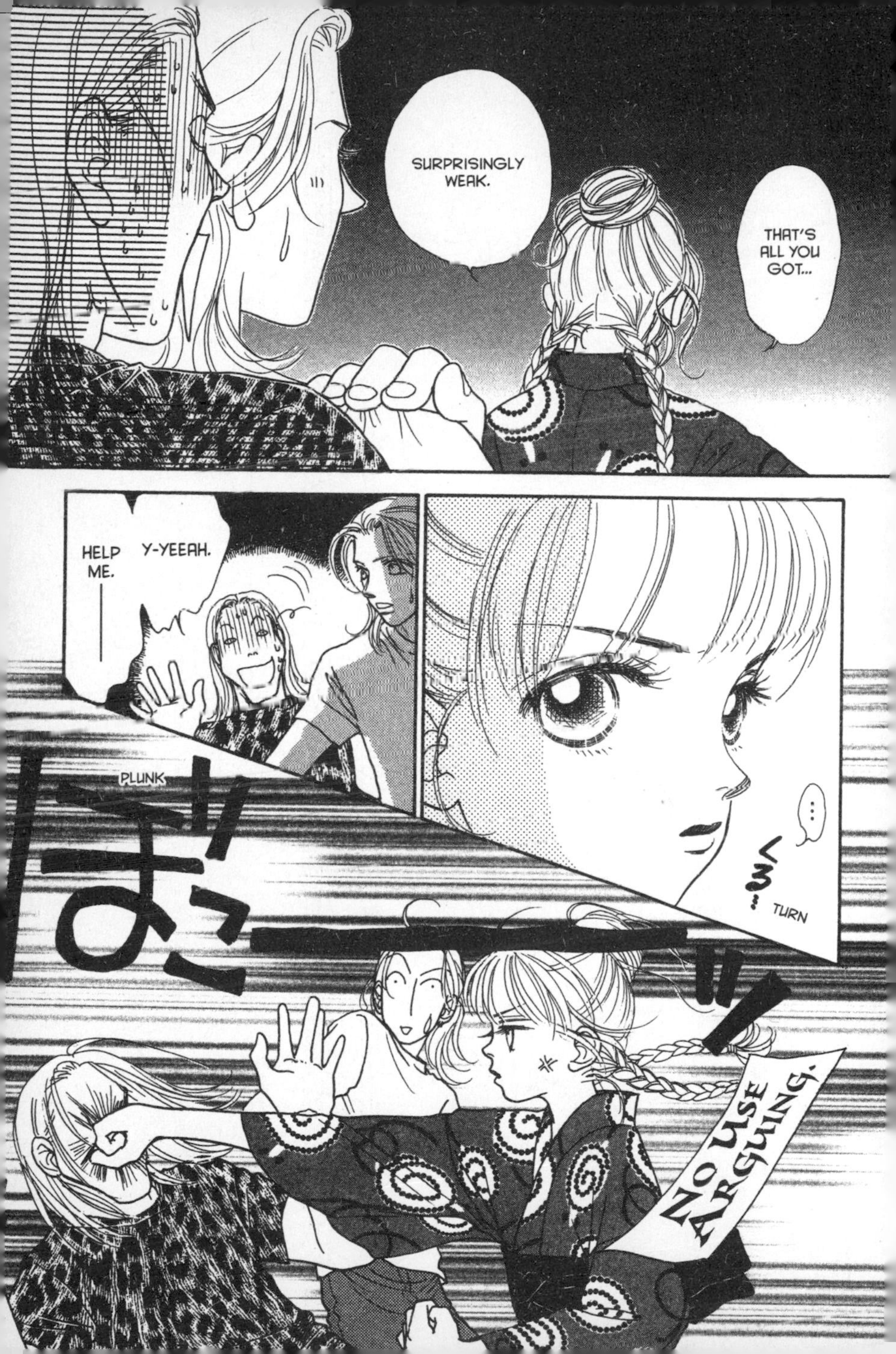
THAT'S ALL YOU GOT...
SURPRISINGLY WEAK.
...
TURN
Y-YEEAH.
HELP ME.
ぼこーーッ
PLUNK
NO USE ARGUING.

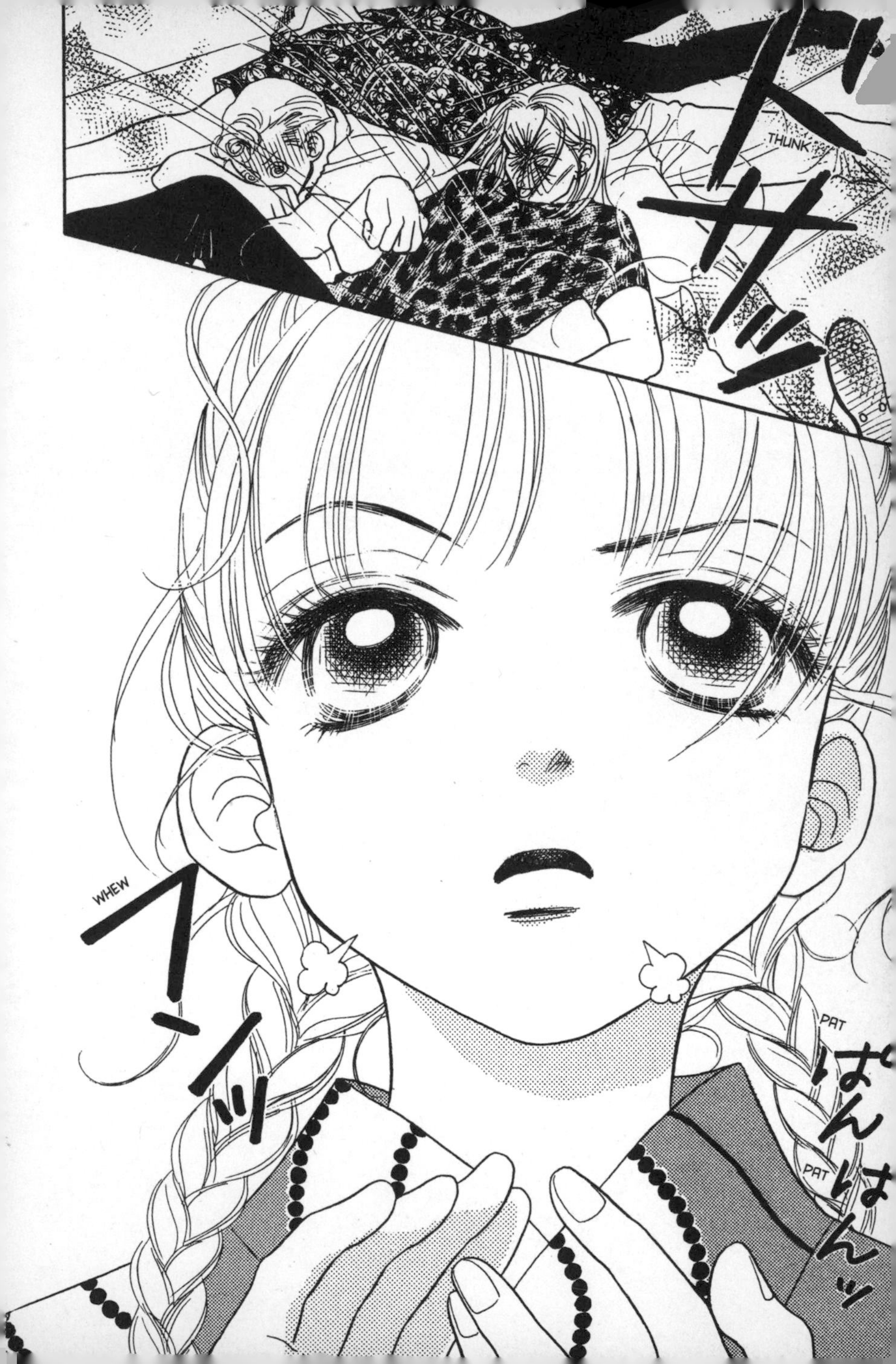
ドサッ
THUNK
WHEW
PAT
ぱんぱんッ
PAT

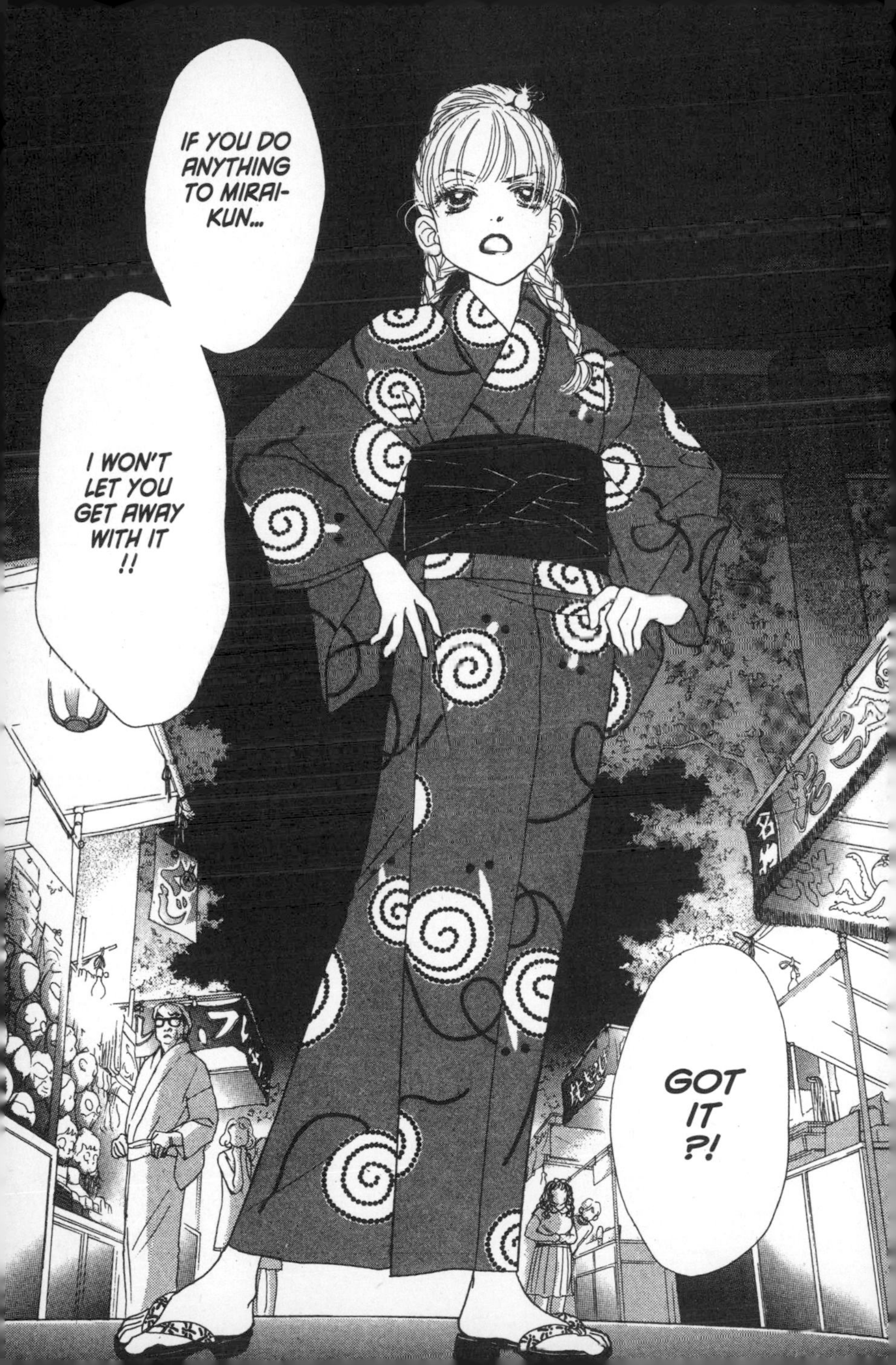
IF YOU DO ANYTHING TO MIRAI-KUN...
I WON'T LET YOU GET AWAY WITH IT !!
GOT IT ?!

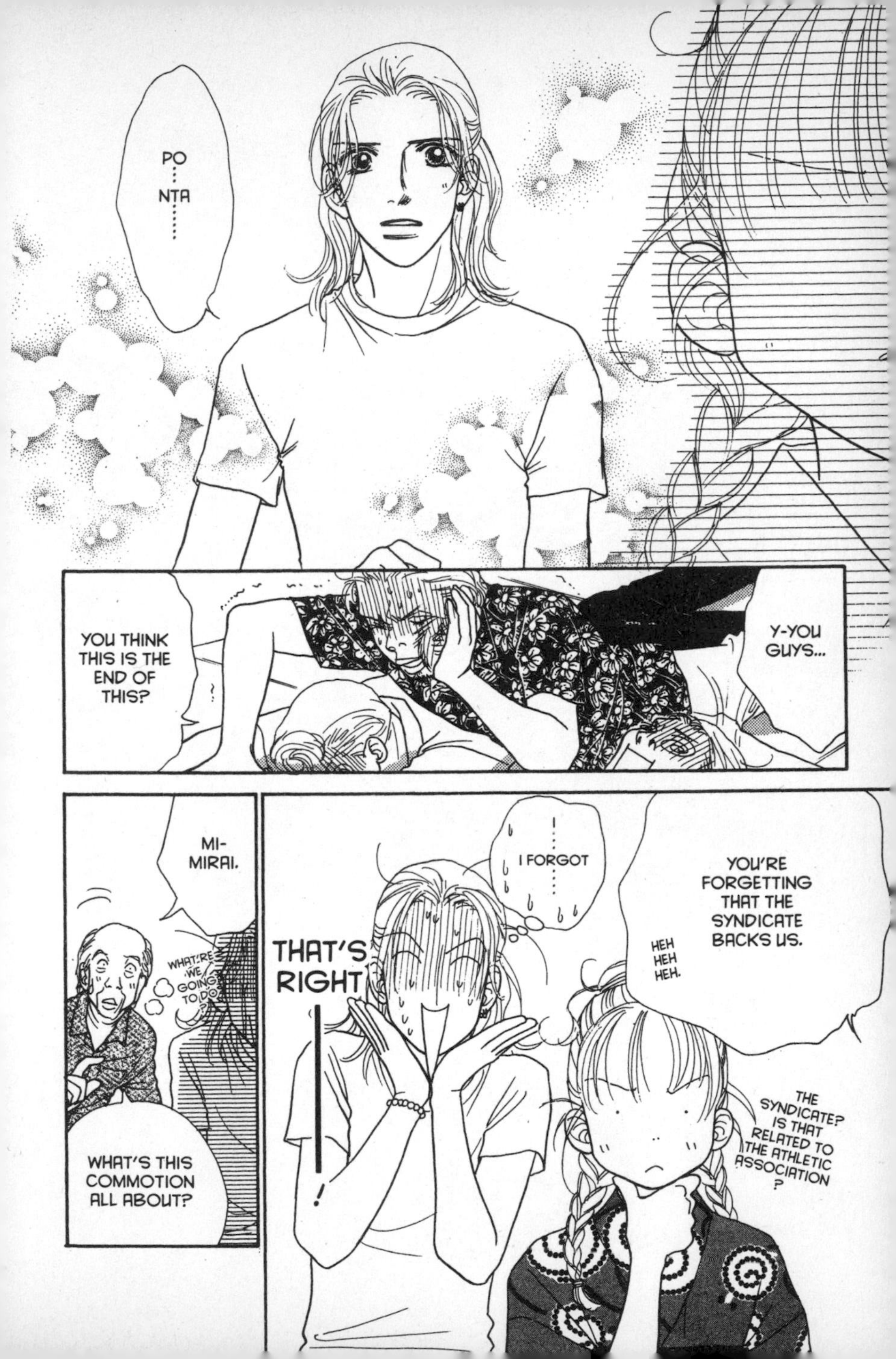
PO... NTA......
Y-YOU GUYS...
YOU THINK THIS IS THE END OF THIS?
YOU'RE FORGETTING THAT THE SYNDICATE BACKS US.
HEH HEH HEH.
I FORGOT......!
THAT'S RIGHT—!
THE SYNDICATE? IS THAT RELATED TO THE ATHLETIC ASSOCIATION?
MI-MIRAI.
WHAT'RE WE GOING TO DO?
WHAT'S THIS COMMOTION ALL ABOUT?

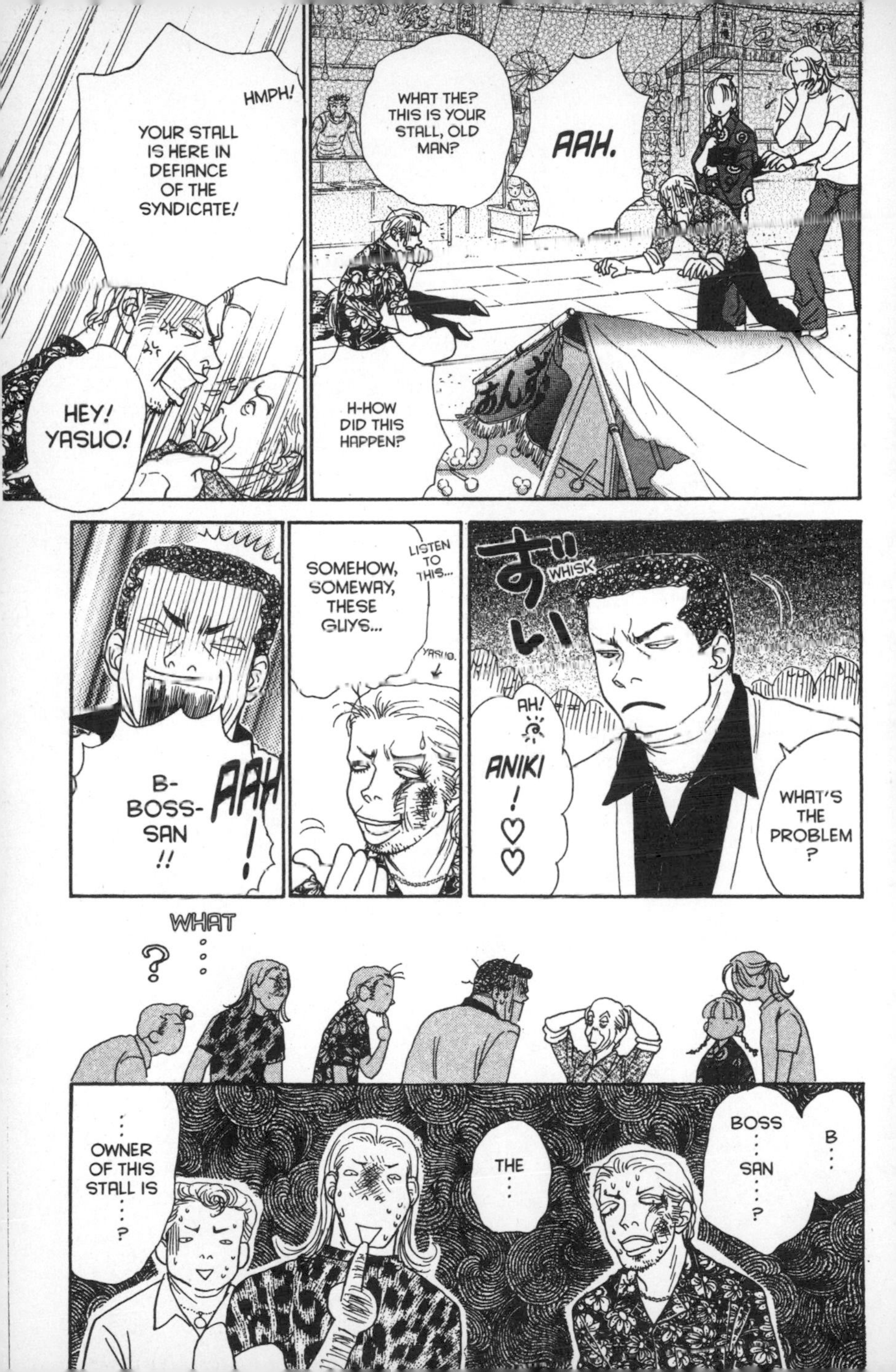
AAH.
WHAT THE? THIS IS YOUR STALL, OLD MAN?
H-HOW DID THIS HAPPEN?
HMPH!
YOUR STALL IS HERE IN DEFIANCE OF THE SYNDICATE!
HEY! YASUO!
すい WHISK
WHAT'S THE PROBLEM?
AH! ANIKI! ♡ ♡
LISTEN TO THIS...
SOMEHOW, SOMEWAY, THESE GUYS...
YASUO.
AAH!
B-BOSS-SAN!!
WHAT...
?
B...
BOSS...SAN...?
THE...
...OWNER OF THIS STALL IS...?

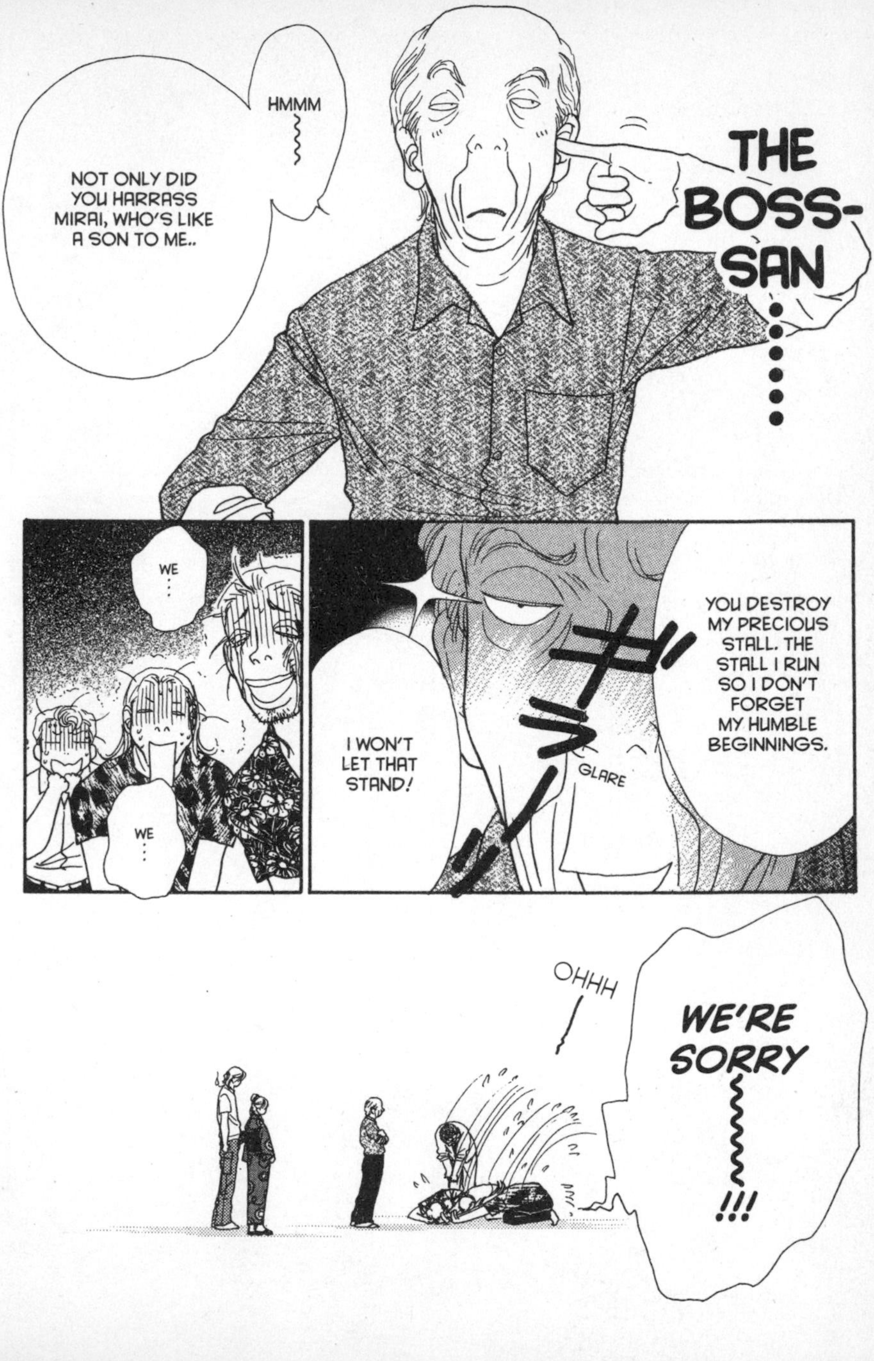
THE BOSS-SAN......
HMMM~
NOT ONLY DID YOU HARRASS MIRAI, WHO'S LIKE A SON TO ME..
YOU DESTROY MY PRECIOUS STALL. THE STALL I RUN SO I DON'T FORGET MY HUMBLE BEGINNINGS.
GLARE
I WON'T LET THAT STAND!
WE...
WE...
OHHH!
WE'RE SORRY~!!!

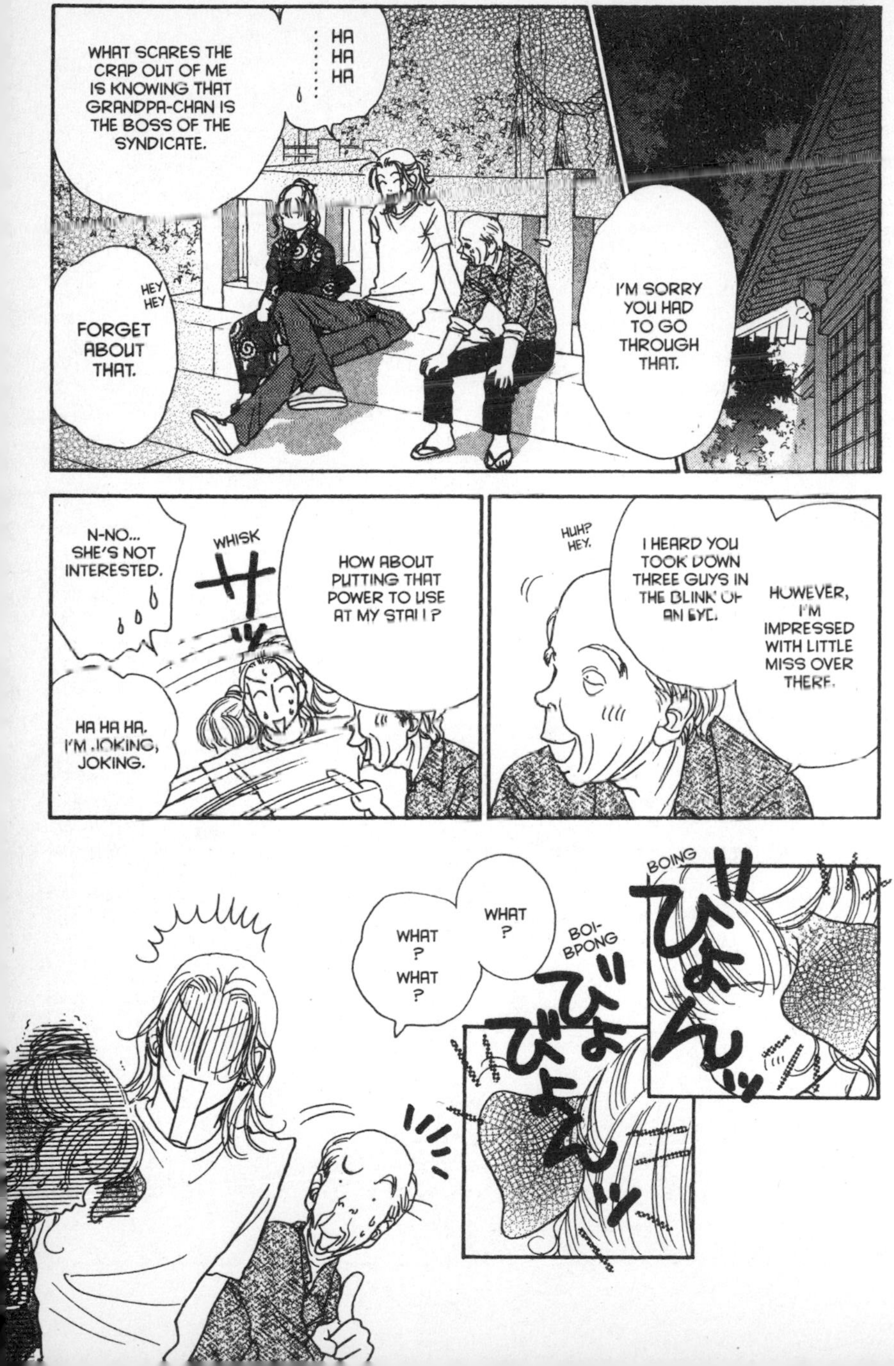
I'M SORRY YOU HAD TO GO THROUGH THAT.
HA HA HA
WHAT SCARES THE CRAP OUT OF ME IS KNOWING THAT GRANDPA-CHAN IS THE BOSS OF THE SYNDICATE.
HEY HEY
FORGET ABOUT THAT.
HOWEVER, I'M IMPRESSED WITH LITTLE MISS OVER THERE.
I HEARD YOU TOOK DOWN THREE GUYS IN THE BLINK OF AN EYE.
HUH? HEY.
HOW ABOUT PUTTING THAT POWER TO USE AT MY STALL?
WHISK
サッ
N-NO... SHE'S NOT INTERESTED.
HA HA HA. I'M JOKING, JOKING.
BOING
ぴょんッ
BOI-BPONG
ぴょんぴょんッ
WHAT?
WHAT? WHAT?

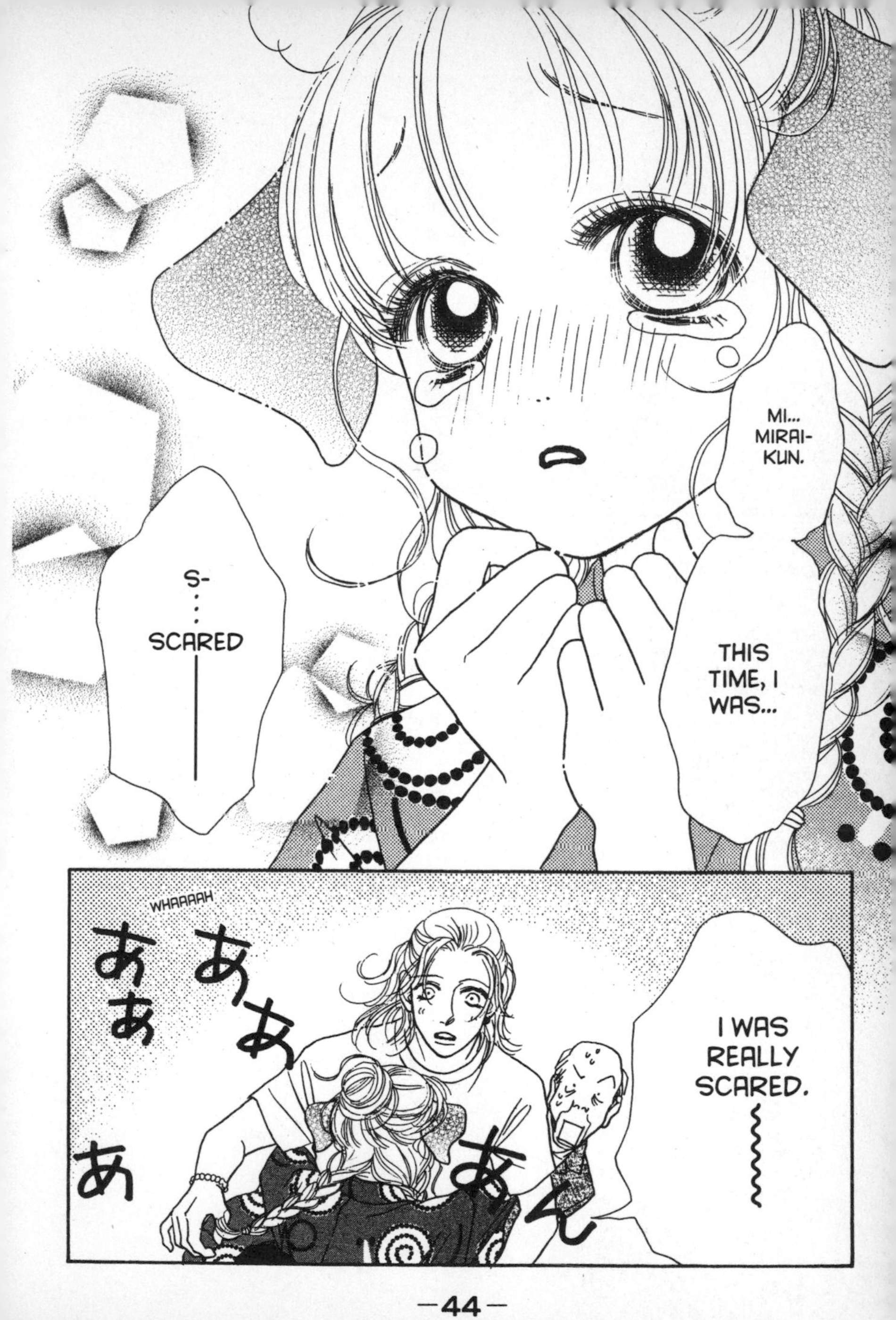
MI... MIRAI-KUN.
THIS TIME, I WAS...
S-... SCARED
I WAS REALLY SCARED.
WHAAAAH

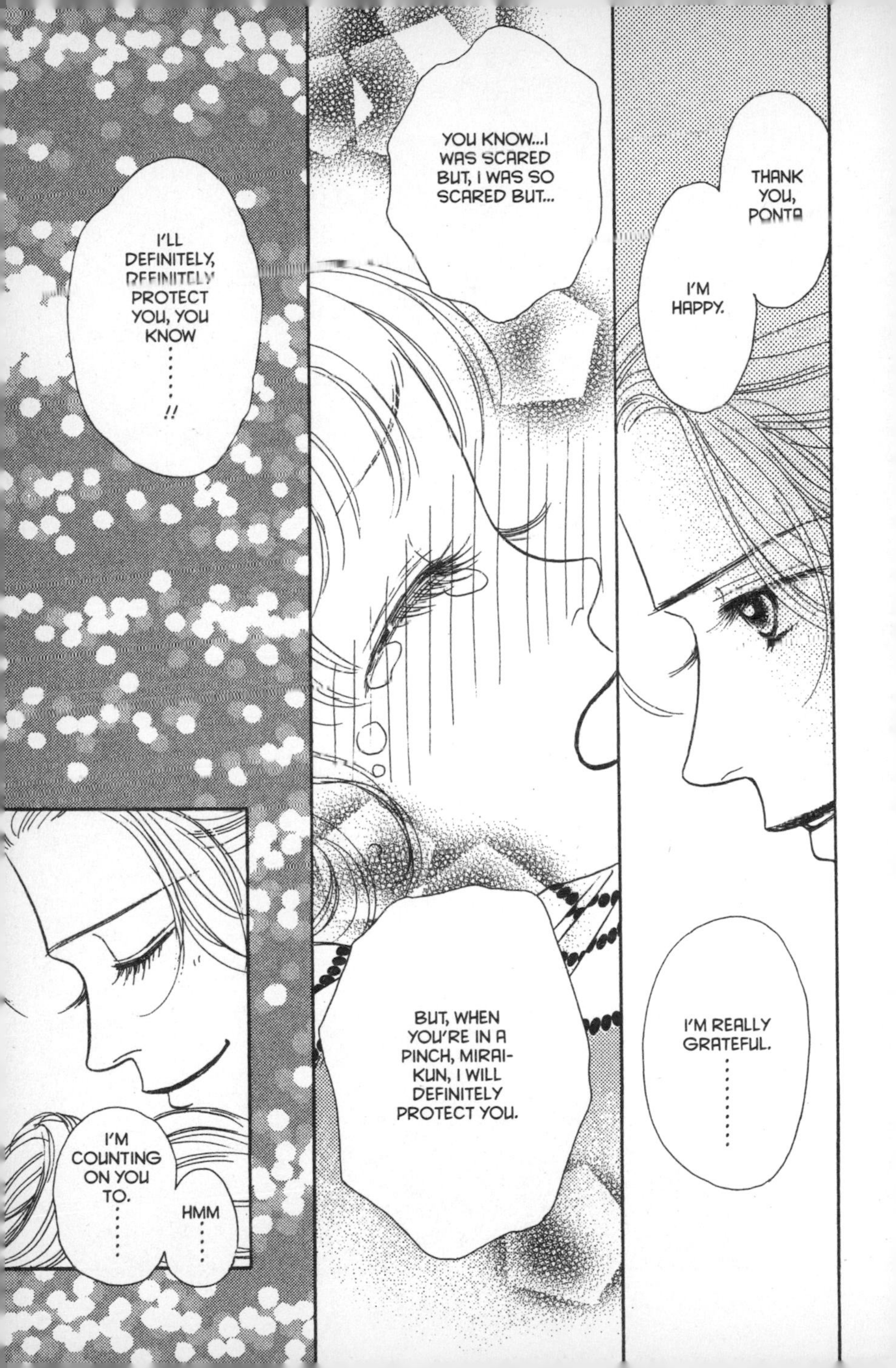
THANK YOU, PONTA
I'M HAPPY.
I'M REALLY GRATEFUL. ……
YOU KNOW...I WAS SCARED BUT, I WAS SO SCARED BUT...
BUT, WHEN YOU'RE IN A PINCH, MIRAI-KUN, I WILL DEFINITELY PROTECT YOU.
I'LL DEFINITELY, DEFINITELY PROTECT YOU, YOU KNOW……!!
I'M COUNTING ON YOU TO. ……
HMM ……

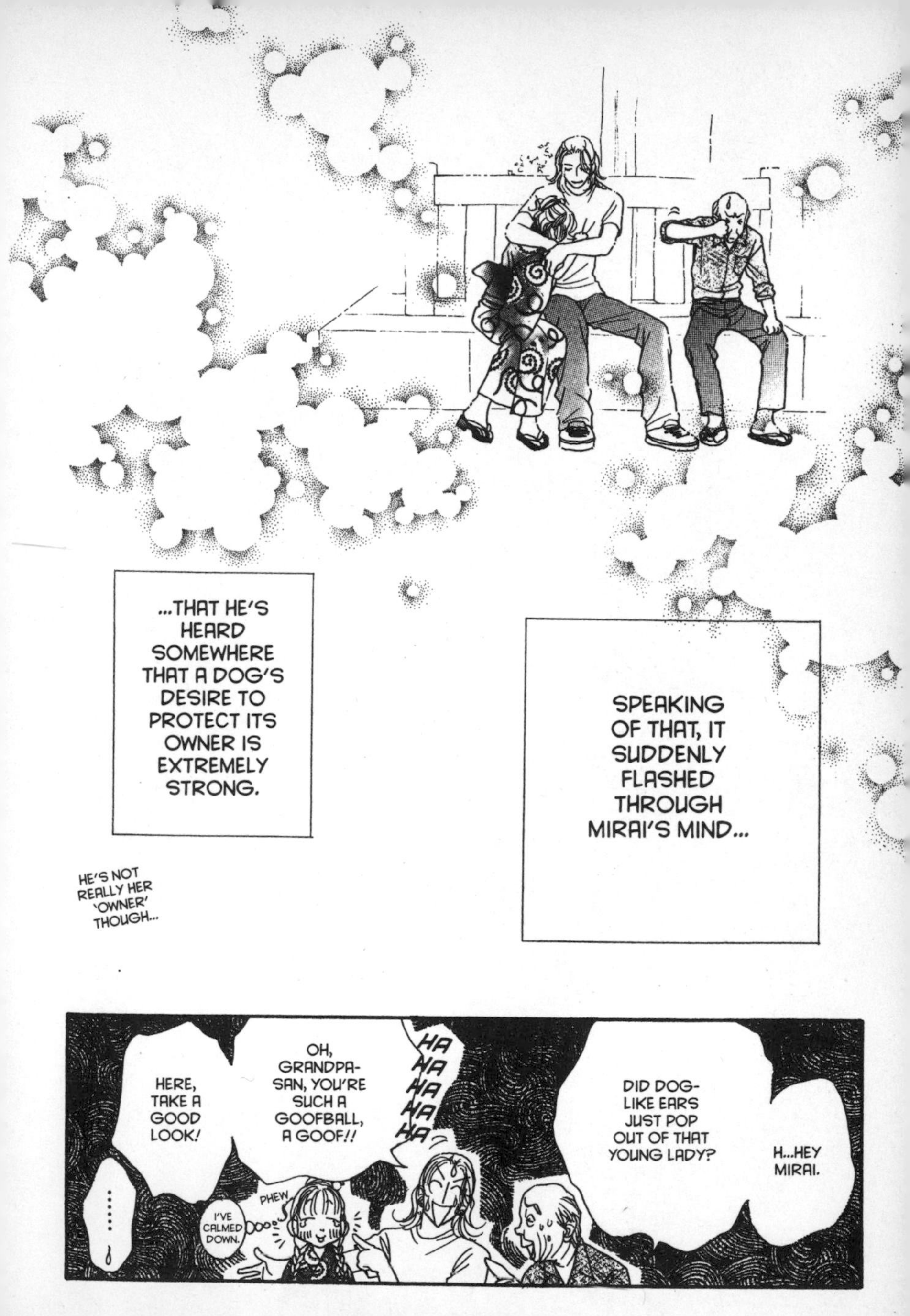
SPEAKING OF THAT, IT SUDDENLY FLASHED THROUGH MIRAI'S MIND...
...THAT HE'S HEARD SOMEWHERE THAT A DOG'S DESIRE TO PROTECT ITS OWNER IS EXTREMELY STRONG.
HE'S NOT REALLY HER 'OWNER' THOUGH...
H...HEY MIRAI.
DID DOG-LIKE EARS JUST POP OUT OF THAT YOUNG LADY?
HA HA HA HA HA HA
OH, GRANDPA-SAN, YOU'RE SUCH A GOOFBALL, A GOOF!!
HERE, TAKE A GOOD LOOK!
PHEW
I'VE CALMED DOWN.
......

END OF CHAPTER 22

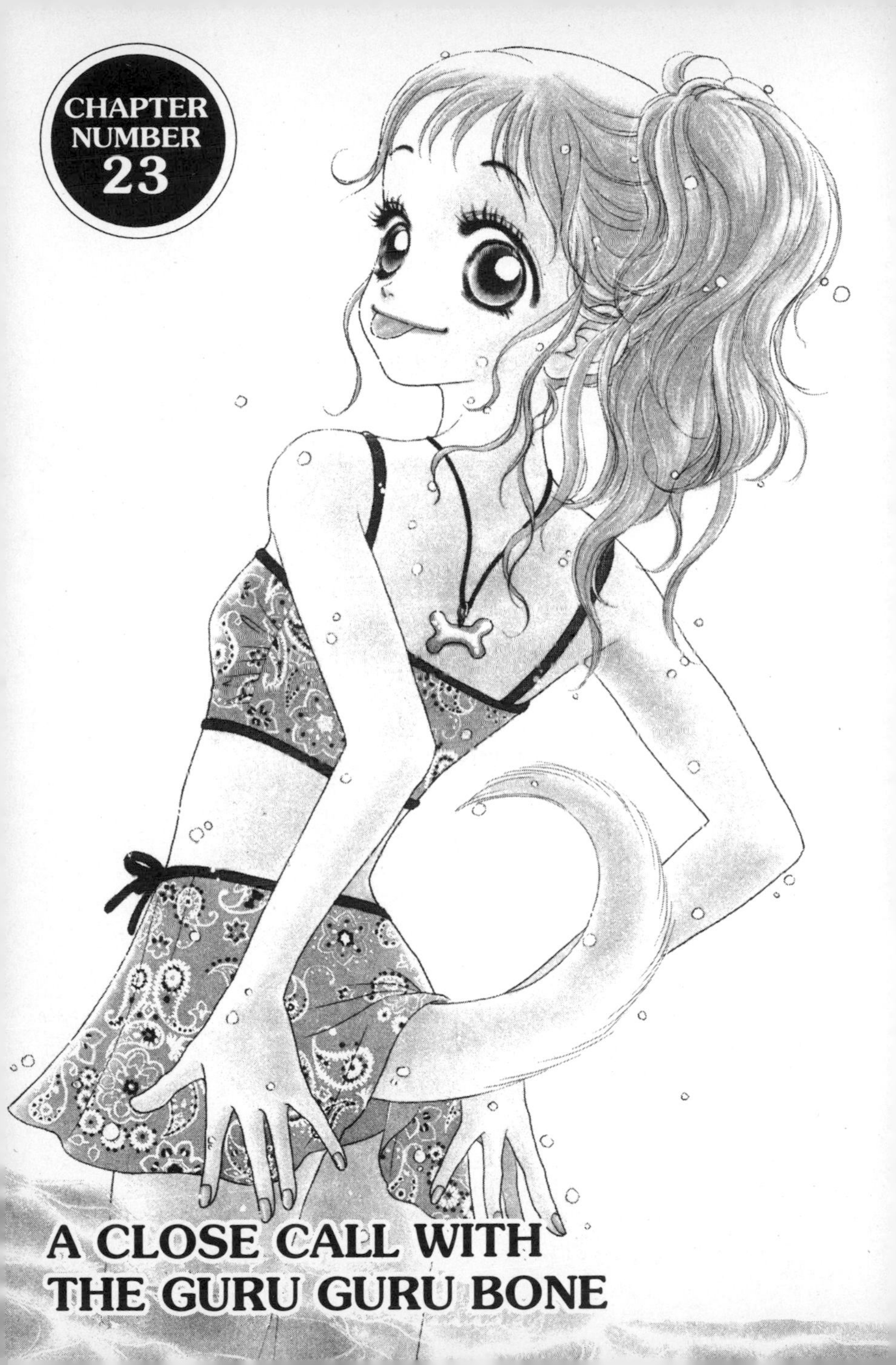
CHAPTER NUMBER 23
A CLOSE CALL WITH THE GURU GURU BONE

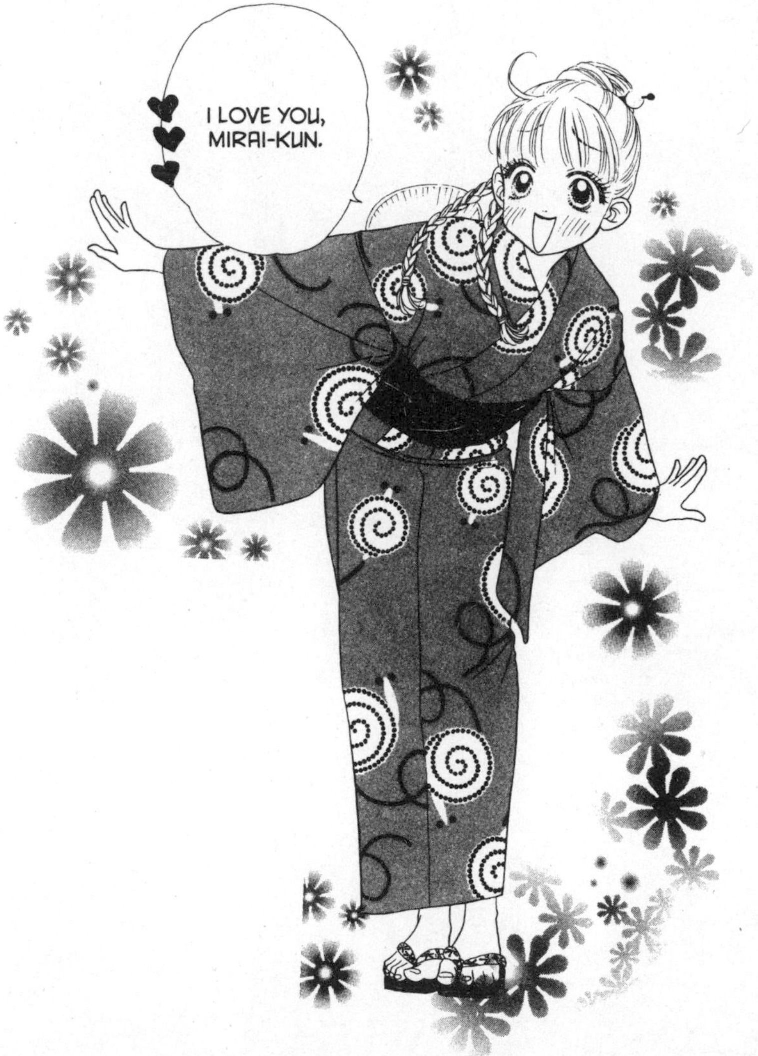
I LOVE YOU, MIRAI-KUN.

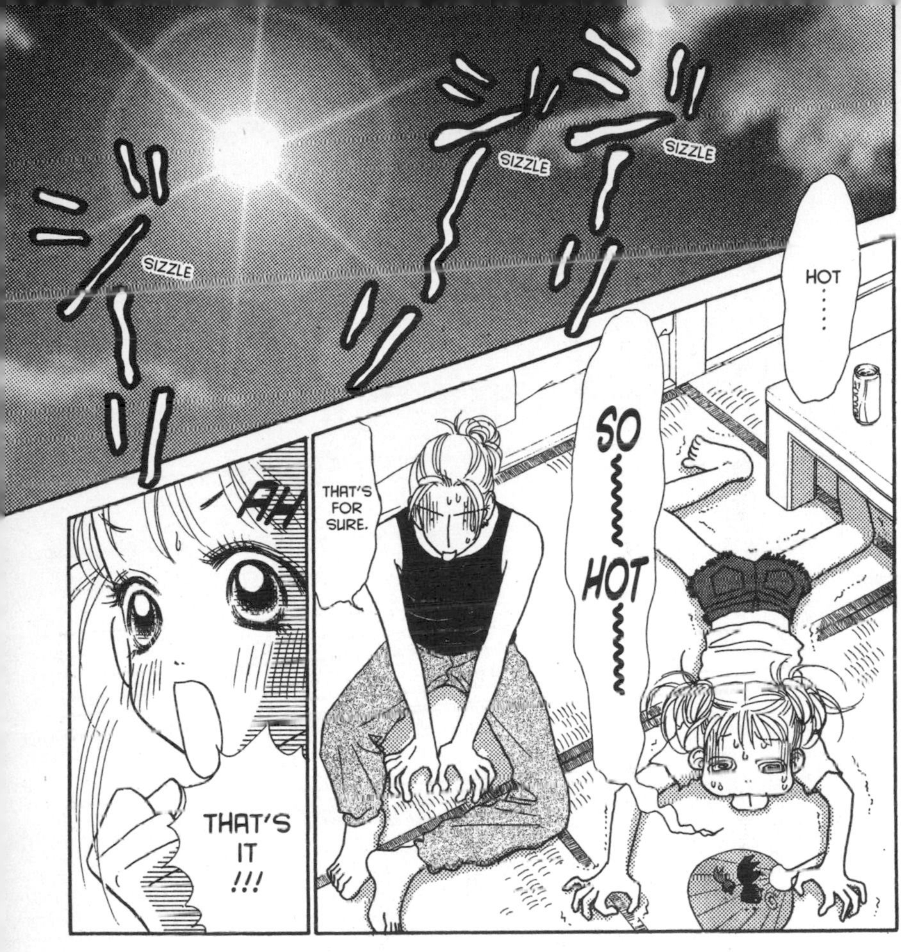
SIZZLE
SIZZLE
SIZZLE
HOT.....
SO~~~ HOT~~~
THAT'S FOR SURE.
AH
THAT'S IT !!!

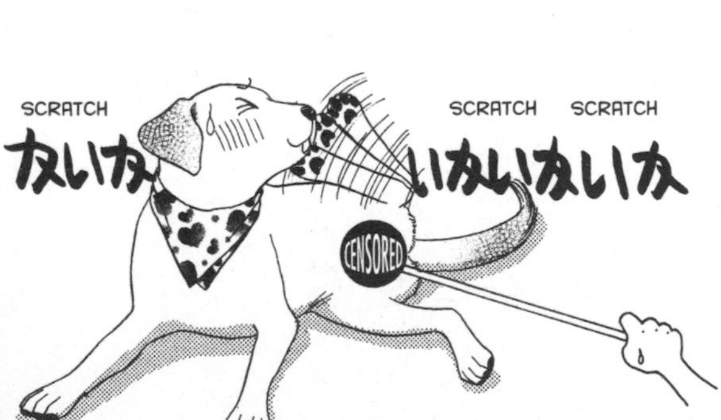
SCRATCH
SCRATCH SCRATCH
CENSORED

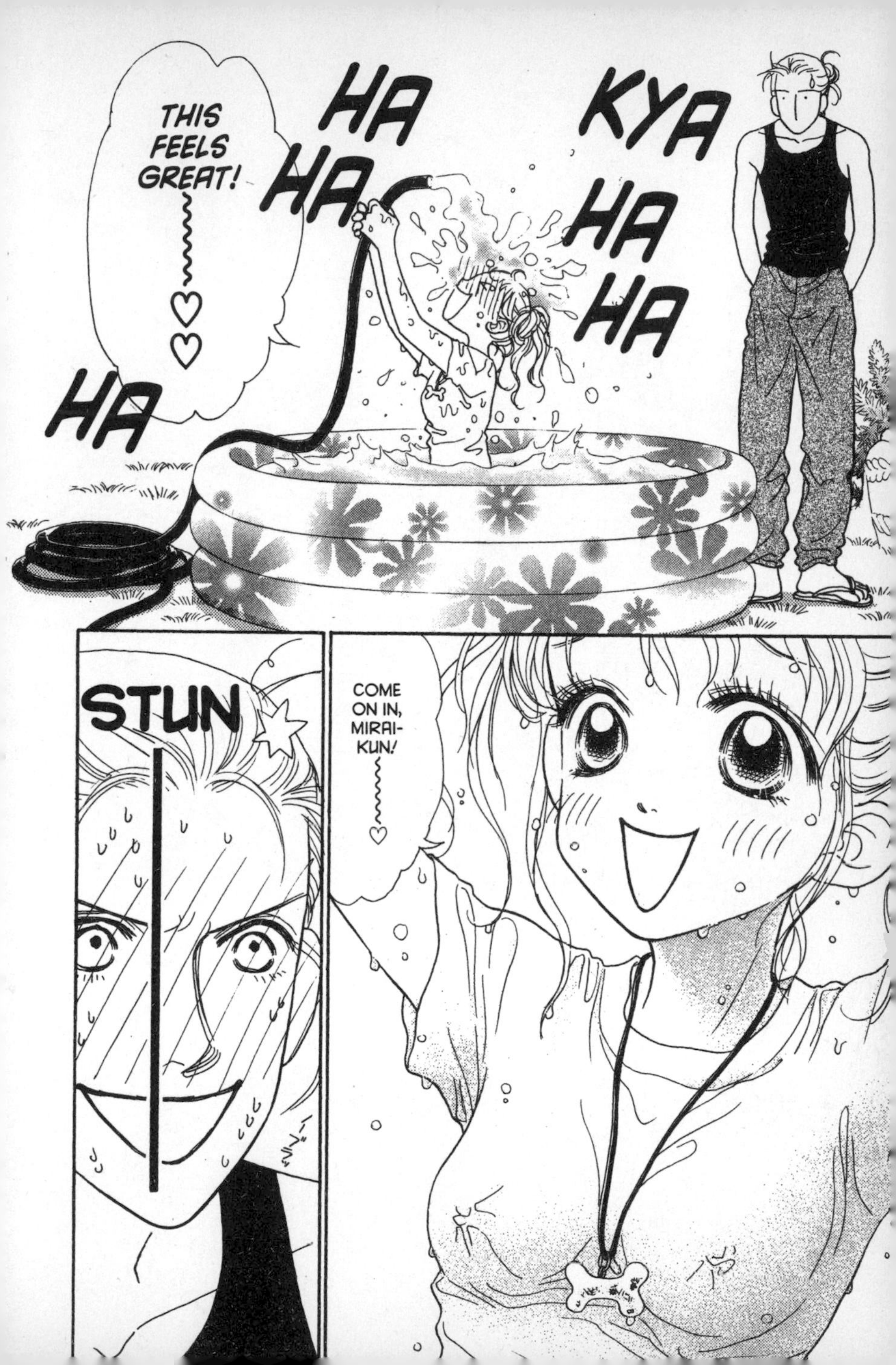
KYA HA HA HA
HA HA
THIS FEELS GREAT!
HA
COME ON IN, MIRAI-KUN!
STUN

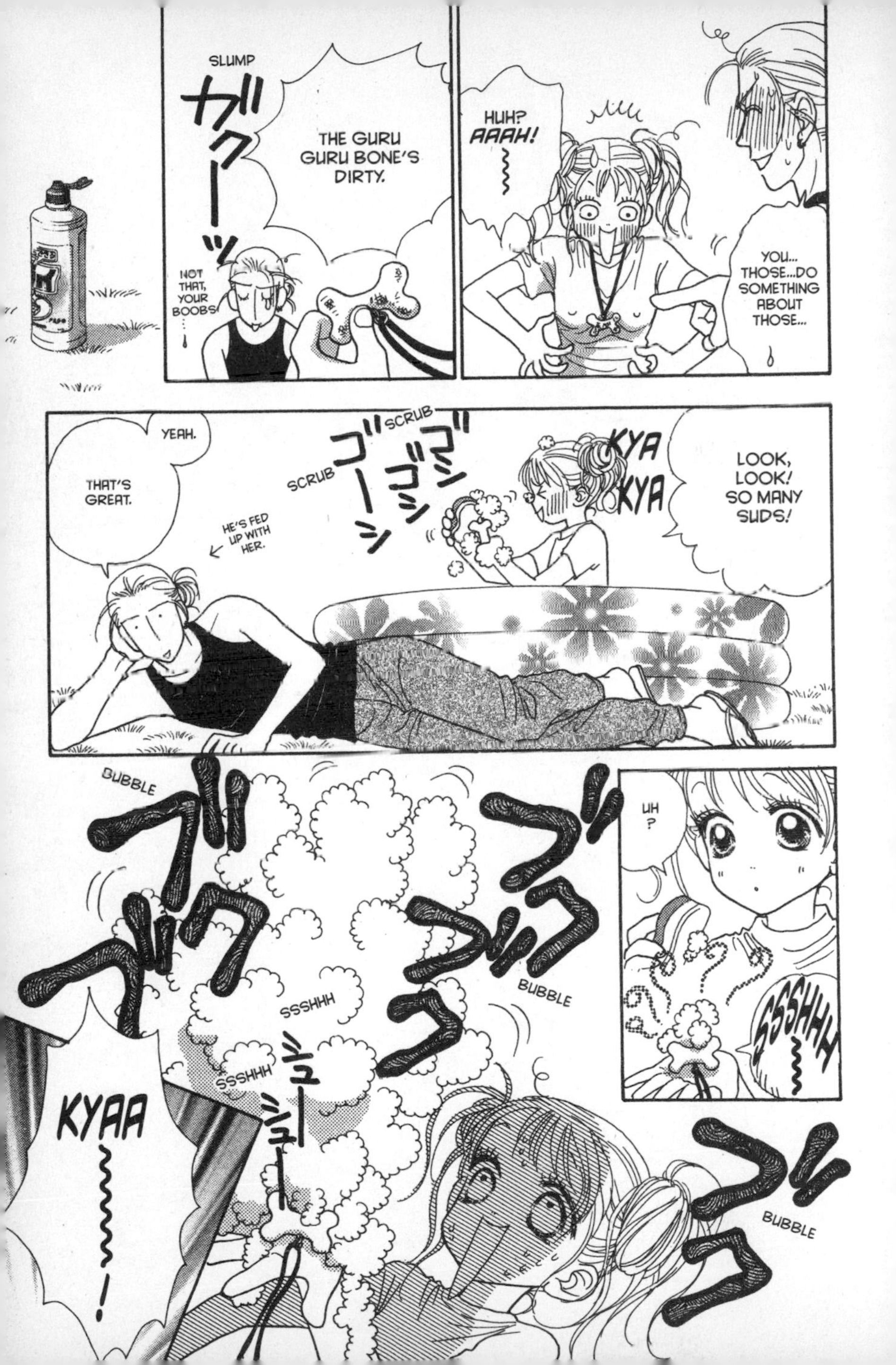
YOU... THOSE...DO SOMETHING ABOUT THOSE...
HUH? AAAH!
THE GURU GURU BONE'S DIRTY.
SLUMP
NOT THAT, YOUR BOOBS!...
LOOK, LOOK! SO MANY SUDS!
KYA KYA
SCRUB
SCRUB
YEAH.
THAT'S GREAT.
HE'S FED UP WITH HER.
UH?
SSSHHH
BUBBLE
BUBBLE
BUBBLE
SSSHHH
SSSHHH
KYAA~!

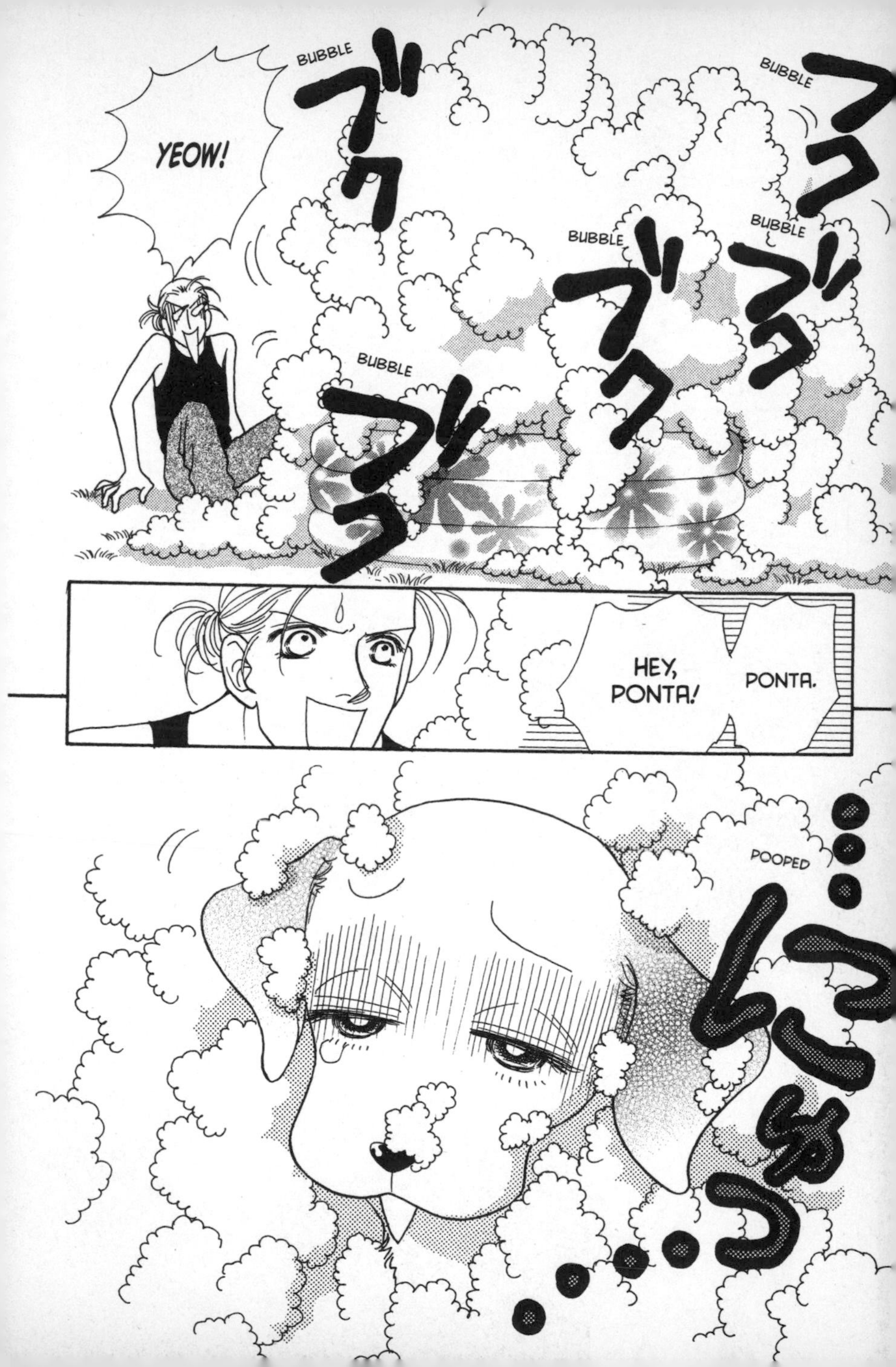
BUBBLE
BUBBLE
BUBBLE
BUBBLE
BUBBLE
YEOW!
PONTA.
HEY, PONTA!
POOPED

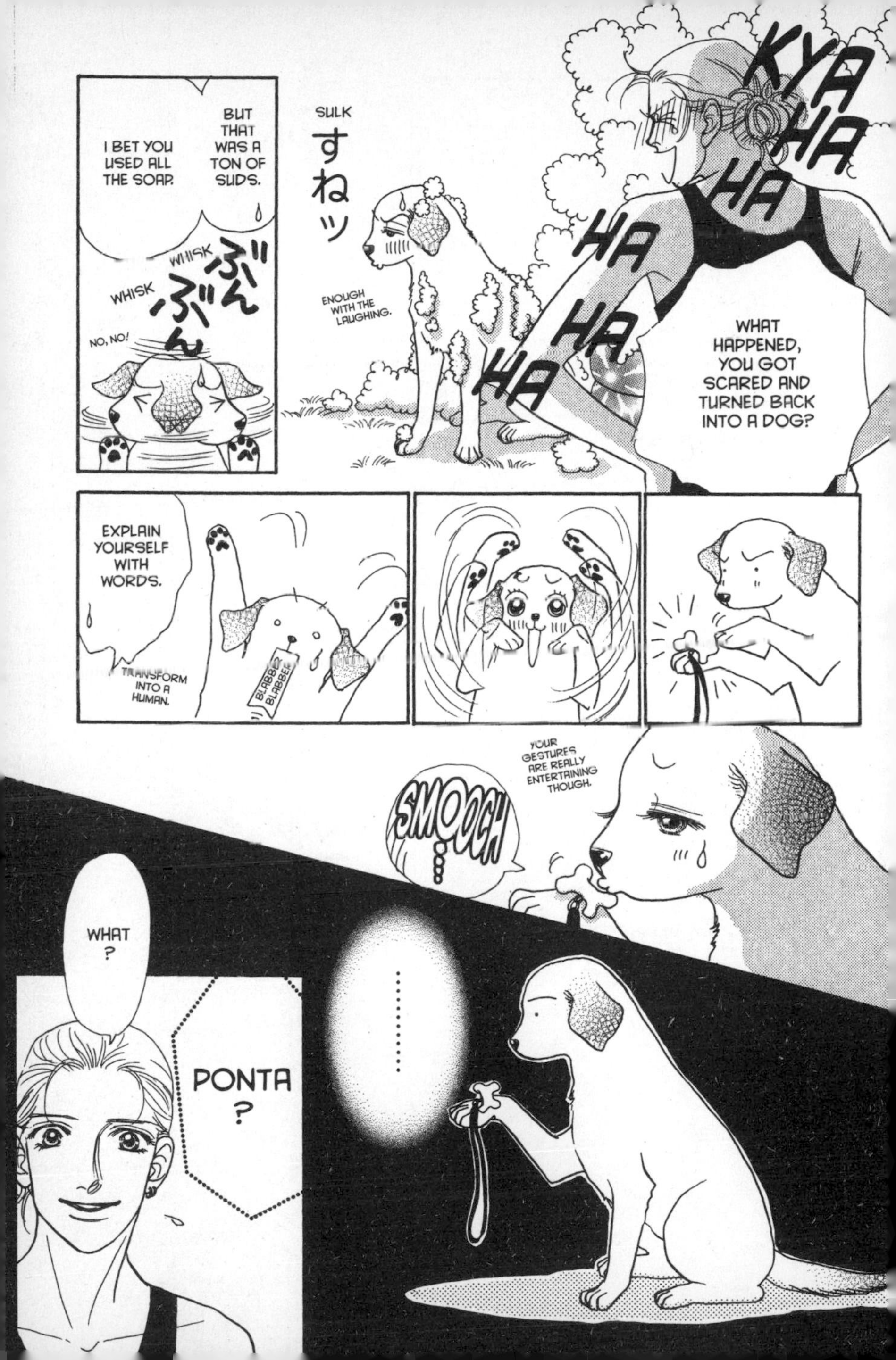
KYA HA HA HA HA HA
WHAT HAPPENED, YOU GOT SCARED AND TURNED BACK INTO A DOG?
SULK
すねッ
ENOUGH WITH THE LAUGHING.
BUT THAT WAS A TON OF SUDS.
I BET YOU USED ALL THE SOAP.
WHISK ぶん
WHISK ぶん
NO, NO!
EXPLAIN YOURSELF WITH WORDS.
TRANSFORM INTO A HUMAN.
BLABBER BLABBER
YOUR GESTURES ARE REALLY ENTERTAINING THOUGH.
SMOOCH
……
PONTA ?
WHAT ?

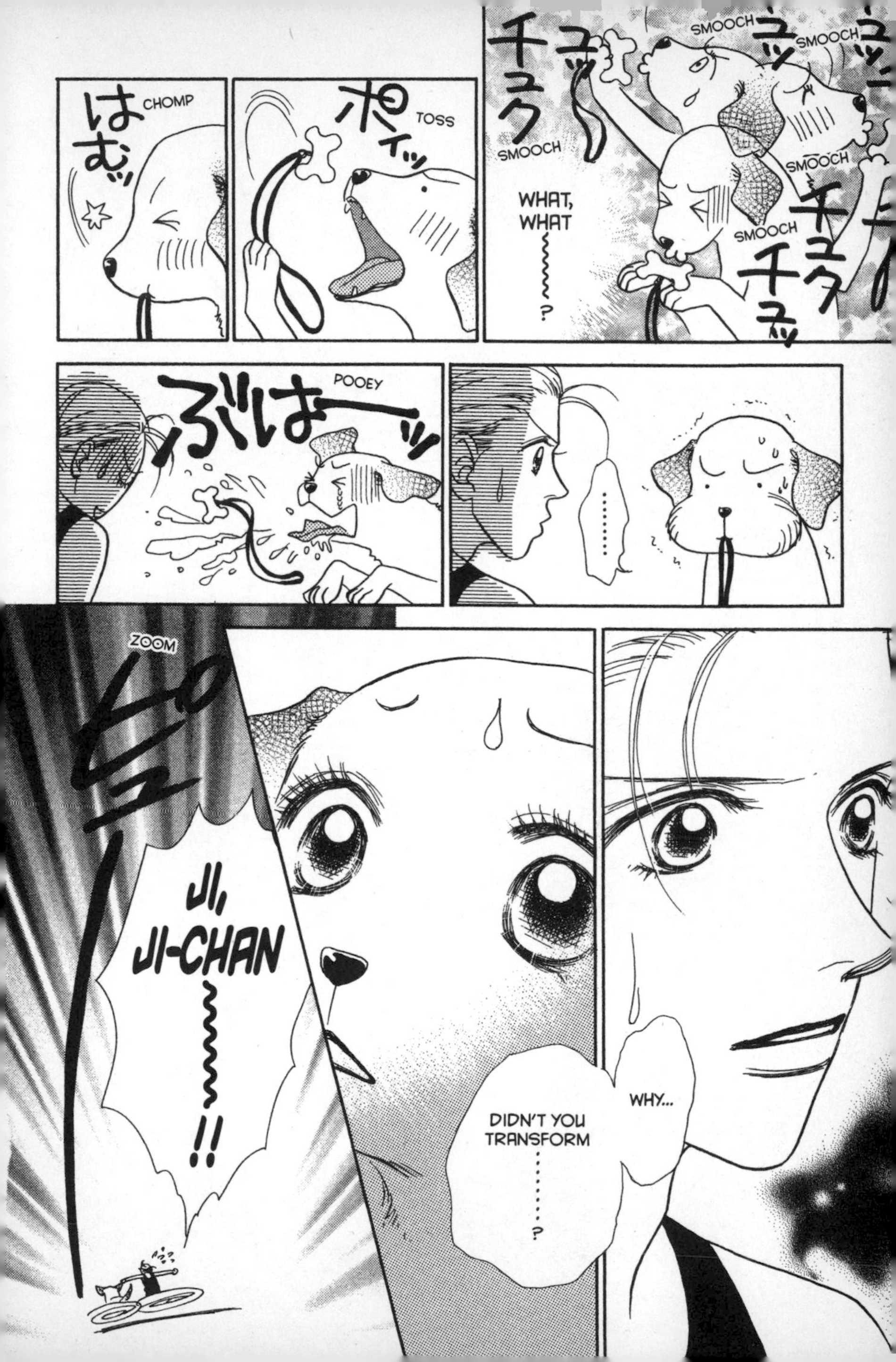
SMOOCH
SMOOCH
SMOOCH
SMOOCH
SMOOCH
WHAT, WHAT~~~?
ポイッ
TOSS
はむッ
CHOMP
......
ぶはーッ
POOEY
WHY...
DIDN'T YOU TRANSFORM......?
ZOOM
JI, JI-CHAN~~~!!

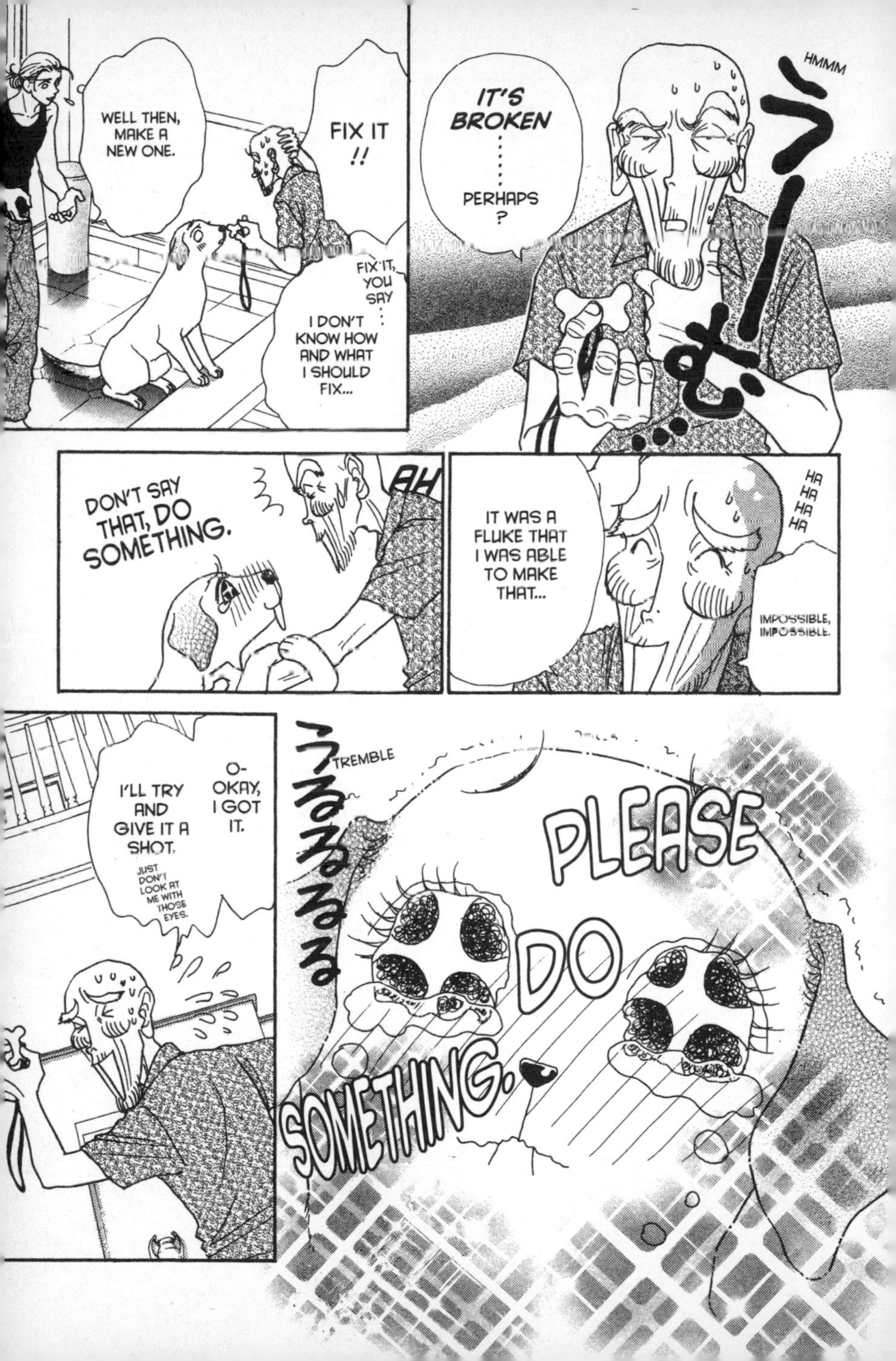
HMMM
IT'S BROKEN ...... PERHAPS ?
FIX IT !!
WELL THEN, MAKE A NEW ONE.
FIX IT, YOU SAY...
I DON'T KNOW HOW AND WHAT I SHOULD FIX...
HA HA HA HA
IT WAS A FLUKE THAT I WAS ABLE TO MAKE THAT...
IMPOSSIBLE, IMPOSSIBLE.
AH
DON'T SAY THAT, DO SOMETHING.
TREMBLE
PLEASE DO SOMETHING.
O-OKAY, I GOT IT.
I'LL TRY AND GIVE IT A SHOT.
JUST DON'T LOOK AT ME WITH THOSE EYES.

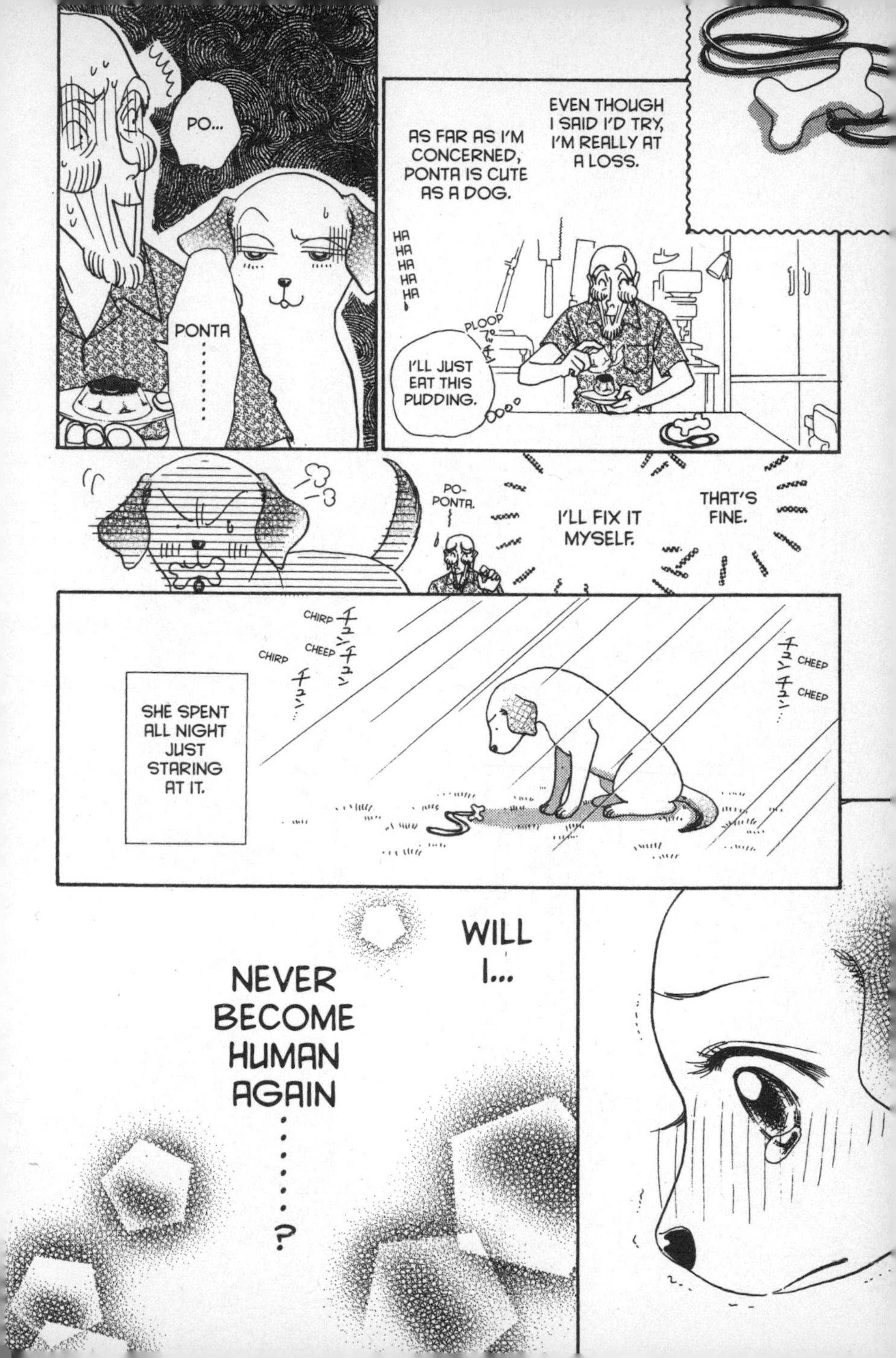
EVEN THOUGH I SAID I'D TRY, I'M REALLY AT A LOSS.
AS FAR AS I'M CONCERNED, PONTA IS CUTE AS A DOG.
HA HA HA HA HA
PLOOP
I'LL JUST EAT THIS PUDDING.
PO...
PONTA......
THAT'S FINE.
I'LL FIX IT MYSELF.
PO-PONTA.
チュンチュン...
CHEEP
CHEEP
CHIRP
チュンチュン
CHEEP
CHIRP
チュン...
SHE SPENT ALL NIGHT JUST STARING AT IT.
WILL I...
NEVER BECOME HUMAN AGAIN......?

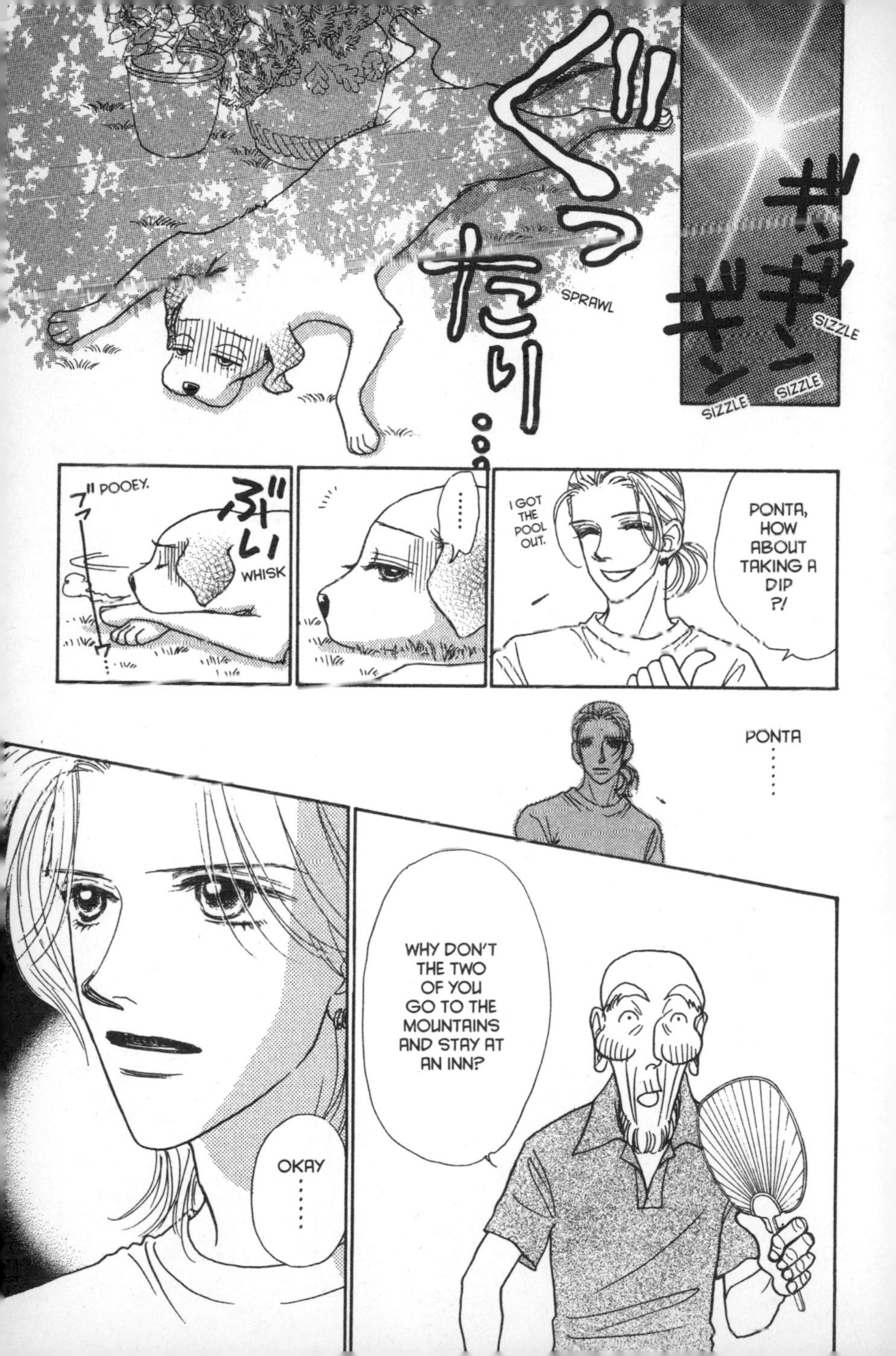

ギンギン
SIZZLE
SIZZLE
SIZZLE
ぐったり。。。
SPRAWL
PONTA, HOW ABOUT TAKING A DIP ?!
I GOT THE POOL OUT.
......
ぶい
WHISK
POOEY.
PONTA ......
WHY DON'T THE TWO OF YOU GO TO THE MOUNTAINS AND STAY AT AN INN?
OKAY ......

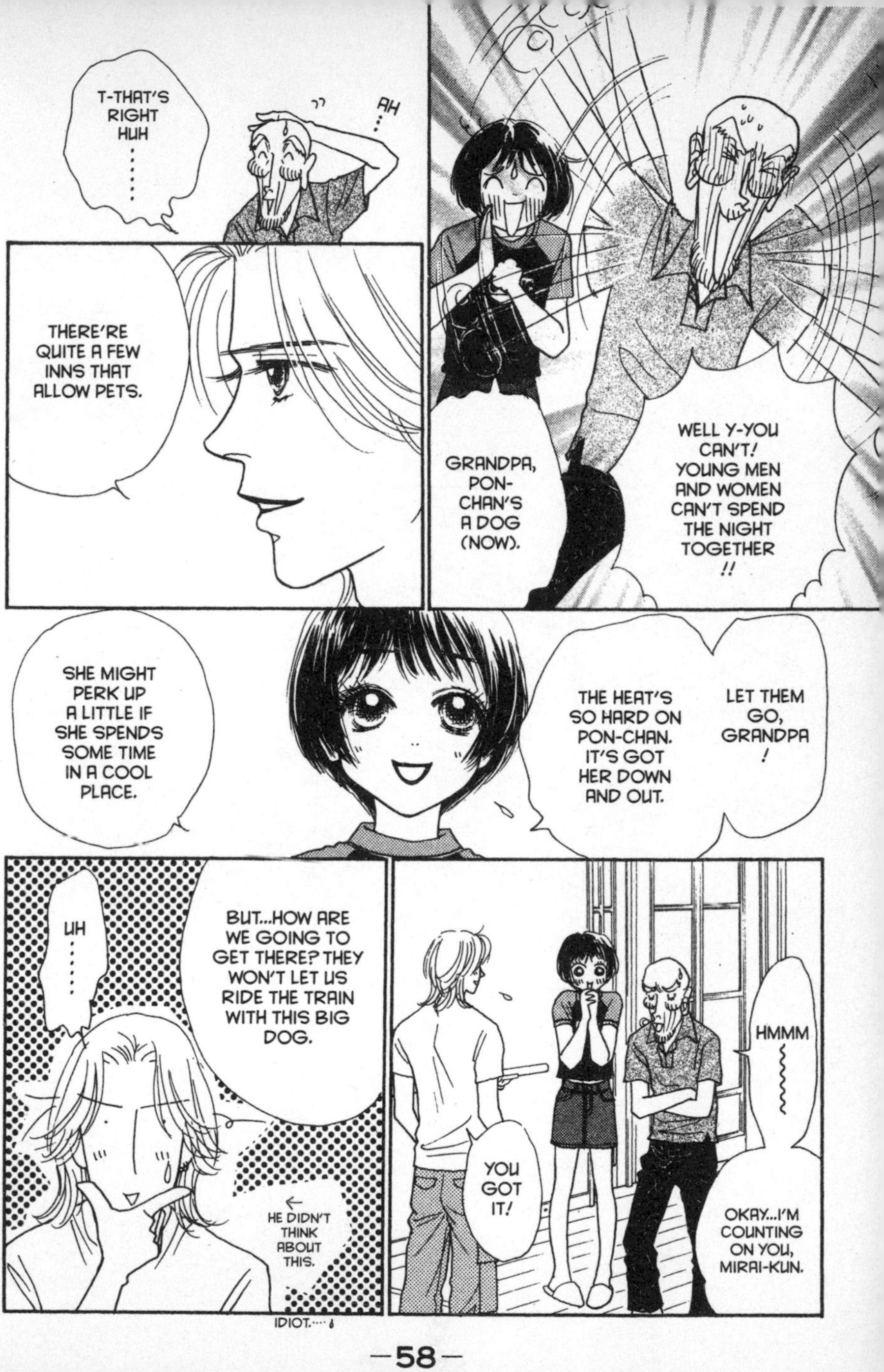
WELL Y-YOU CAN'T! YOUNG MEN AND WOMEN CAN'T SPEND THE NIGHT TOGETHER!!
GRANDPA, PON-CHAN'S A DOG (NOW).
AH...
T-THAT'S RIGHT HUH......
THERE'RE QUITE A FEW INNS THAT ALLOW PETS.
LET THEM GO, GRANDPA!
THE HEAT'S SO HARD ON PON-CHAN. IT'S GOT HER DOWN AND OUT.
SHE MIGHT PERK UP A LITTLE IF SHE SPENDS SOME TIME IN A COOL PLACE.
HMMM~
OKAY...I'M COUNTING ON YOU, MIRAI-KUN.
YOU GOT IT!
BUT...HOW ARE WE GOING TO GET THERE? THEY WON'T LET US RIDE THE TRAIN WITH THIS BIG DOG.
UH......
← HE DIDN'T THINK ABOUT THIS.
IDIOT.....

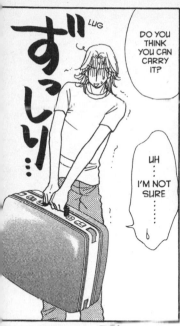

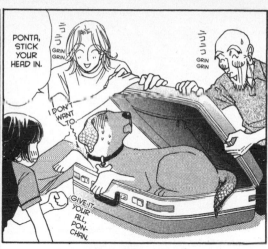

PONTA, STICK YOUR HEAD IN.
GRIN GRIN
GRIN GRIN
I DON'T WANT TO.
GIVE IT YOUR ALL, PON-CHAN.
LATCH
IT WORKED!
ずっしり…
LUG
DO YOU THINK YOU CAN CARRY IT?
UH… I'M NOT SURE……
PLOP
ROLL
WHEEZE WHEEZE WHEEZE
THIS ISN'T GOING TO WORK……
I GOT IT!!!
AH!

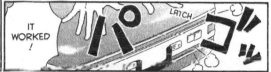

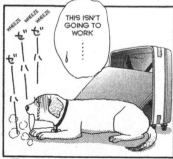

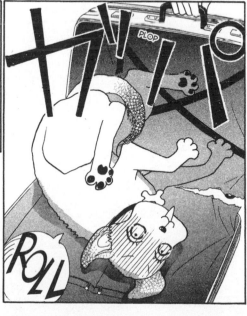

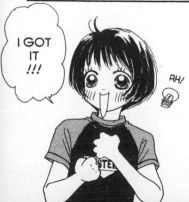

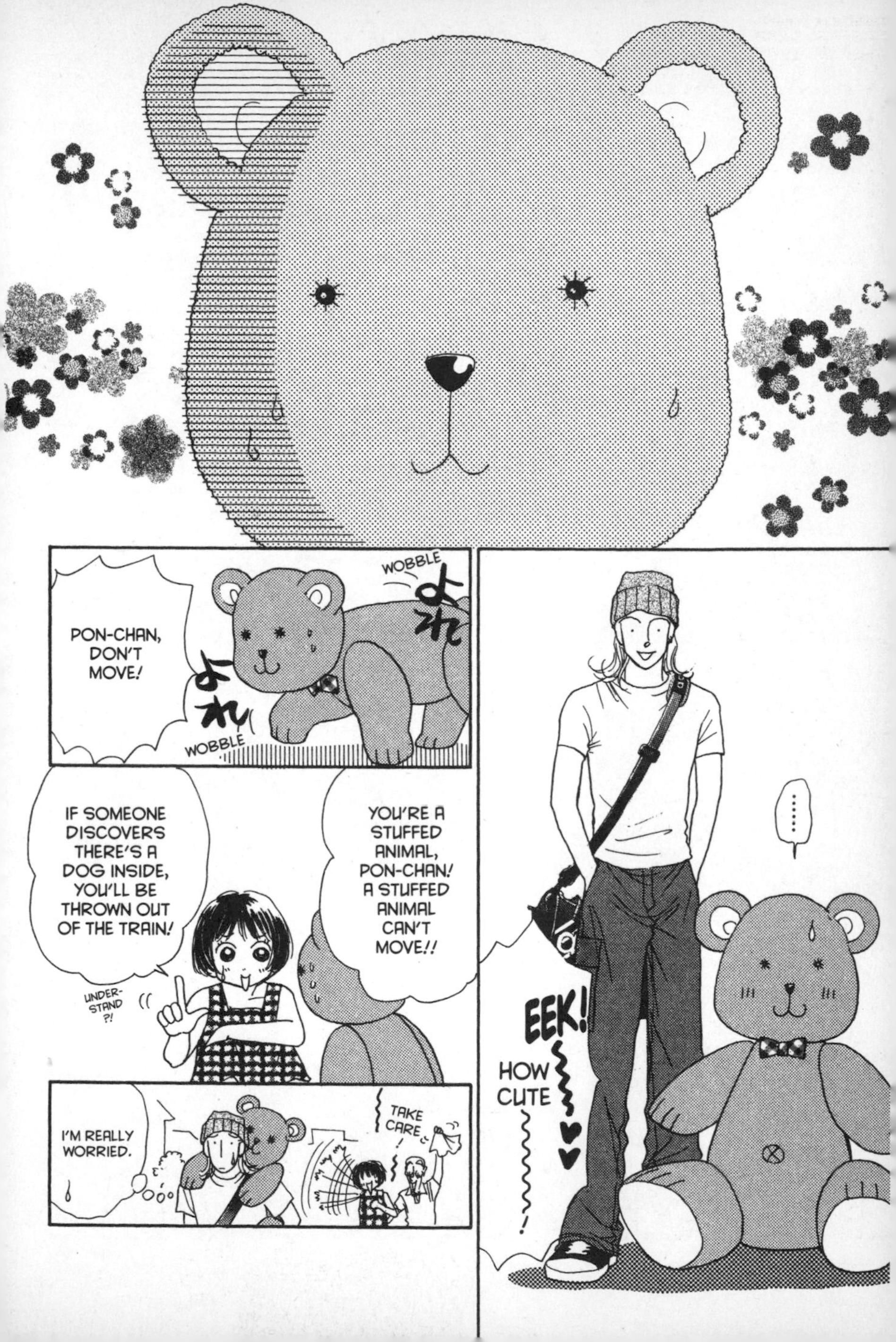
......
EEK!
HOW CUTE
PON-CHAN, DON'T MOVE!
WOBBLE
よれ
よれ
WOBBLE
YOU'RE A STUFFED ANIMAL, PON-CHAN! A STUFFED ANIMAL CAN'T MOVE!!
IF SOMEONE DISCOVERS THERE'S A DOG INSIDE, YOU'LL BE THROWN OUT OF THE TRAIN!
UNDERSTAND?!
TAKE CARE!
I'M REALLY WORRIED.

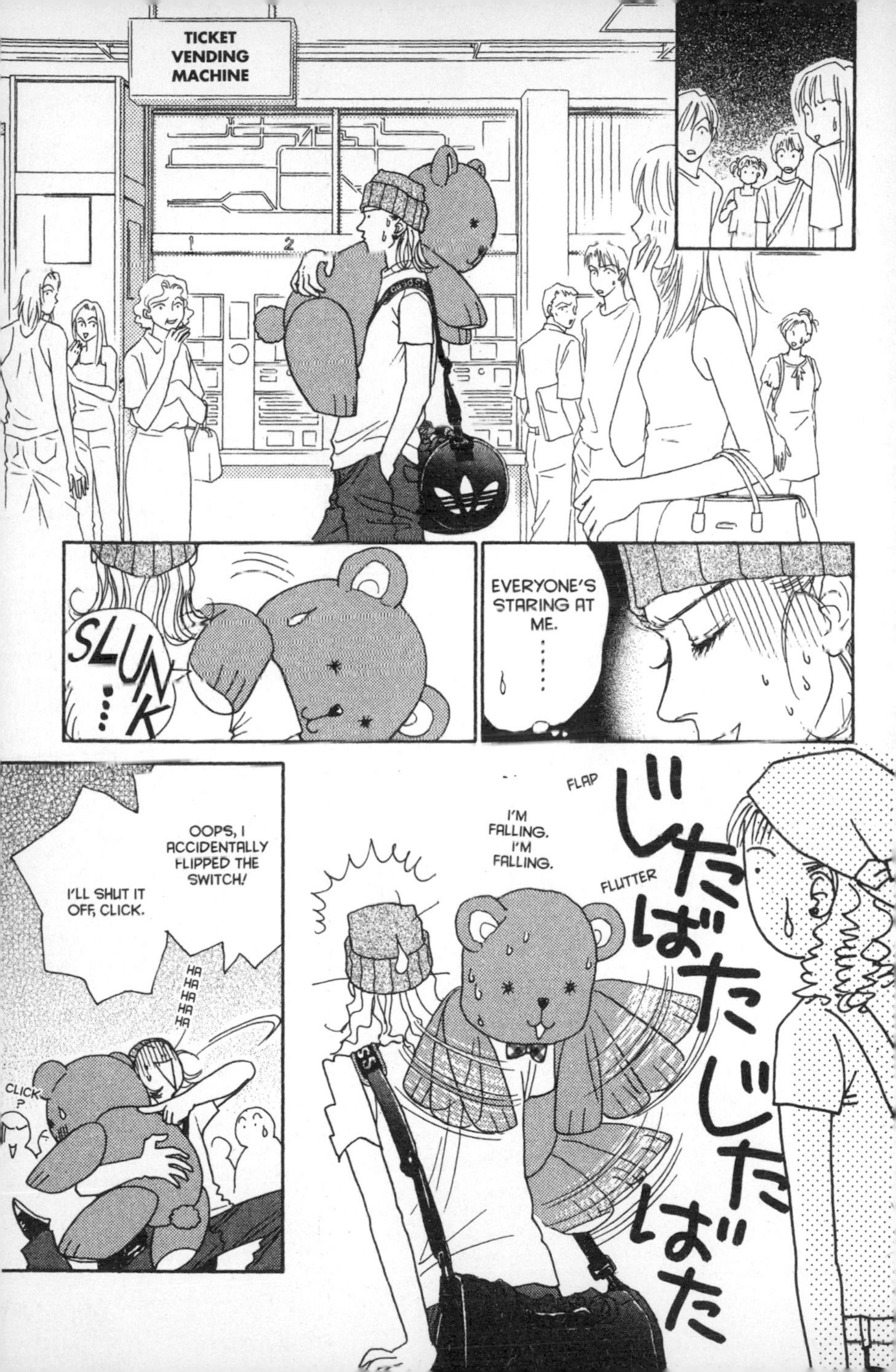
TICKET VENDING MACHINE
EVERYONE'S STARING AT ME. ......
SLUNK...
じたばたじたばた
FLAP
FLUTTER
I'M FALLING. I'M FALLING.
OOPS, I ACCIDENTALLY FLIPPED THE SWITCH!
I'LL SHUT IT OFF, CLICK.
HA HA HA HA HA
CLICK?

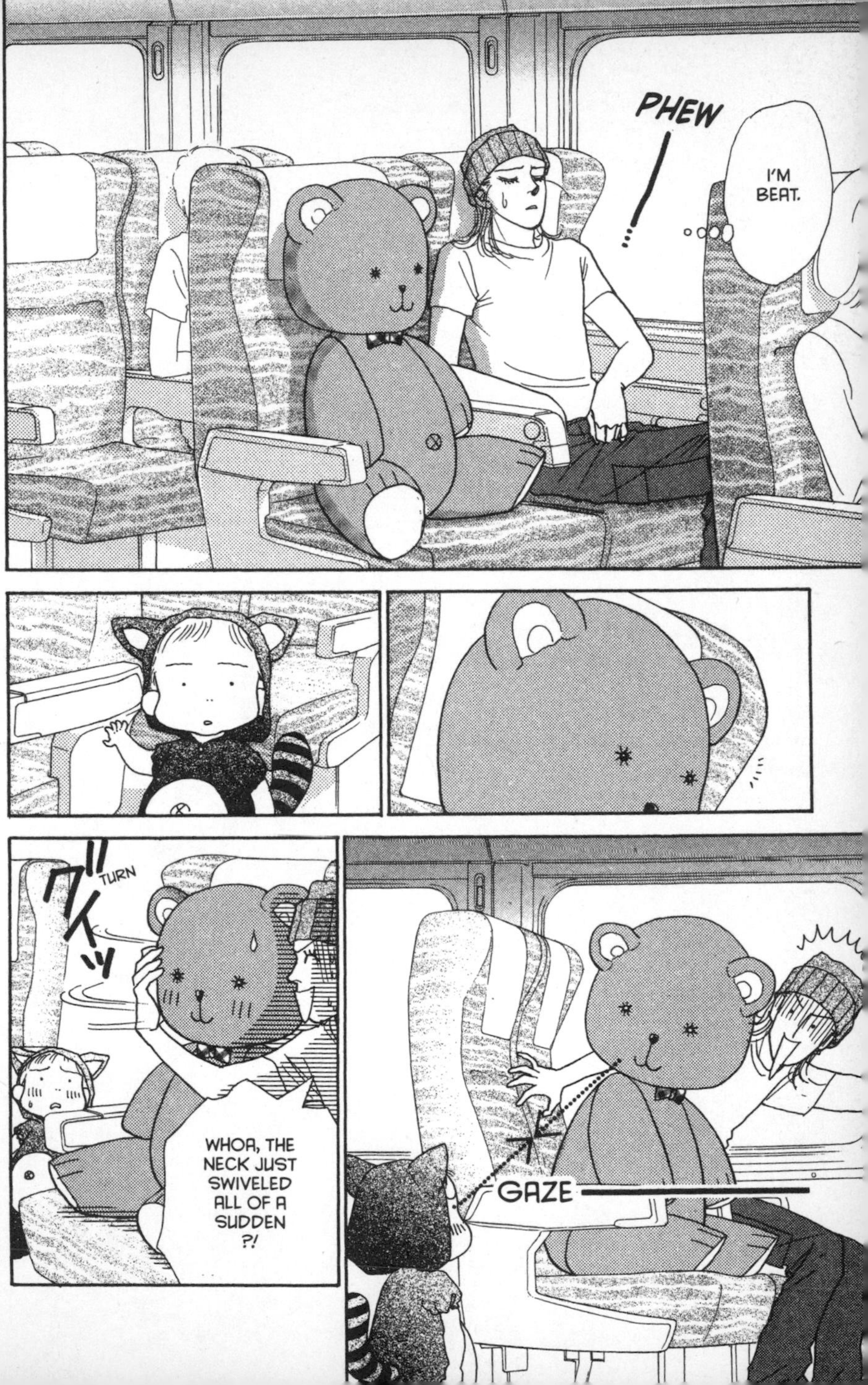
PHEW
I'M BEAT.
GAZE
TURN
WHOA, THE NECK JUST SWIVELED ALL OF A SUDDEN ?!

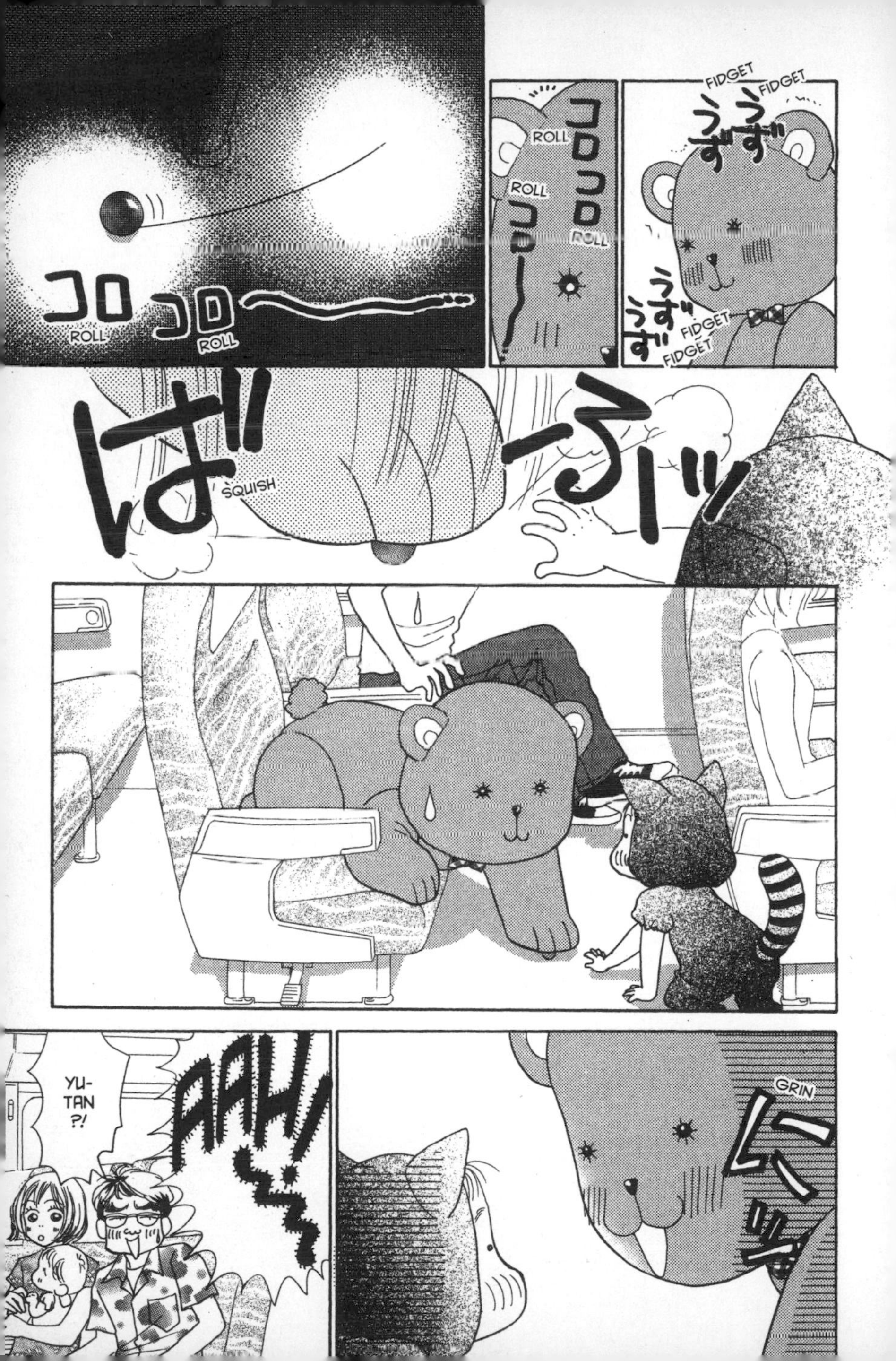
FIDGET FIDGET
うずうず
うずうず
FIDGET FIDGET
ROLL
コロコロ
ROLL
ROLL
コロー
コロ
ROLL
コロ
ROLL
ばーふッ
SQUISH
GRIN
にーッ
AAH!
YU-TAN ?!

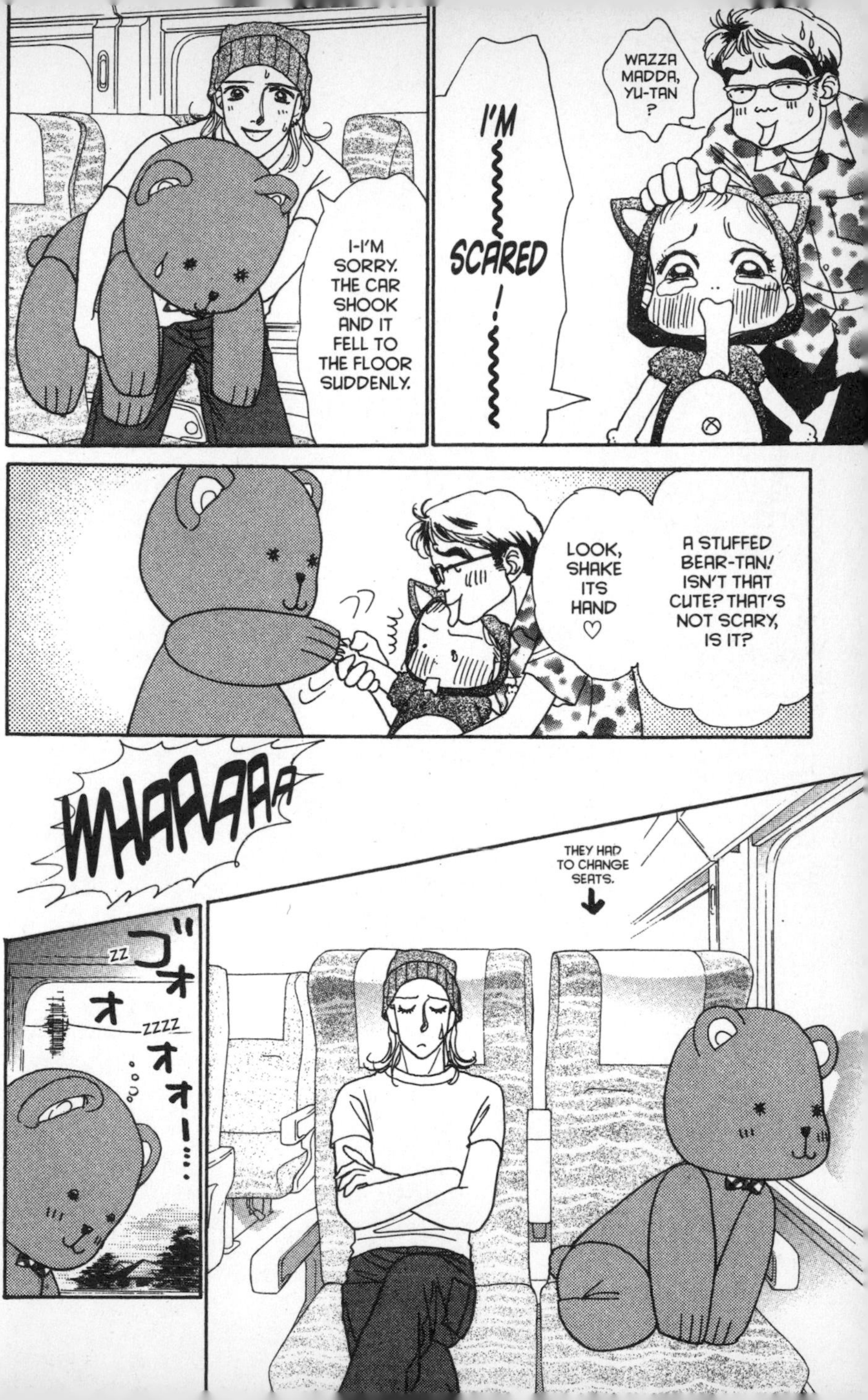
WAZZA MADDA, YU-TAN?
I'M SCARED!
I-I'M SORRY. THE CAR SHOOK AND IT FELL TO THE FLOOR SUDDENLY.
A STUFFED BEAR-TAN! ISN'T THAT CUTE? THAT'S NOT SCARY, IS IT?
LOOK, SHAKE ITS HAND ♡
WHAAAAA
THEY HAD TO CHANGE SEATS.
ZZ
ゴオオオオー……
ZZZZ

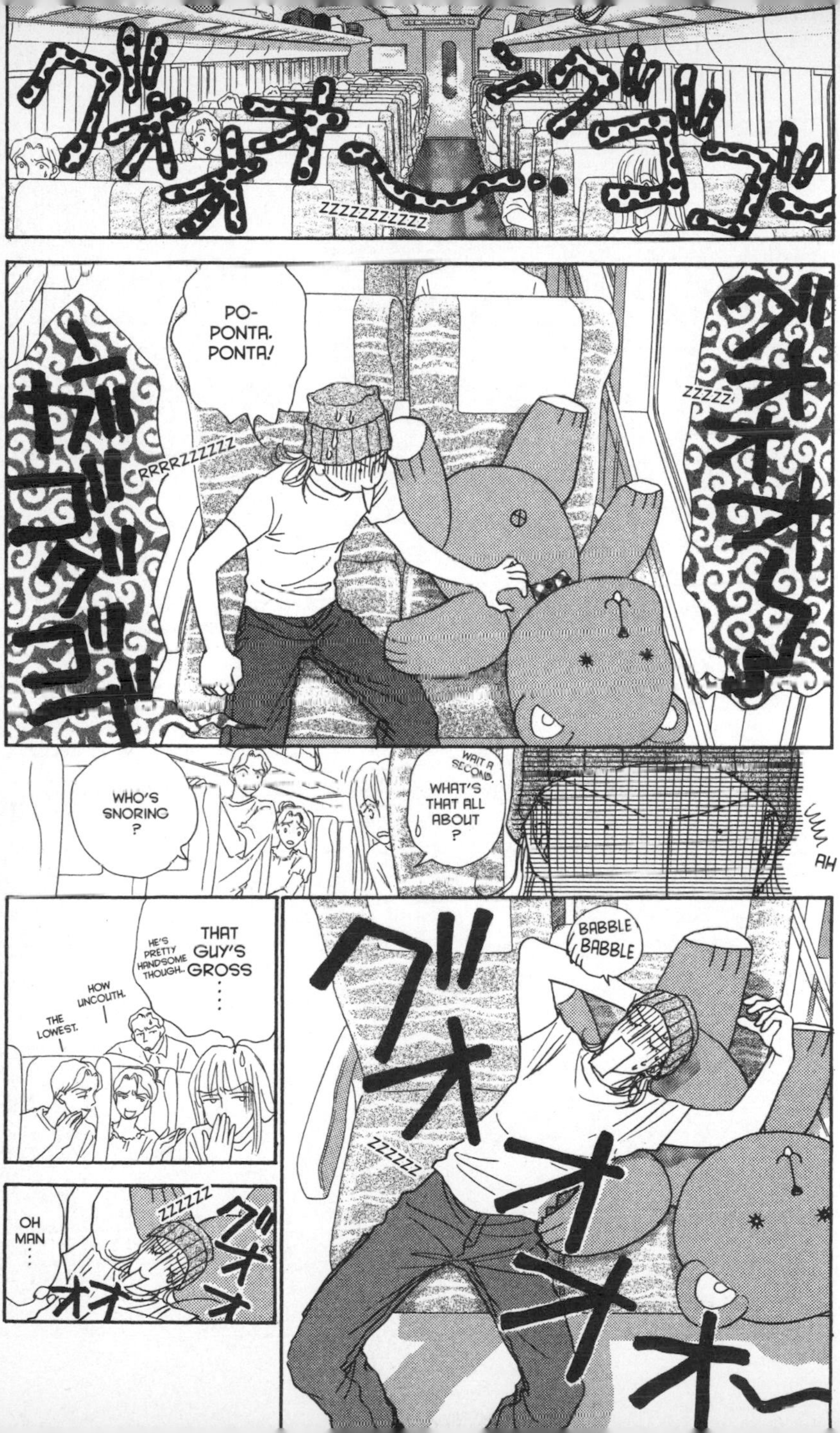
ZZZZZZZZZZZ
ZZZZZ
PO-PONTA, PONTA!
RRRRZZZZZZ
AH
WAIT A SECOND.
WHAT'S THAT ALL ABOUT?
WHO'S SNORING?
BABBLE BABBLE
ZZZZZZ
THAT GUY'S GROSS ...
HE'S PRETTY HANDSOME THOUGH..
HOW UNCOUTH.
THE LOWEST.
ZZZZZZ
OH MAN ...

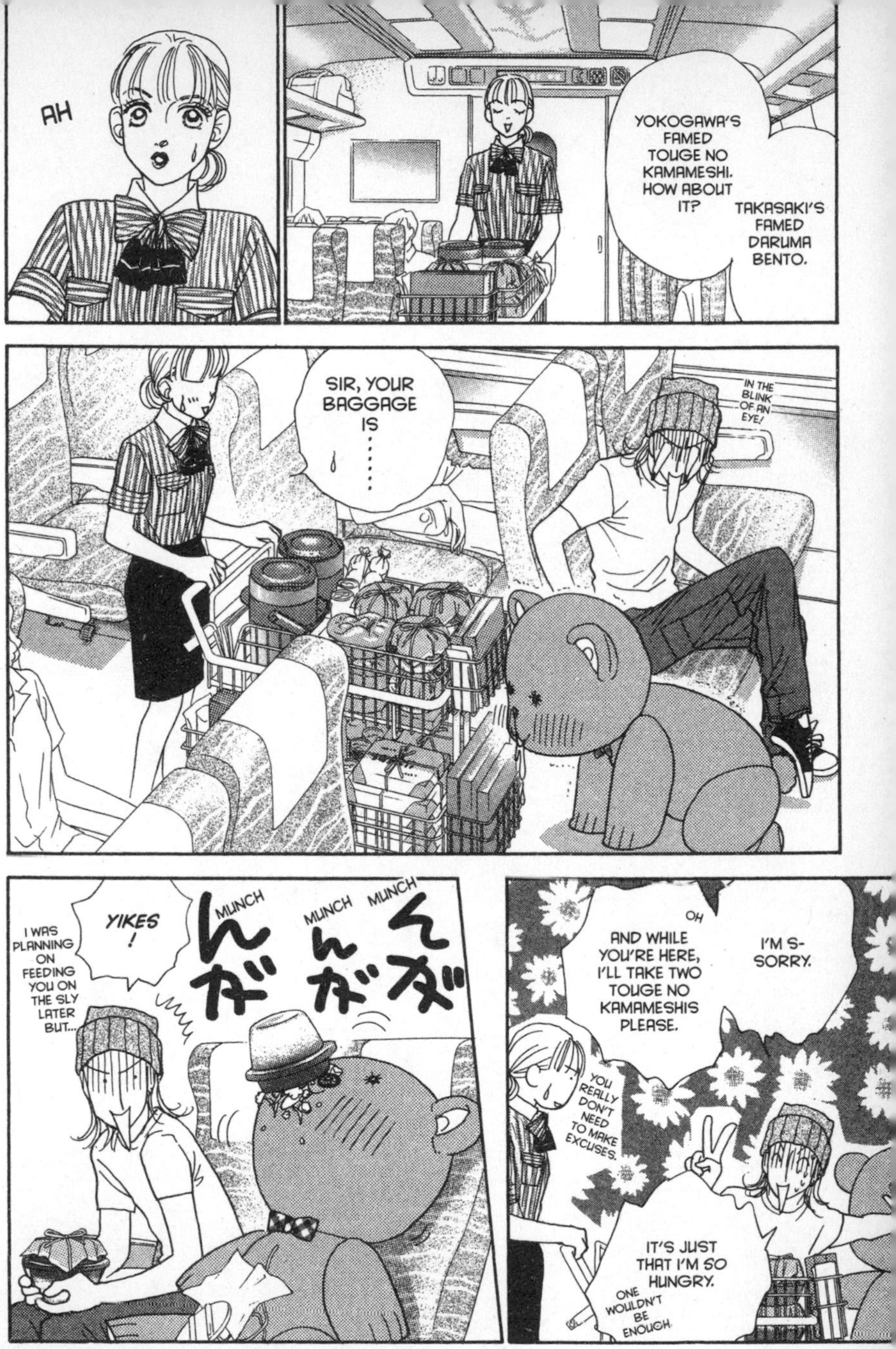
YOKOGAWA'S FAMED TOUGE NO KAMAMESHI. HOW ABOUT IT?
TAKASAKI'S FAMED DARUMA BENTO.
AH
IN THE BLINK OF AN EYE!
SIR, YOUR BAGGAGE IS ......
OH
I'M S-SORRY.
AND WHILE YOU'RE HERE, I'LL TAKE TWO TOUGE NO KAMAMESHIS PLEASE.
YOU REALLY DON'T NEED TO MAKE EXCUSES.
IT'S JUST THAT I'M SO HUNGRY.
ONE WOULDN'T BE ENOUGH.
MUNCH MUNCH MUNCH
YIKES!
I WAS PLANNING ON FEEDING YOU ON THE SLY LATER BUT...

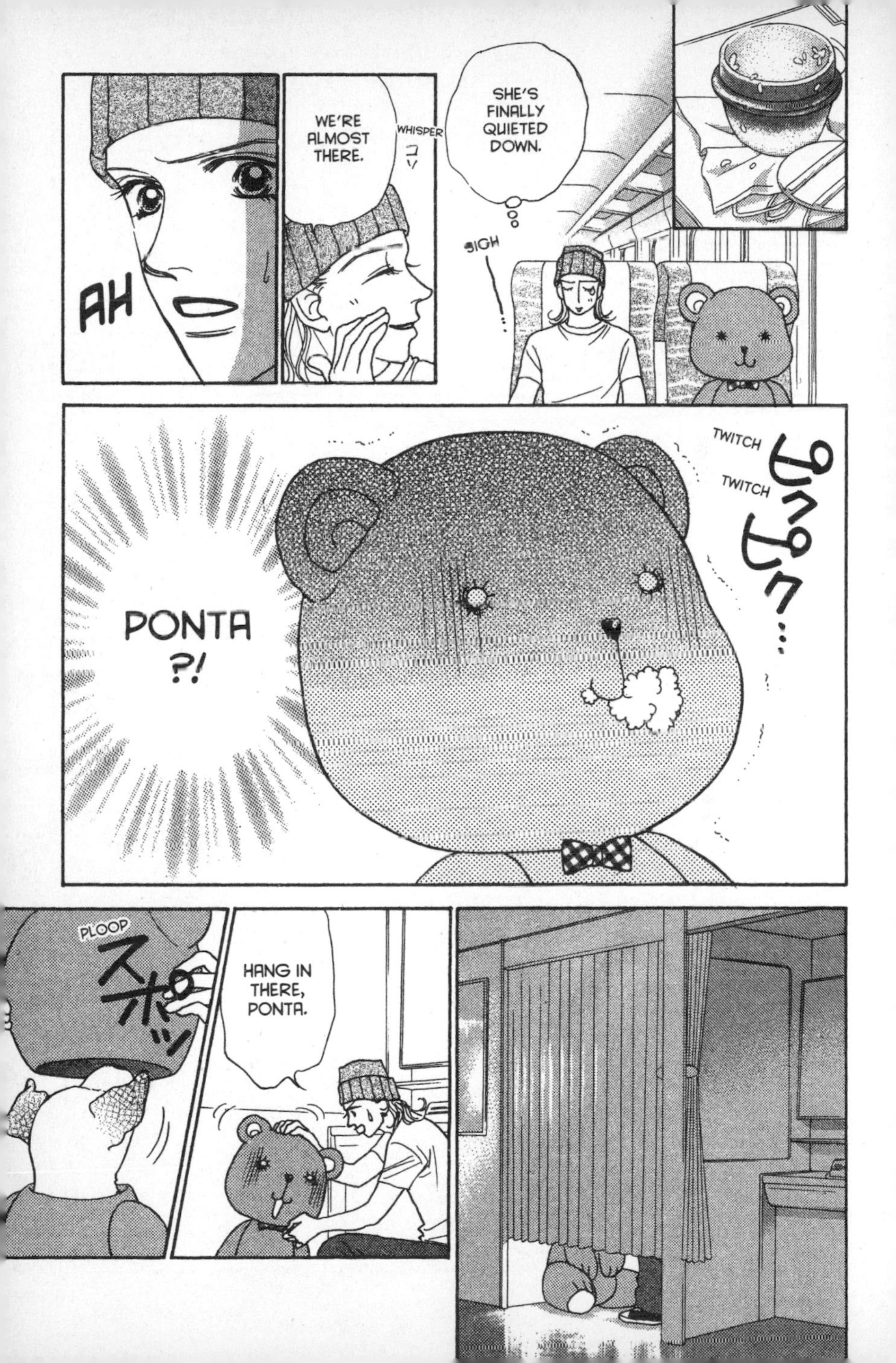
SHE'S FINALLY QUIETED DOWN.
SIGH
WE'RE ALMOST THERE.
WHISPER
コソ
AH
TWITCH TWITCH
ピクピク…
PONTA ?!
HANG IN THERE, PONTA.
PLOOP
スポッ

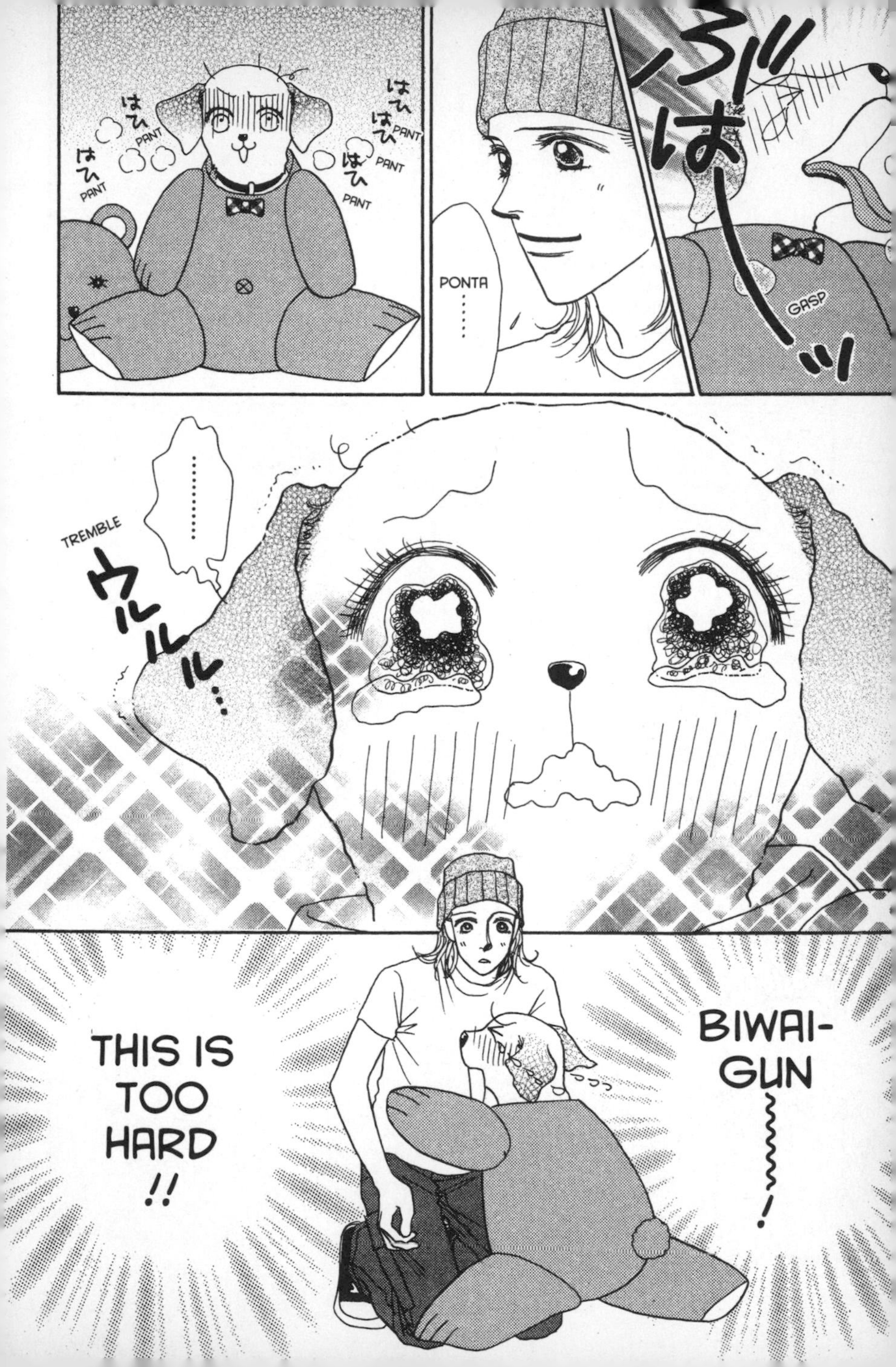
GASP
PONTA
......
はひ
はひ
はひ
はひ
はひ
PANT
PANT
PANT
PANT
PANT
......
TREMBLE
ウルルル...
BIWAI-GUN~~~!
THIS IS TOO HARD!!

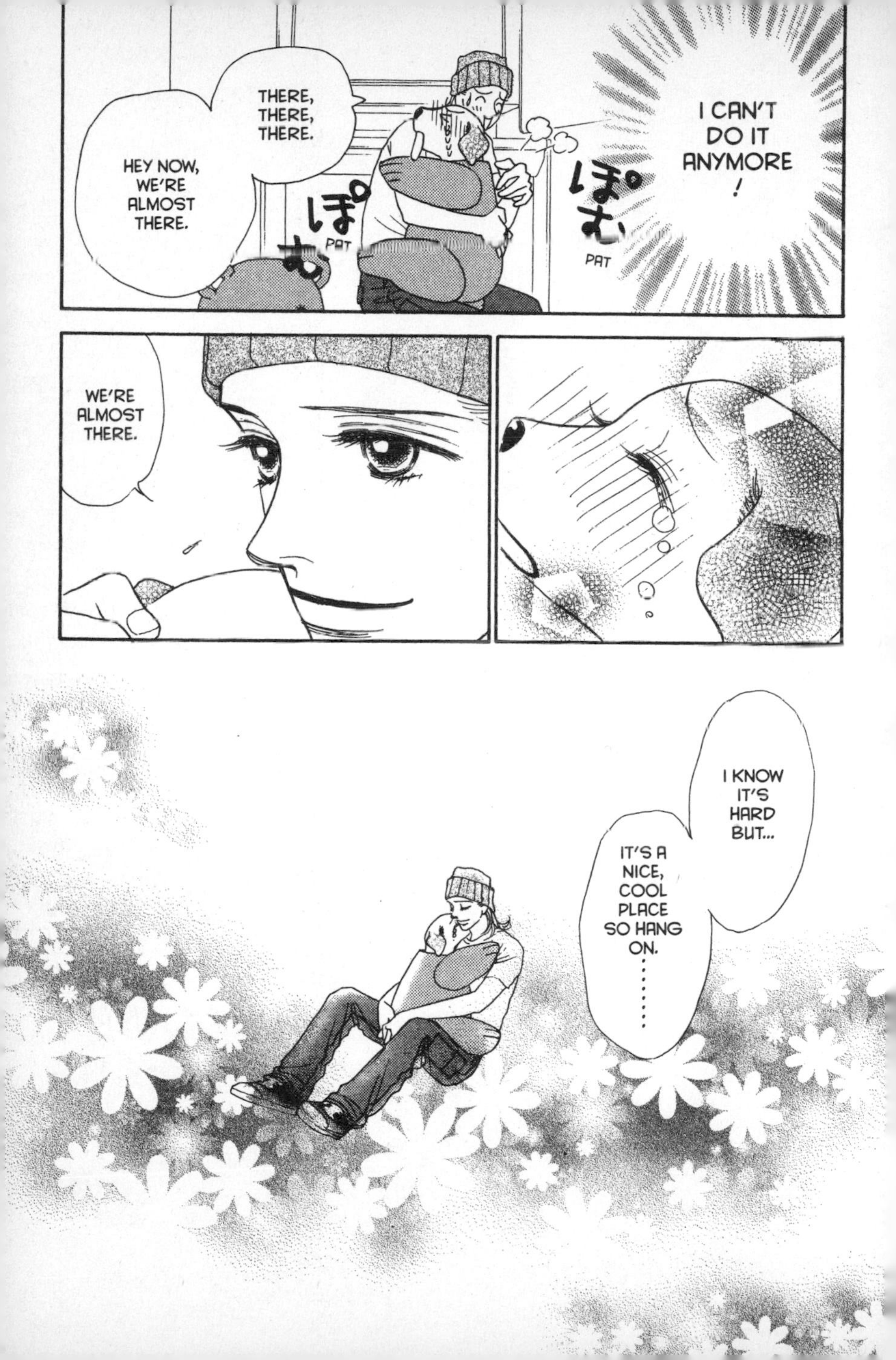
I CAN'T DO IT ANYMORE!
ぽむ PAT
THERE, THERE, THERE.
ぽむ PAT
HEY NOW, WE'RE ALMOST THERE.
WE'RE ALMOST THERE.
I KNOW IT'S HARD BUT...
IT'S A NICE, COOL PLACE SO HANG ON. ......

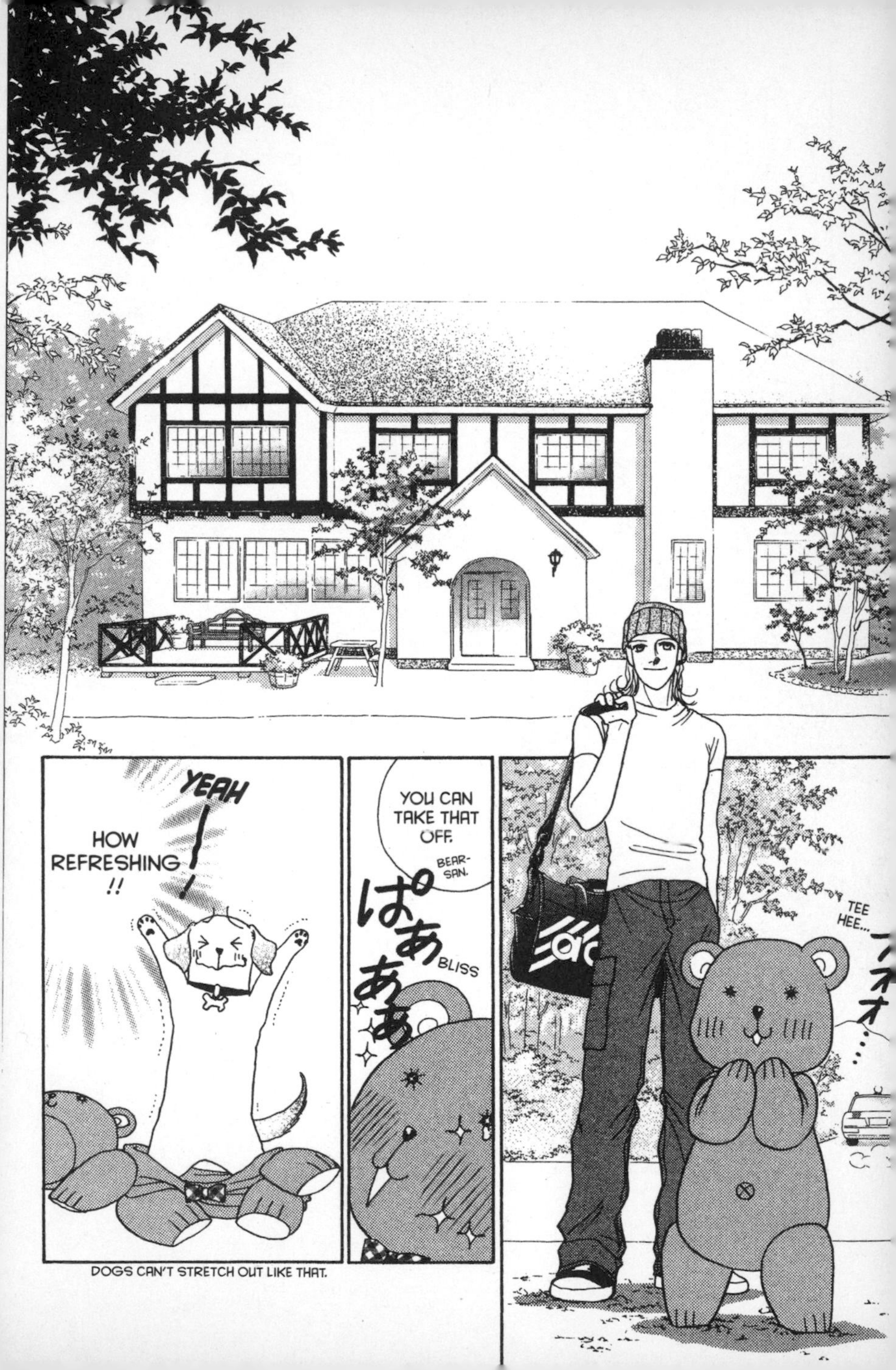
TEE HEE...
YOU CAN TAKE THAT OFF.
BEAR-SAN.
ぱあああ
BLISS
YEAH
HOW REFRESHING!!
DOGS CAN'T STRETCH OUT LIKE THAT.

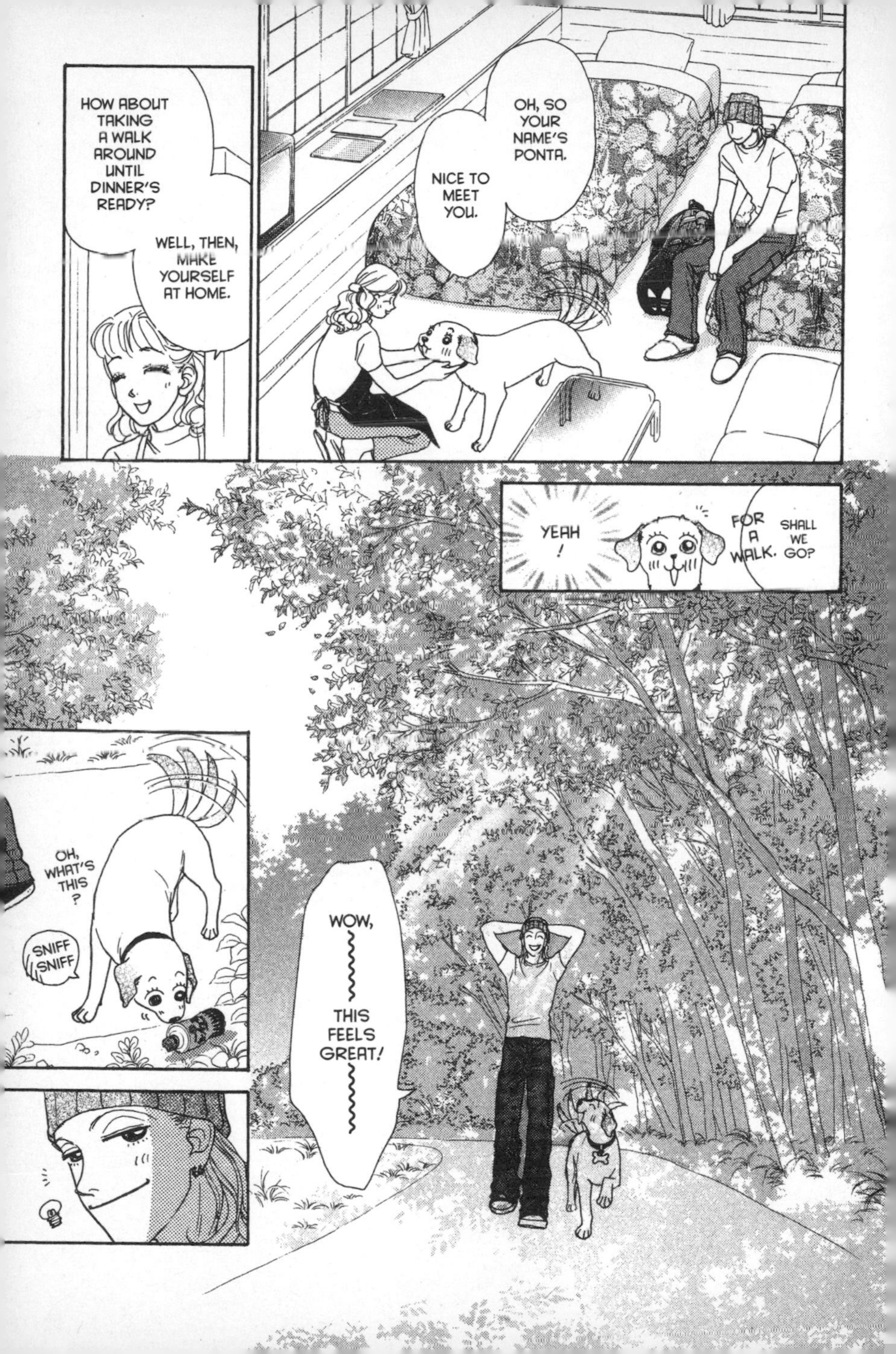
OH, SO YOUR NAME'S PONTA.
NICE TO MEET YOU.
HOW ABOUT TAKING A WALK AROUND UNTIL DINNER'S READY?
WELL, THEN, MAKE YOURSELF AT HOME.
SHALL WE GO?
FOR A WALK.
YEAH!
WOW, THIS FEELS GREAT!
OH, WHAT'S THIS?
SNIFF SNIFF

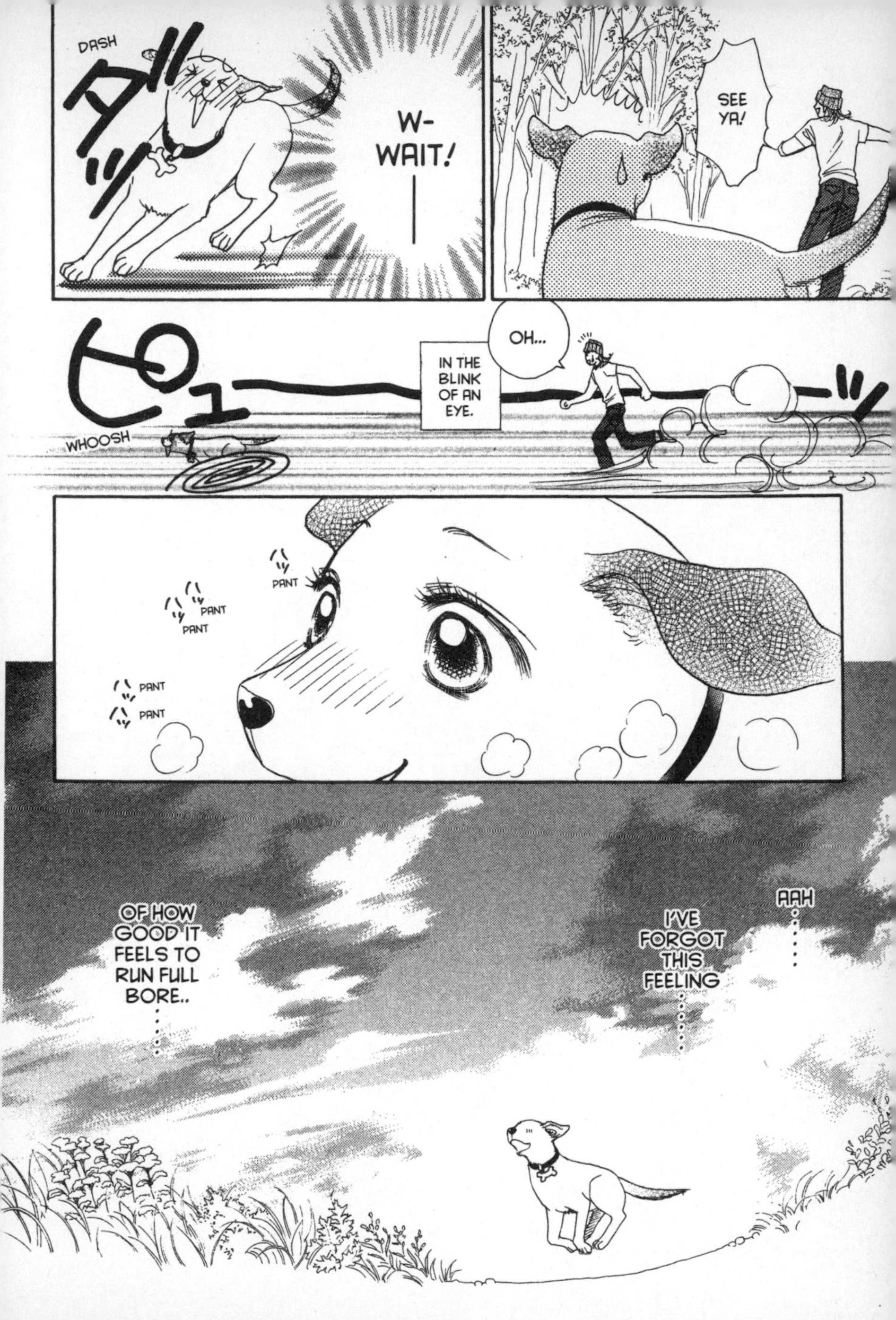

SEE YA!
DASH
W-WAIT!
OH...
IN THE BLINK OF AN EYE.
WHOOSH
PANT
PANT
PANT
PANT
PANT
AAH.....
I'VE FORGOT THIS FEELING......
OF HOW GOOD IT FEELS TO RUN FULL BORE.......

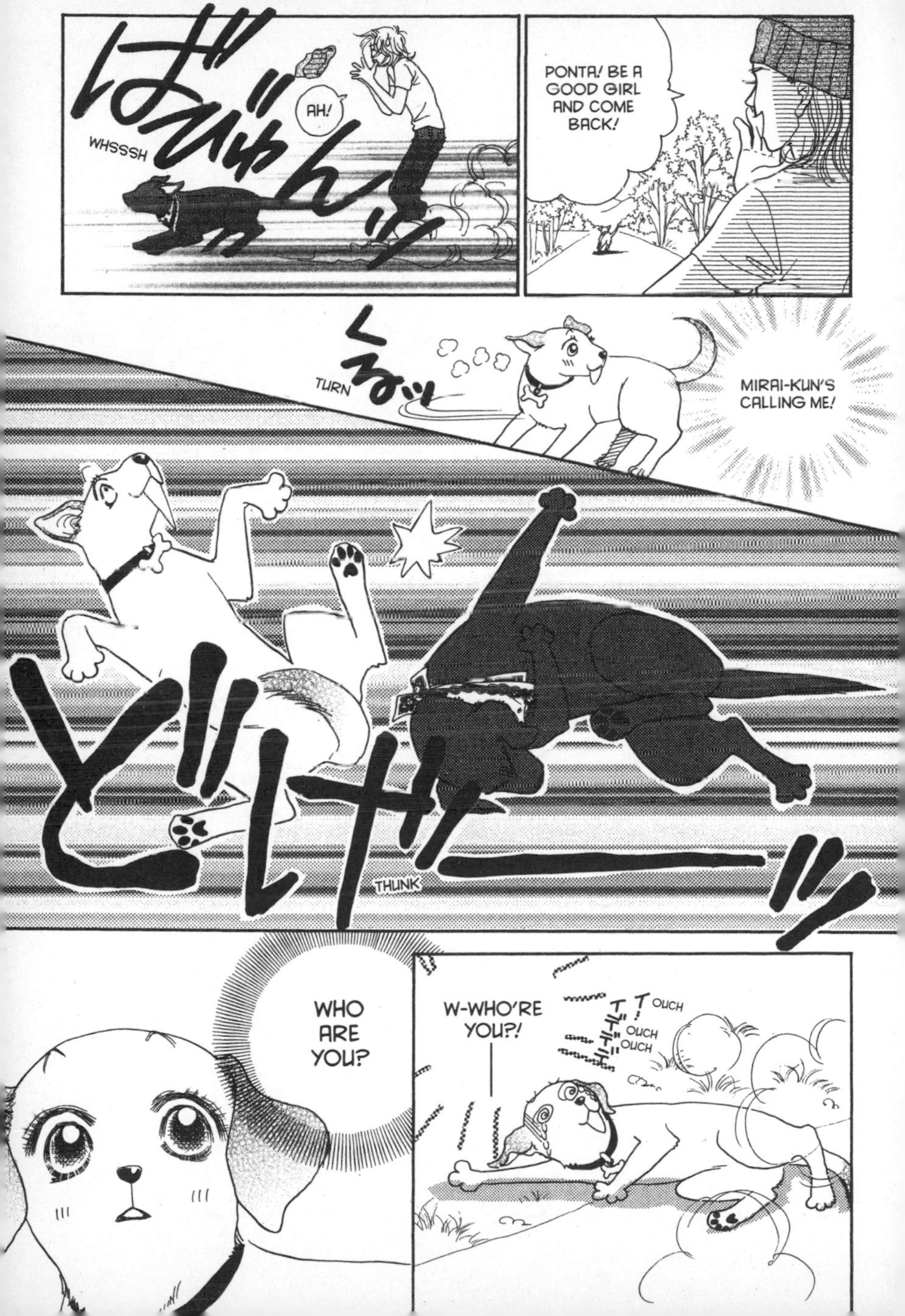
PONTA! BE A GOOD GIRL AND COME BACK!
AH!
ばびゅんッ
WHSSSH
くるッ
TURN
MIRAI-KUN'S CALLING ME!
THUNK
W-WHO'RE YOU?!
OUCH
OUCH
OUCH
WHO ARE YOU?

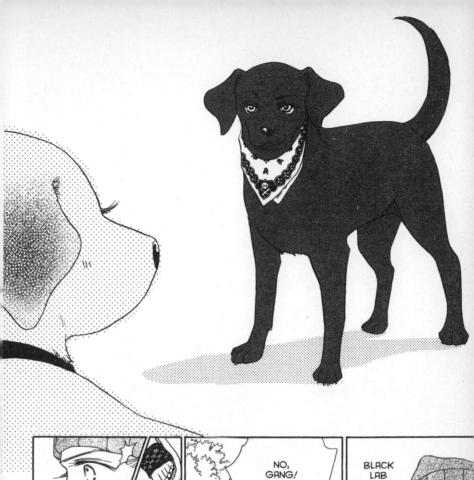

NO, GANG! GET BACK HERE!

KYA!!

CLACK

BLACK LAB .....

JUST LIKE THE CHARACTERS INDICATE, THIS IS AN ABBREVIATION FOR BLACK LABRADOR RETRIEVER.

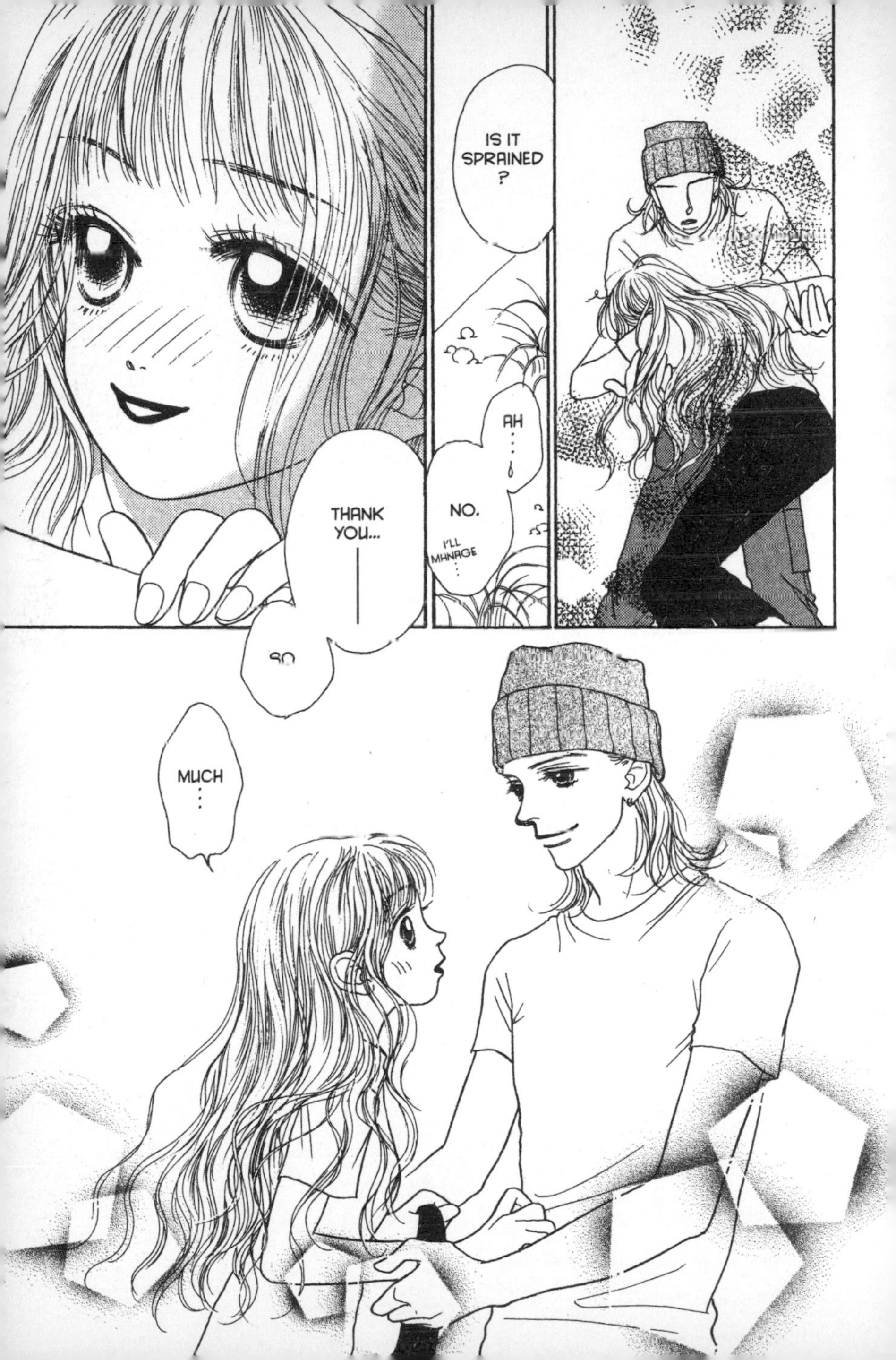

IS IT SPRAINED?
AH...
NO.
I'LL MANAGE...
THANK YOU...
SO
MUCH...

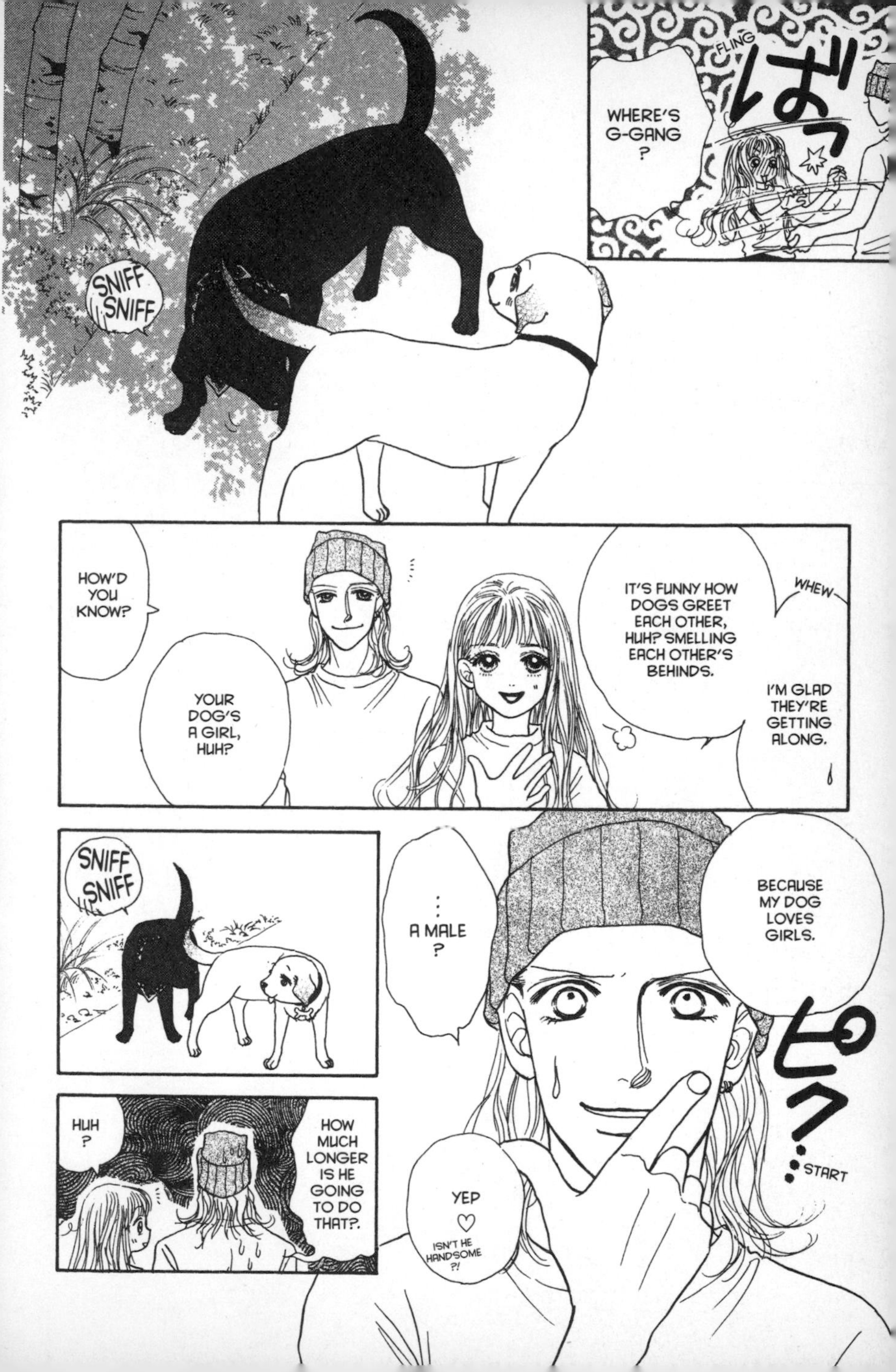
FLING
ばっ
WHERE'S G-GANG ?
SNIFF SNIFF
WHEW
IT'S FUNNY HOW DOGS GREET EACH OTHER, HUH? SMELLING EACH OTHER'S BEHINDS.
I'M GLAD THEY'RE GETTING ALONG.
YOUR DOG'S A GIRL, HUH?
HOW'D YOU KNOW?
BECAUSE MY DOG LOVES GIRLS.
ピクッ
START
... A MALE ?
YEP ♡
ISN'T HE HANDSOME ?!
SNIFF SNIFF
HOW MUCH LONGER IS HE GOING TO DO THAT?.
HUH ?

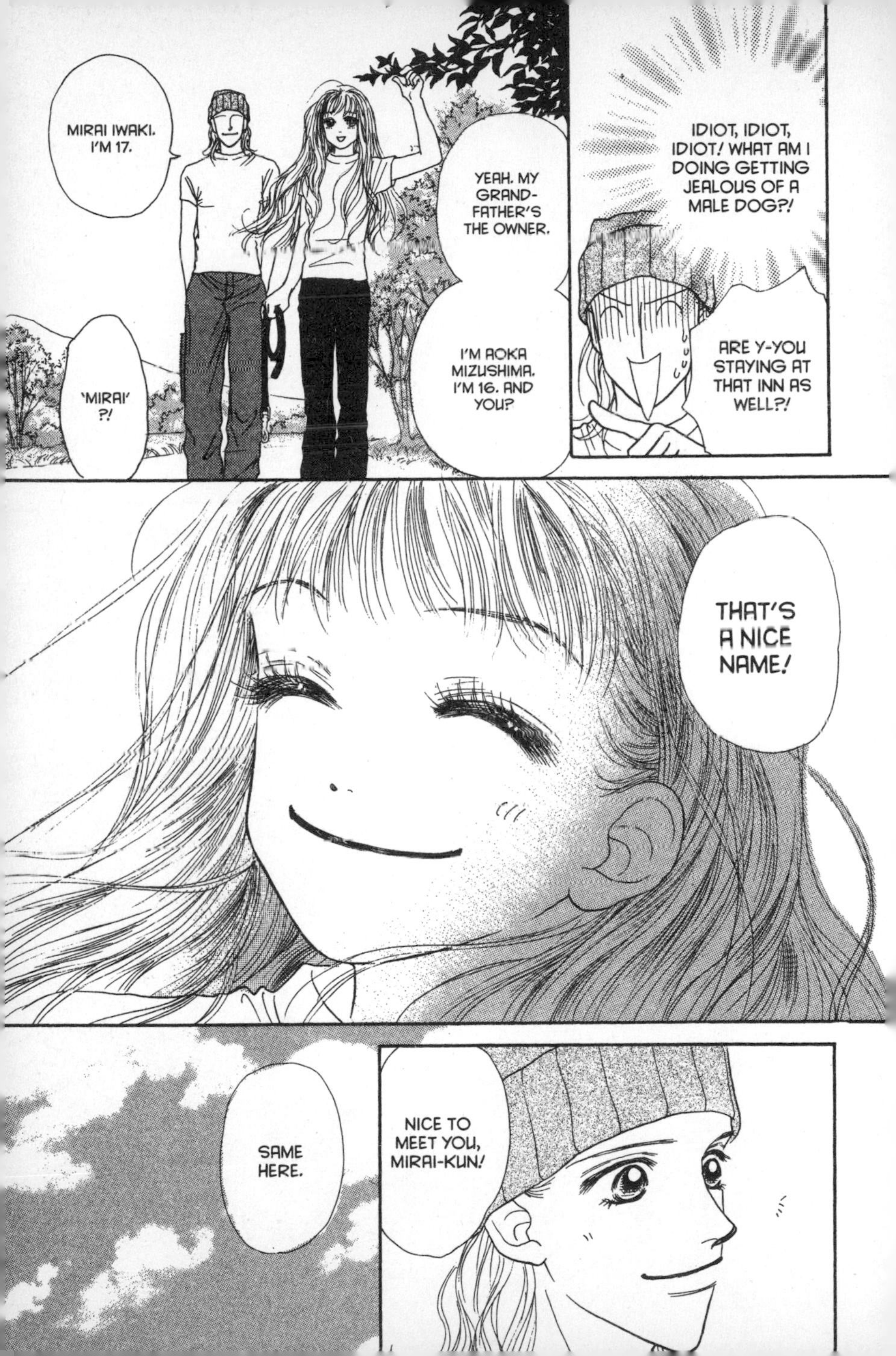
IDIOT, IDIOT, IDIOT! WHAT AM I DOING GETTING JEALOUS OF A MALE DOG?!
ARE Y-YOU STAYING AT THAT INN AS WELL?!
YEAH. MY GRAND-FATHER'S THE OWNER.
I'M AOKA MIZUSHIMA. I'M 16. AND YOU?
MIRAI IWAKI. I'M 17.
'MIRAI' ?!
THAT'S A NICE NAME!
NICE TO MEET YOU, MIRAI-KUN!
SAME HERE.

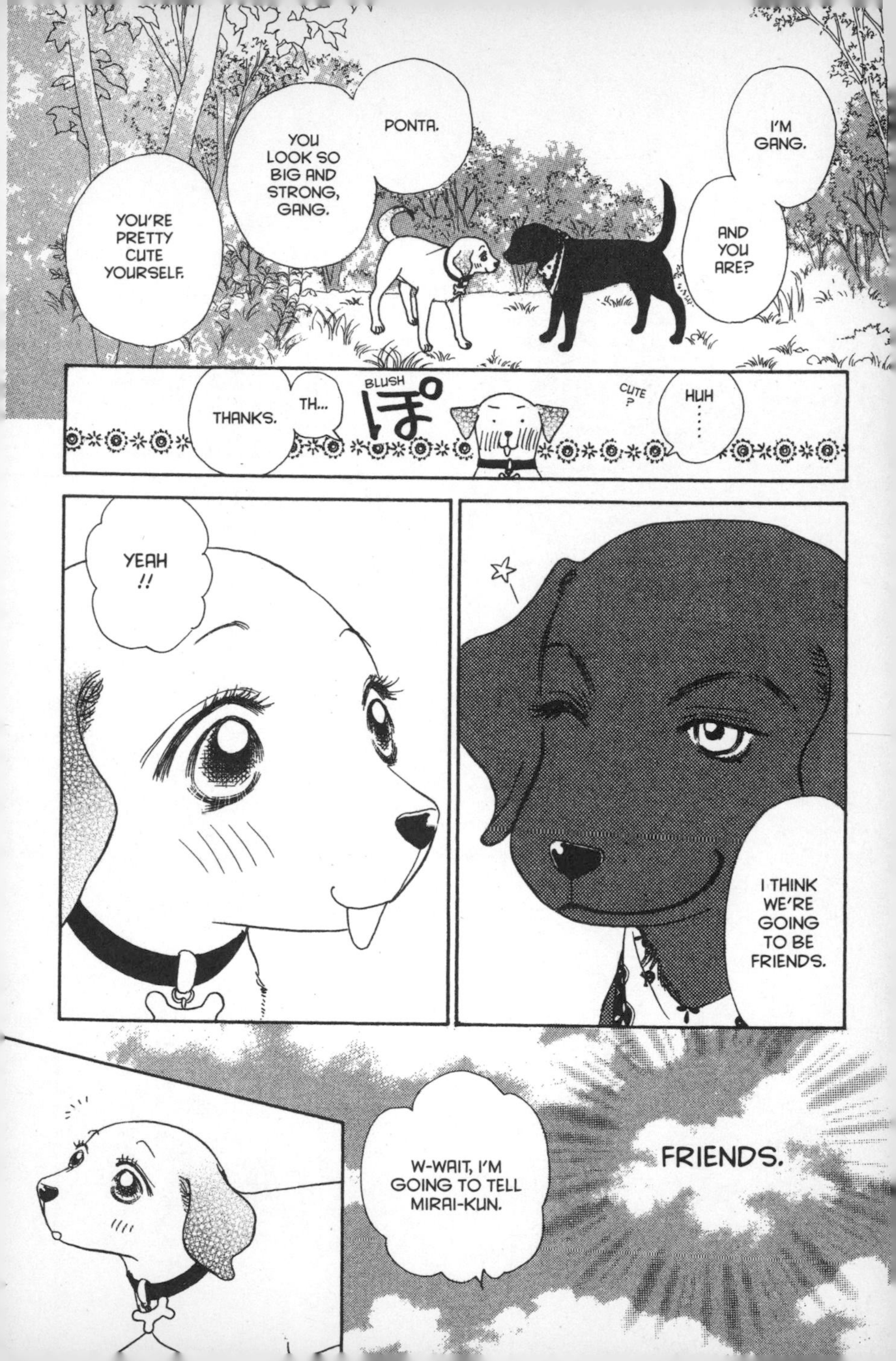
I'M GANG.
AND YOU ARE?
PONTA.
YOU LOOK SO BIG AND STRONG, GANG.
YOU'RE PRETTY CUTE YOURSELF.
HUH ......
CUTE ?
BLUSH
ぽ
TH...
THANKS.
I THINK WE'RE GOING TO BE FRIENDS.
YEAH !!
FRIENDS.
W-WAIT, I'M GOING TO TELL MIRAI-KUN.

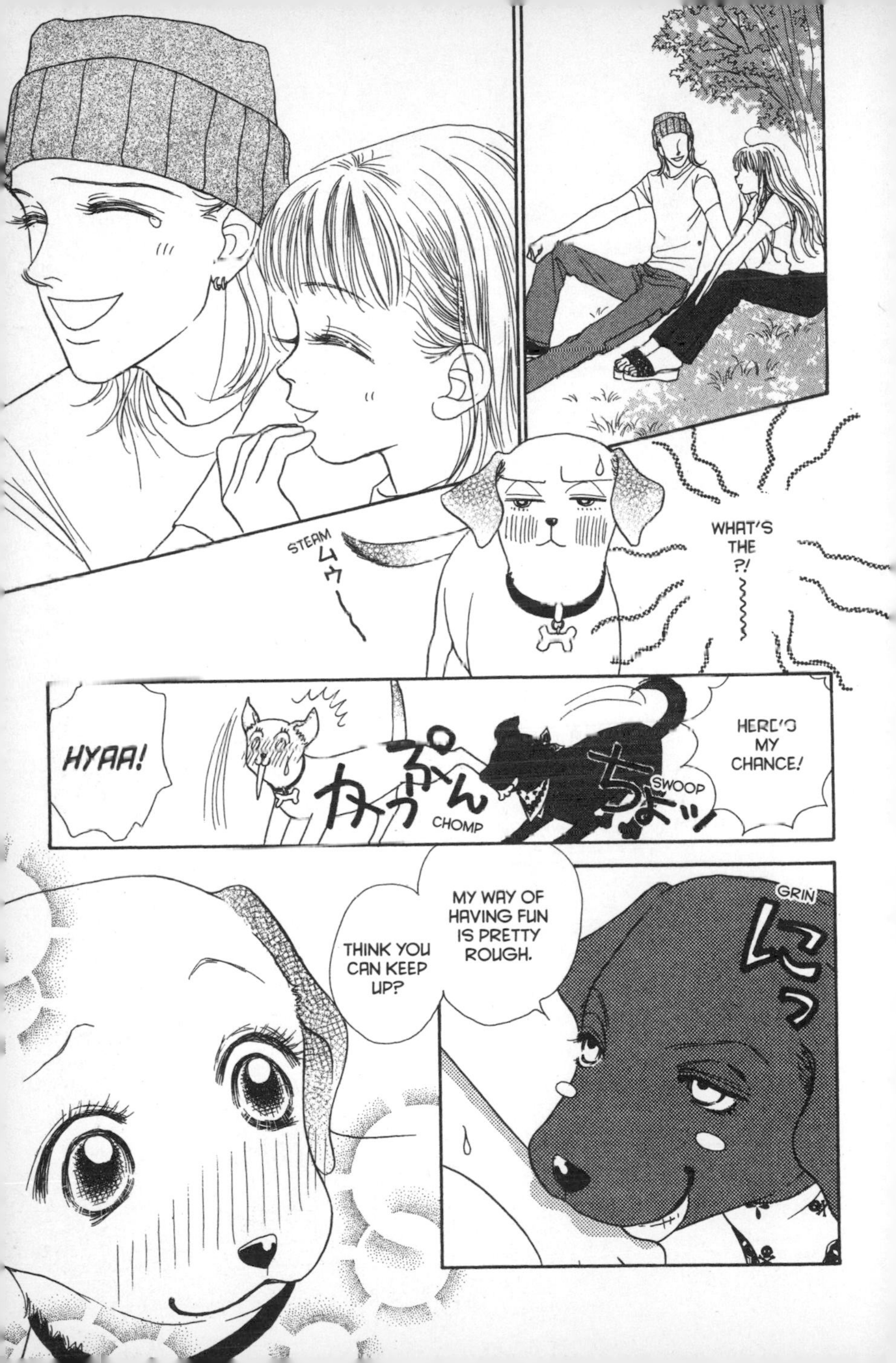
WHAT'S THE ?!
STEAM
ムウー
HERE'S MY CHANCE!
SWOOP
ちょッ
かっぷん
CHOMP
HYAA!
GRIN
にっ
MY WAY OF HAVING FUN IS PRETTY ROUGH.
THINK YOU CAN KEEP UP?

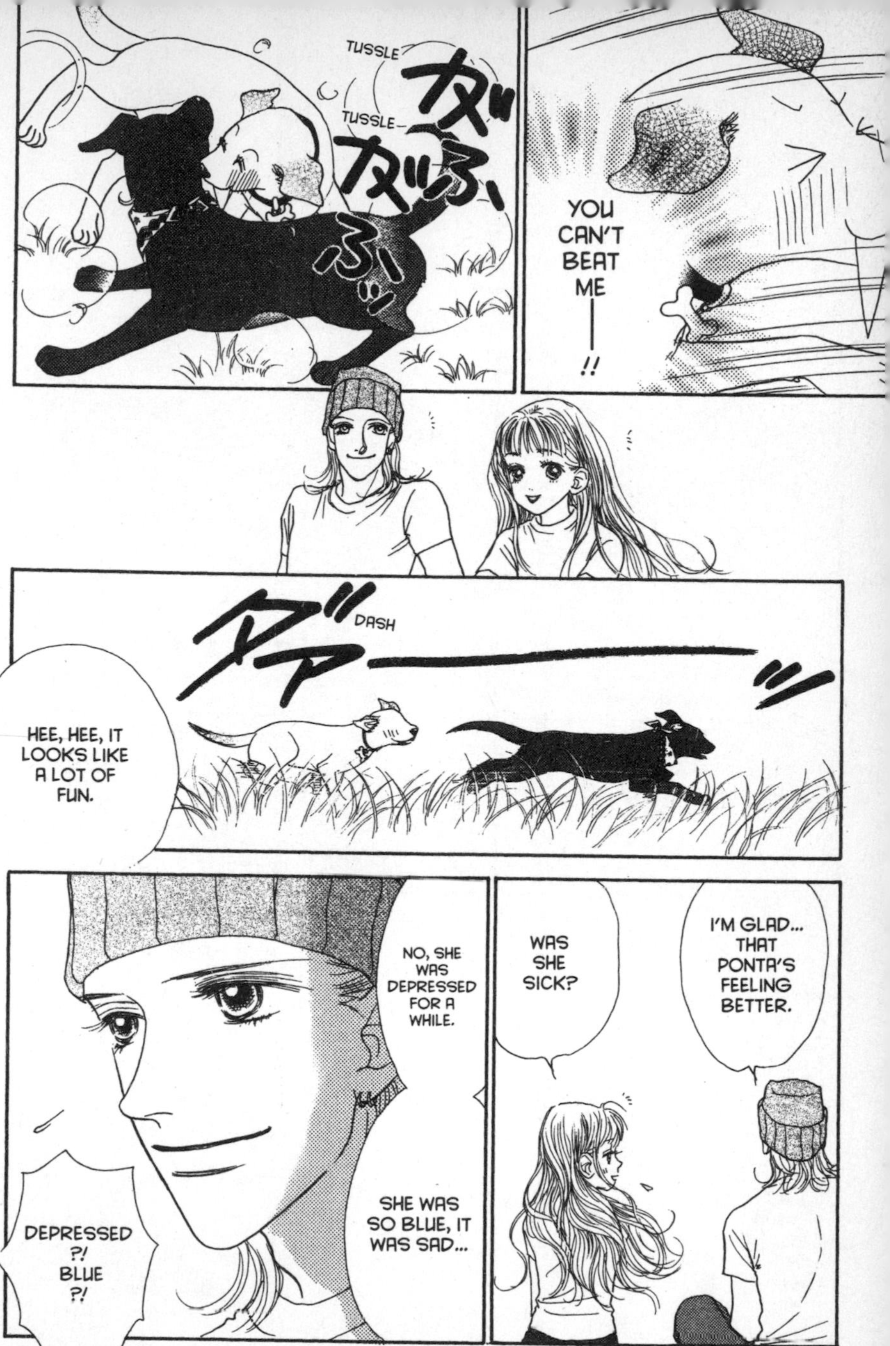
YOU CAN'T BEAT ME—!!
TUSSLE
TUSSLE
DASH
HEE, HEE, IT LOOKS LIKE A LOT OF FUN.
I'M GLAD... THAT PONTA'S FEELING BETTER.
WAS SHE SICK?
NO, SHE WAS DEPRESSED FOR A WHILE.
SHE WAS SO BLUE, IT WAS SAD...
DEPRESSED?! BLUE?!

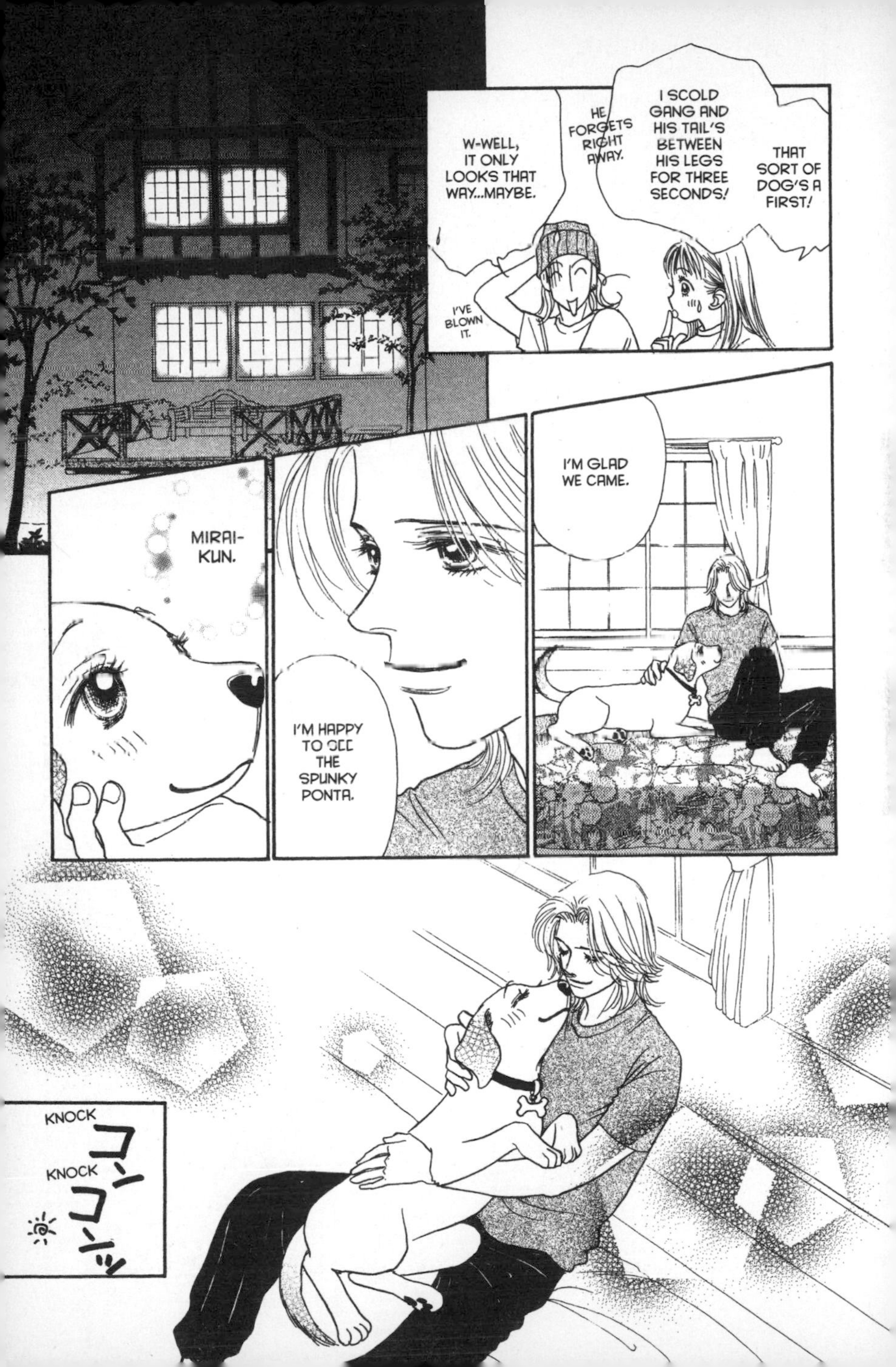
THAT SORT OF DOG'S A FIRST!
I SCOLD GANG AND HIS TAIL'S BETWEEN HIS LEGS FOR THREE SECONDS!
HE FORGETS RIGHT AWAY.
W-WELL, IT ONLY LOOKS THAT WAY...MAYBE.
I'VE BLOWN IT.
I'M GLAD WE CAME.
I'M HAPPY TO SEE THE SPUNKY PONTA.
MIRAI-KUN.
KNOCK
KNOCK
コンコンッ

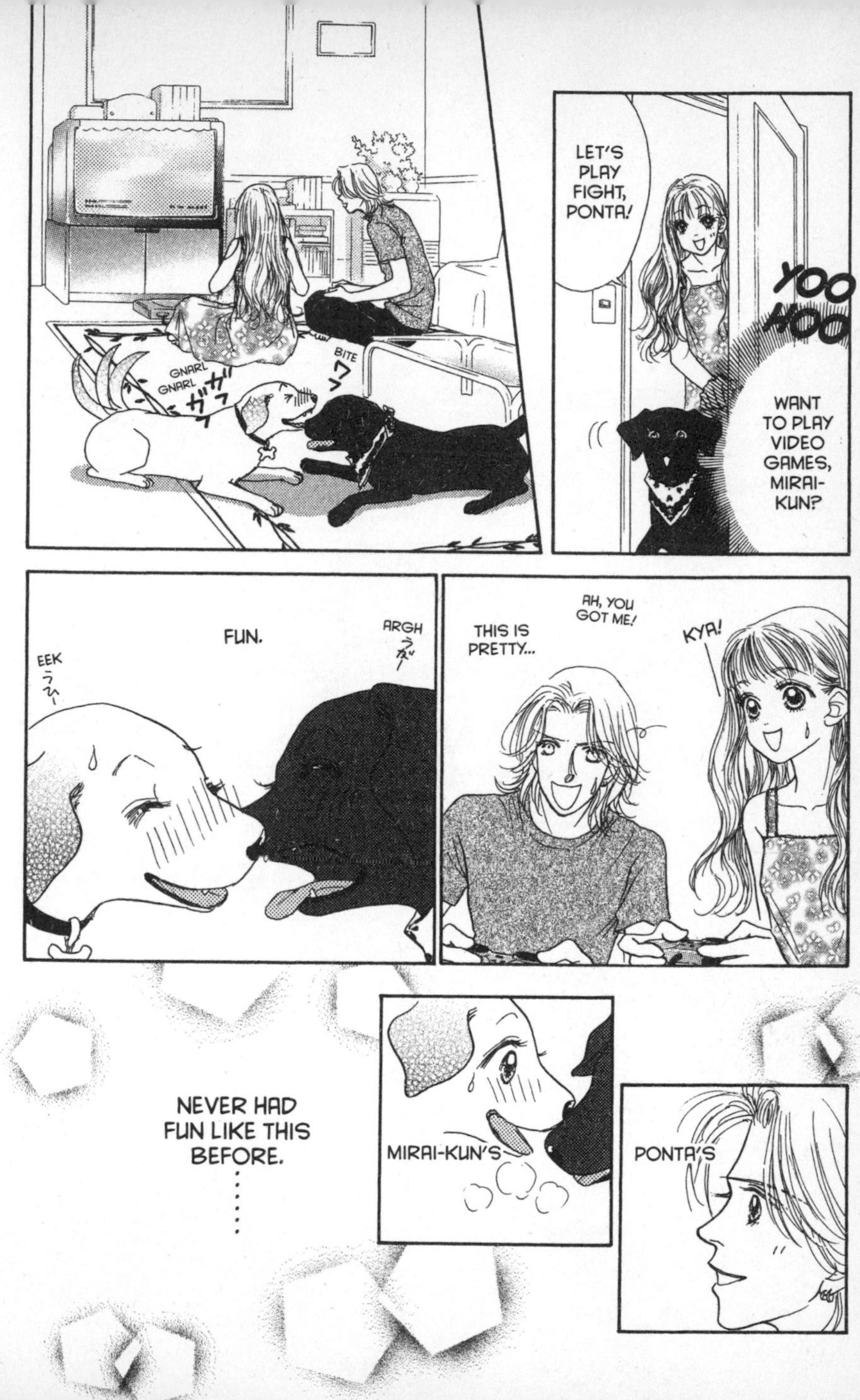
YOO HOO
WANT TO PLAY VIDEO GAMES, MIRAI-KUN?
LET'S PLAY FIGHT, PONTA!
BITE
GNARL GNARL
KYA!
AH, YOU GOT ME!
THIS IS PRETTY...
ARGH
FUN.
EEK
PONTA'S
MIRAI-KUN'S
NEVER HAD FUN LIKE THIS BEFORE.
......

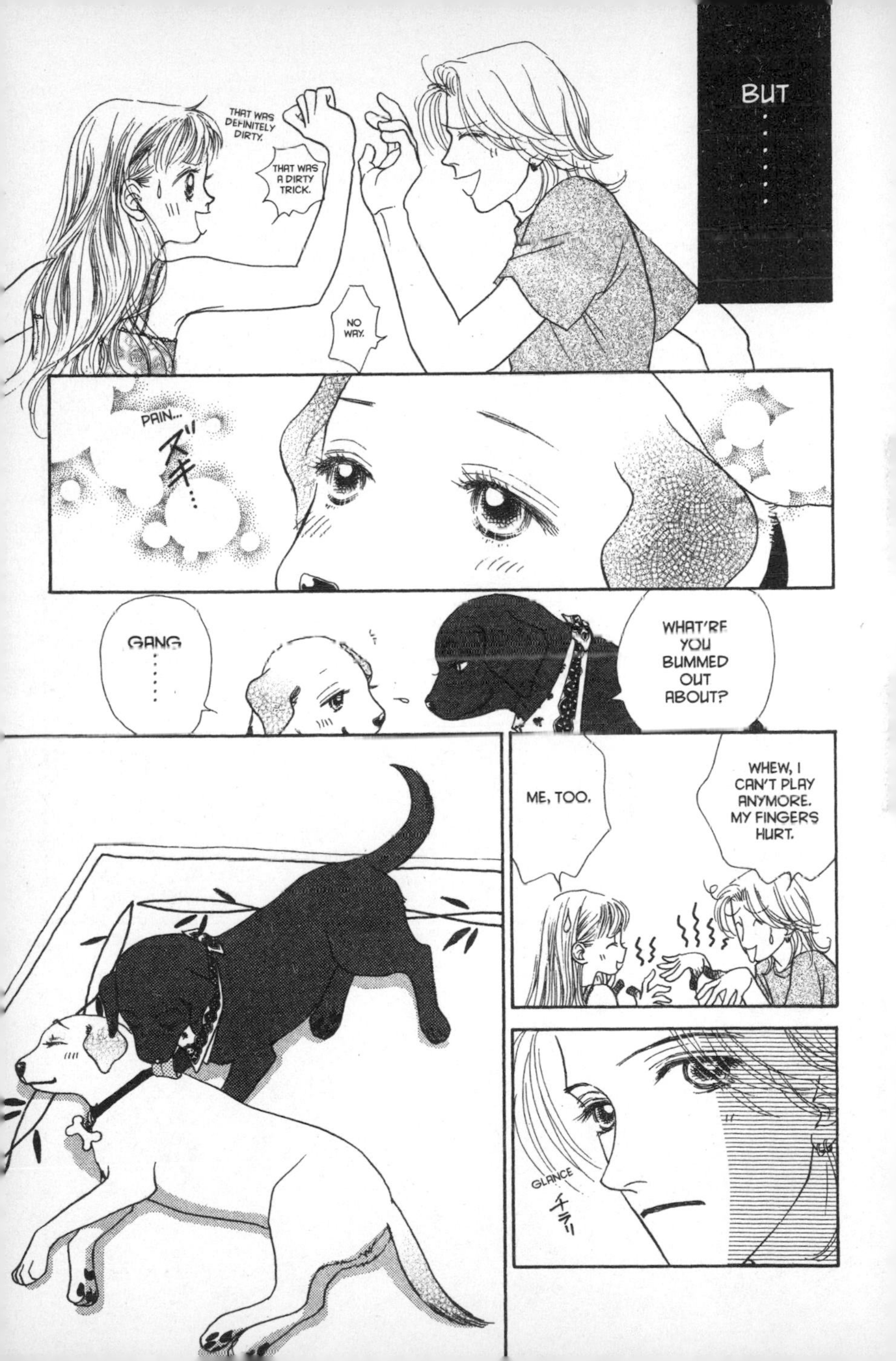
BUT ......
THAT WAS A DIRTY TRICK.
THAT WAS DEFINITELY DIRTY.
NO WAY.
PAIN...
ズキ...
WHAT'RE YOU BUMMED OUT ABOUT?
GANG ......
WHEW, I CAN'T PLAY ANYMORE. MY FINGERS HURT.
ME, TOO.
GLANCE
チラリ

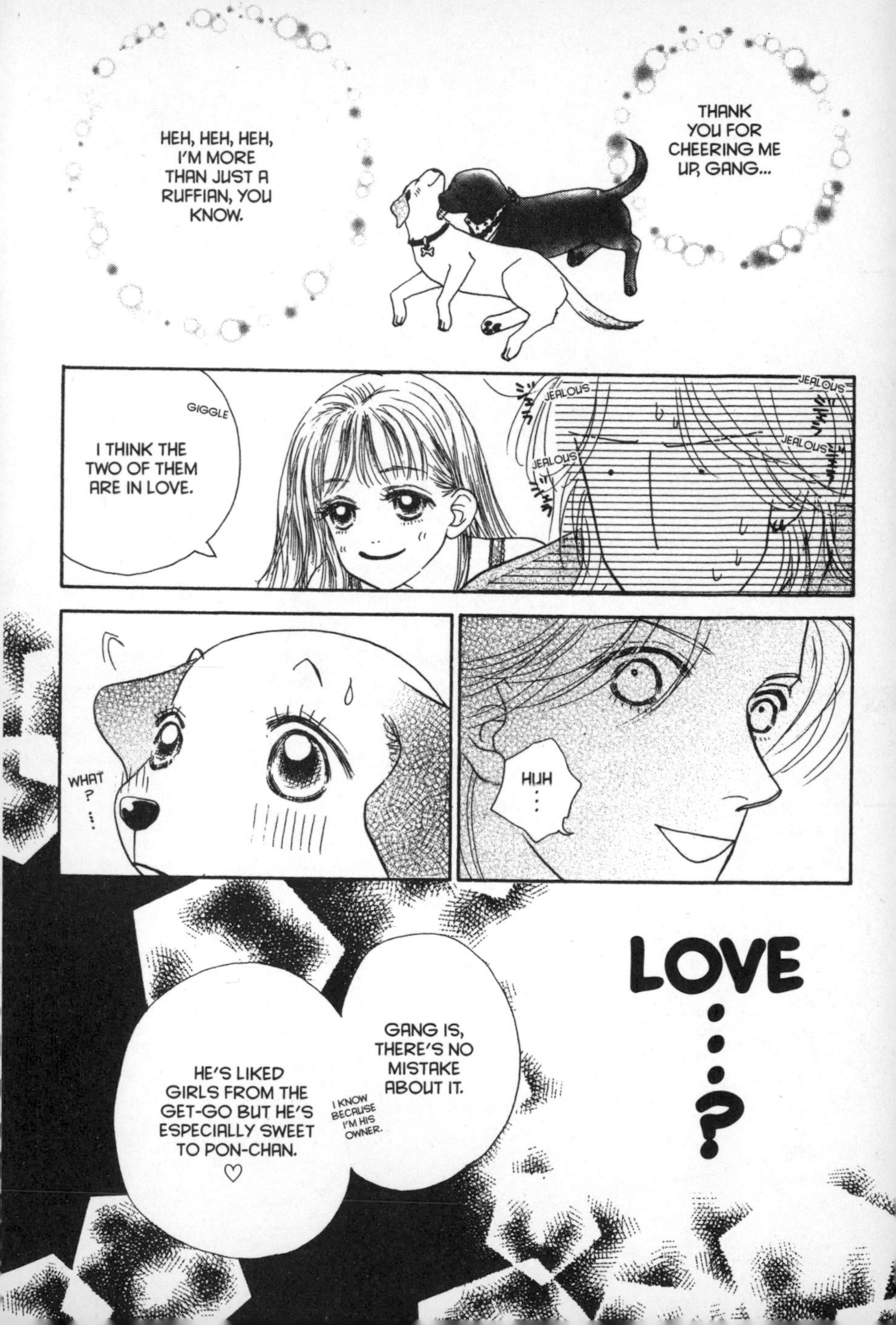
THANK YOU FOR CHEERING ME UP, GANG...
HEH, HEH, HEH, I'M MORE THAN JUST A RUFFIAN, YOU KNOW.
JEALOUS
JEALOUS
JEALOUS
JEALOUS
GIGGLE
I THINK THE TWO OF THEM ARE IN LOVE.
HUH ...
WHAT ? ...
LOVE ...?
GANG IS, THERE'S NO MISTAKE ABOUT IT.
I KNOW BECAUSE I'M HIS OWNER.
HE'S LIKED GIRLS FROM THE GET-GO BUT HE'S ESPECIALLY SWEET TO PON-CHAN. ♡

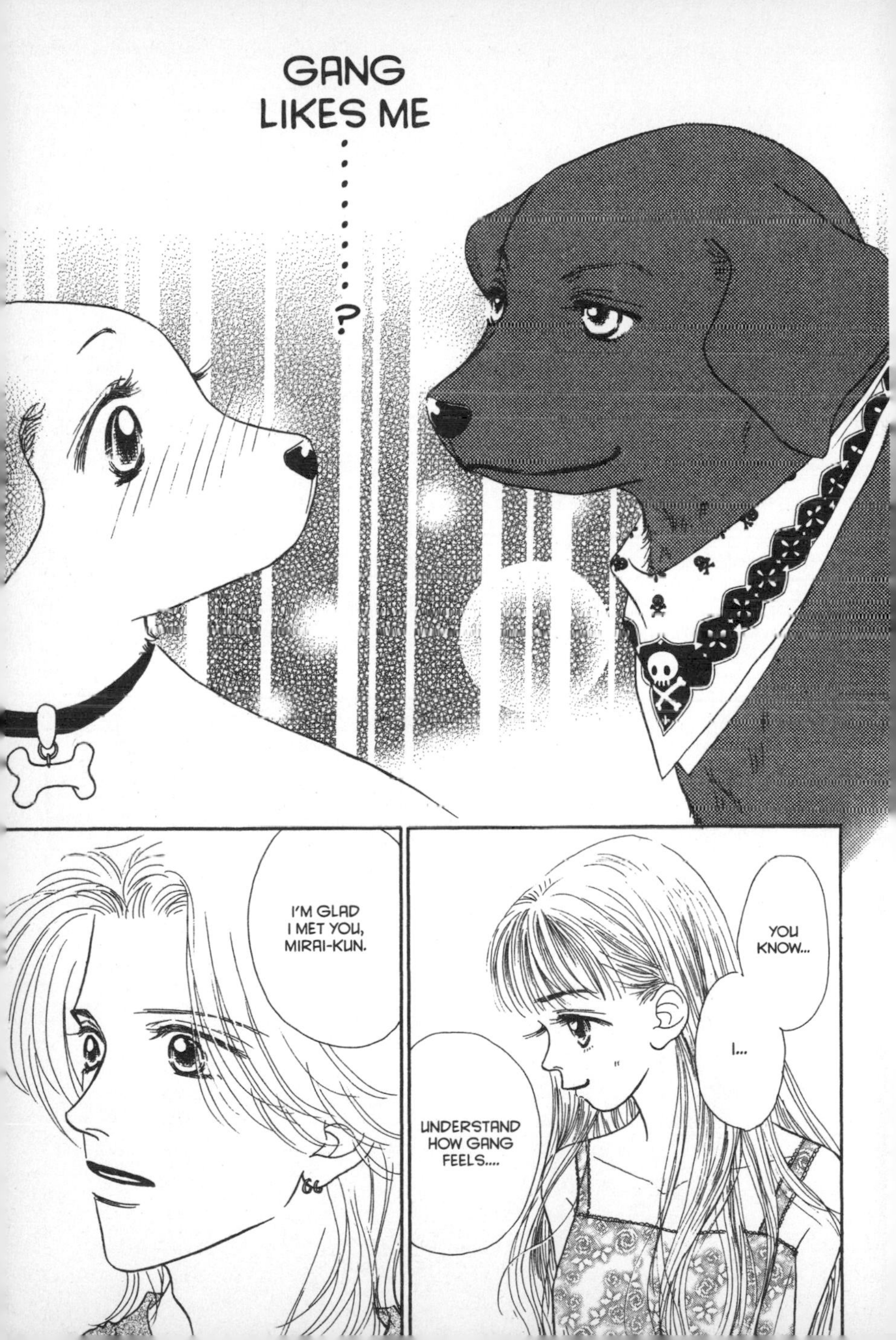
GANG LIKES ME
......?
YOU KNOW...
I...
UNDERSTAND HOW GANG FEELS....
I'M GLAD I MET YOU, MIRAI-KUN.

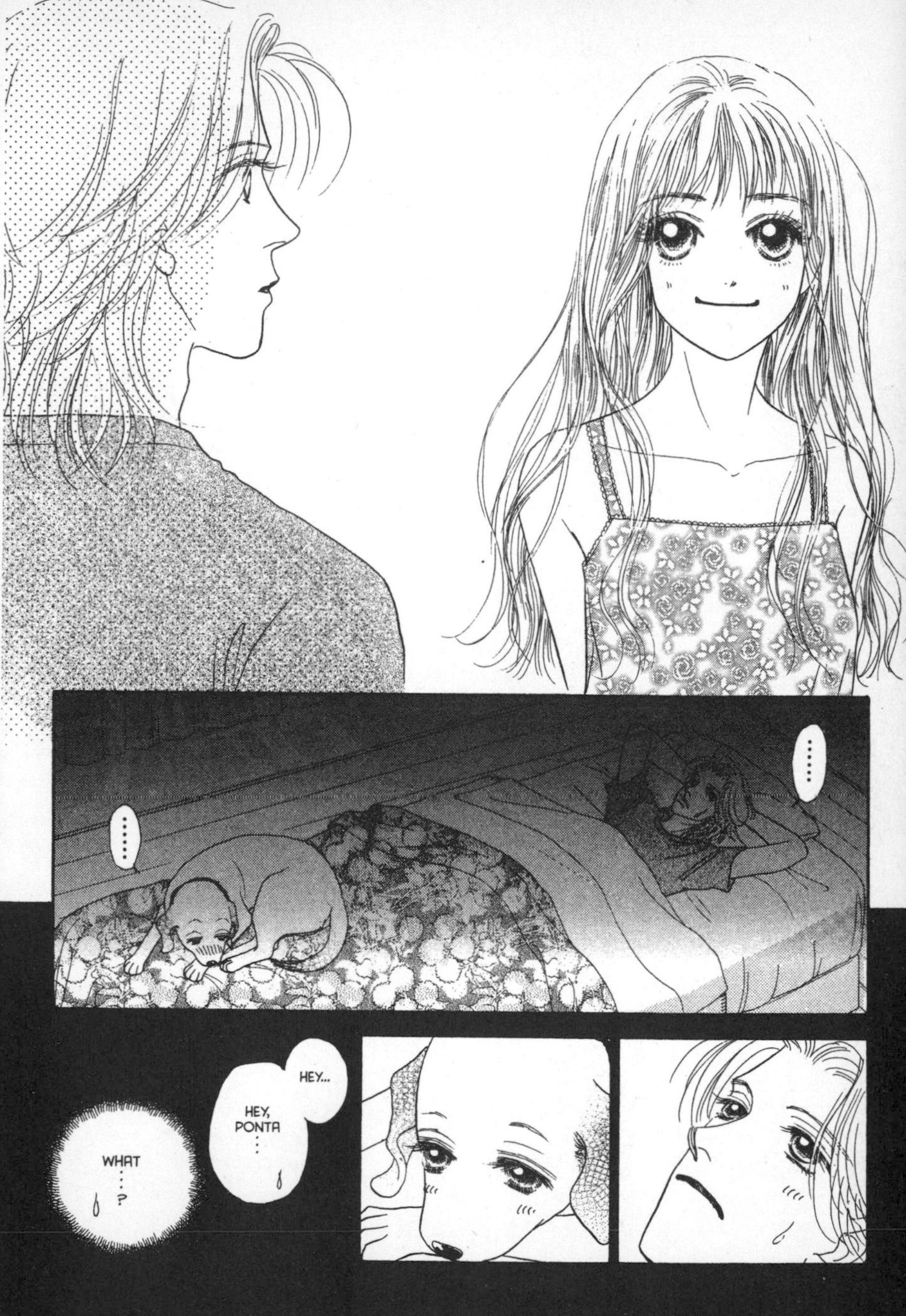
......
......
HEY...
HEY, PONTA...
WHAT...?

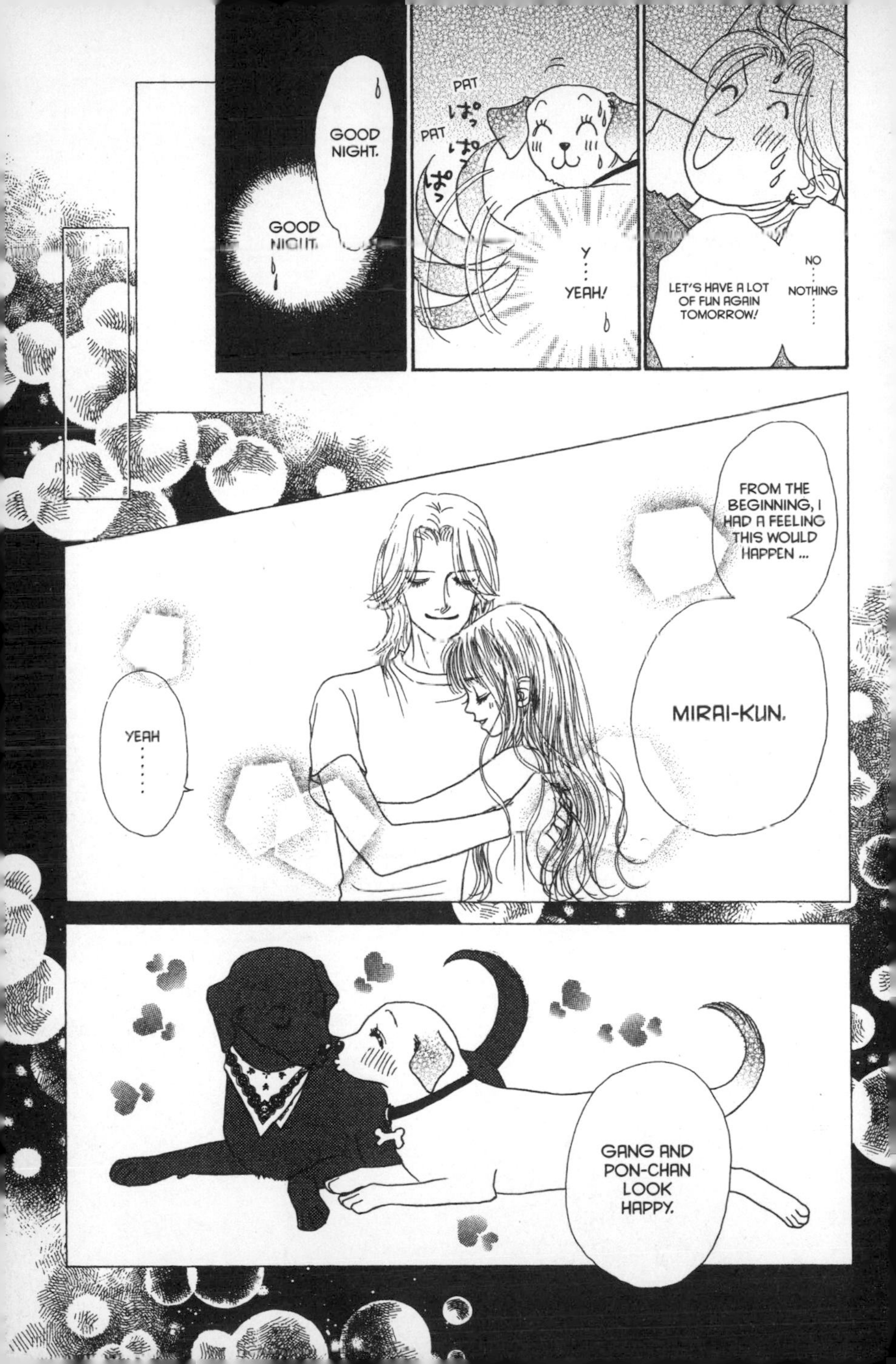
NO...... NOTHING......
LET'S HAVE A LOT OF FUN AGAIN TOMORROW!
PAT ぱっ
PAT ぱっ
ぱっ
Y... YEAH!
GOOD NIGHT.
GOOD NIGHT.
FROM THE BEGINNING, I HAD A FEELING THIS WOULD HAPPEN ...
MIRAI-KUN.
YEAH ......
GANG AND PON-CHAN LOOK HAPPY.

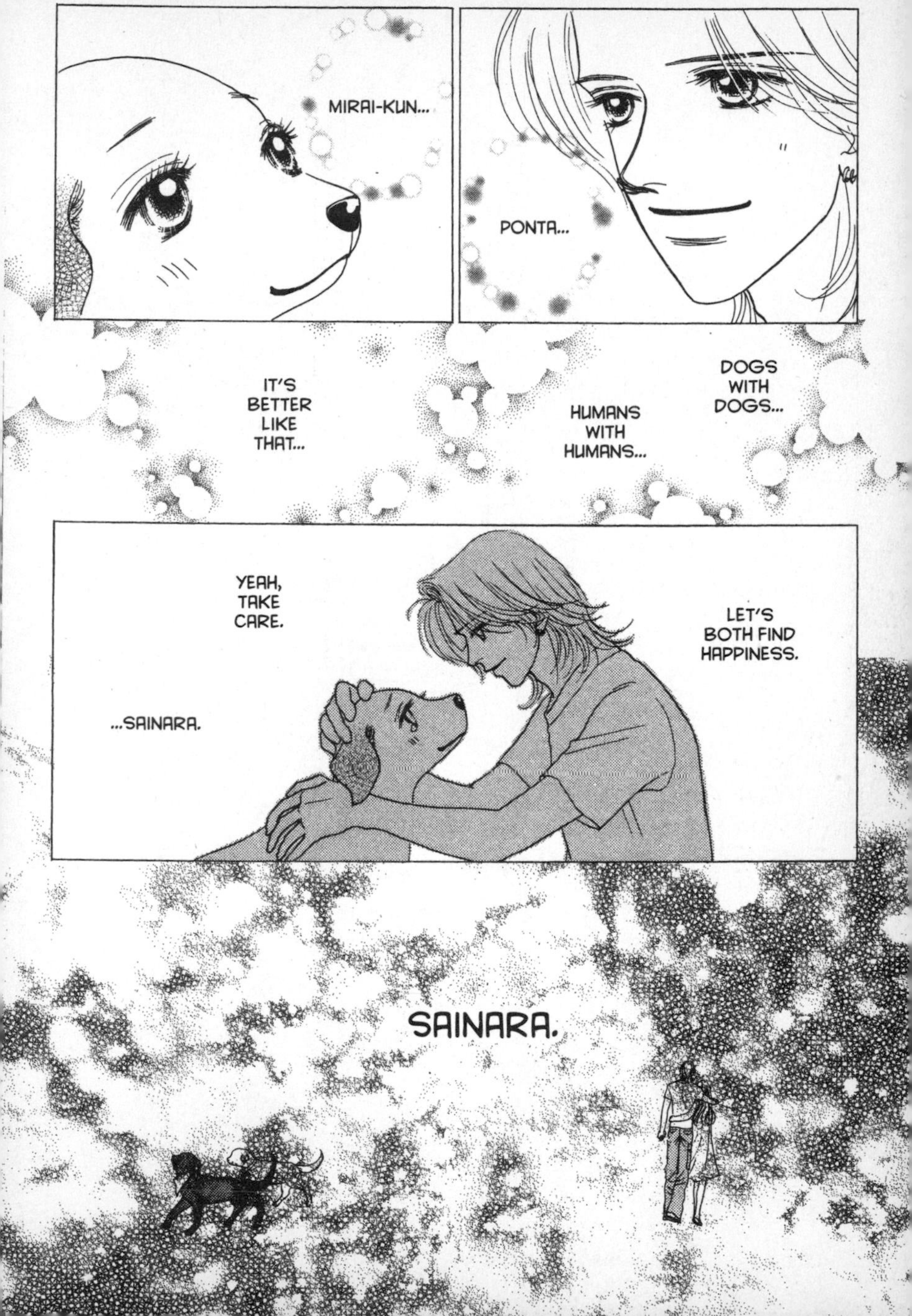
PONTA...
MIRAI-KUN...
DOGS WITH DOGS...
HUMANS WITH HUMANS...
IT'S BETTER LIKE THAT...
LET'S BOTH FIND HAPPINESS.
YEAH, TAKE CARE.
...SAINARA.
SAINARA.

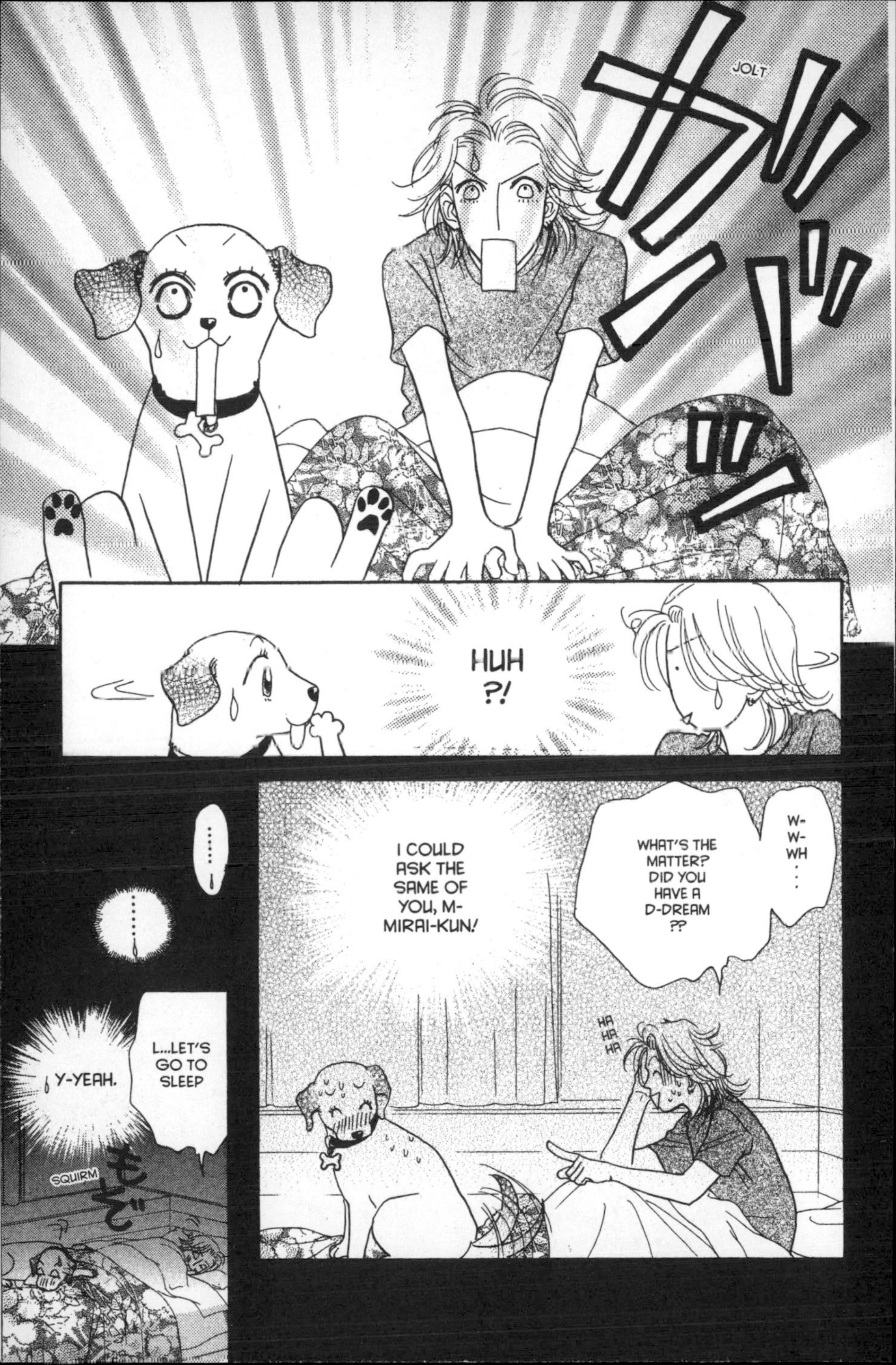
JOLT
HUH ?!
W- W- WH . . .
WHAT'S THE MATTER? DID YOU HAVE A D-DREAM ??
I COULD ASK THE SAME OF YOU, M-MIRAI-KUN!
HA HA HA
......
......
L...LET'S GO TO SLEEP
Y-YEAH.
SQUIRM

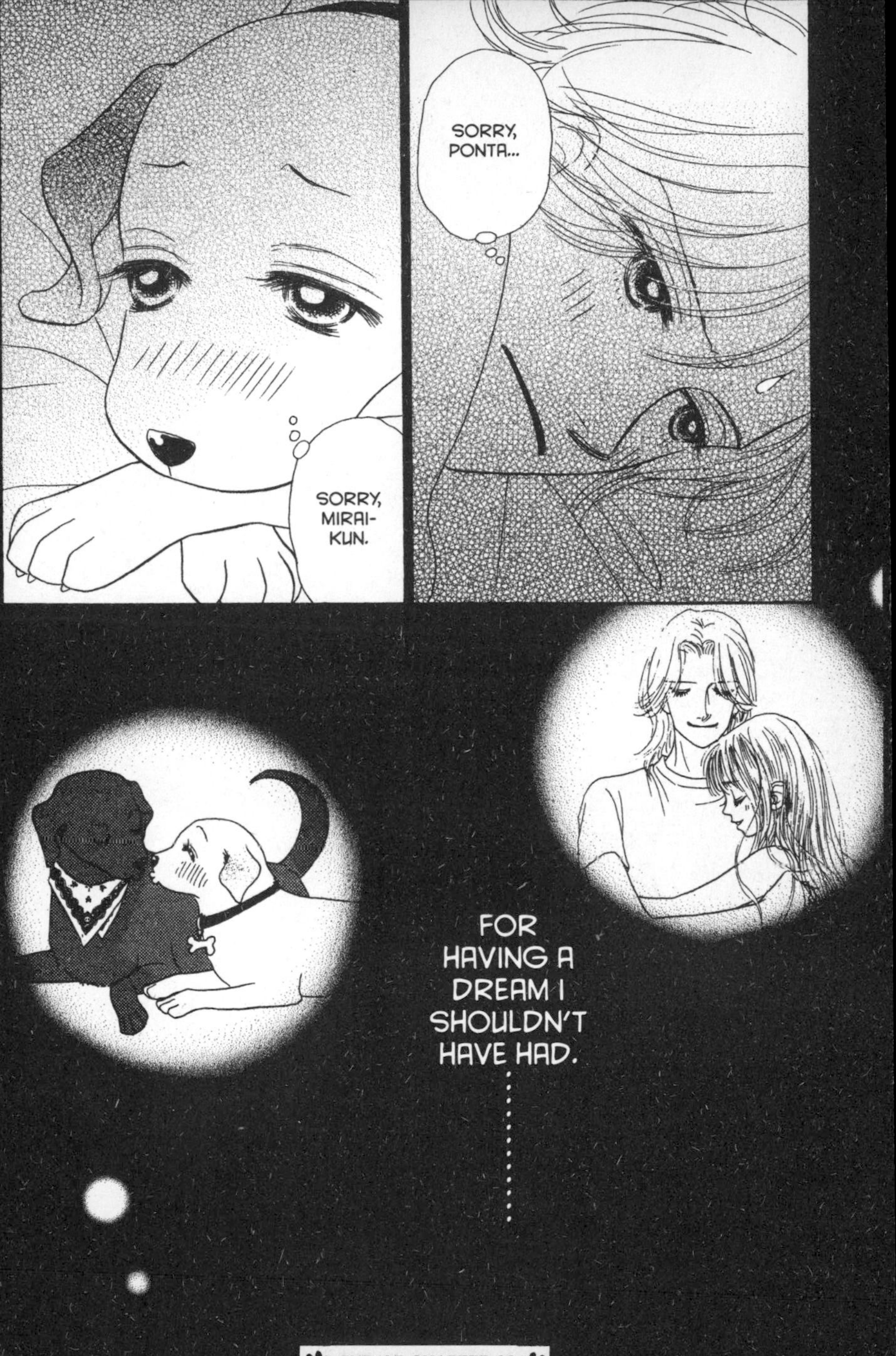
SORRY, PONTA...
SORRY, MIRAI-KUN.
FOR HAVING A DREAM I SHOULDN'T HAVE HAD.

END OF CHAPTER 23

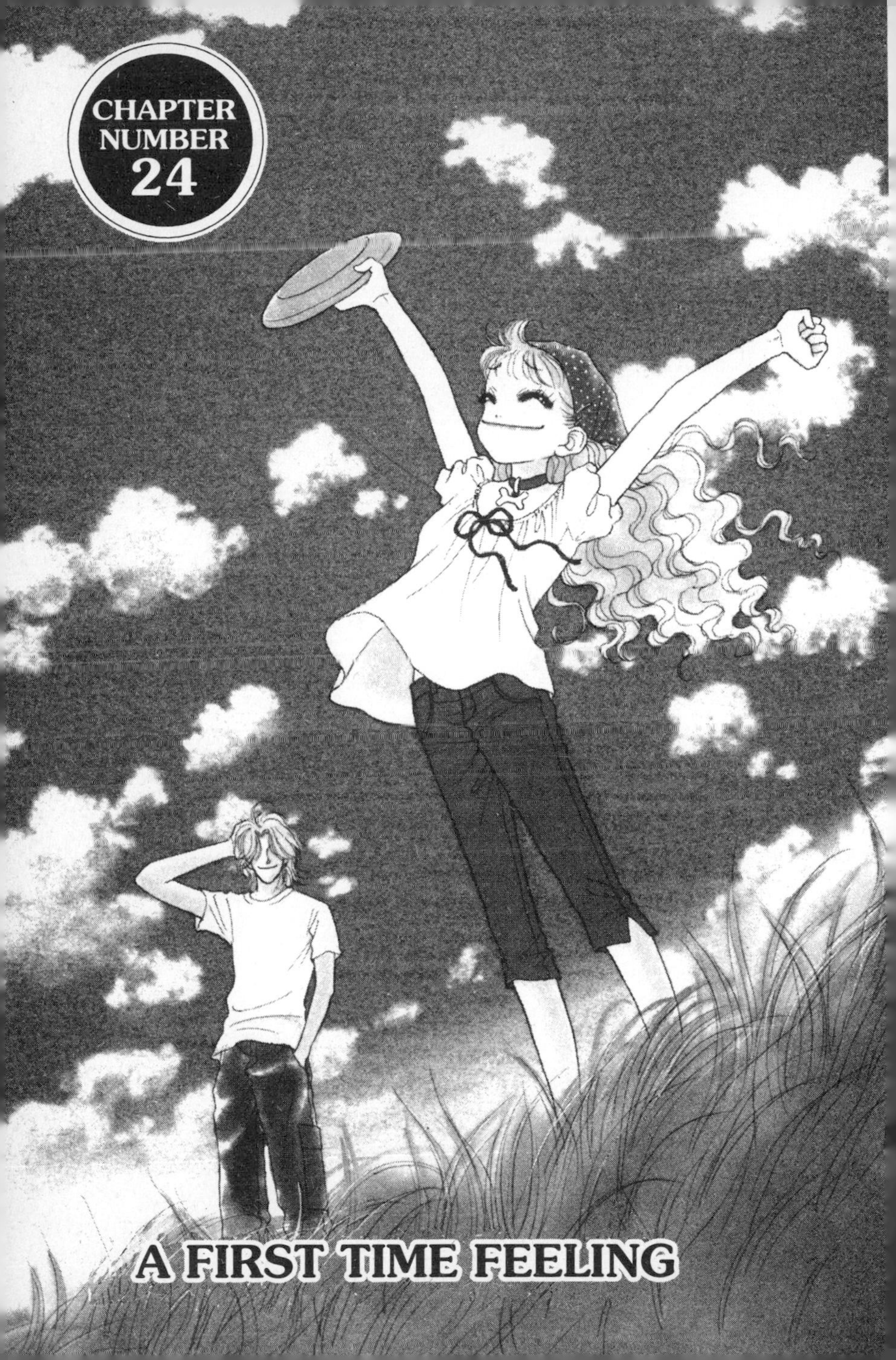
CHAPTER NUMBER 24
A FIRST TIME FEELING

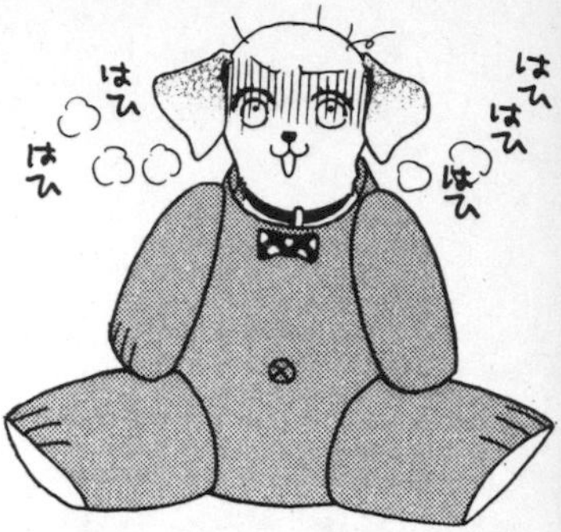
はひ
はひ
はひ
はひ
はひ

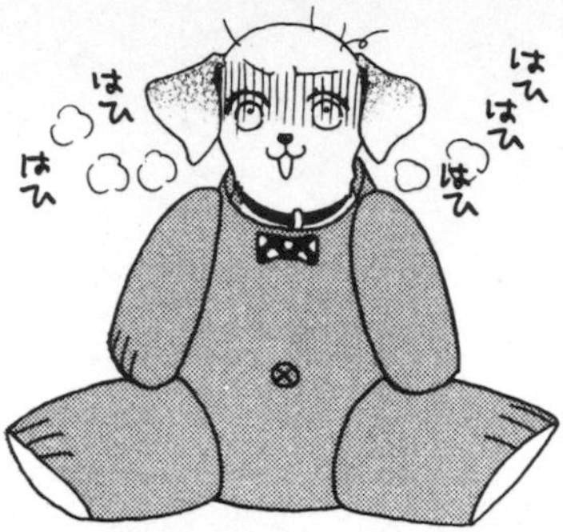
はひ
はひ
はひ
はひ
はひ

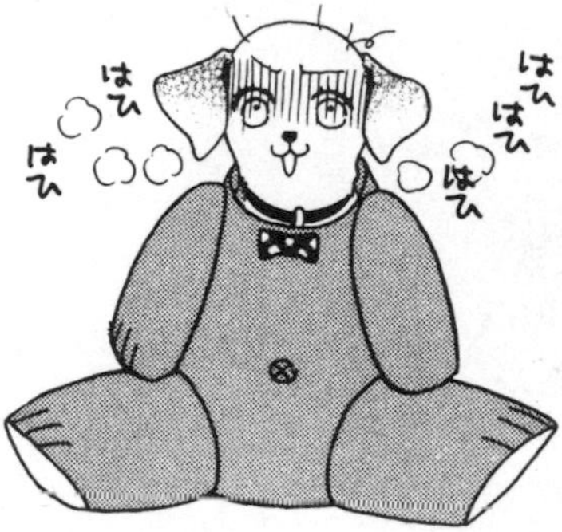
はひ
はひ
はひ
はひ
はひ

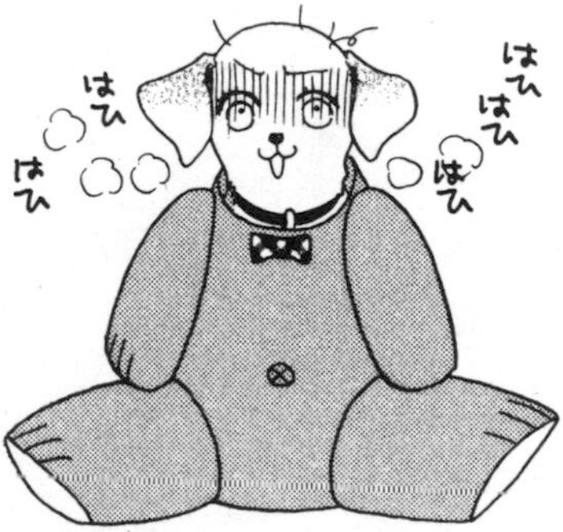
はひ
はひ
はひ
はひ
はひ

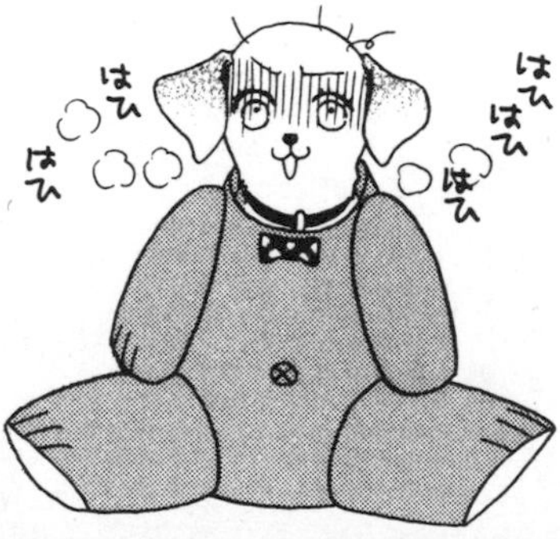
はひ
はひ
はひ
はひ
はひ

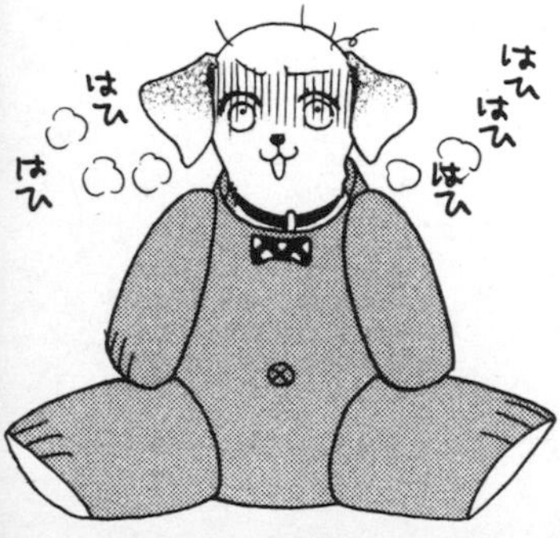
はひ
はひ
はひ
はひ
はひ

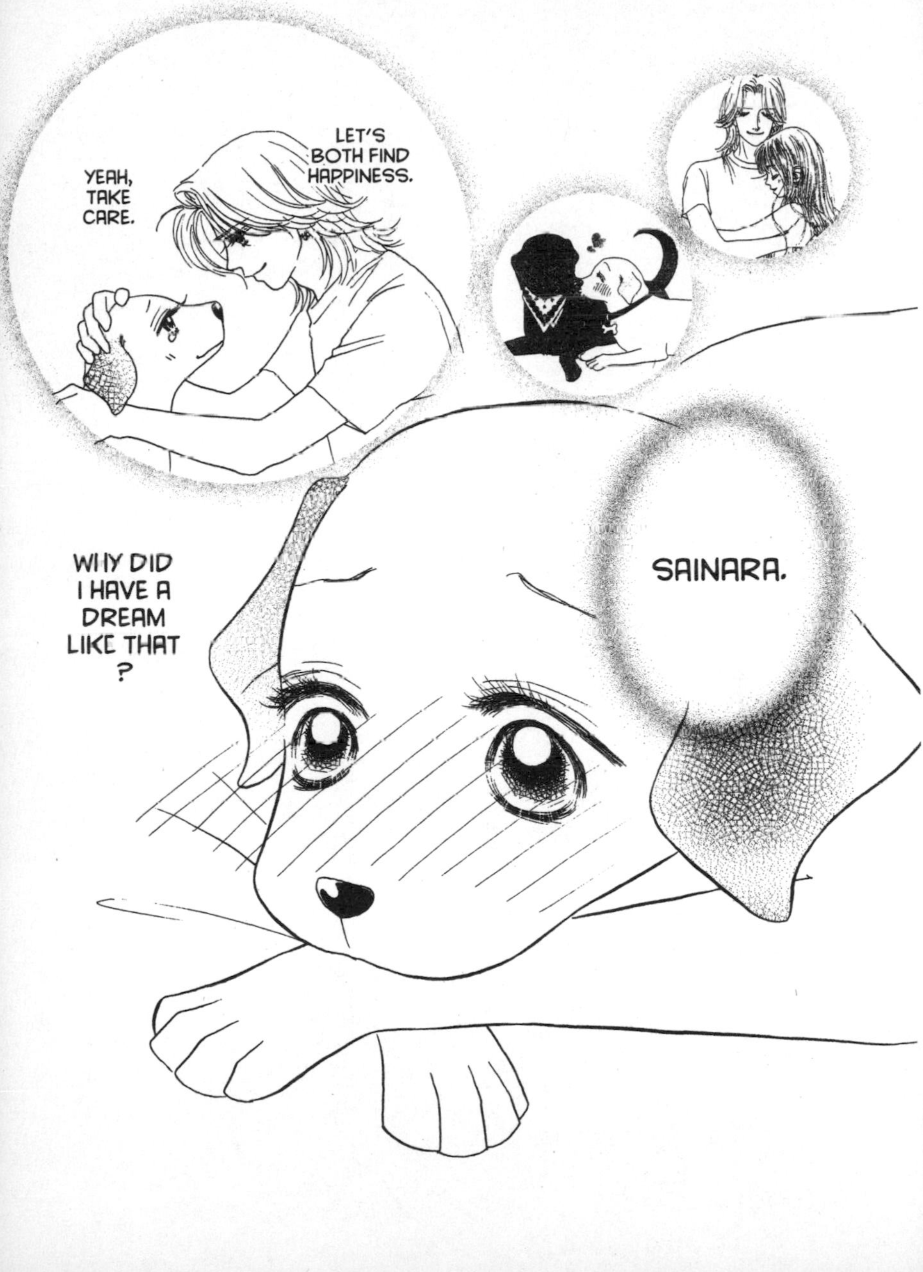
LET'S BOTH FIND HAPPINESS.
YEAH, TAKE CARE.
SAINARA.
WHY DID I HAVE A DREAM LIKE THAT?

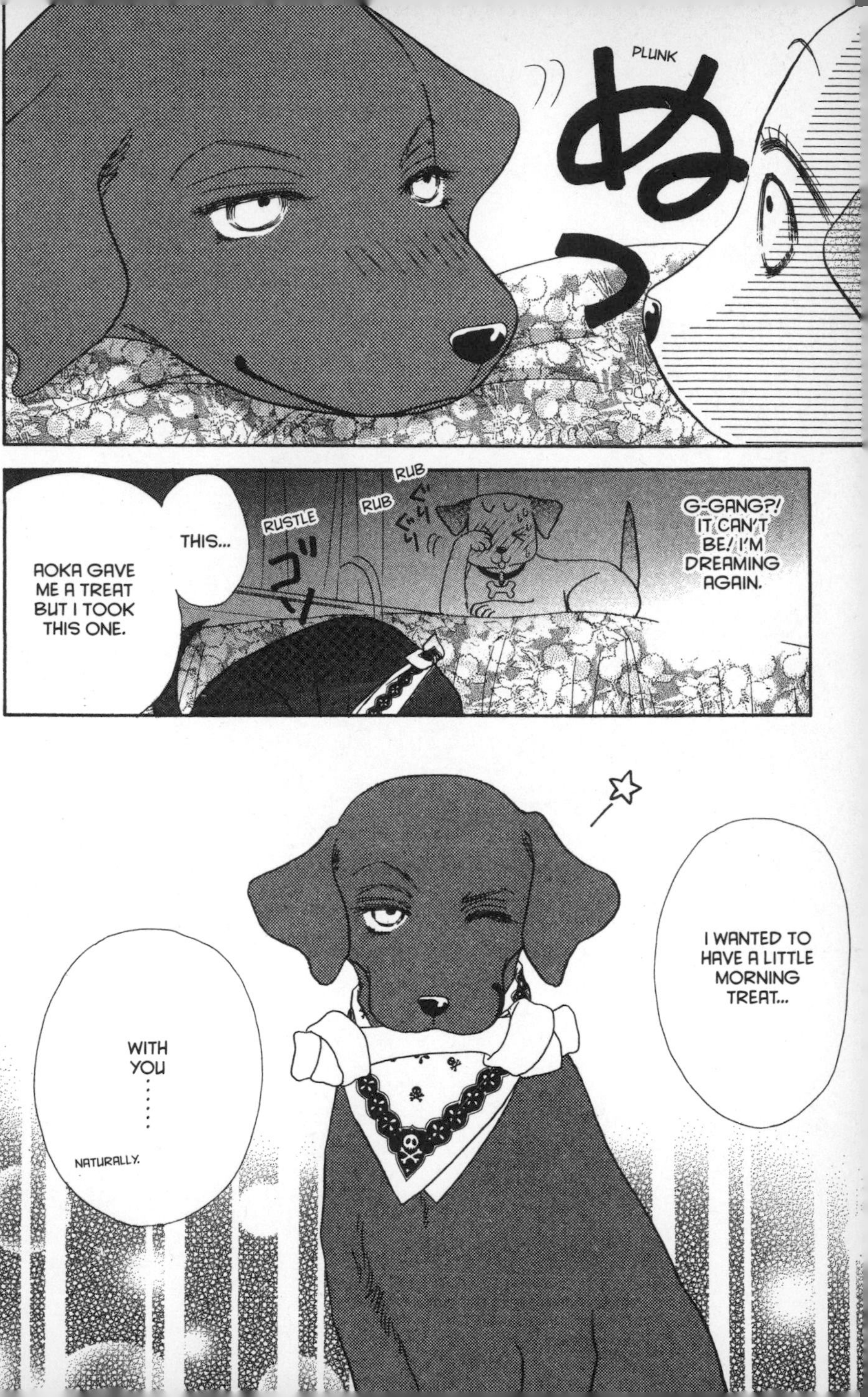
PLUNK
ぬっ
G-GANG?! IT CAN'T BE! I'M DREAMING AGAIN.
RUB
RUB
ぐりぐり
RUSTLE
THIS...
AOKA GAVE ME A TREAT BUT I TOOK THIS ONE.
I WANTED TO HAVE A LITTLE MORNING TREAT...
WITH YOU......
NATURALLY.

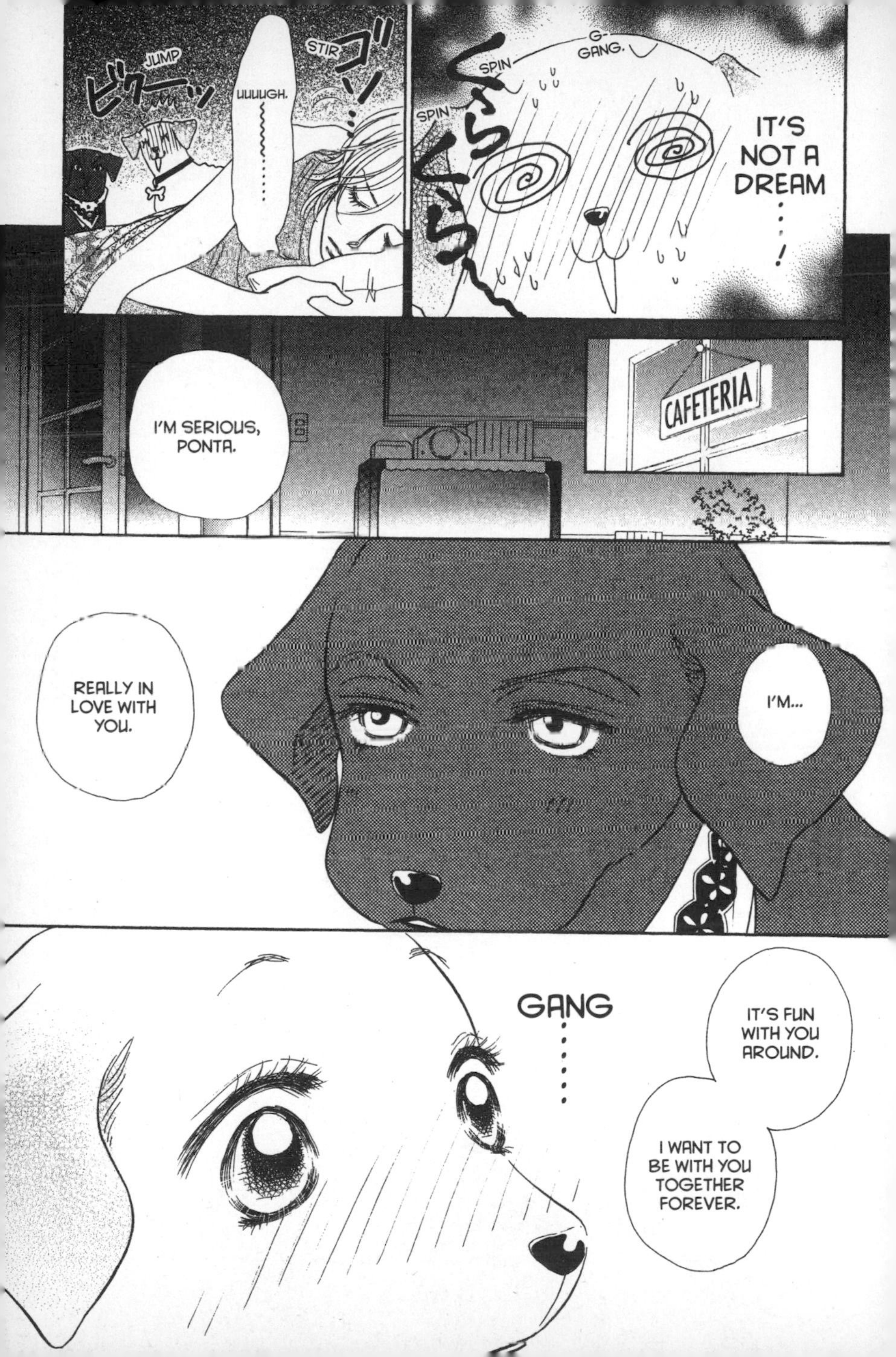
G-GANG.
SPIN
SPIN
くらくら
IT'S NOT A DREAM...!
STIR
ゴソッ
UUUUGH......
JUMP
ビクーッ
CAFETERIA
I'M SERIOUS, PONTA.
I'M...
REALLY IN LOVE WITH YOU.
GANG......
IT'S FUN WITH YOU AROUND.
I WANT TO BE WITH YOU TOGETHER FOREVER.

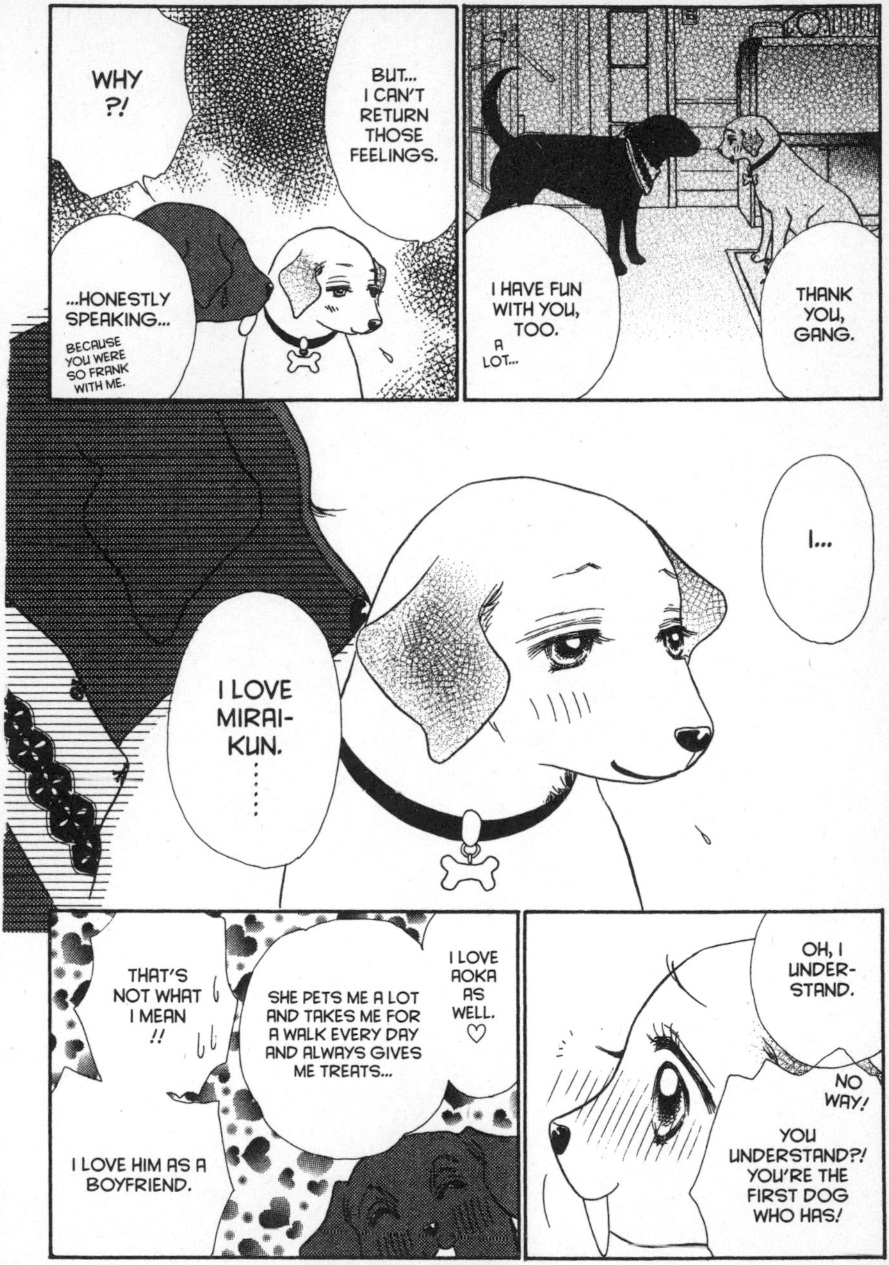
THANK YOU, GANG.
I HAVE FUN WITH YOU, TOO.
A LOT...
BUT... I CAN'T RETURN THOSE FEELINGS.
WHY?!
...HONESTLY SPEAKING...
BECAUSE YOU WERE SO FRANK WITH ME.
I...
I LOVE MIRAI-KUN.
......
OH, I UNDER-STAND.
NO WAY!
YOU UNDERSTAND?! YOU'RE THE FIRST DOG WHO HAS!
I LOVE AOKA AS WELL. ♡
SHE PETS ME A LOT AND TAKES ME FOR A WALK EVERY DAY AND ALWAYS GIVES ME TREATS...
THAT'S NOT WHAT I MEAN!!
I LOVE HIM AS A BOYFRIEND.

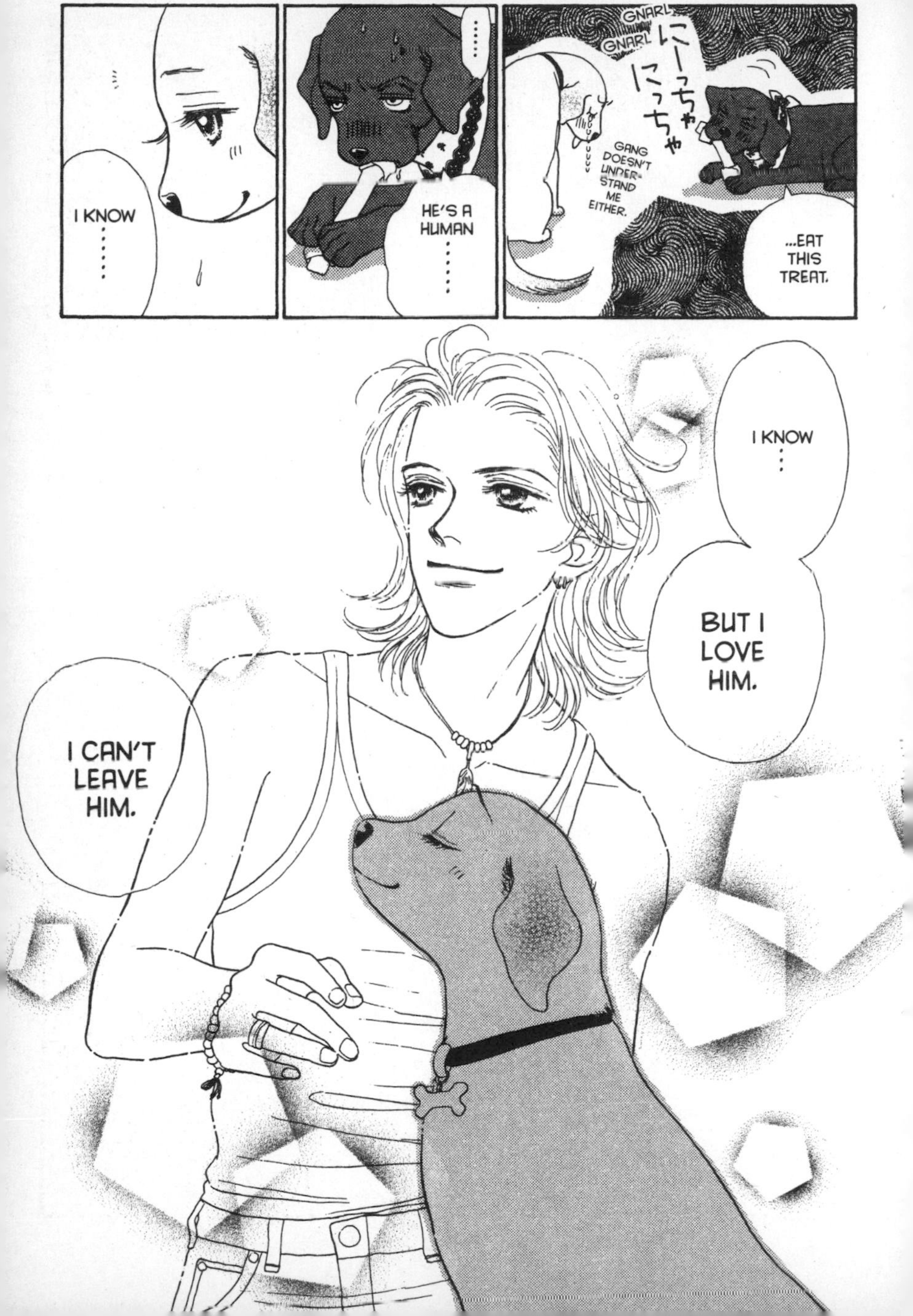
GNARL
GNARL
にーっちゃにっちゃ
GANG DOESN'T UNDERSTAND ME EITHER.
...EAT THIS TREAT.
HE'S A HUMAN……
I KNOW……
I KNOW…
BUT I LOVE HIM.
I CAN'T LEAVE HIM.

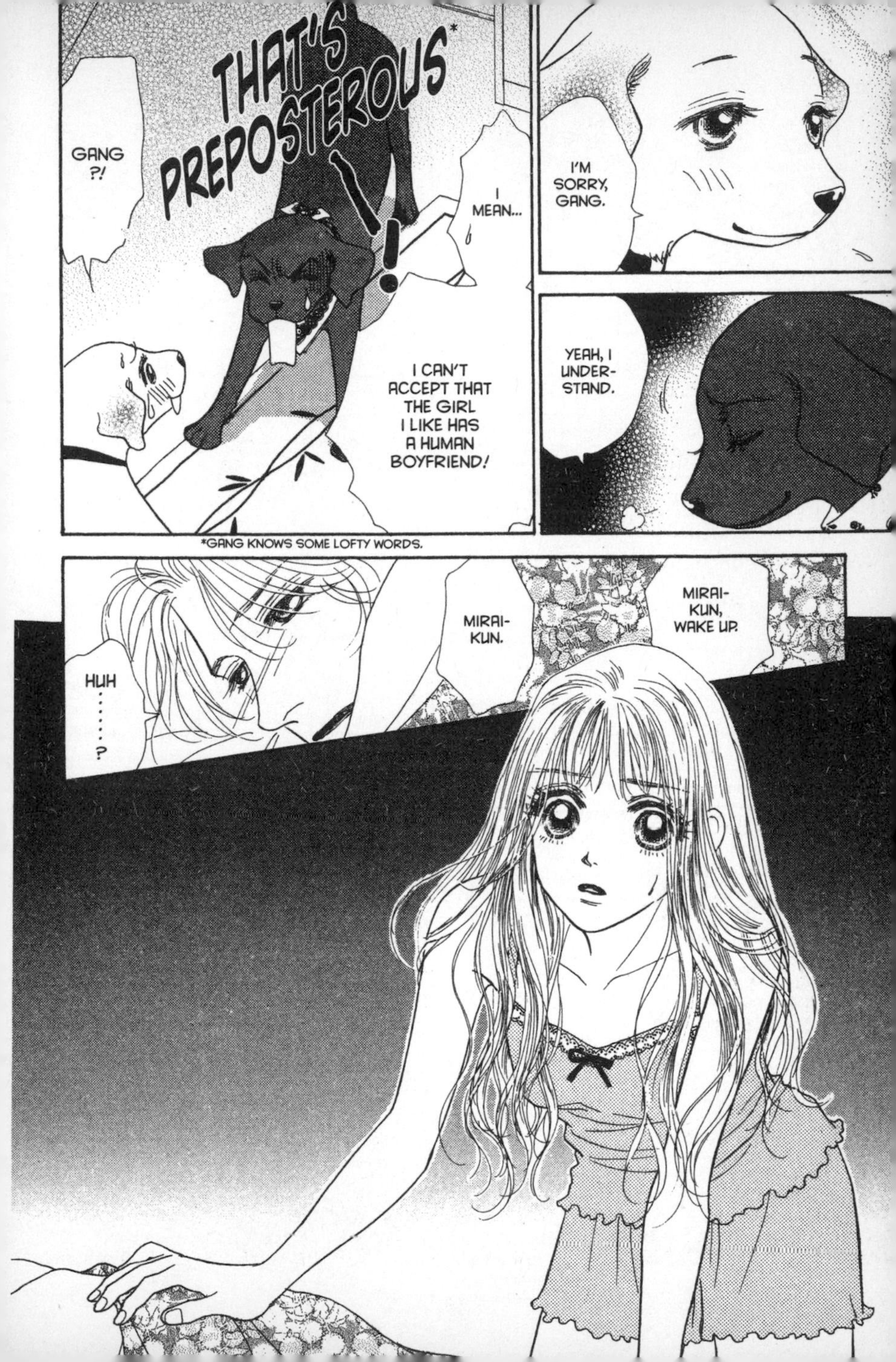
I'M SORRY, GANG.
YEAH, I UNDERSTAND.
I MEAN...
I CAN'T ACCEPT THAT THE GIRL I LIKE HAS A HUMAN BOYFRIEND!
THAT'S PREPOSTEROUS*
!
GANG ?!
MIRAI-KUN, WAKE UP.
MIRAI-KUN.
HUH......?
*GANG KNOWS SOME LOFTY WORDS.

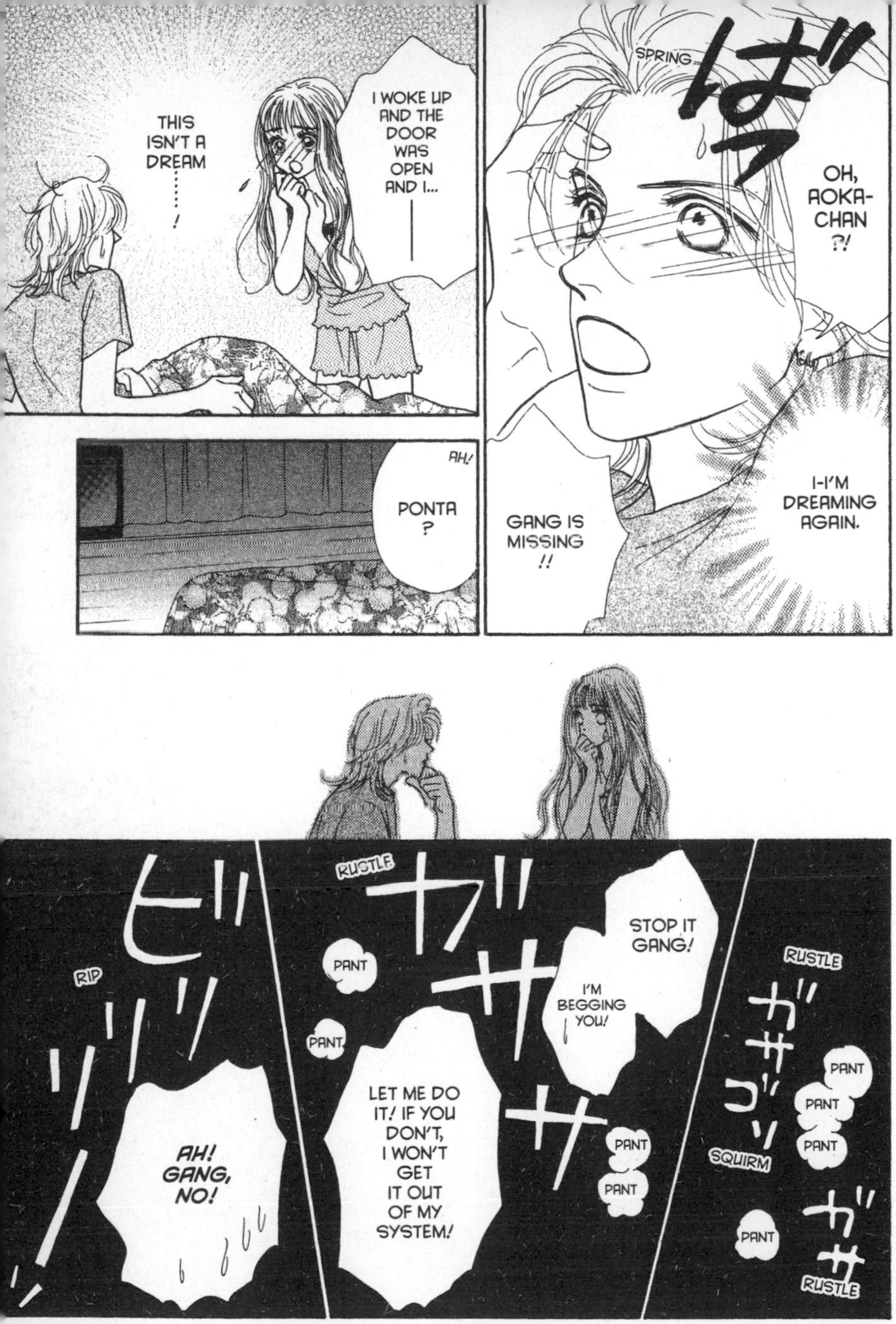

SPRING
OH, AOKA-CHAN ?!
I-I'M DREAMING AGAIN.
GANG IS MISSING !!
I WOKE UP AND THE DOOR WAS OPEN AND I...
THIS ISN'T A DREAM......!
AH!
PONTA ?
RUSTLE
PANT
PANT
PANT
SQUIRM
PANT
RUSTLE
RUSTLE
STOP IT GANG!
I'M BEGGING YOU!
PANT
PANT
LET ME DO IT! IF YOU DON'T, I WON'T GET IT OUT OF MY SYSTEM!
PANT
PANT
RIP
AH! GANG, NO!

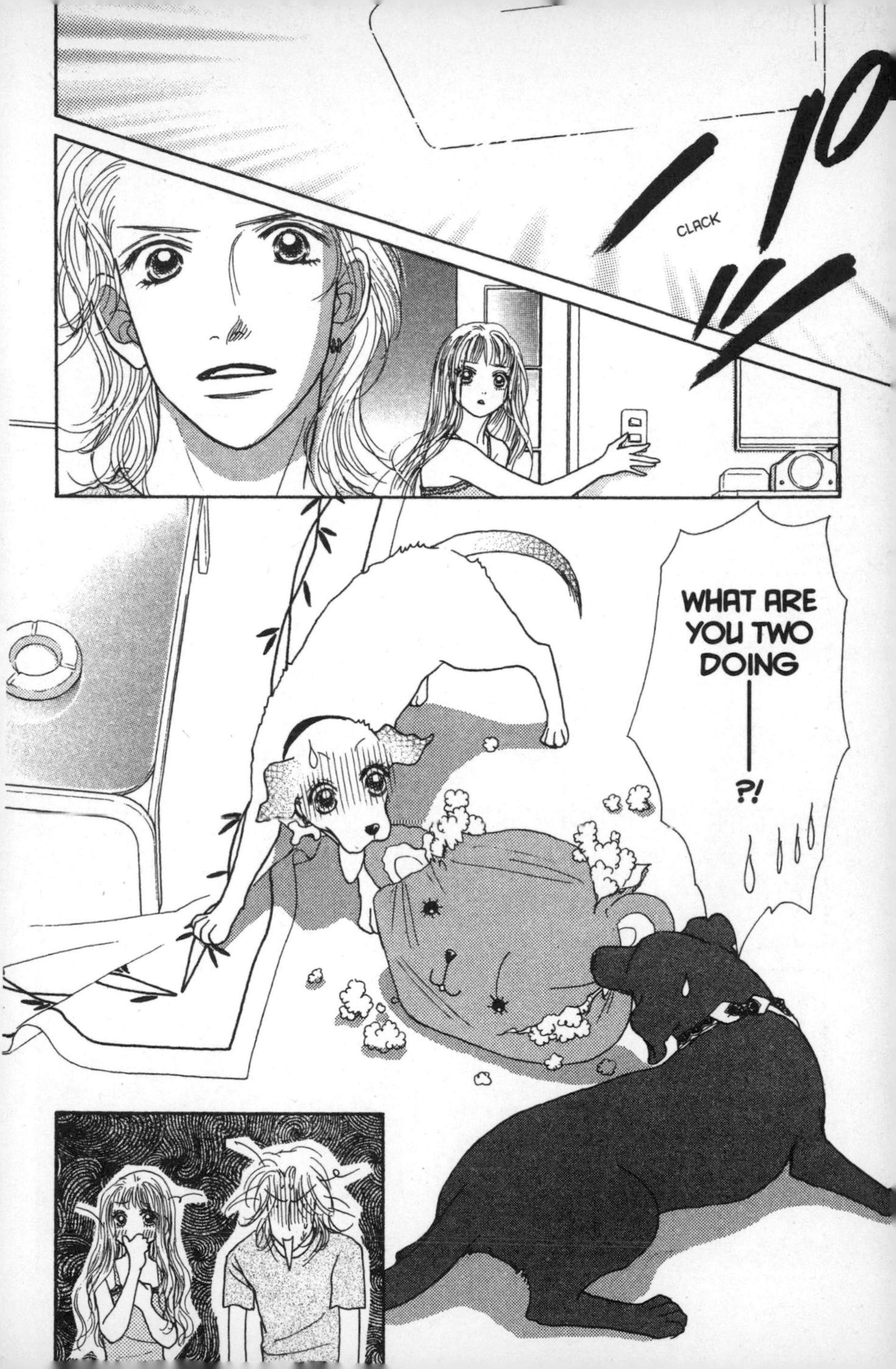
CLACK
WHAT ARE YOU TWO DOING ?!

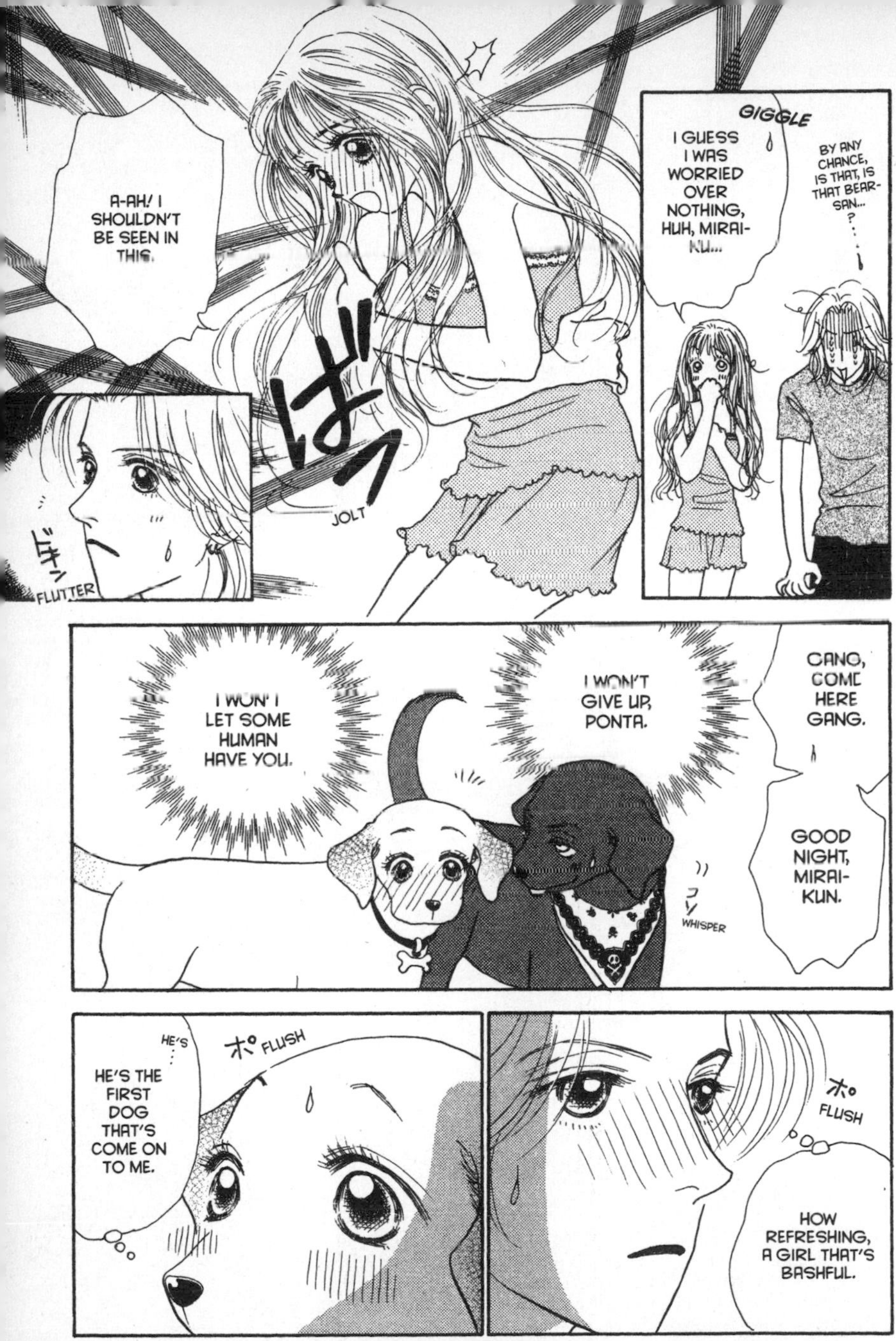
BY ANY CHANCE, IS THAT, IS THAT BEAR-SAN...?
GIGGLE
I GUESS I WAS WORRIED OVER NOTHING, HUH, MIRAI-KU...
ぱっ
JOLT
A-AH! I SHOULDN'T BE SEEN IN THIS.
ドキン
FLUTTER
GANG, COME HERE GANG.
GOOD NIGHT, MIRAI-KUN.
I WON'T GIVE UP, PONTA.
I WON'T LET SOME HUMAN HAVE YOU.
コソ
WHISPER
ポ
FLUSH
HOW REFRESHING, A GIRL THAT'S BASHFUL.
ポ
FLUSH
HE'S...
HE'S THE FIRST DOG THAT'S COME ON TO ME.

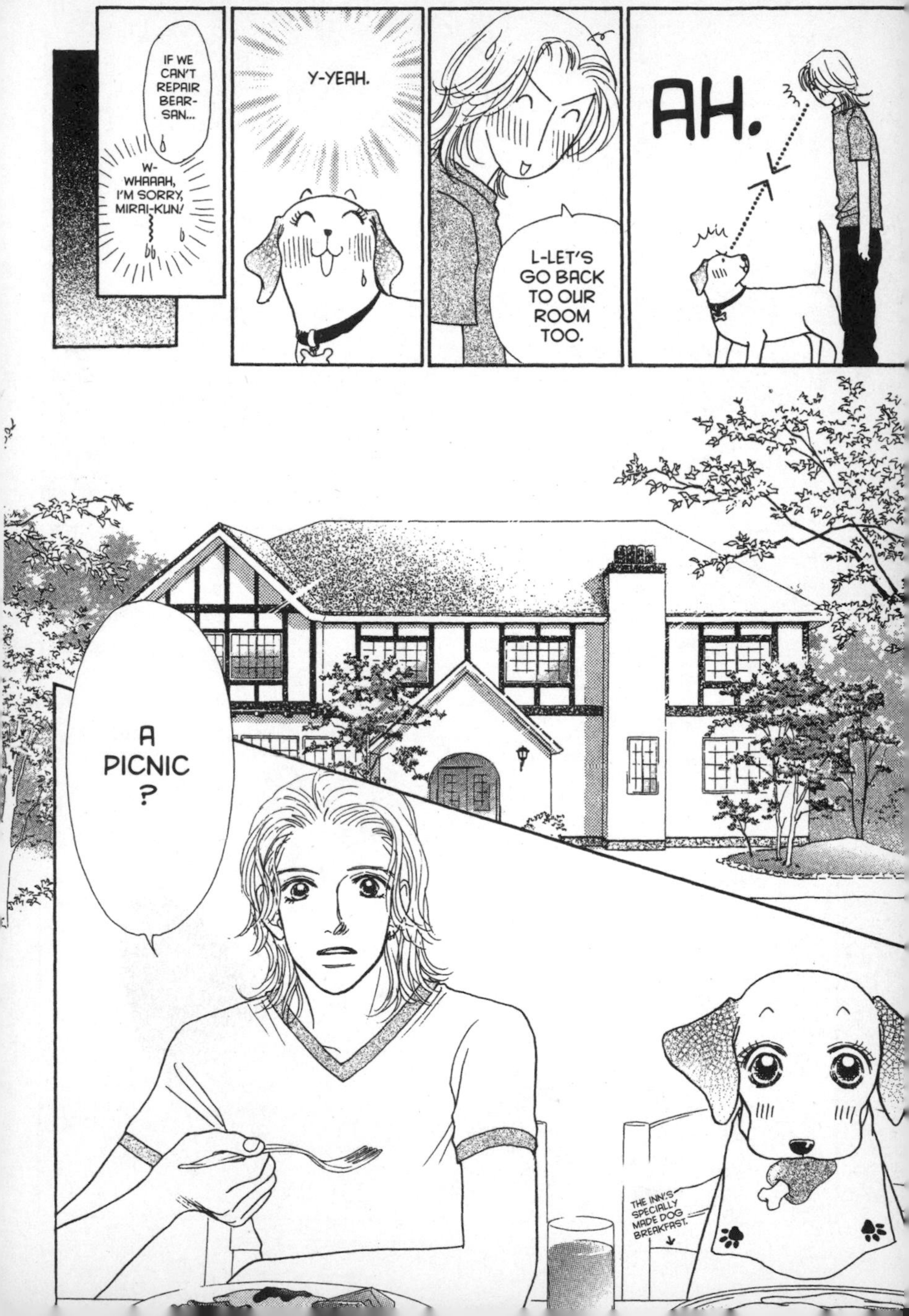
AH.
L-LET'S GO BACK TO OUR ROOM TOO.
Y-YEAH.
IF WE CAN'T REPAIR BEAR-SAN...
W-WHAAAH, I'M SORRY, MIRAI-KUN!
A PICNIC?
THE INN'S SPECIALLY MADE DOG BREAKFAST.

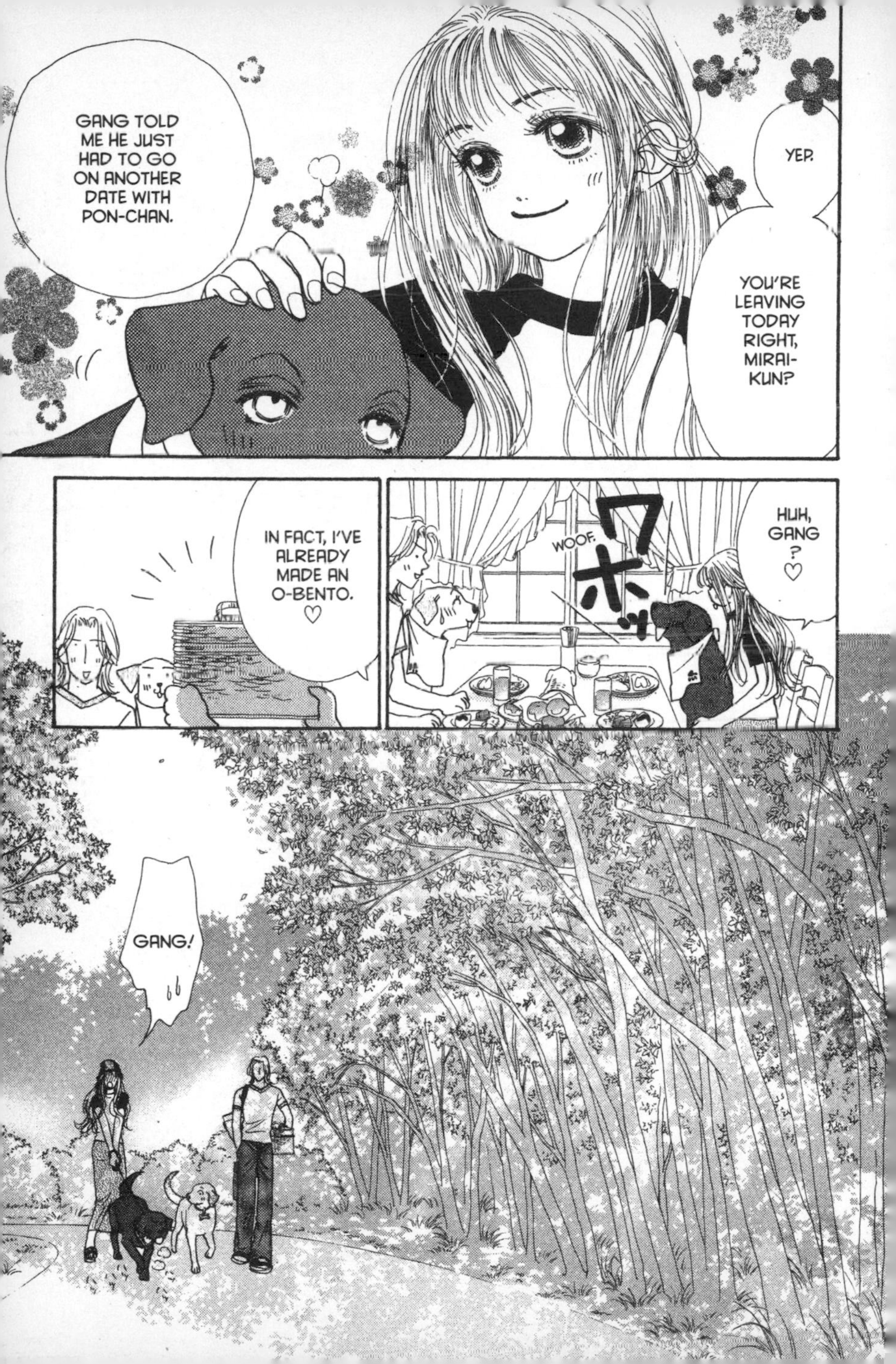
YEP.
YOU'RE LEAVING TODAY RIGHT, MIRAI-KUN?
GANG TOLD ME HE JUST HAD TO GO ON ANOTHER DATE WITH PON-CHAN.
HUH, GANG? ♡
WOOF.
ワホッ
IN FACT, I'VE ALREADY MADE AN O-BENTO. ♡
GANG!

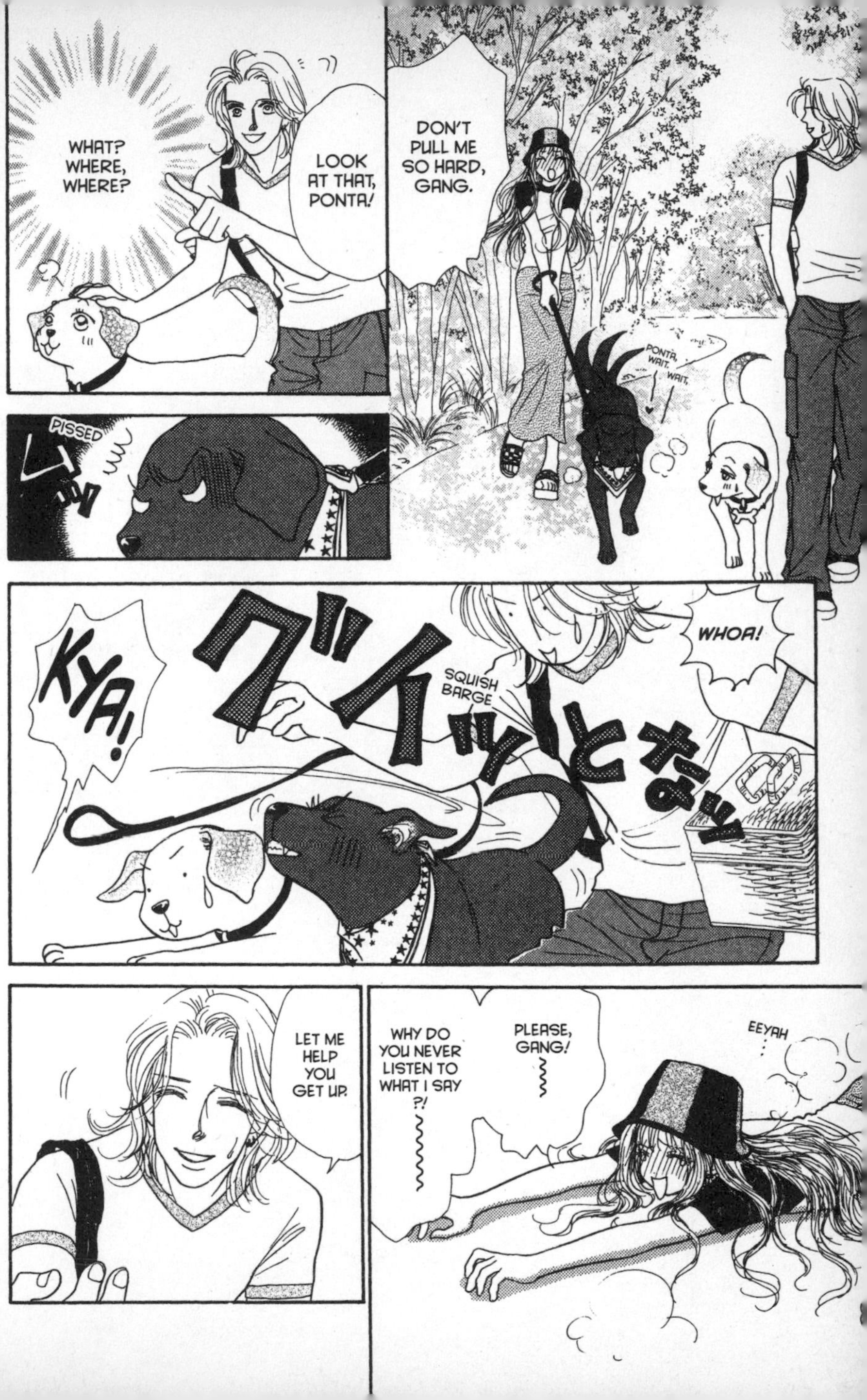
DON'T PULL ME SO HARD, GANG.
PONTA, WAIT. WAIT.
LOOK AT THAT, PONTA!
WHAT? WHERE, WHERE?
PISSED
WHOA!
SQUISH BARGE
グイッとなッ
KYA!
EEYAH
PLEASE, GANG!
WHY DO YOU NEVER LISTEN TO WHAT I SAY ?!
LET ME HELP YOU GET UP.

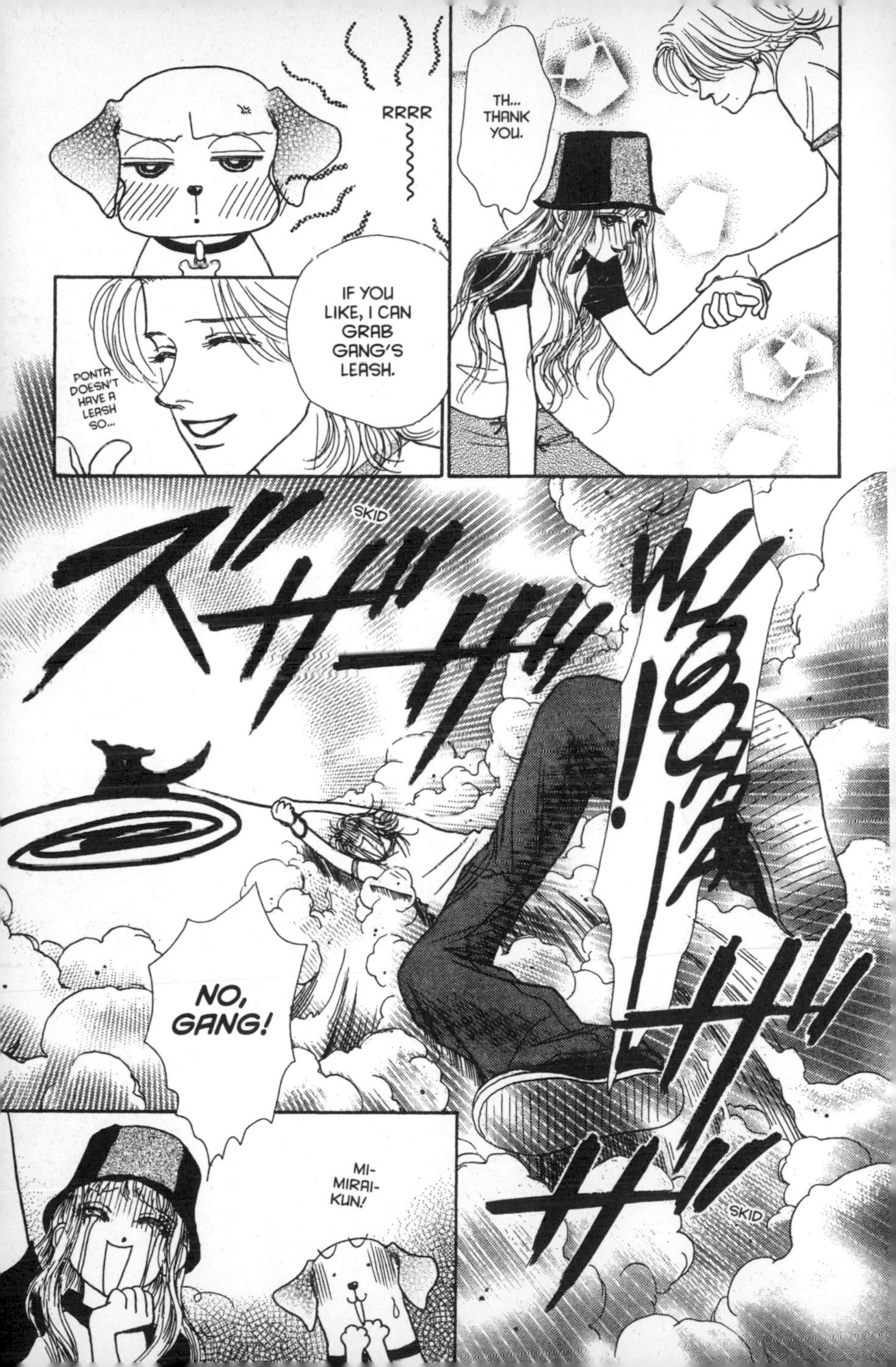
TH... THANK YOU.
RRRR
IF YOU LIKE, I CAN GRAB GANG'S LEASH.
PONTA DOESN'T HAVE A LEASH SO...
SKID
SKID
NO, GANG!
MI-MIRAI-KUN!

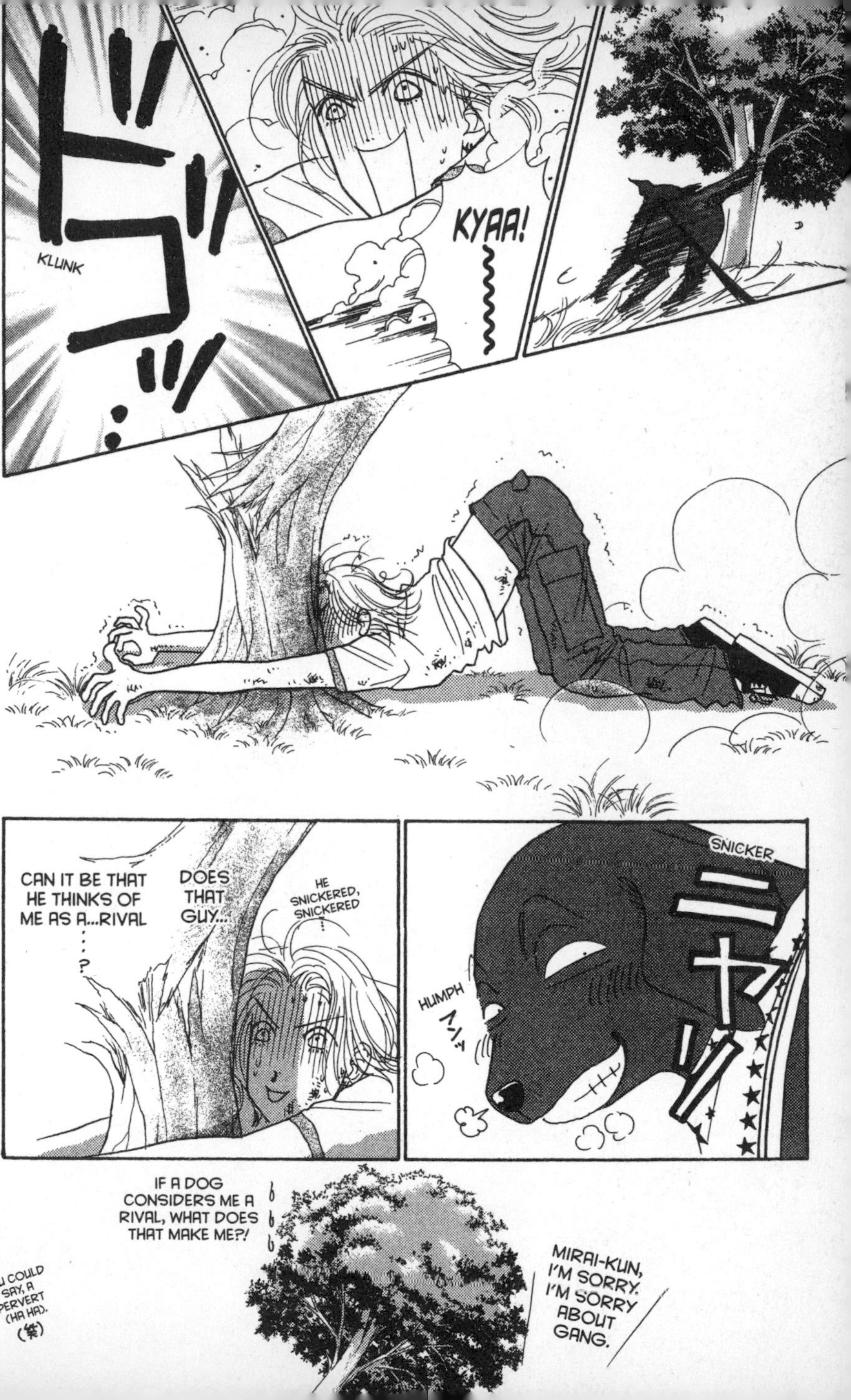
KYAA!
KLUNK
ドゴッ
SNICKER
ニヤッ
HUMPH
フンッ
HE SNICKERED, SNICKERED
DOES THAT GUY...
CAN IT BE THAT HE THINKS OF ME AS A...RIVAL ...?
MIRAI-KUN, I'M SORRY. I'M SORRY ABOUT GANG.
IF A DOG CONSIDERS ME A RIVAL, WHAT DOES THAT MAKE ME?!
YOU COULD SAY, A PERVERT (HA HA).
(笑)

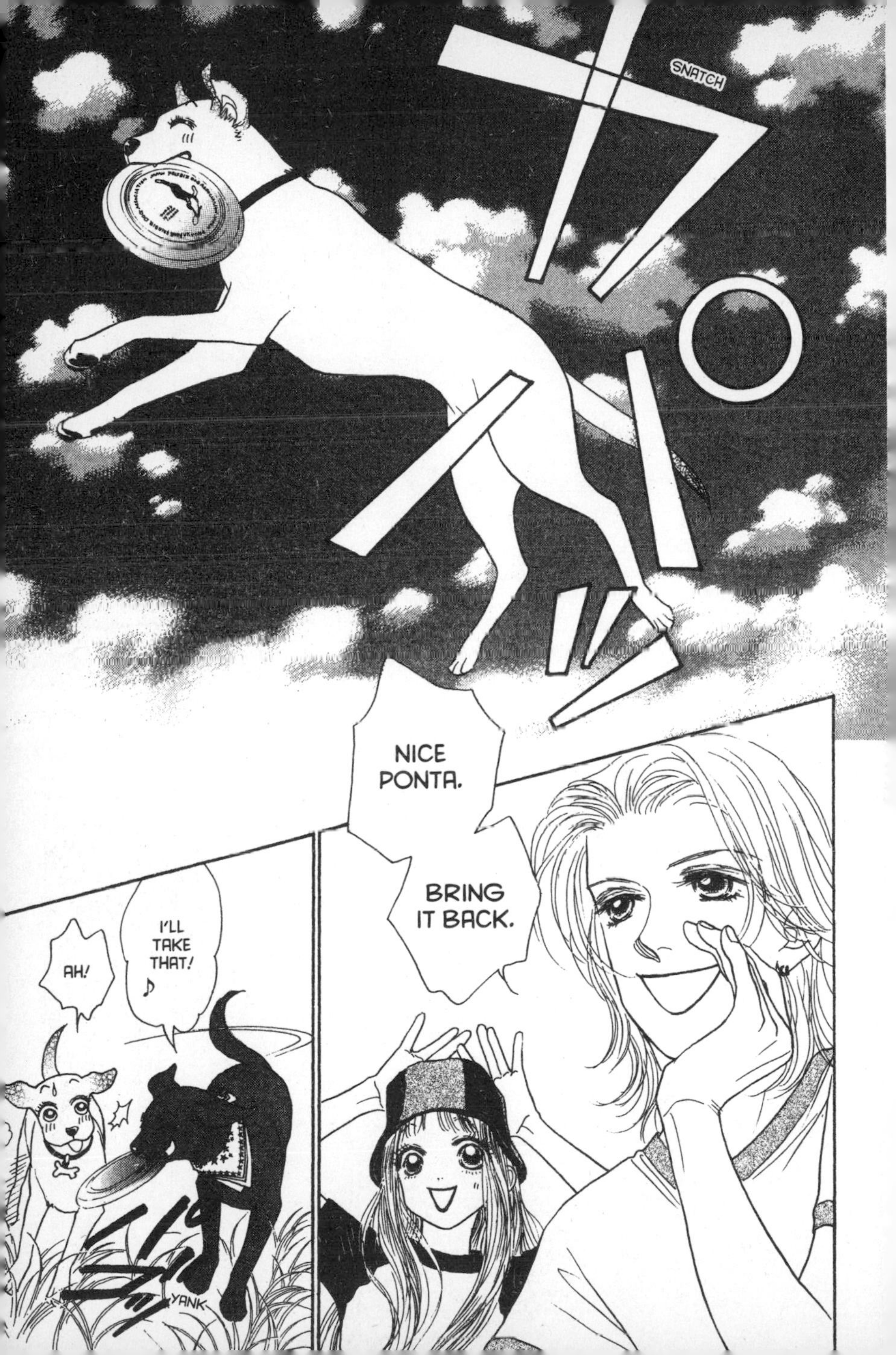
SNATCH
NICE PONTA.
BRING IT BACK.
I'LL TAKE THAT! ♪
AH!
YANK

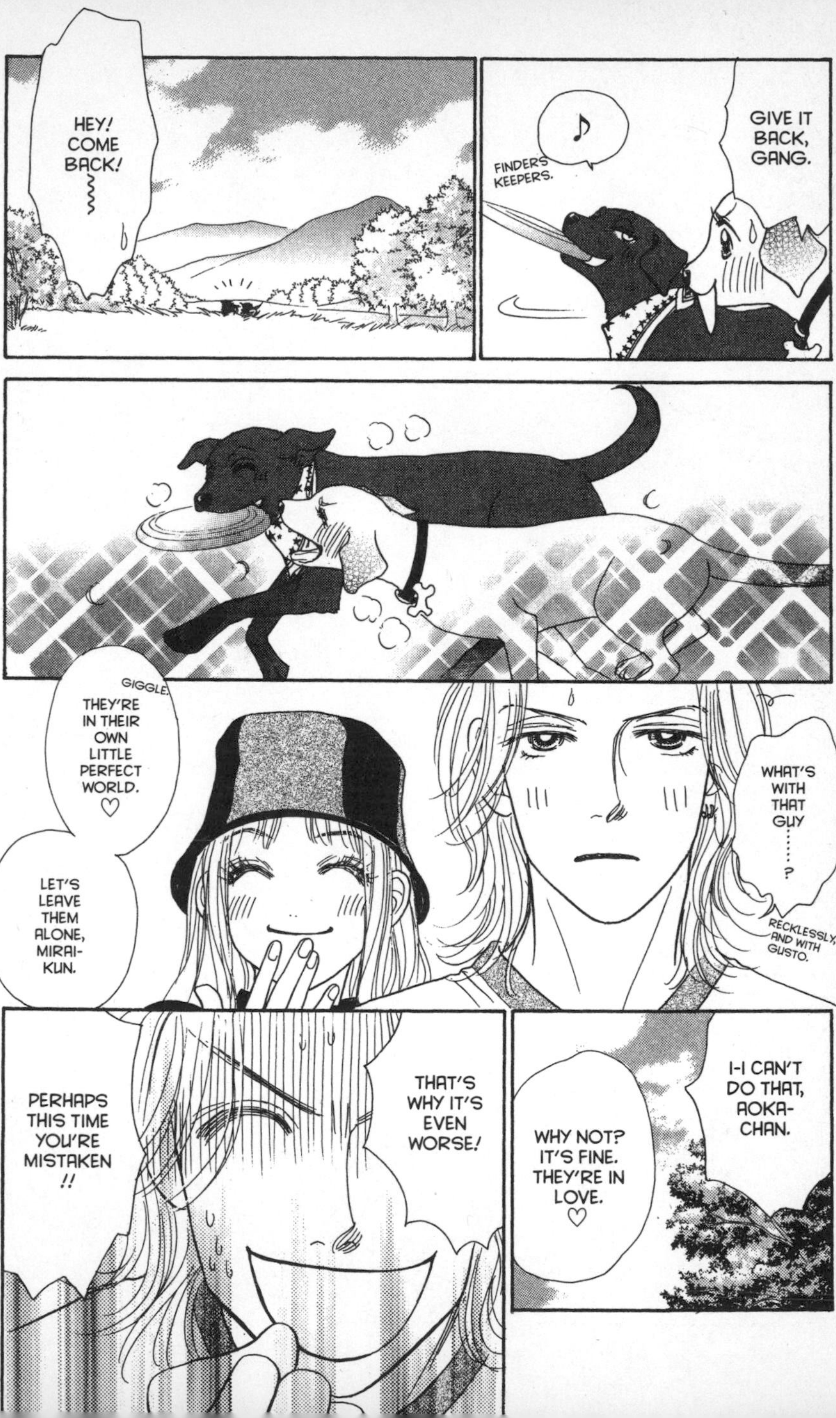
GIVE IT BACK, GANG.
♪
FINDERS KEEPERS.
HEY! COME BACK!
WHAT'S WITH THAT GUY......?
RECKLESSLY, AND WITH GUSTO.
GIGGLE.
THEY'RE IN THEIR OWN LITTLE PERFECT WORLD. ♡
LET'S LEAVE THEM ALONE, MIRAI-KUN.
I-I CAN'T DO THAT, AOKA-CHAN.
WHY NOT? IT'S FINE. THEY'RE IN LOVE. ♡
THAT'S WHY IT'S EVEN WORSE!
PERHAPS THIS TIME YOU'RE MISTAKEN!!

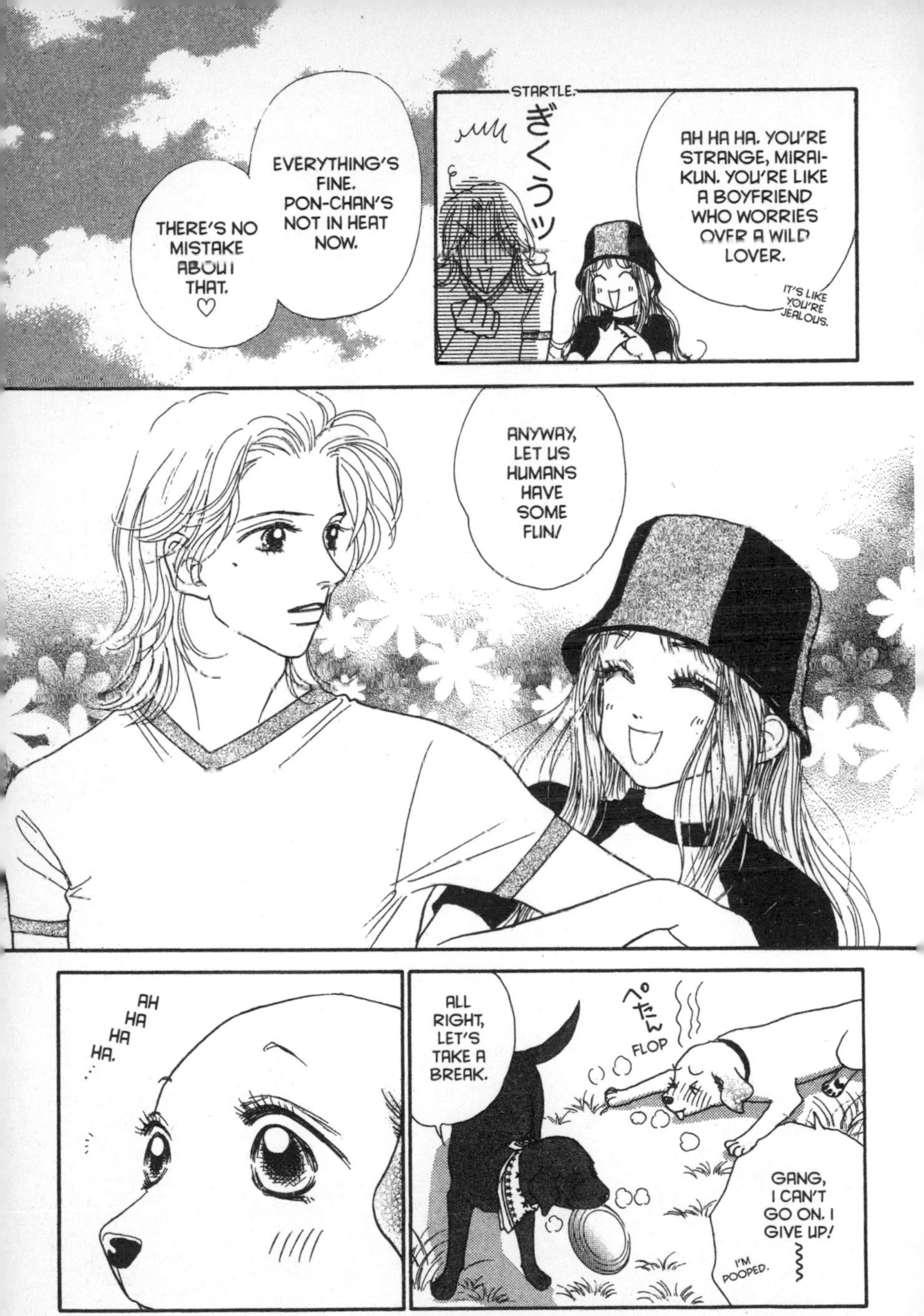
AH HA HA. YOU'RE STRANGE, MIRAI-KUN. YOU'RE LIKE A BOYFRIEND WHO WORRIES OVER A WILD LOVER.
ぎくうッ
STARTLE.
IT'S LIKE YOU'RE JEALOUS.
EVERYTHING'S FINE. PON-CHAN'S NOT IN HEAT NOW.
THERE'S NO MISTAKE ABOUT THAT. ♡
ANYWAY, LET US HUMANS HAVE SOME FUN!
ぺたん
FLOP
ALL RIGHT, LET'S TAKE A BREAK.
GANG, I CAN'T GO ON. I GIVE UP!
I'M POOPED.
AH HA HA HA. ...

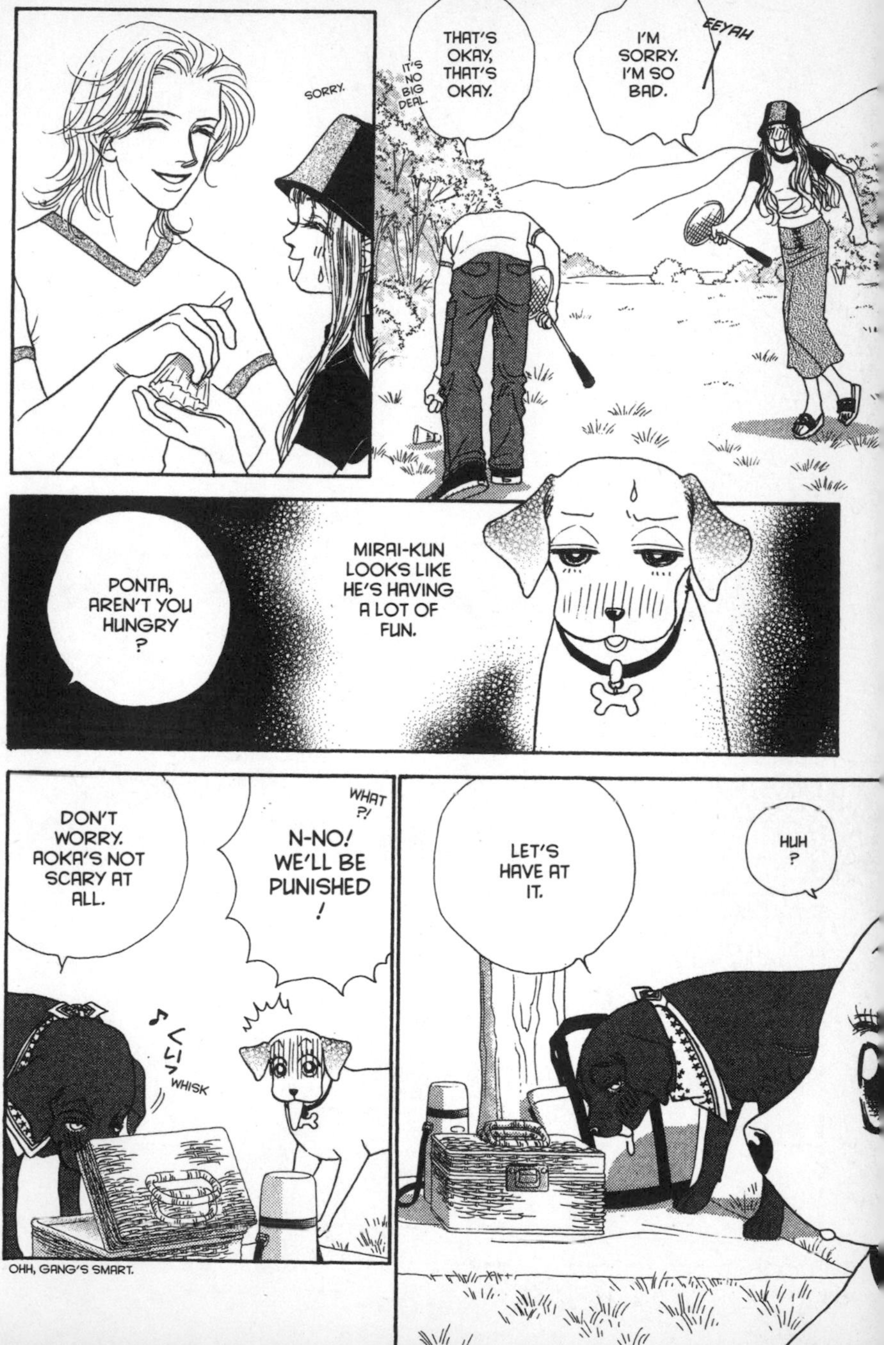
EEYAH
I'M SORRY. I'M SO BAD.
THAT'S OKAY, THAT'S OKAY.
IT'S NO BIG DEAL.
SORRY.
MIRAI-KUN LOOKS LIKE HE'S HAVING A LOT OF FUN.
PONTA, AREN'T YOU HUNGRY?
HUH?
LET'S HAVE AT IT.
WHAT?!
N-NO! WE'LL BE PUNISHED!
DON'T WORRY. AOKA'S NOT SCARY AT ALL.
WHISK
OHH, GANG'S SMART.

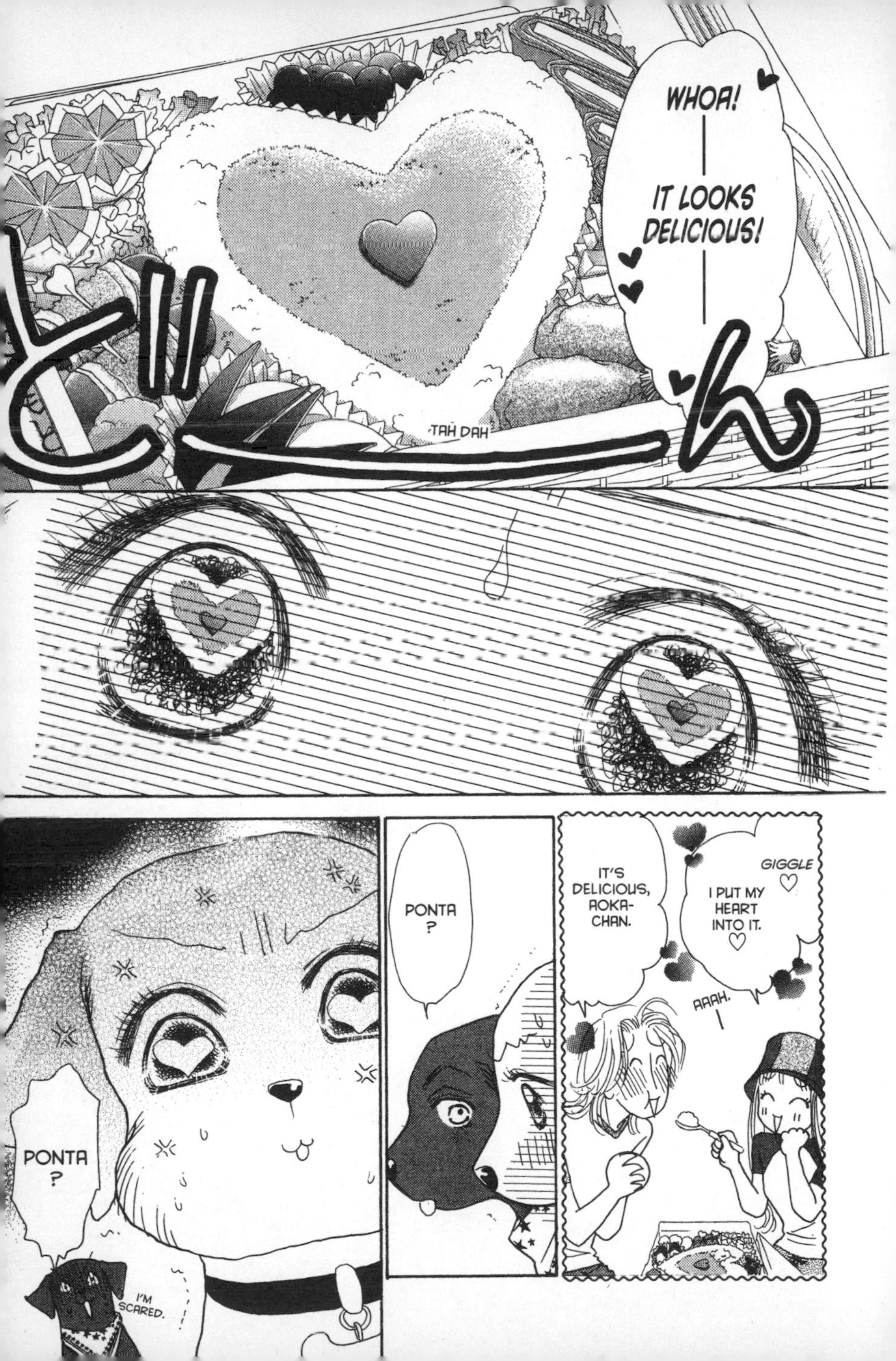
WHOA! IT LOOKS DELICIOUS!
TAH DAH
GIGGLE
I PUT MY HEART INTO IT.
IT'S DELICIOUS, AOKA-CHAN.
AAAH.
PONTA?
PONTA?
I'M SCARED.

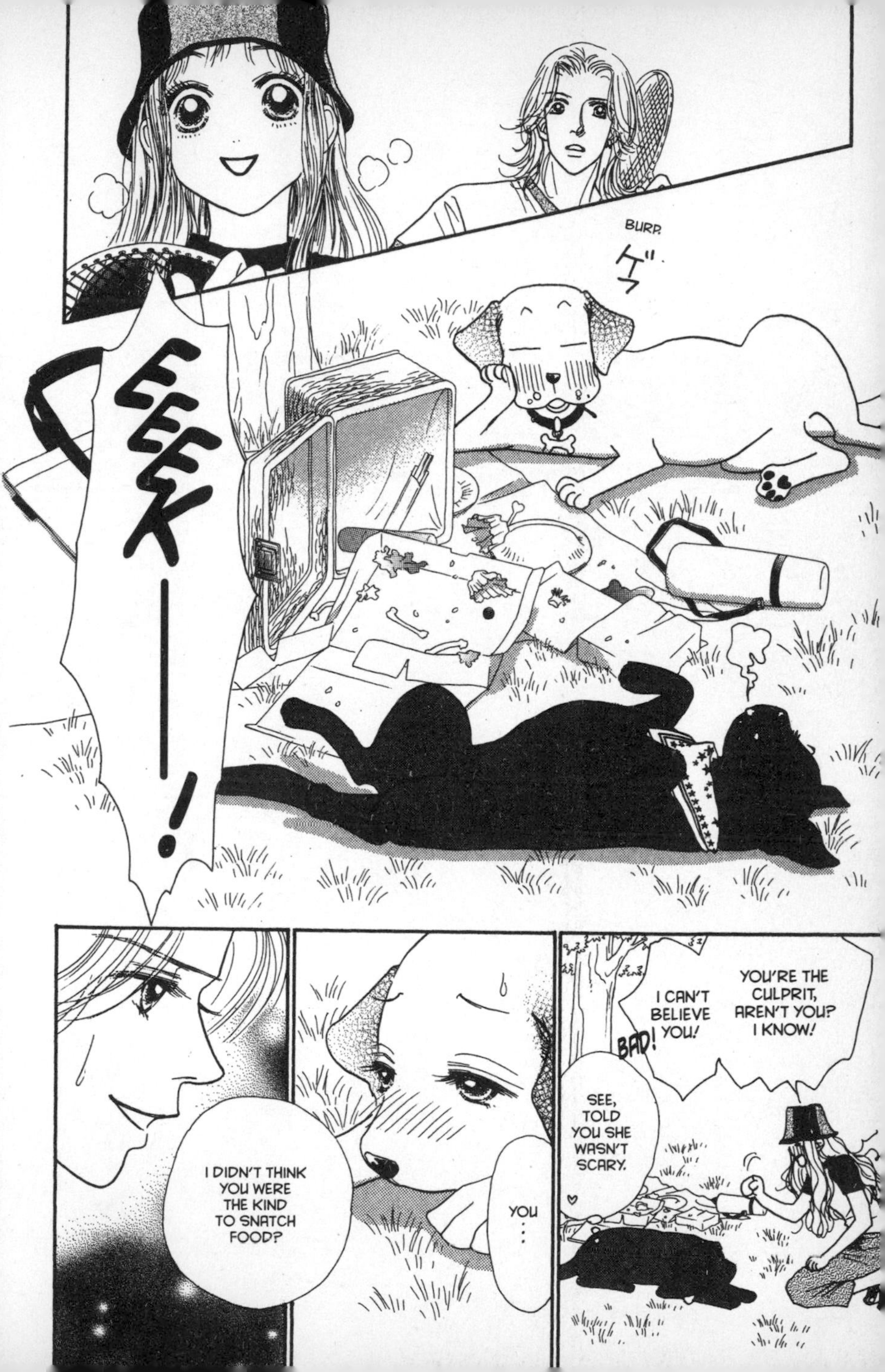
BURP.
ゲフ
EEEEK——!
YOU'RE THE CULPRIT, AREN'T YOU? I KNOW!
I CAN'T BELIEVE YOU!
BAD!
SEE, TOLD YOU SHE WASN'T SCARY.
YOU...
I DIDN'T THINK YOU WERE THE KIND TO SNATCH FOOD?

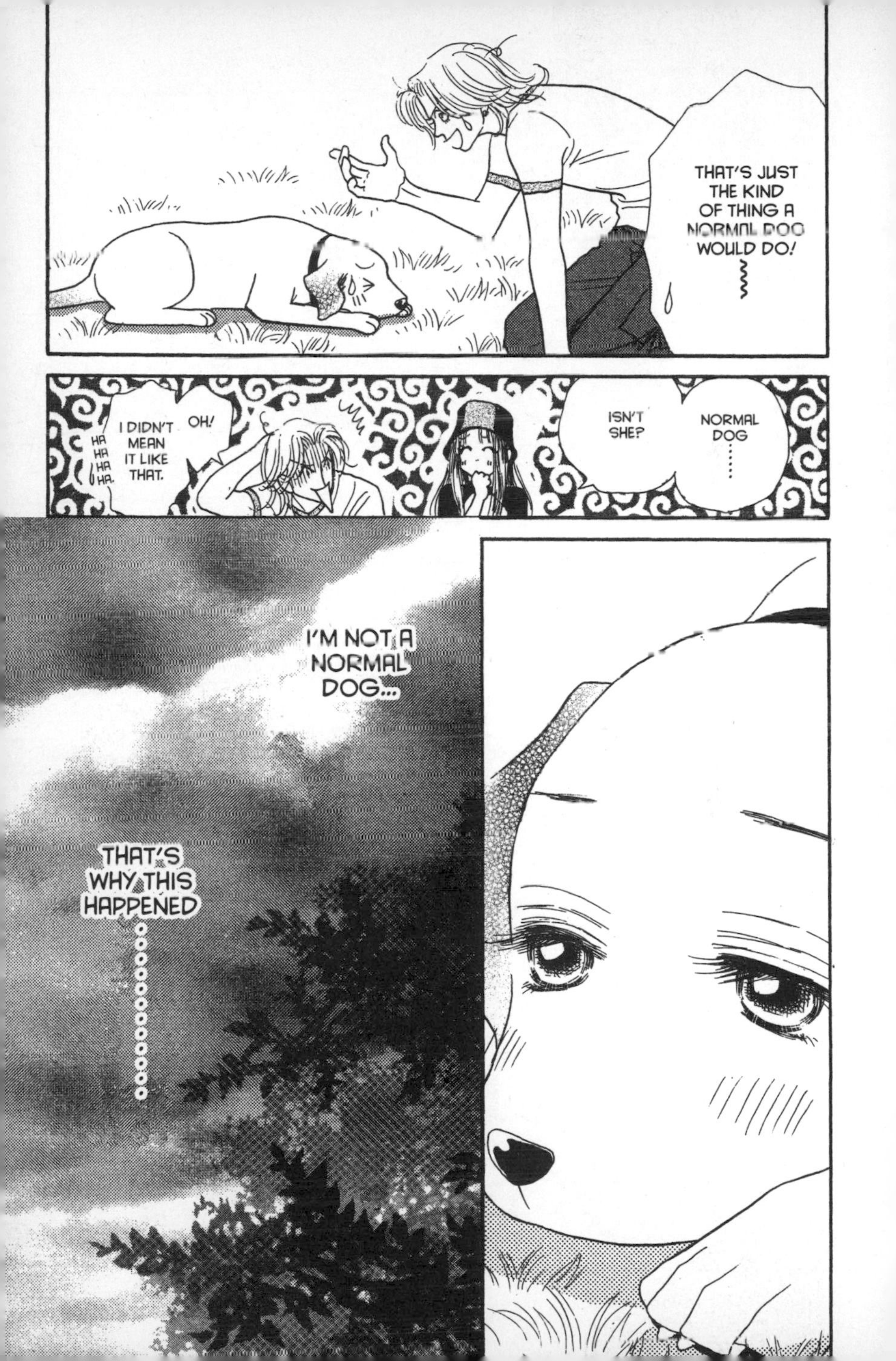
THAT'S JUST THE KIND OF THING A NORMAL DOG WOULD DO!
NORMAL DOG ......
ISN'T SHE?
OH!
I DIDN'T MEAN IT LIKE THAT.
HA HA HA HA.
I'M NOT A NORMAL DOG...
THAT'S WHY THIS HAPPENED ....

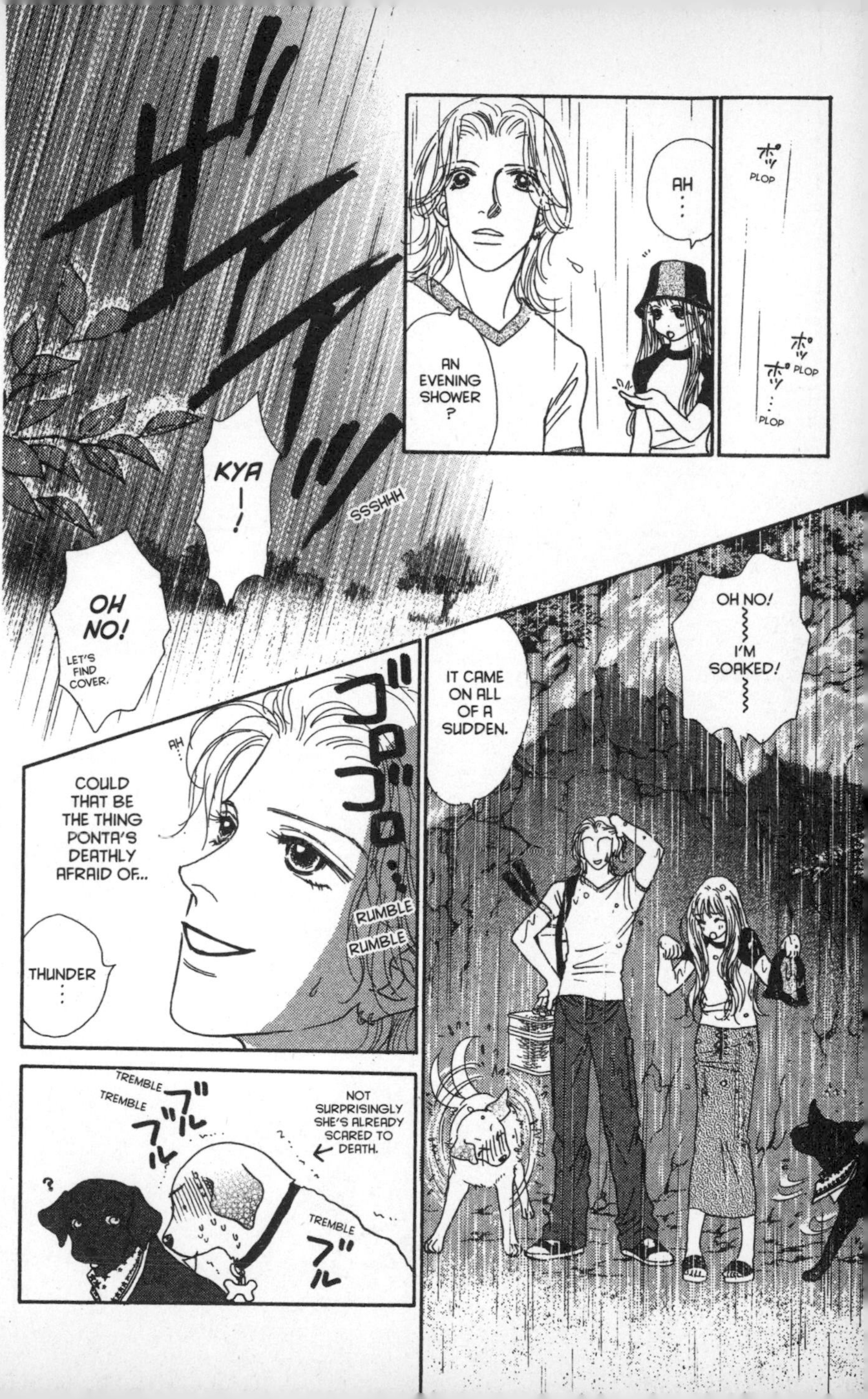

ポッ
PLOP
ポッ
PLOP
ポッ…
PLOP
AH…
AN EVENING SHOWER?
ザアアッ
KYA—!
SSSHHH
OH NO!
LET'S FIND COVER.
OH NO! I'M SOAKED!
IT CAME ON ALL OF A SUDDEN.
AH
ゴロゴロ…
RUMBLE RUMBLE
COULD THAT BE THE THING PONTA'S DEATHLY AFRAID OF…
THUNDER…
NOT SURPRISINGLY SHE'S ALREADY SCARED TO DEATH.
ブル
TREMBLE
ブル
TREMBLE
ブル
TREMBLE

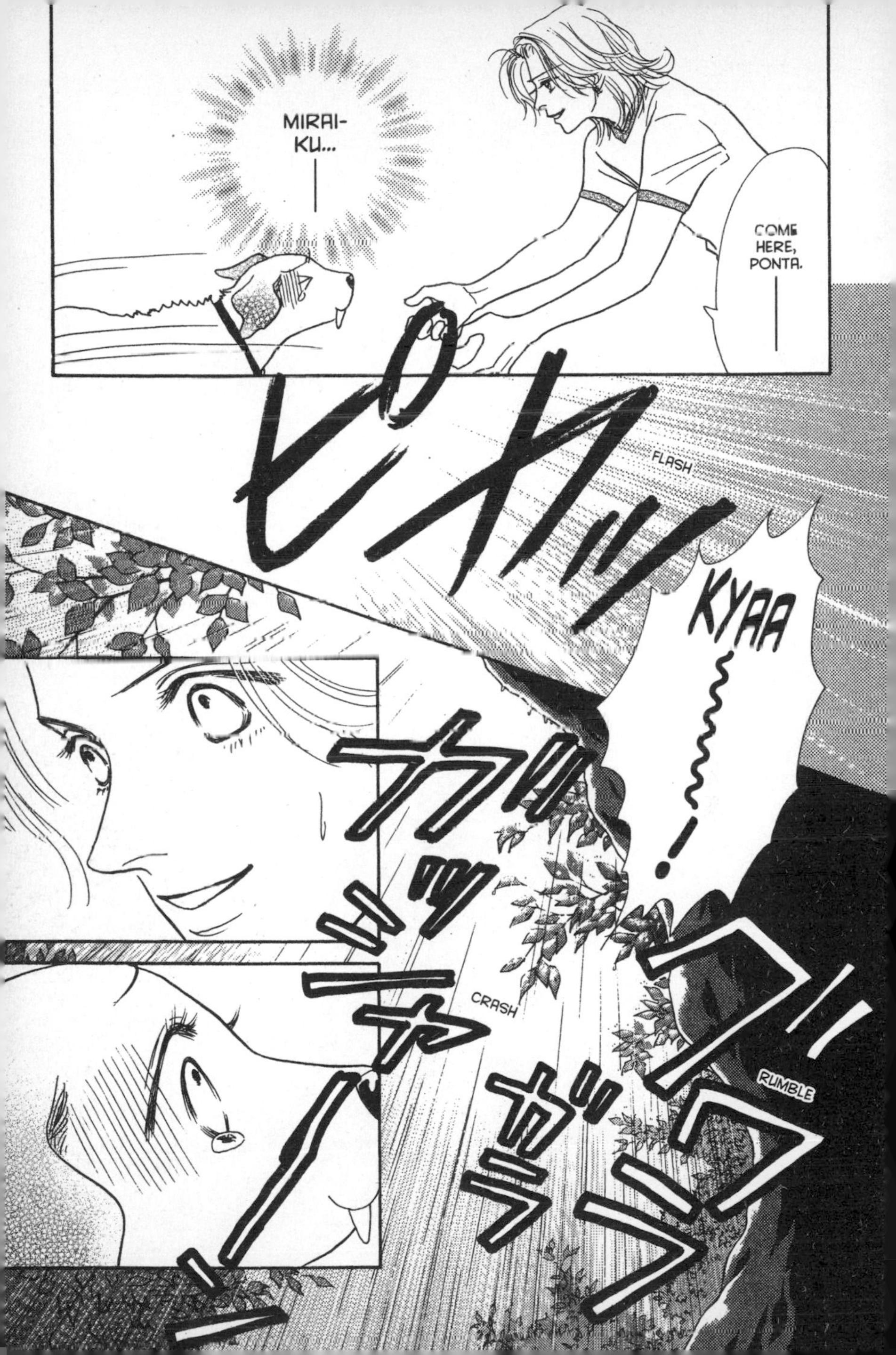
COME HERE, PONTA.
MIRAI-KU...
FLASH
KYAA~~~!
RUMBLE
CRASH

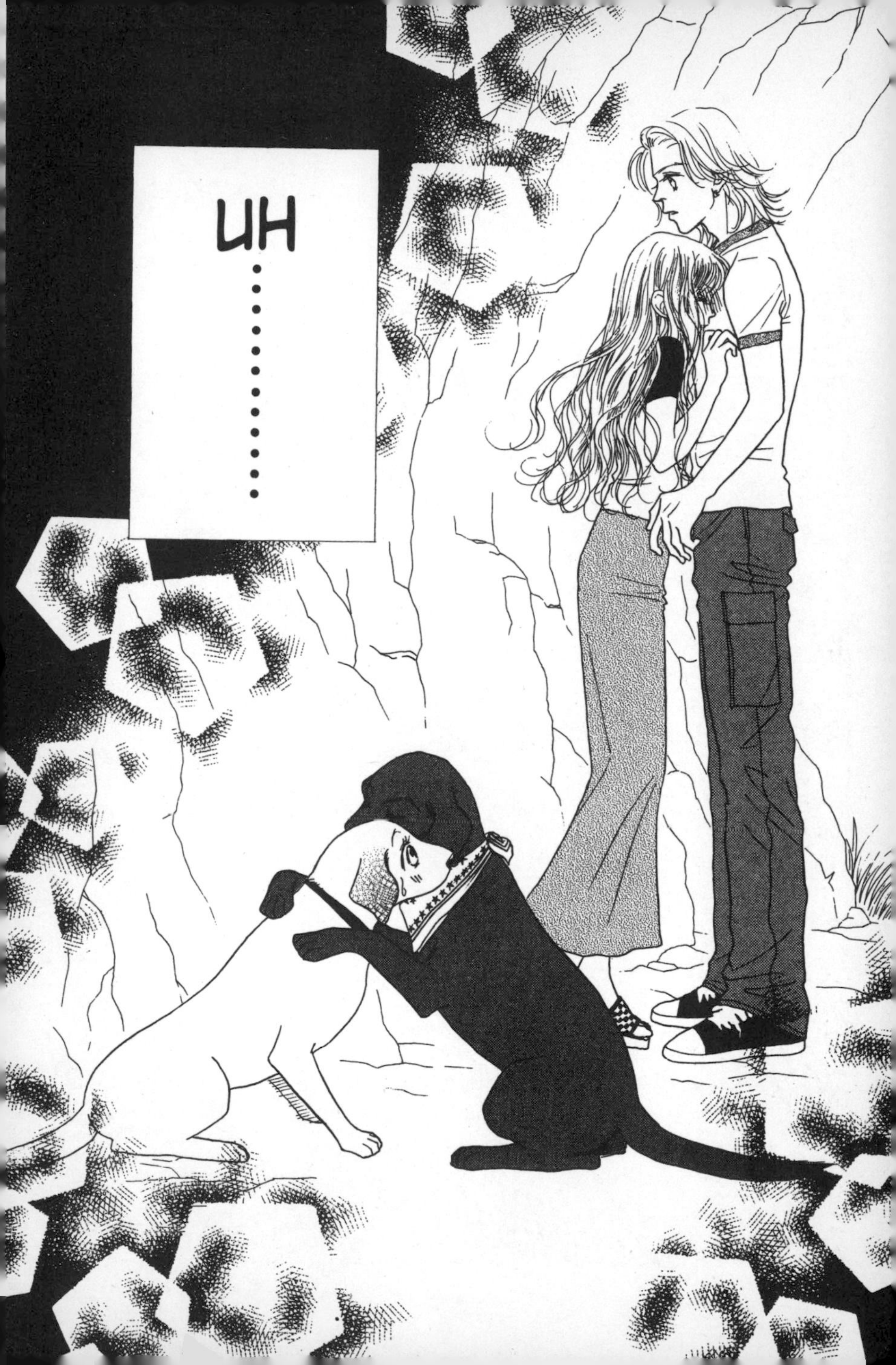
UH……

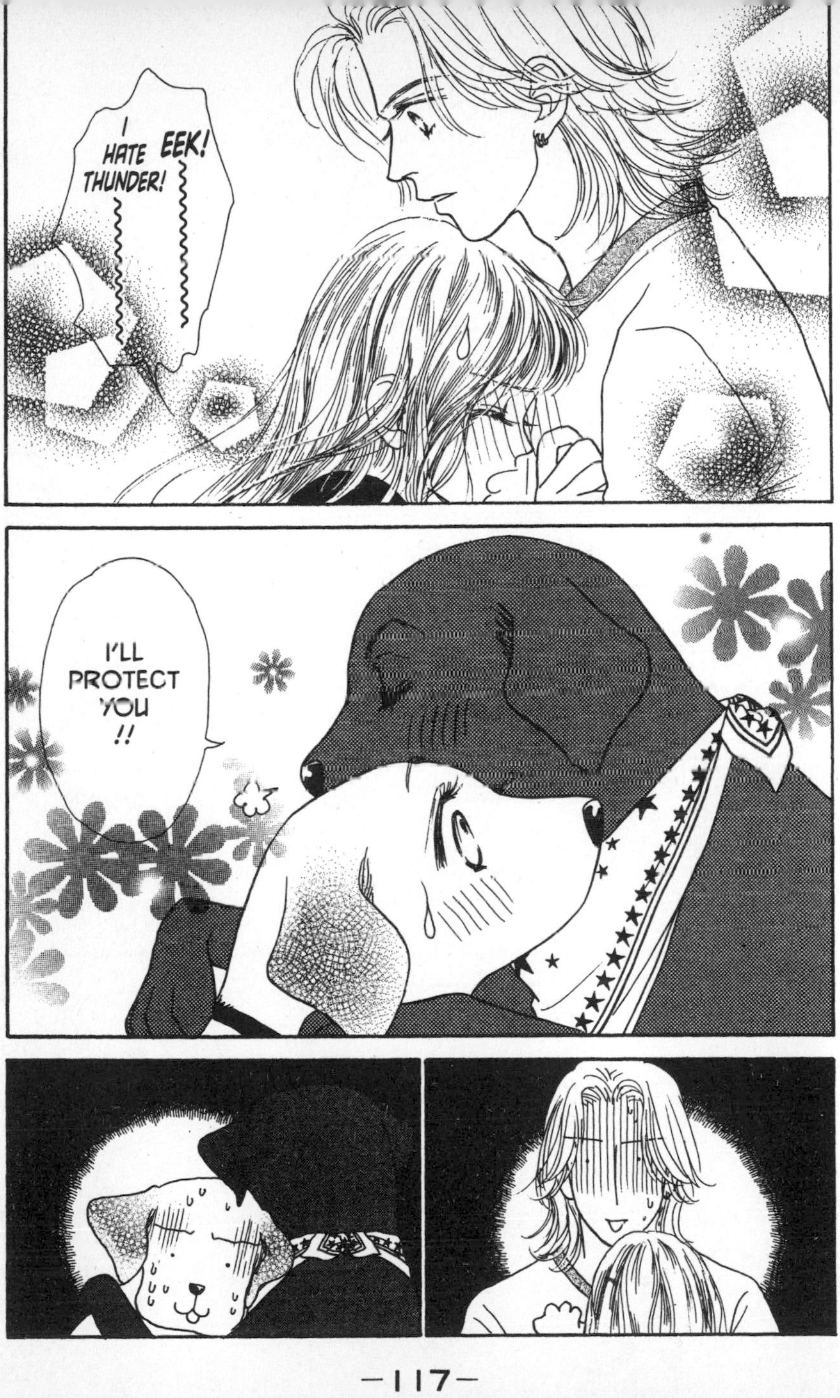
EEK!
I HATE THUNDER!
I'LL PROTECT YOU !!

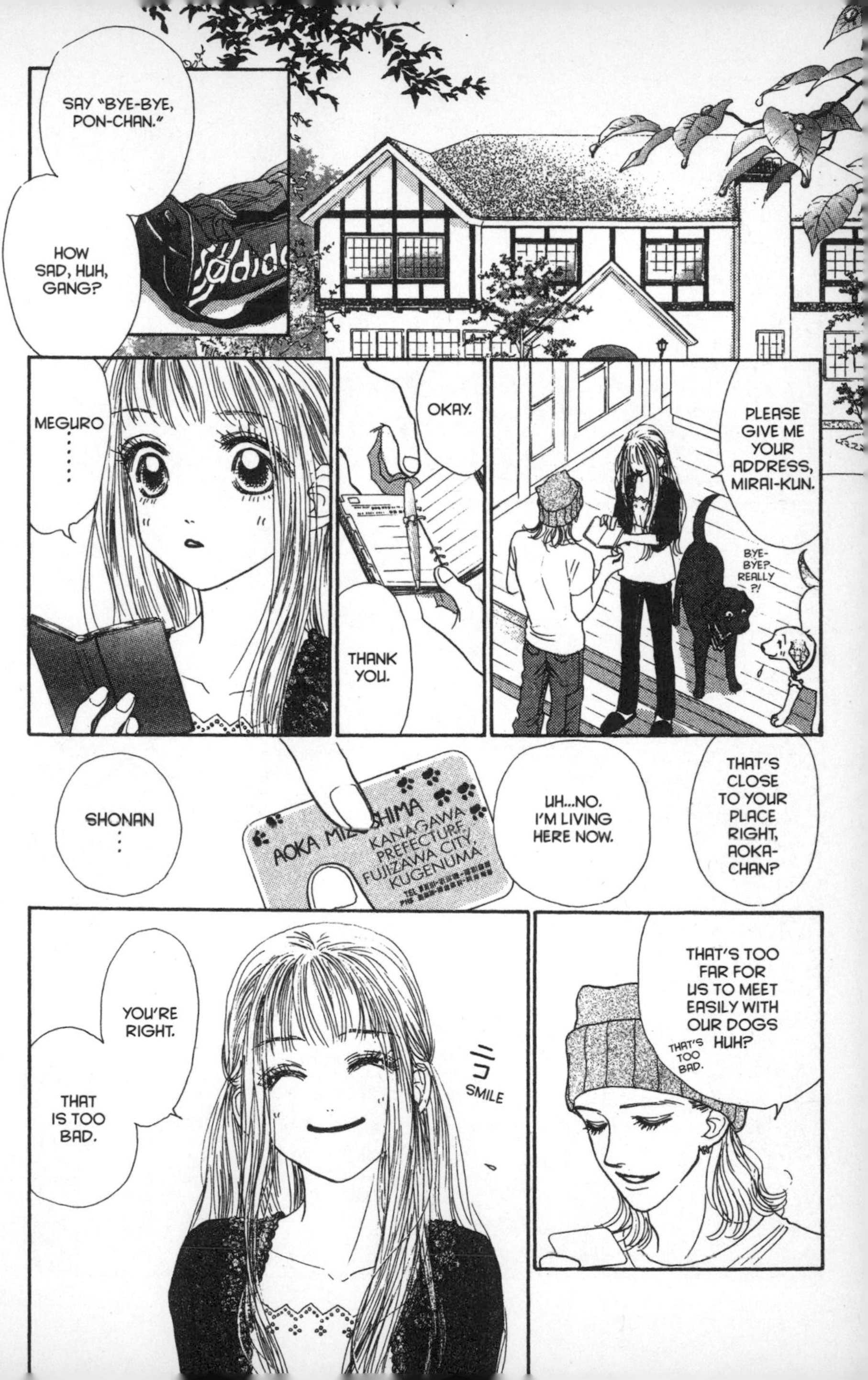
SAY "BYE-BYE, PON-CHAN."
HOW SAD, HUH, GANG?
PLEASE GIVE ME YOUR ADDRESS, MIRAI-KUN.
BYE-BYE? REALLY ?!
OKAY.
THANK YOU.
MEGURO ......
THAT'S CLOSE TO YOUR PLACE RIGHT, AOKA-CHAN?
UH...NO. I'M LIVING HERE NOW.
AOKA MIZ SHIMA
KANAGAWA PREFECTURE, FUJIZAWA CITY, KUGENUMA
SHONAN ...
THAT'S TOO FAR FOR US TO MEET EASILY WITH OUR DOGS HUH?
THAT'S TOO BAD.
YOU'RE RIGHT.
THAT IS TOO BAD.
ニコ
SMILE

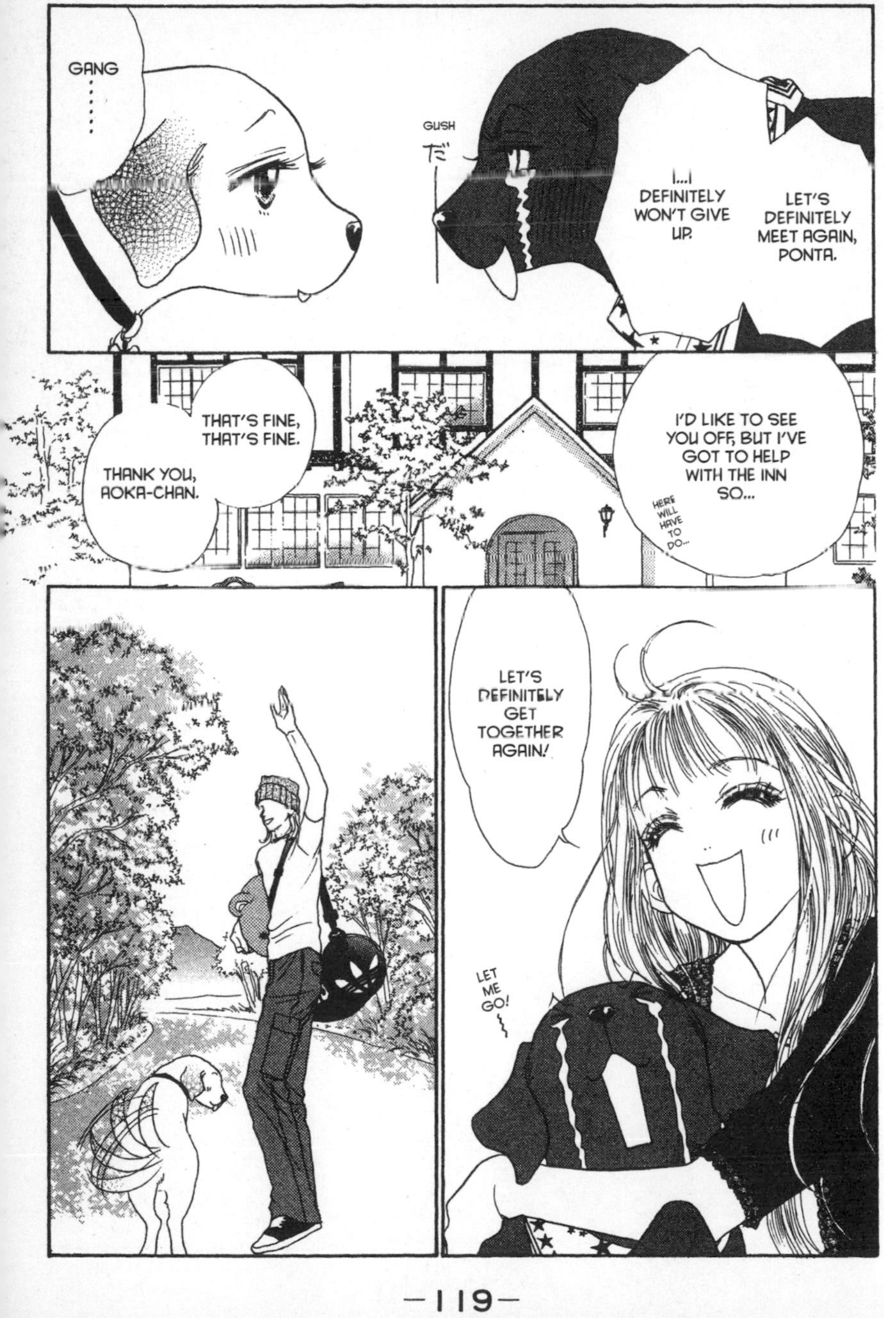
LET'S DEFINITELY MEET AGAIN, PONTA.
I...I DEFINITELY WON'T GIVE UP.
GUSH
だ
GANG
......
I'D LIKE TO SEE YOU OFF, BUT I'VE GOT TO HELP WITH THE INN SO...
HERE WILL HAVE TO DO...
THAT'S FINE, THAT'S FINE.
THANK YOU, AOKA-CHAN.
LET'S DEFINITELY GET TOGETHER AGAIN!
LET ME GO!

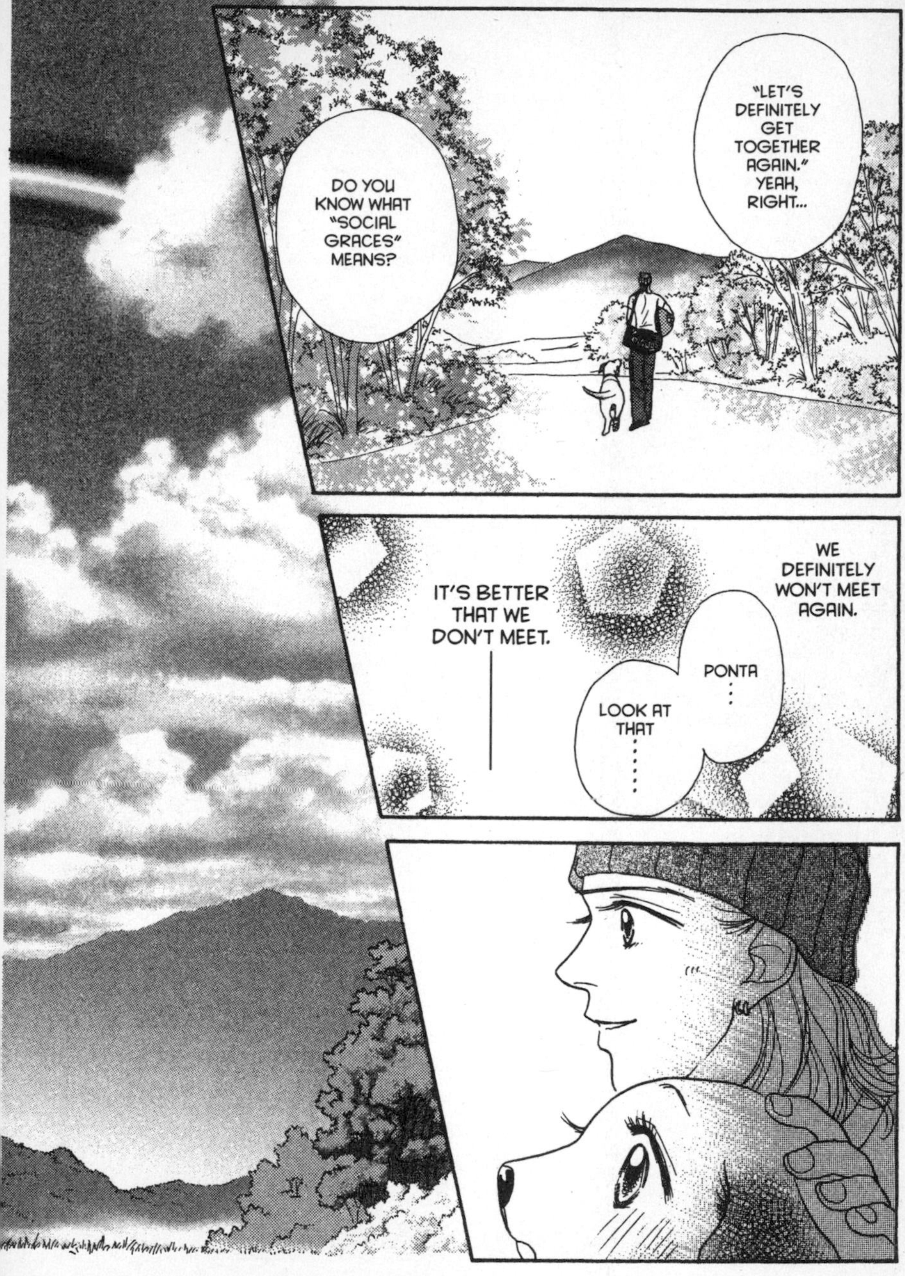
"LET'S DEFINITELY GET TOGETHER AGAIN." YEAH, RIGHT...
DO YOU KNOW WHAT "SOCIAL GRACES" MEANS?
WE DEFINITELY WON'T MEET AGAIN.
PONTA ...
LOOK AT THAT .....
IT'S BETTER THAT WE DON'T MEET.

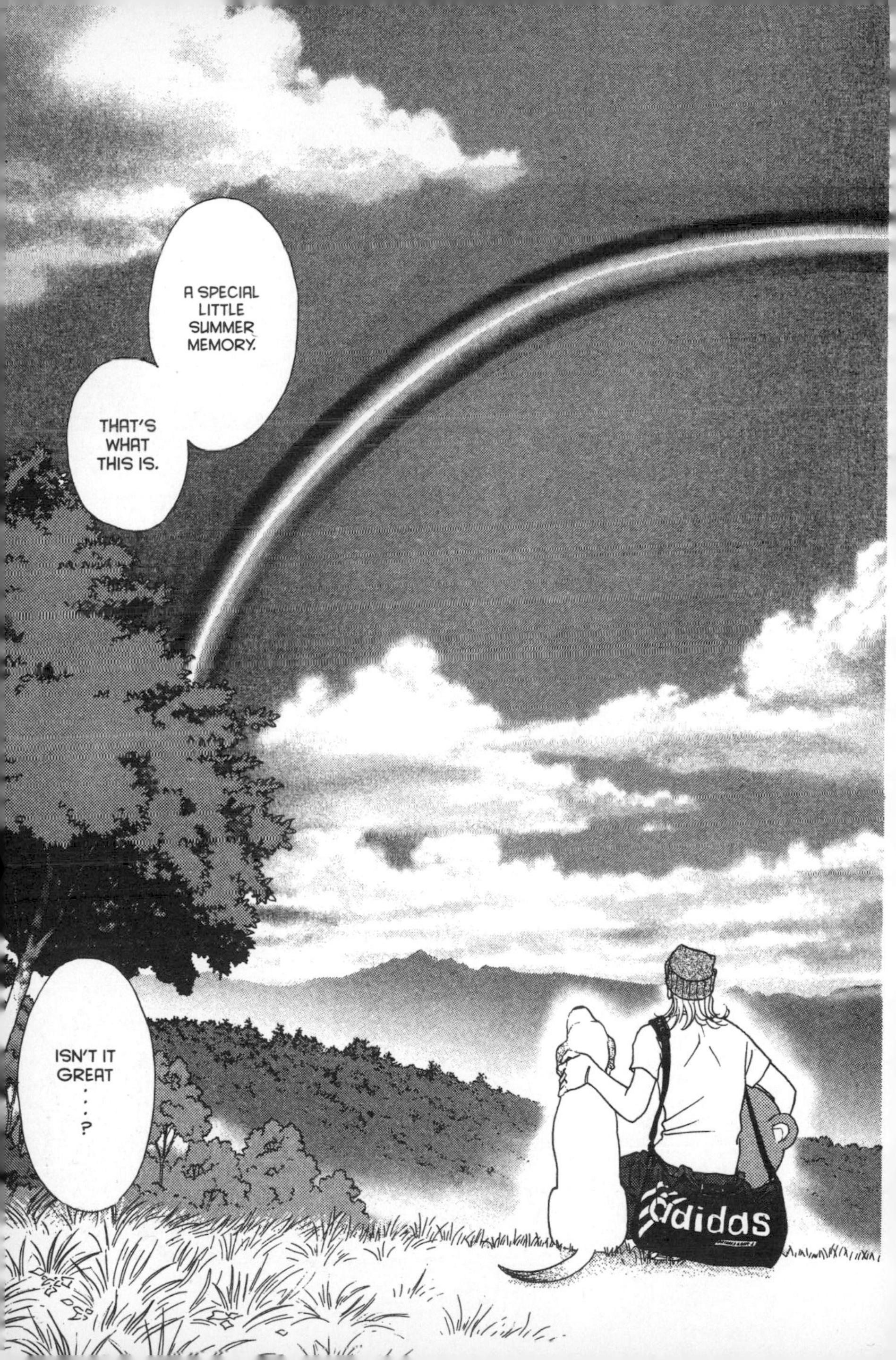
A SPECIAL LITTLE SUMMER MEMORY.
THAT'S WHAT THIS IS.
ISN'T IT GREAT ...?
adidas

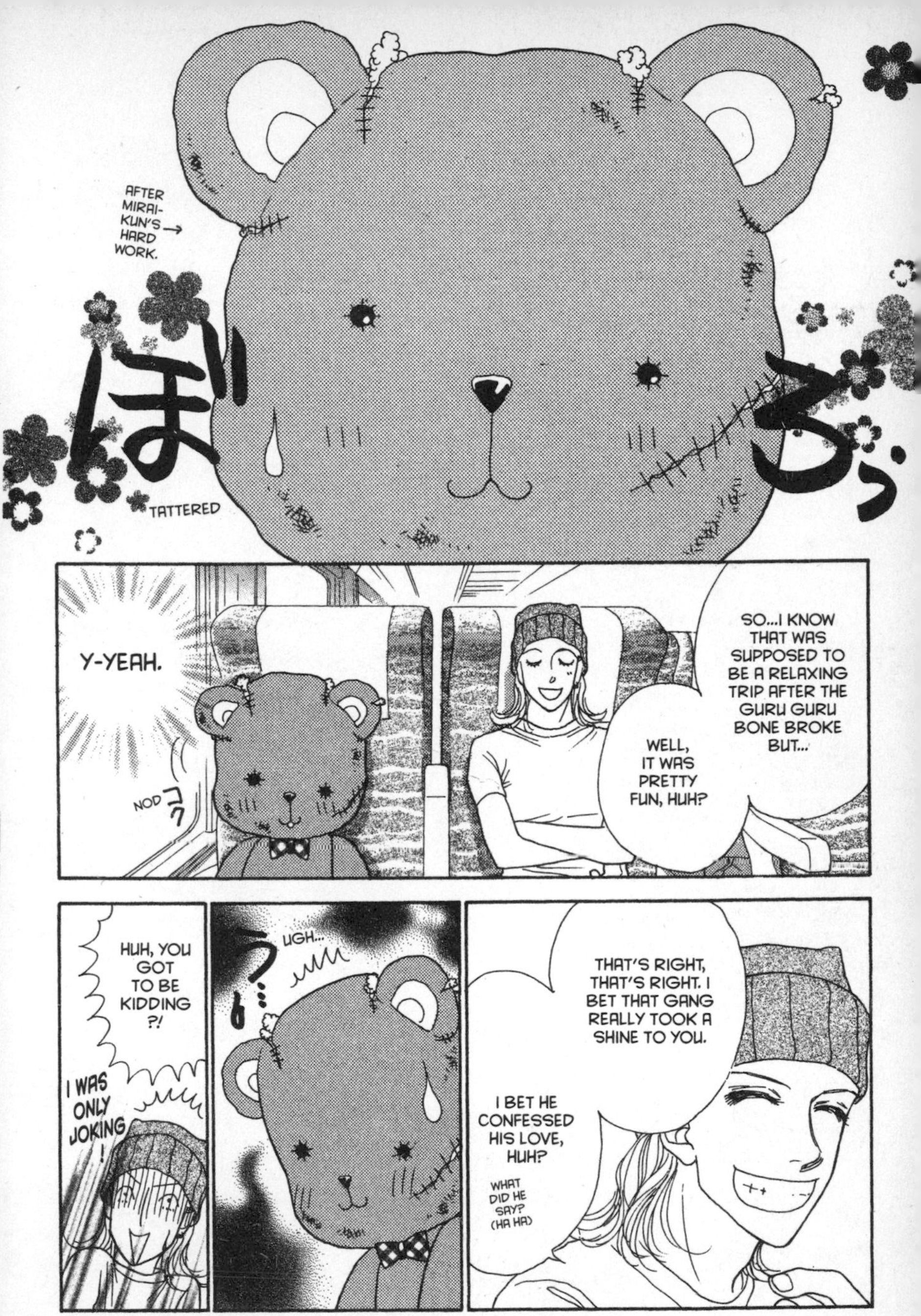

AFTER MIRAI-KUN'S → HARD WORK.
ぼろっ
TATTERED
SO...I KNOW THAT WAS SUPPOSED TO BE A RELAXING TRIP AFTER THE GURU GURU BONE BROKE BUT...
WELL, IT WAS PRETTY FUN, HUH?
Y-YEAH.
NOD コク
THAT'S RIGHT, THAT'S RIGHT. I BET THAT GANG REALLY TOOK A SHINE TO YOU.
I BET HE CONFESSED HIS LOVE, HUH?
WHAT DID HE SAY? (HA HA)
う…
UGH...
HUH, YOU GOT TO BE KIDDING?!
I WAS ONLY JOKING!

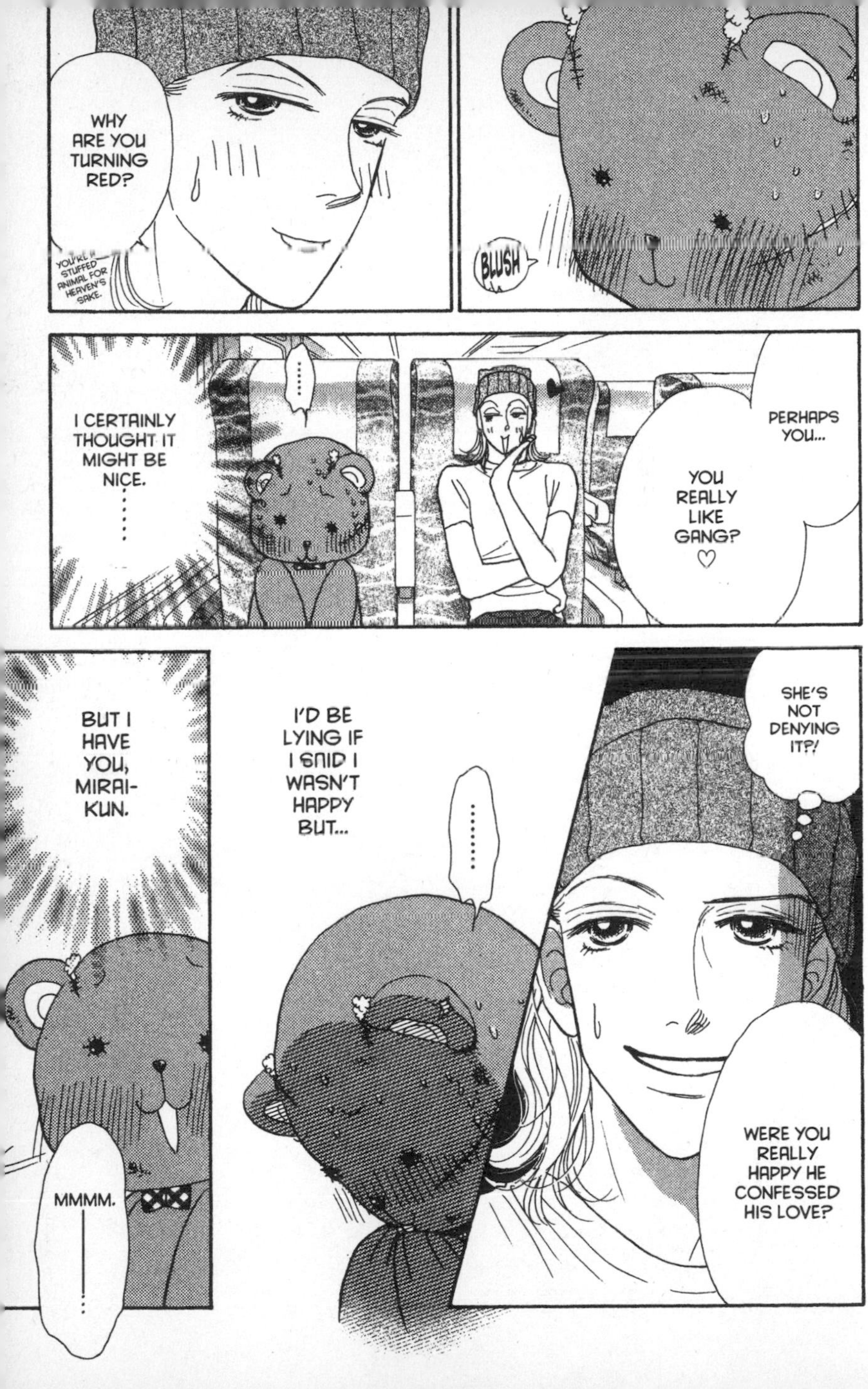
BLUSH
WHY ARE YOU TURNING RED?
YOU'RE A STUFFED ANIMAL FOR HEAVEN'S SAKE.
PERHAPS YOU... YOU REALLY LIKE GANG? ♡
......
I CERTAINLY THOUGHT IT MIGHT BE NICE. ......
SHE'S NOT DENYING IT?!
WERE YOU REALLY HAPPY HE CONFESSED HIS LOVE?
....
I'D BE LYING IF I SAID I WASN'T HAPPY BUT...
BUT I HAVE YOU, MIRAI-KUN.
MMMM. —......

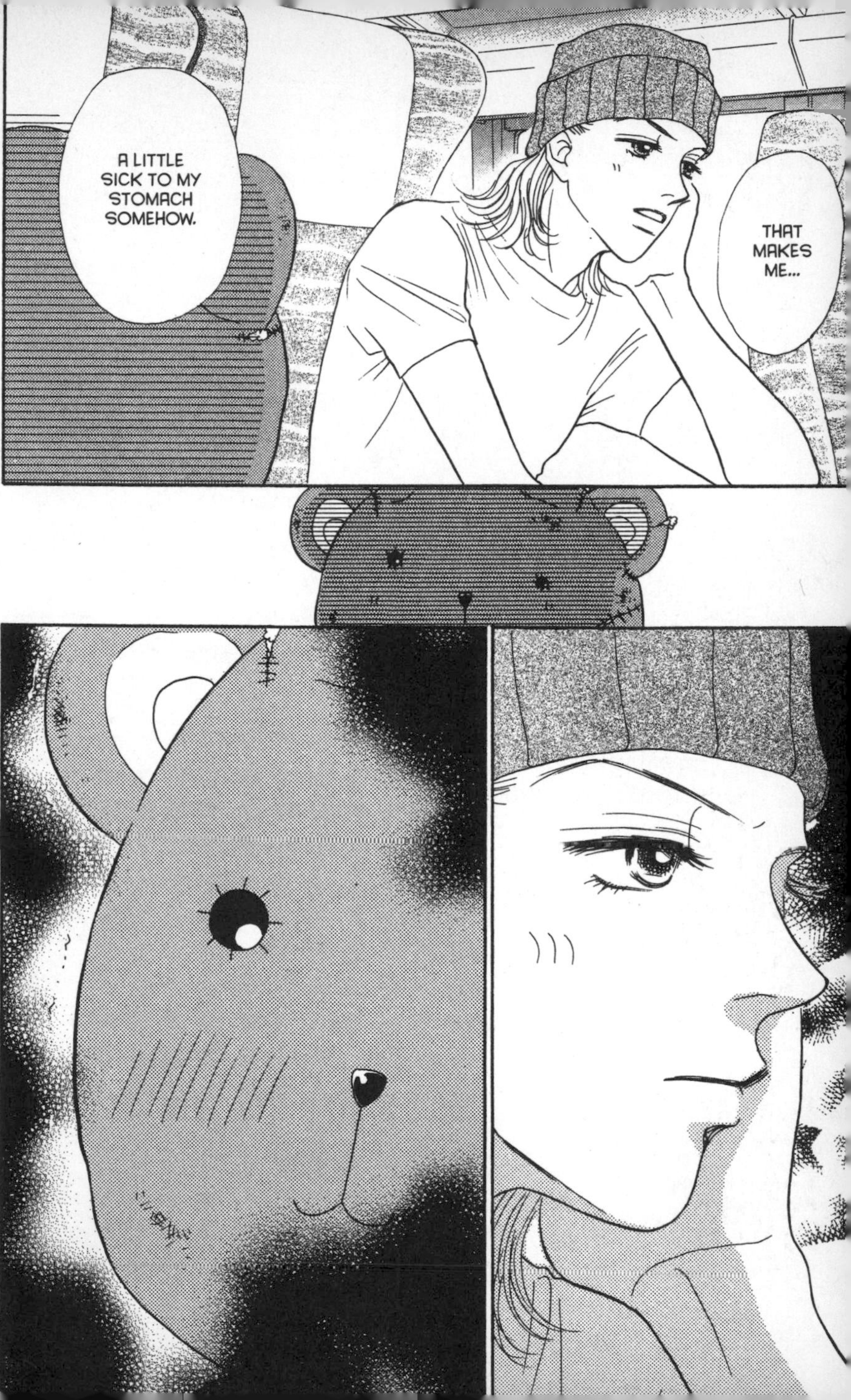
THAT MAKES ME...
A LITTLE SICK TO MY STOMACH SOMEHOW.

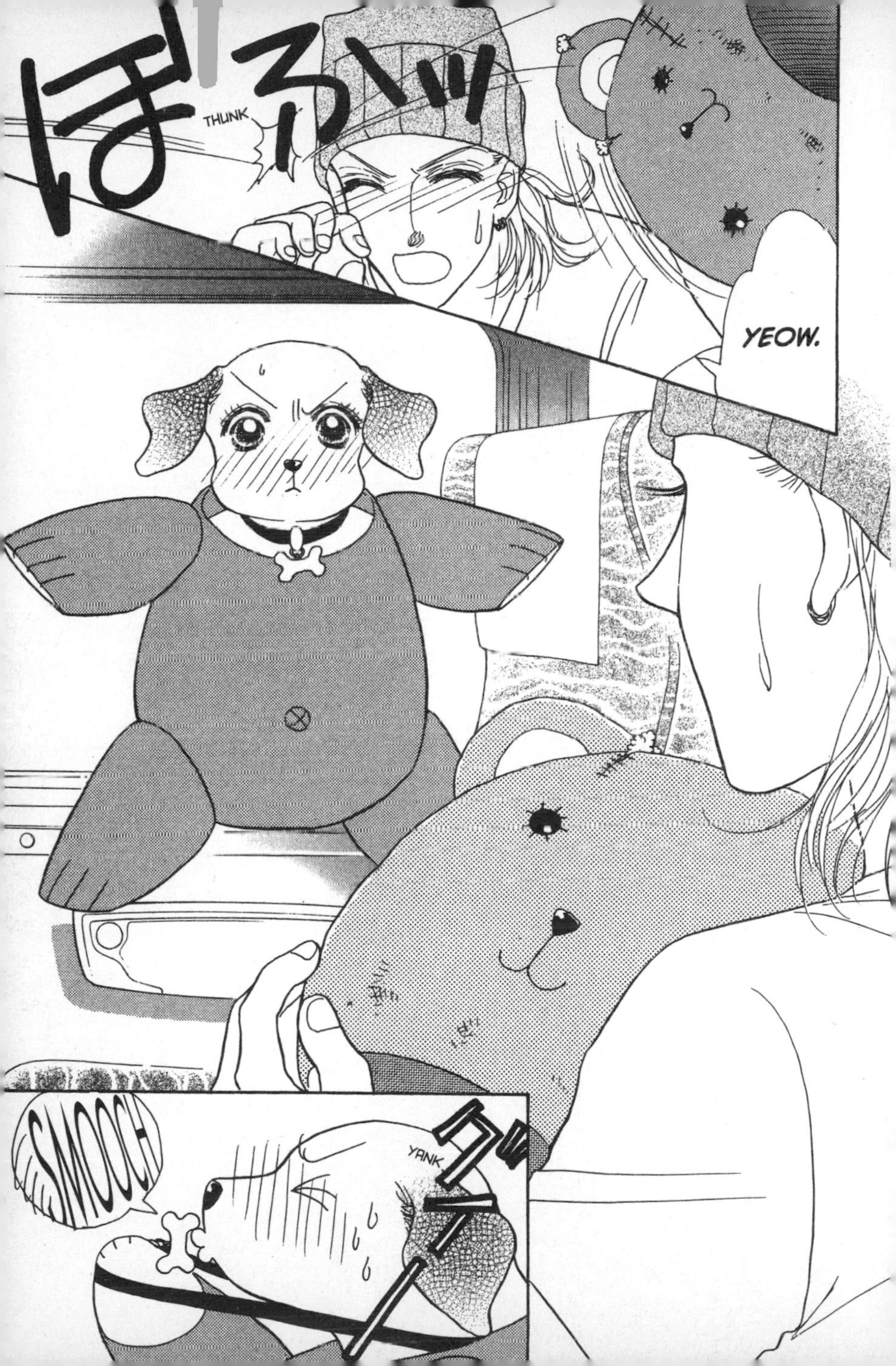
THUNK
YEOW.
YANK
SMOOCH

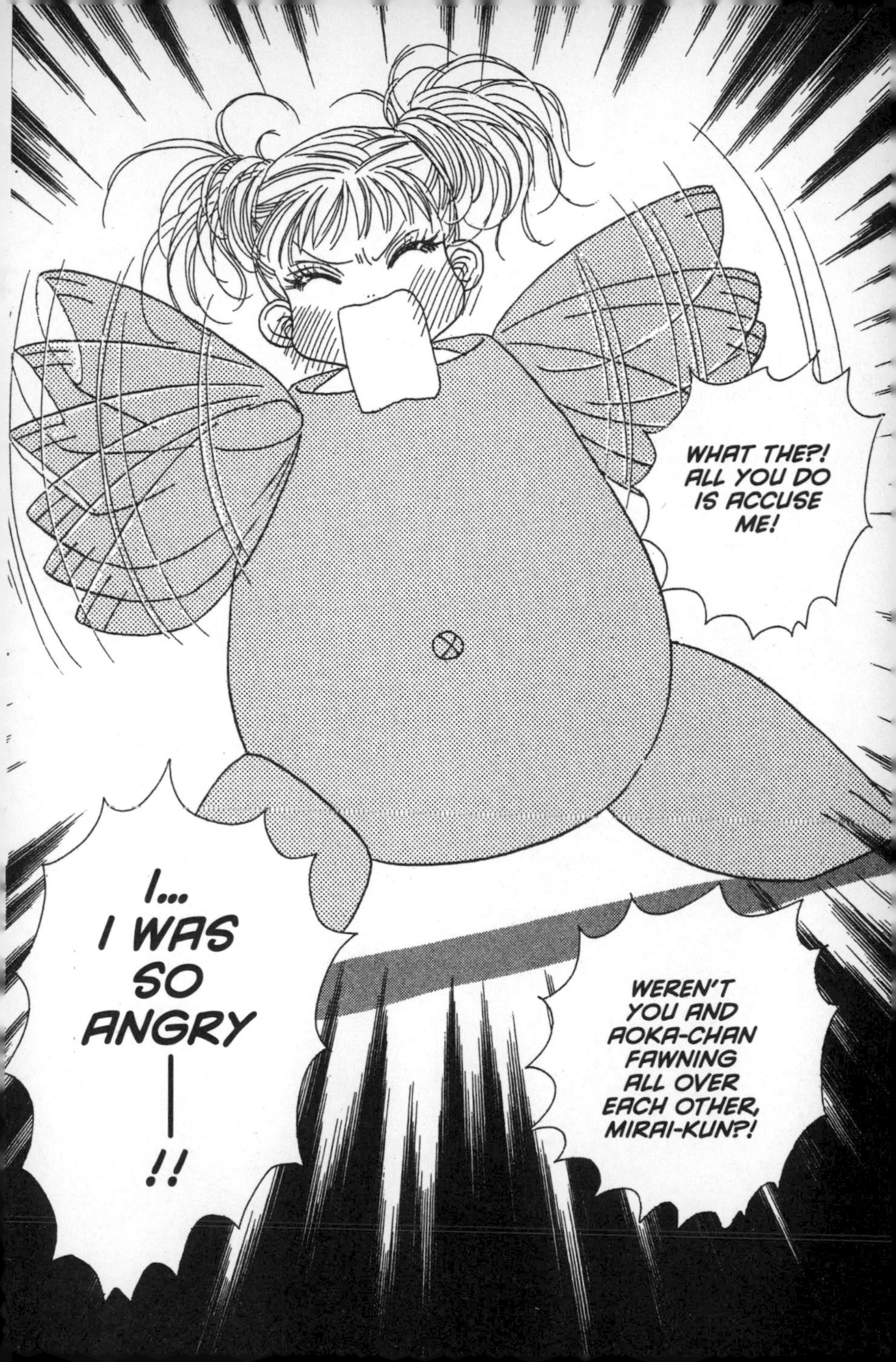
WHAT THE?! ALL YOU DO IS ACCUSE ME!
WEREN'T YOU AND AOKA-CHAN FAWNING ALL OVER EACH OTHER, MIRAI-KUN?!
I... I WAS SO ANGRY — — !!

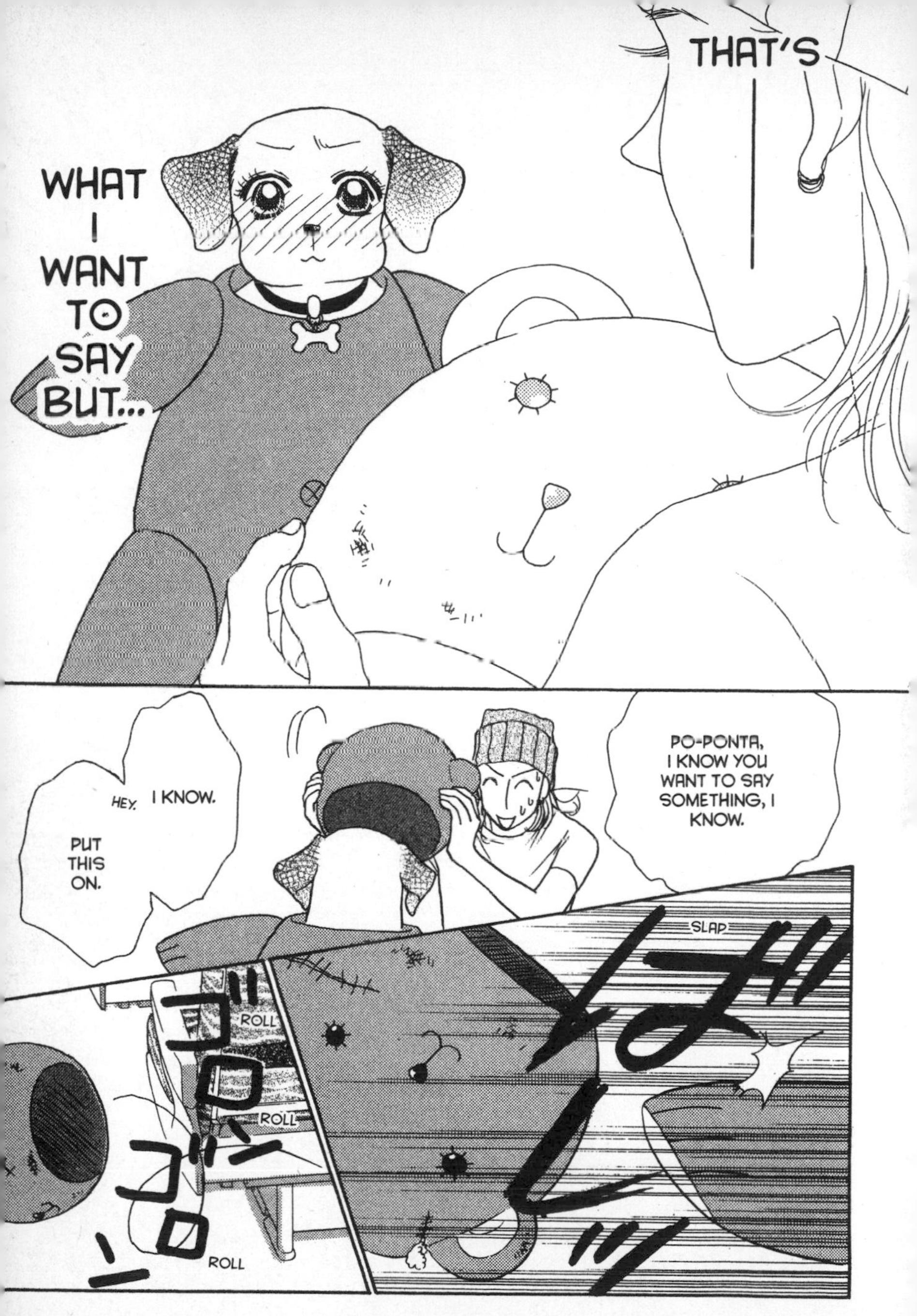
THAT'S
WHAT I WANT TO SAY BUT...
PO-PONTA, I KNOW YOU WANT TO SAY SOMETHING, I KNOW.
HEY. I KNOW.
PUT THIS ON.
SLAP
ROLL
ROLL
ROLL

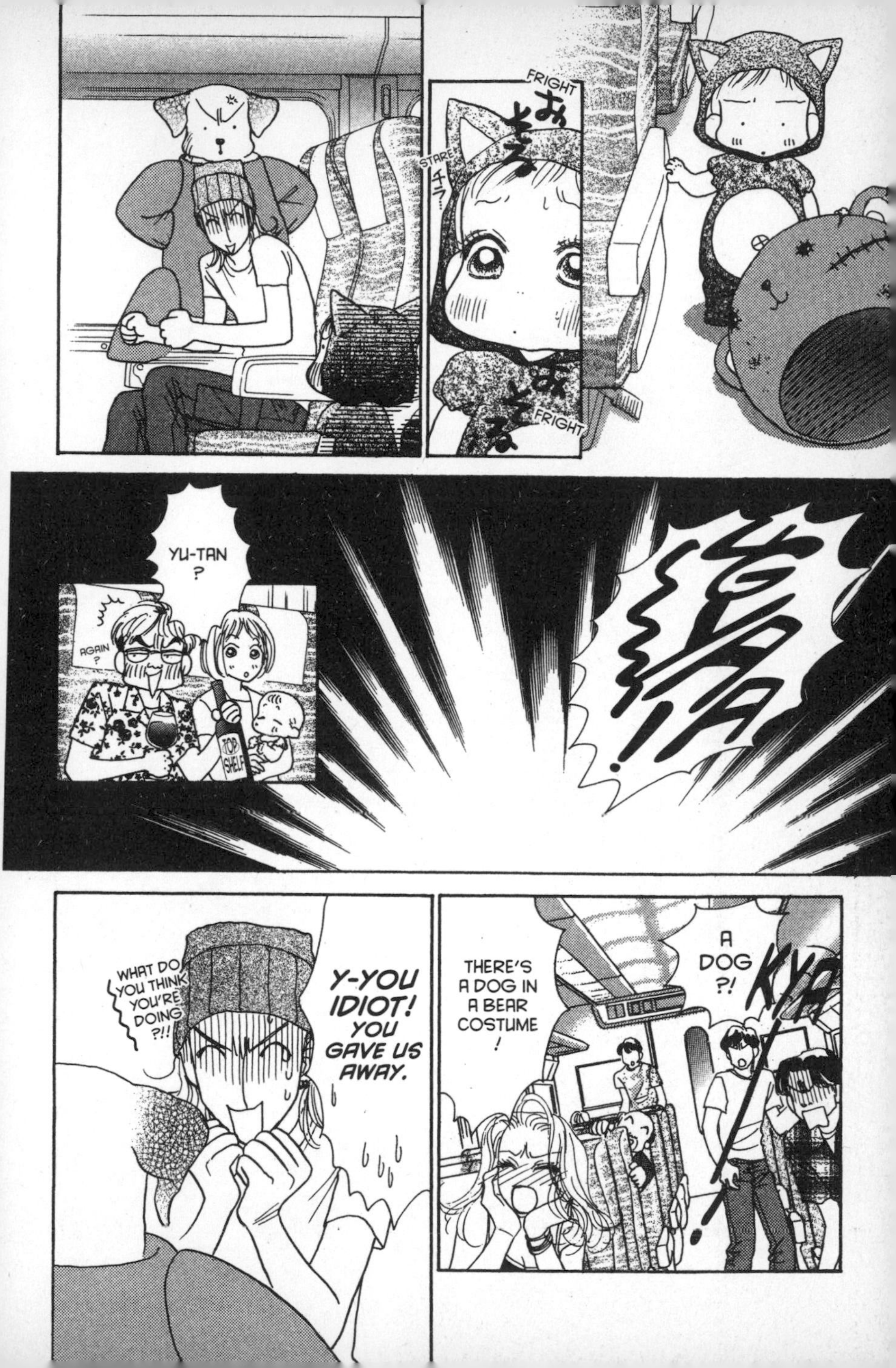

FRIGHT
STARE
チラ…
FRIGHT
YU-TAN ?
AGAIN ?
A DOG ?!
KYA
THERE'S A DOG IN A BEAR COSTUME !
Y-YOU IDIOT! YOU GAVE US AWAY.
WHAT DO YOU THINK YOU'RE DOING ?!!

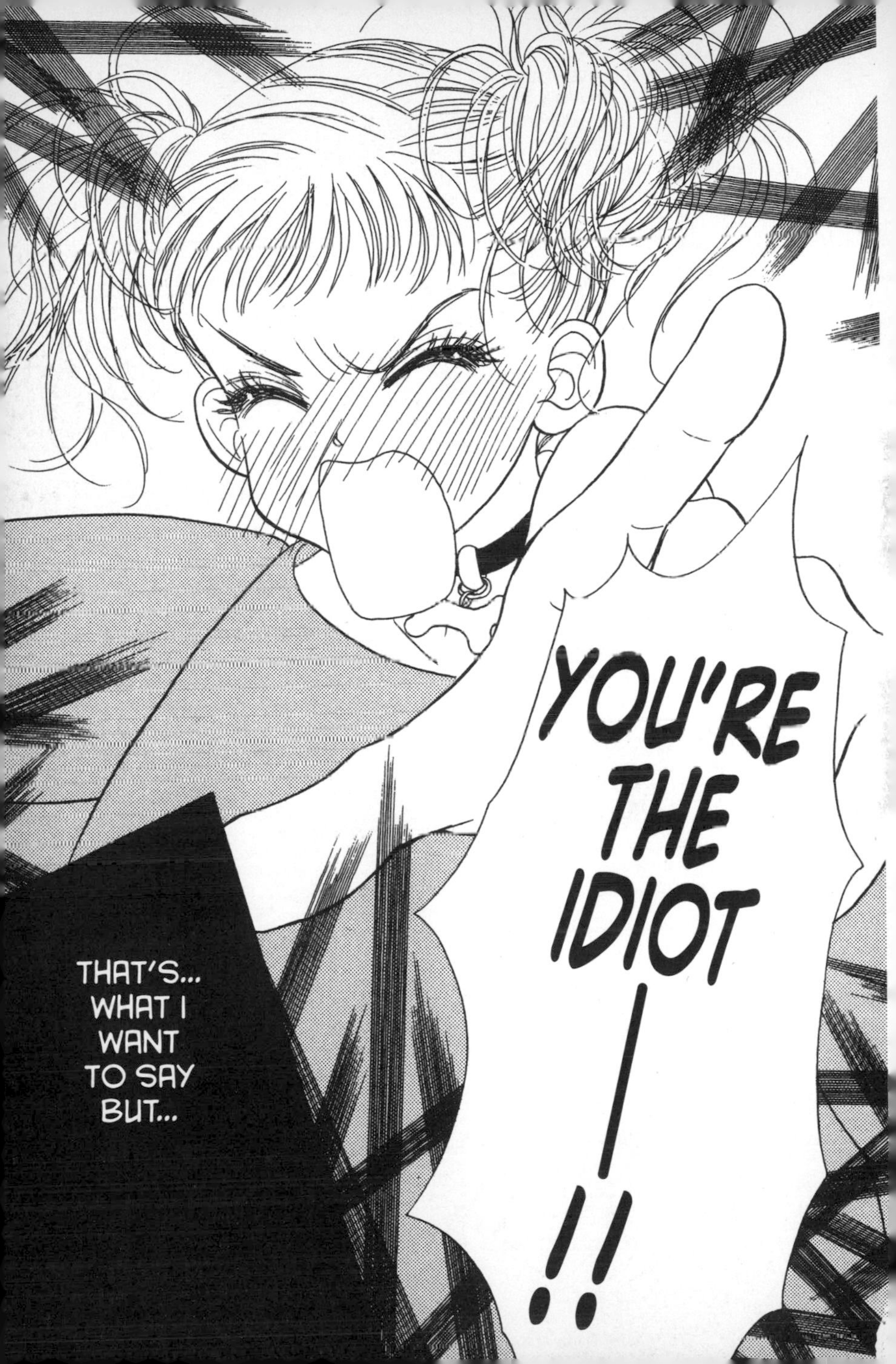
YOU'RE THE IDIOT —!!
THAT'S... WHAT I WANT TO SAY BUT...

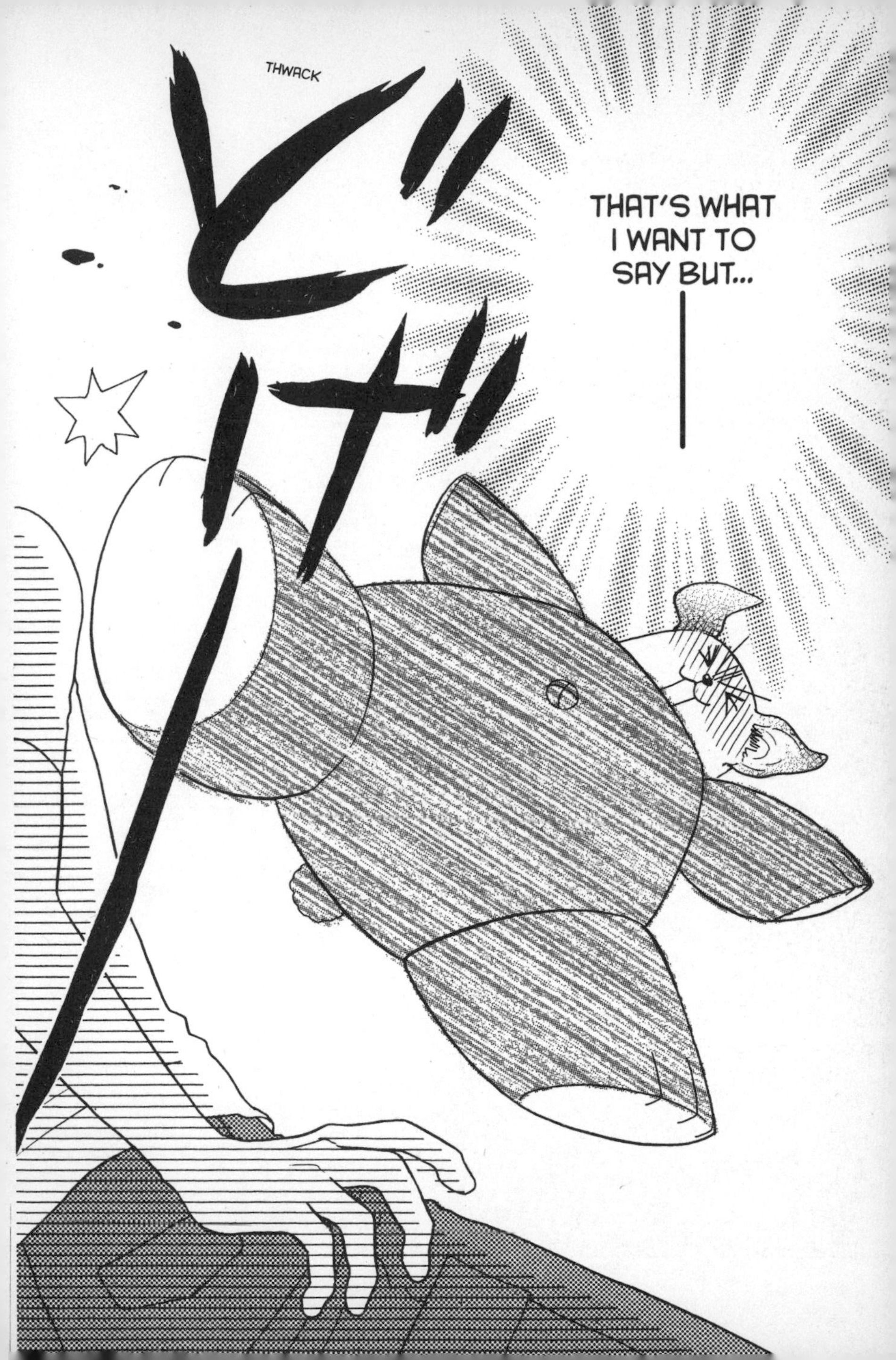
THWACK
THAT'S WHAT I WANT TO SAY BUT...

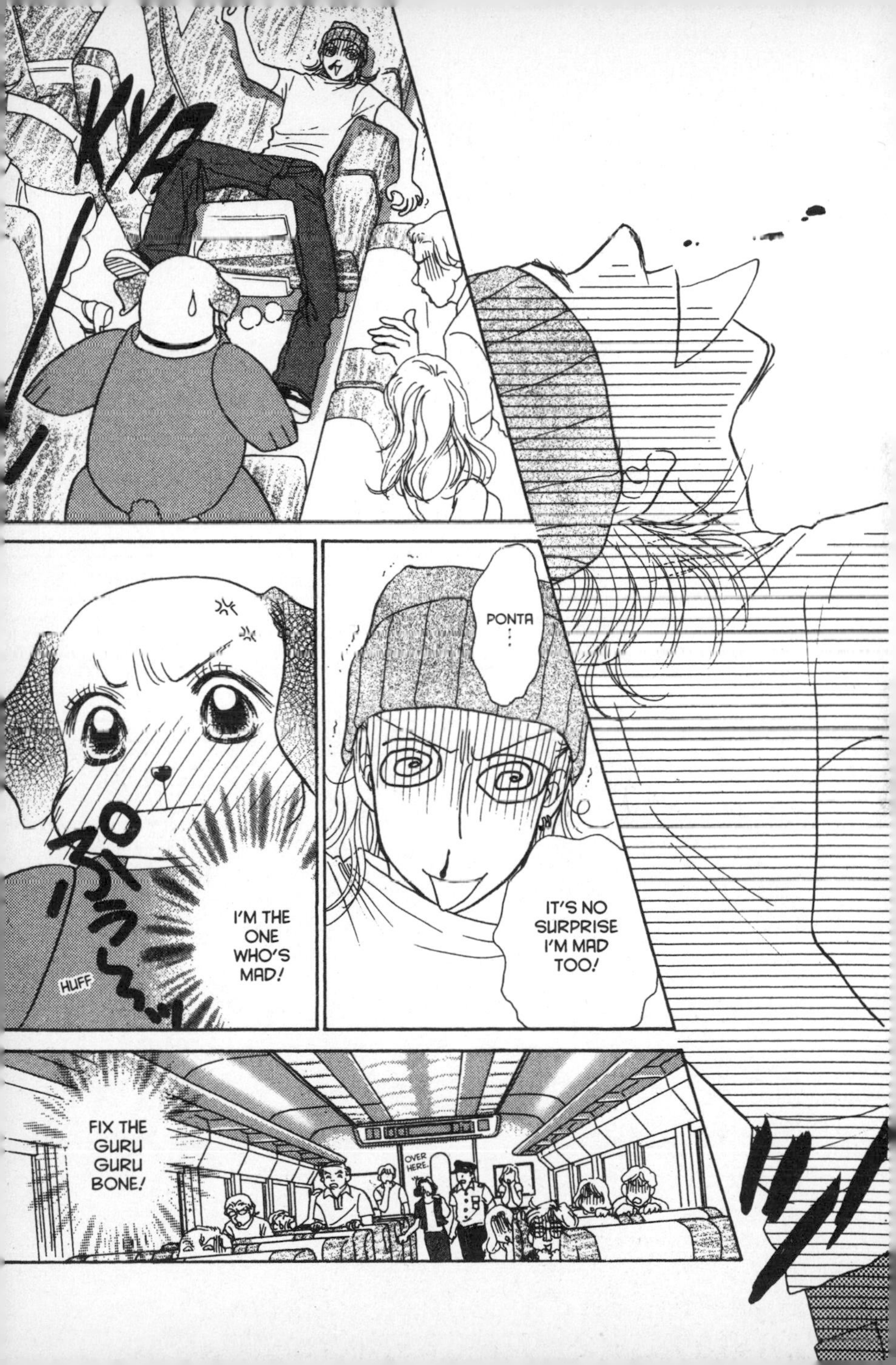
KYA
PONTA...
IT'S NO SURPRISE I'M MAD TOO!
I'M THE ONE WHO'S MAD!
HUFF
FIX THE GURU GURU BONE!
OVER HERE.

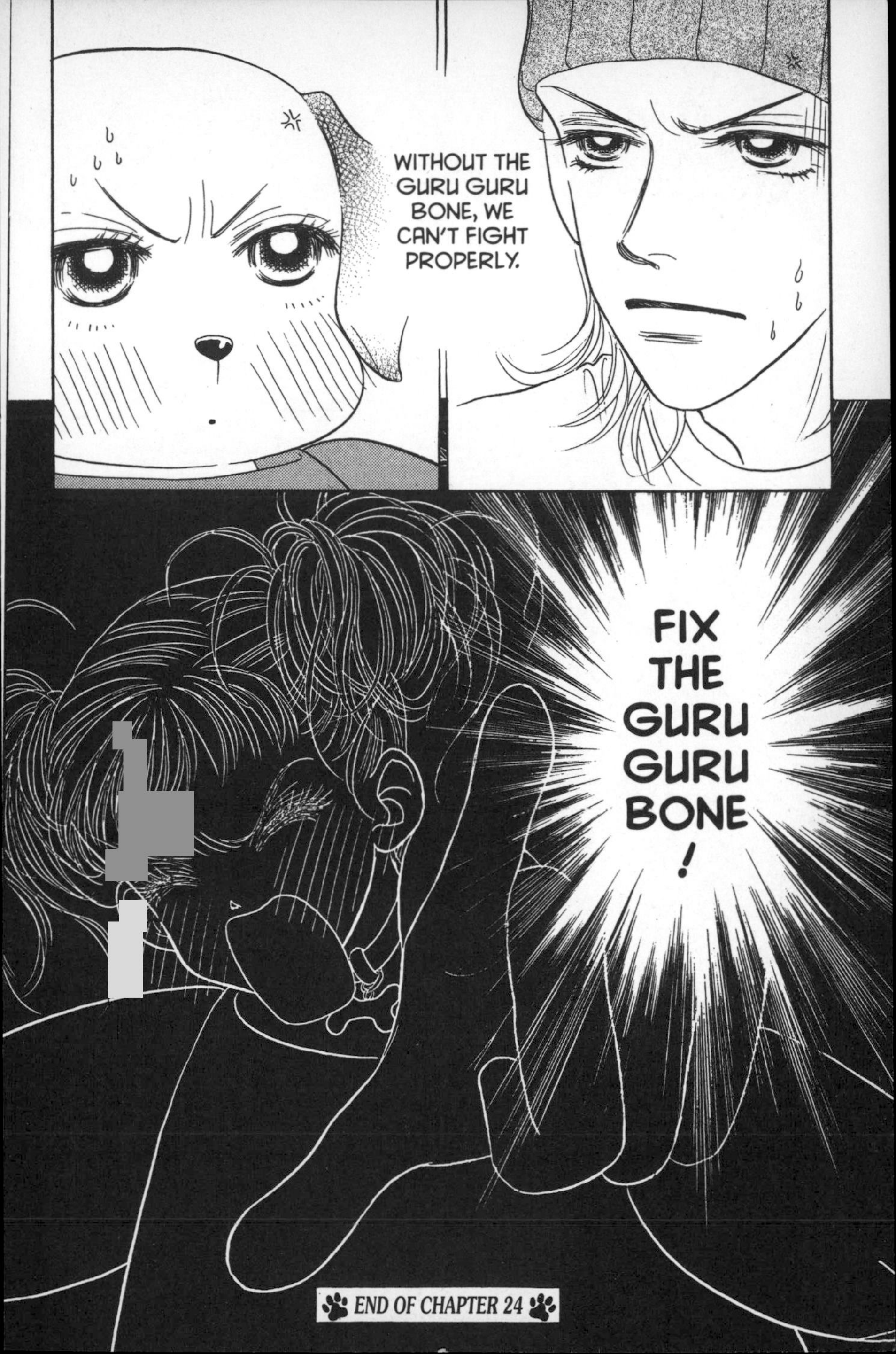
WITHOUT THE GURU GURU BONE, WE CAN'T FIGHT PROPERLY.
FIX THE GURU GURU BONE!
END OF CHAPTER 24

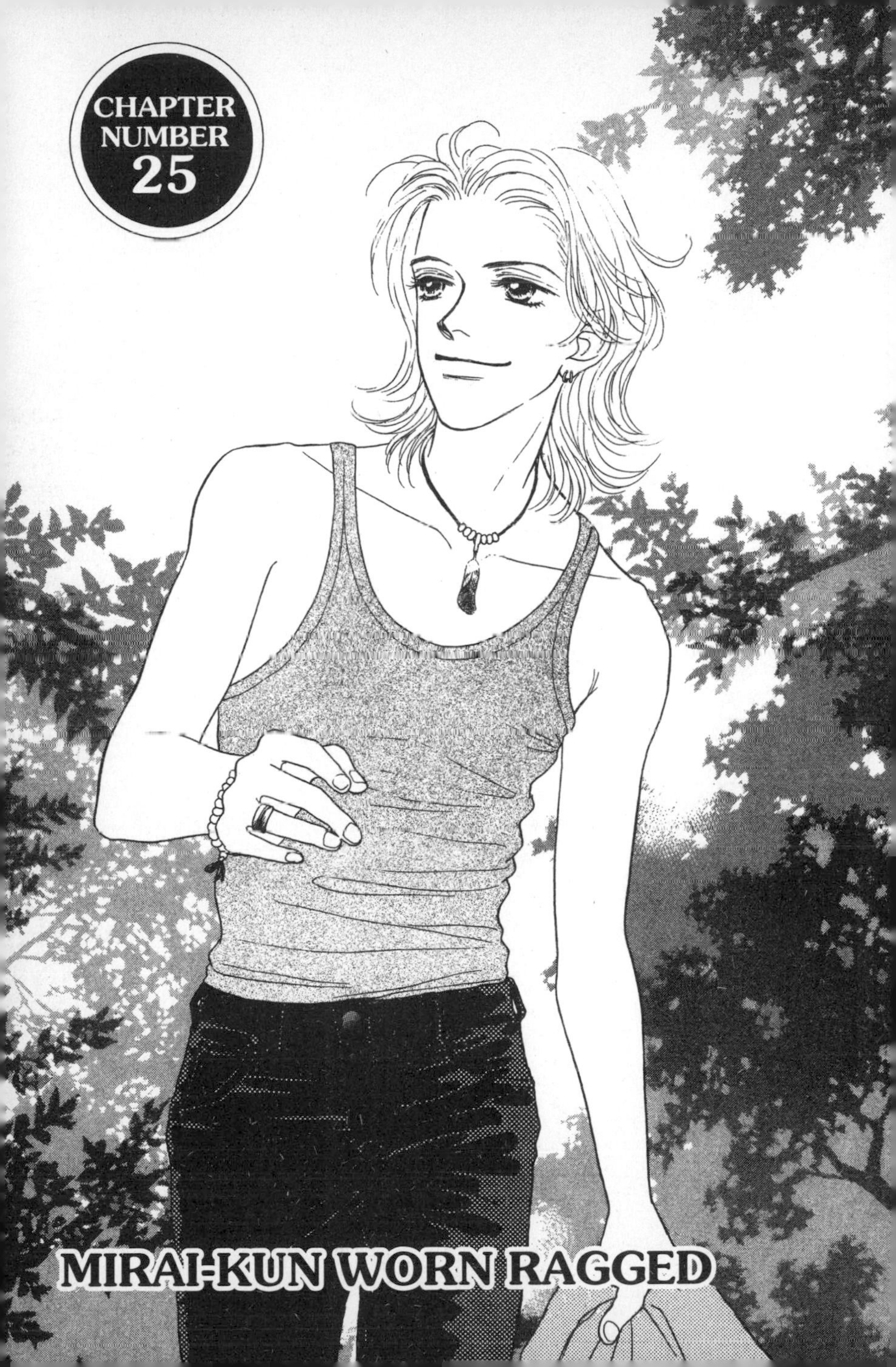
CHAPTER NUMBER 25
MIRAI-KUN WORN RAGGED

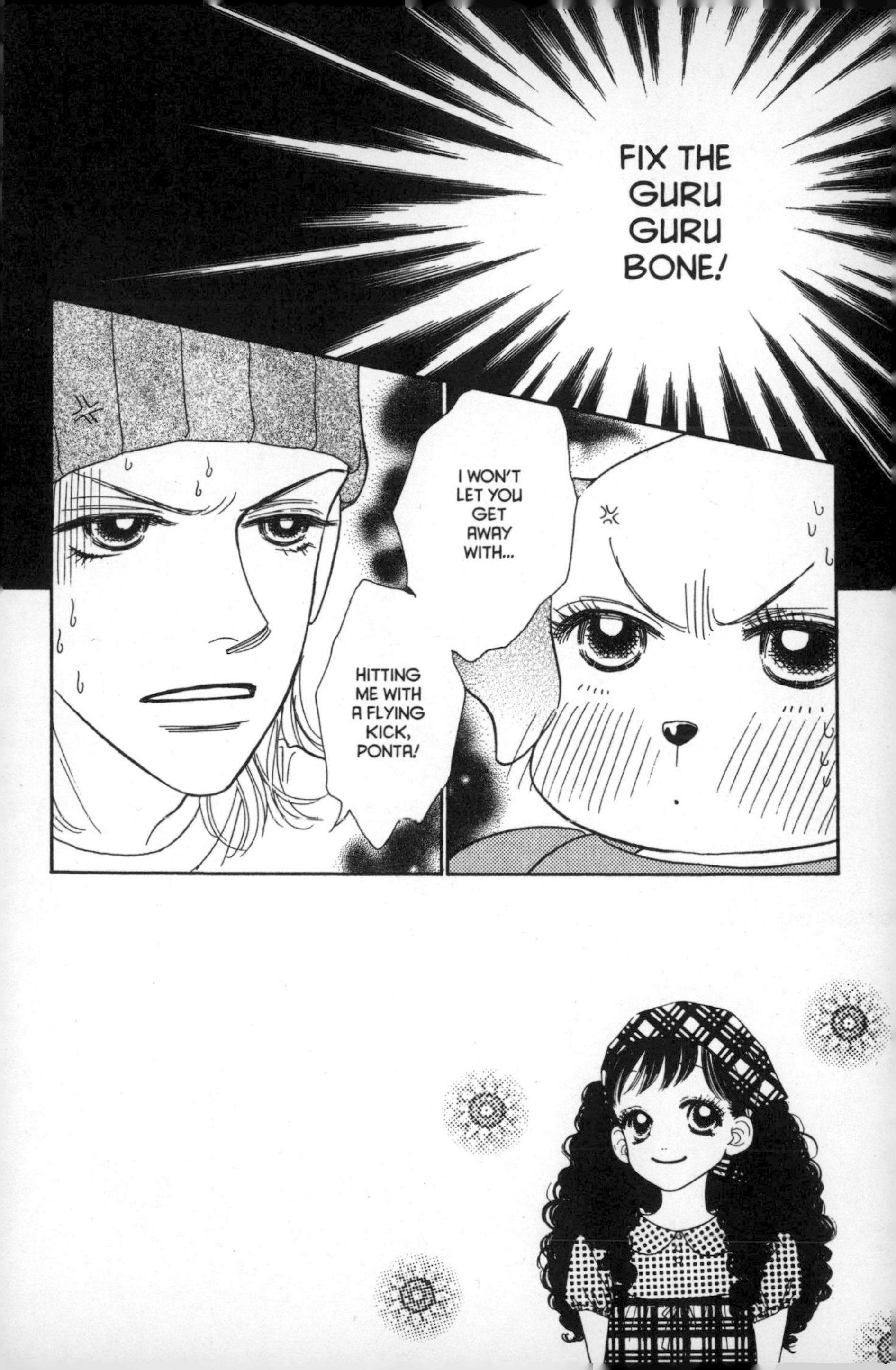
FIX THE GURU GURU BONE!
I WON'T LET YOU GET AWAY WITH...
HITTING ME WITH A FLYING KICK, PONTA!

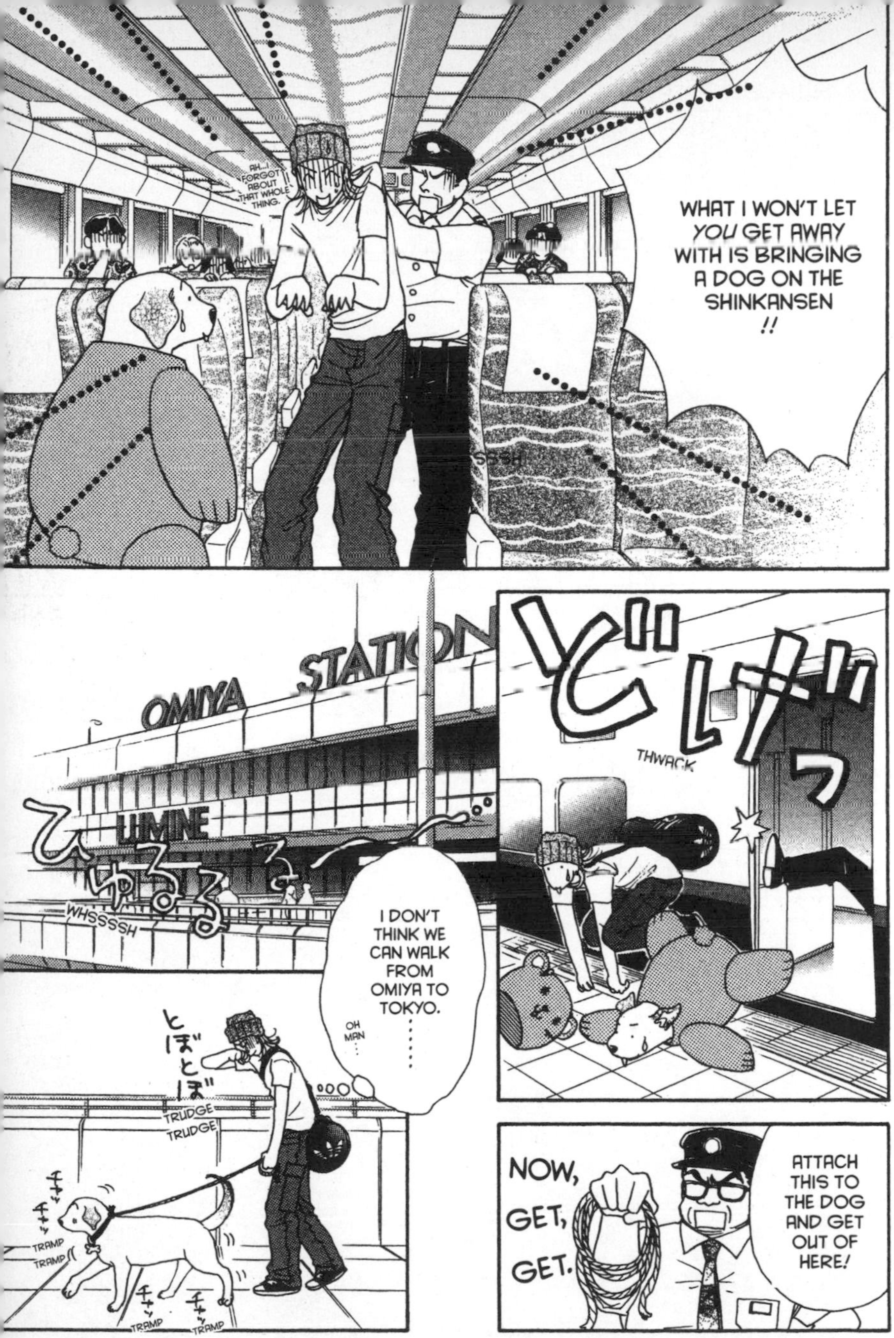
WHAT I WON'T LET *YOU* GET AWAY WITH IS BRINGING A DOG ON THE SHINKANSEN !!
AH...I FORGOT ABOUT THAT WHOLE THING.
SSSH
どげっ
THWACK
OMIYA STATION
LUMINE
ひゅるるる
WHSSSSH
I DON'T THINK WE CAN WALK FROM OMIYA TO TOKYO. ......
OH MAN...
ATTACH THIS TO THE DOG AND GET OUT OF HERE!
NOW, GET, GET.
とぼとぼ
TRUDGE TRUDGE
チャッ チャッ
TRAMP TRAMP
チャッ
TRAMP
チャッ
TRAMP

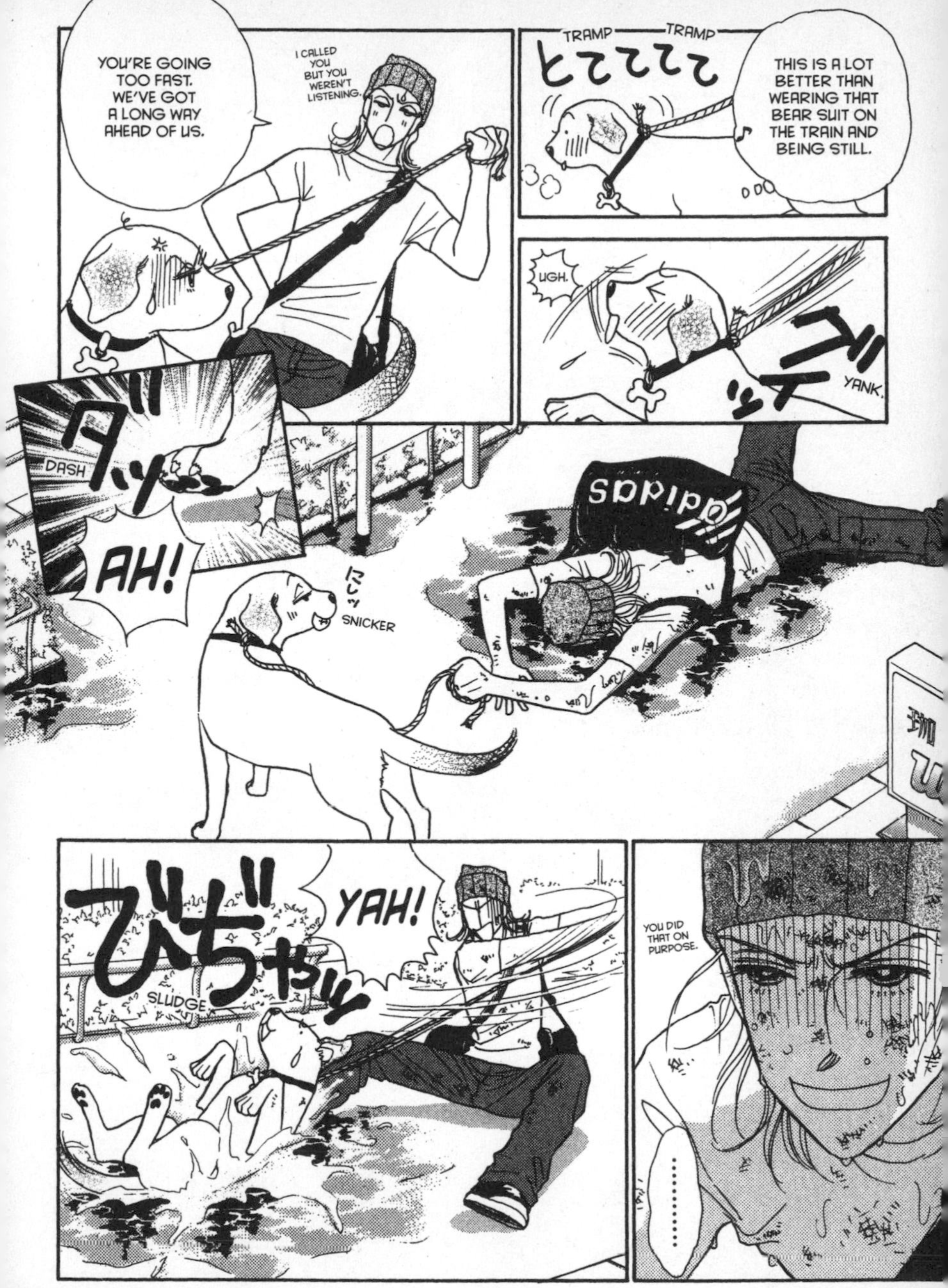

TRAMP
TRAMP
THIS IS A LOT BETTER THAN WEARING THAT BEAR SUIT ON THE TRAIN AND BEING STILL.
UGH.
YANK.
YOU'RE GOING TOO FAST. WE'VE GOT A LONG WAY AHEAD OF US.
I CALLED YOU BUT YOU WEREN'T LISTENING.
DASH
AH!
SNICKER
YOU DID THAT ON PURPOSE.
......
YAH!
SLUDGE

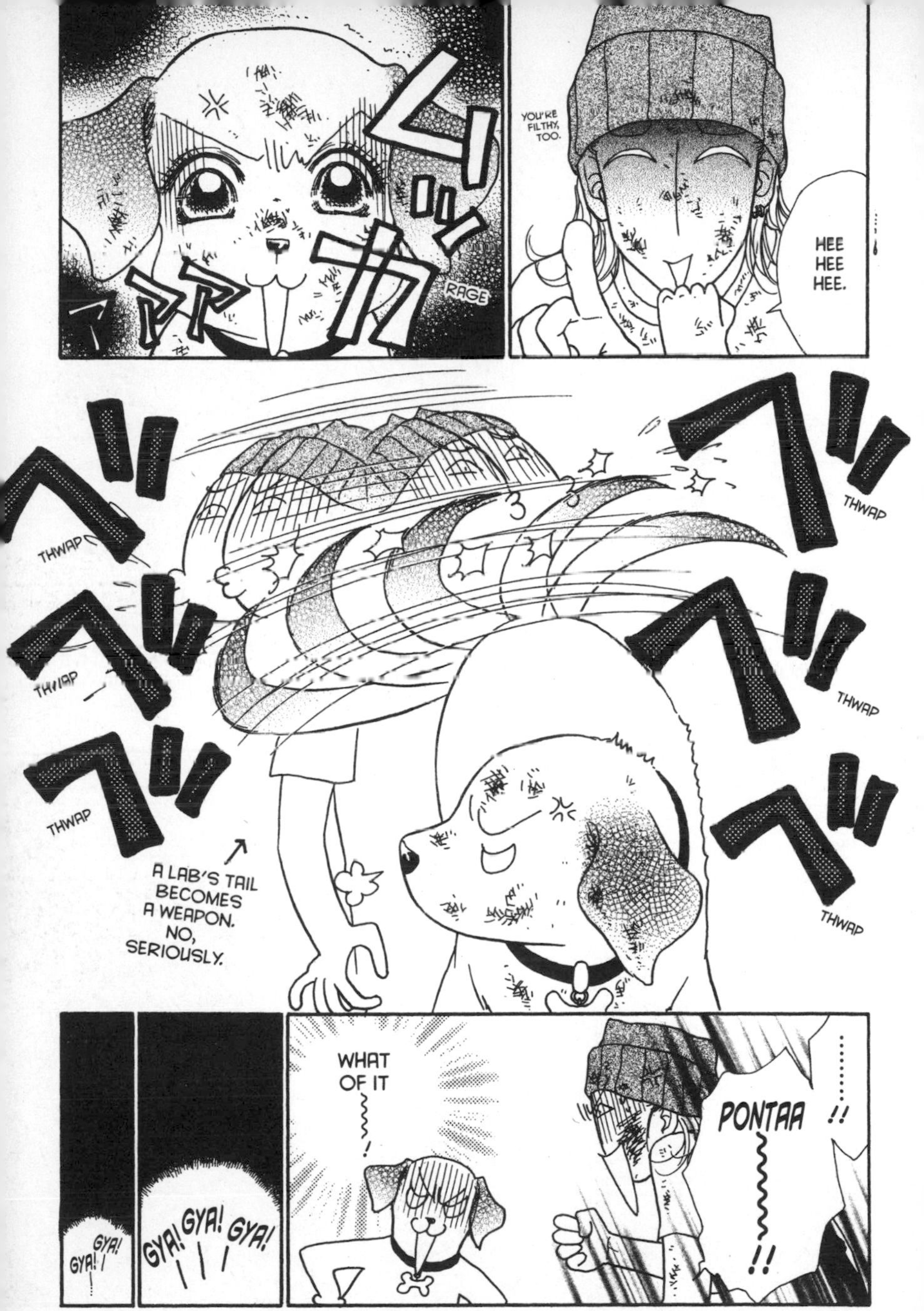
YOU'RE FILTHY, TOO.
HEE HEE HEE.
......!
RAGE
THWAP
THWAP
THWAP
THWAP
THWAP
THWAP
A LAB'S TAIL BECOMES A WEAPON. NO, SERIOUSLY.
......!!
PONTAA~!!
WHAT OF IT~!
GYA! GYA! GYA!
GYA! GYA!

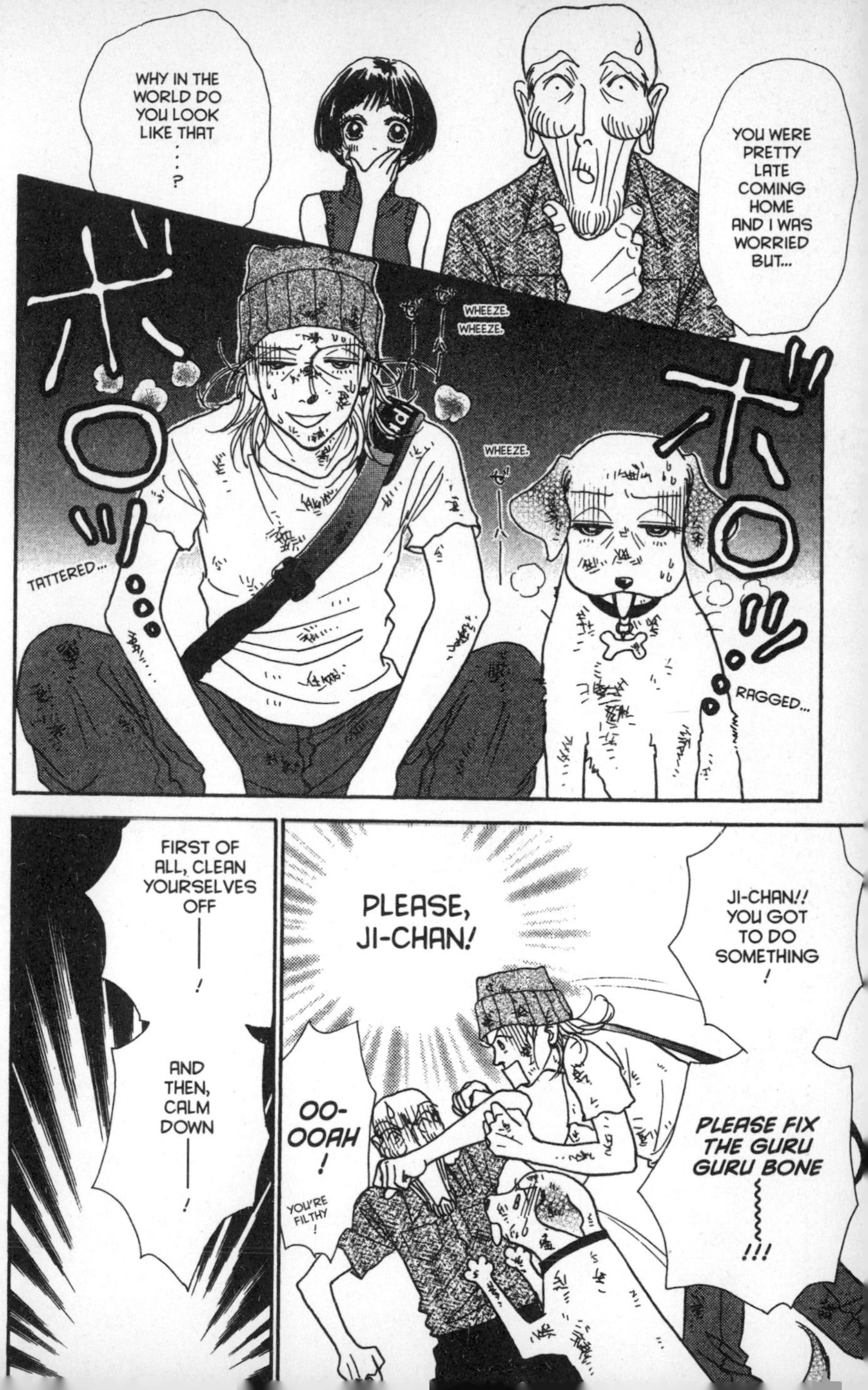
YOU WERE PRETTY LATE COMING HOME AND I WAS WORRIED BUT...
WHY IN THE WORLD DO YOU LOOK LIKE THAT . . . ?
ボロッ
ボロッ
WHEEZE.
WHEEZE.
WHEEZE.
RAGGED...
TATTERED...
JI-CHAN!! YOU GOT TO DO SOMETHING !
PLEASE, JI-CHAN!
PLEASE FIX THE GURU GURU BONE ~~~~ !!!
OO-OOAH !
YOU'RE FILTHY !
FIRST OF ALL, CLEAN YOURSELVES OFF —— !
AND THEN, CALM DOWN —— !

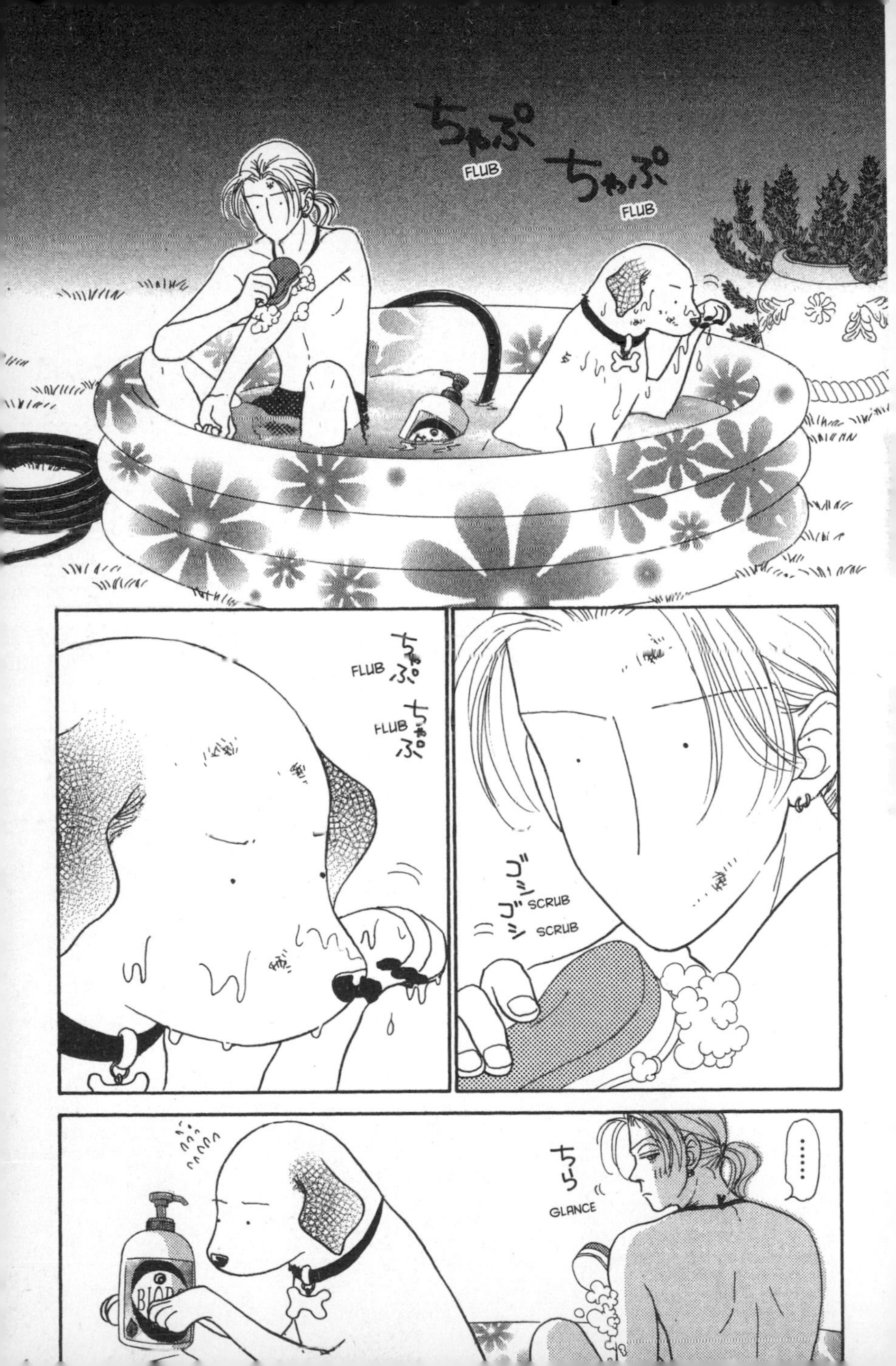
ちゃぷ
FLUB
ちゃぷ
FLUB
ゴシ ゴシ
SCRUB SCRUB
ちゃぷ
FLUB
ちゃぷ
FLUB
……
ちら
GLANCE

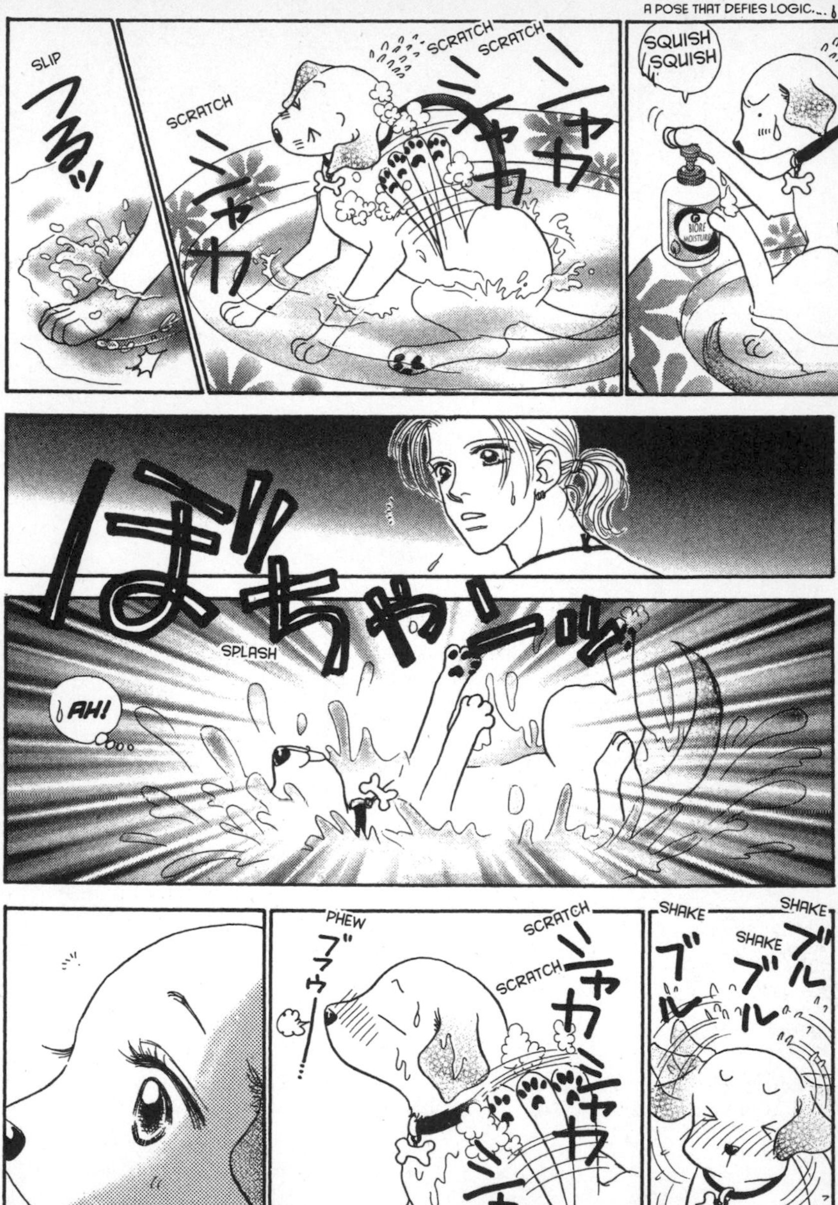

A POSE THAT DEFIES LOGIC...
SQUISH SQUISH
SCRATCH
SCRATCH
SCRATCH
シャカシャカ
シャカ
SLIP
つるッ
ぼちゃーんッ
SPLASH
AH!
SHAKE
SHAKE
SHAKE
ブルブル
ブル
SCRATCH
SCRATCH
SCRATCH
シャカシャカ
シャカ
PHEW
ブフゥー…!!

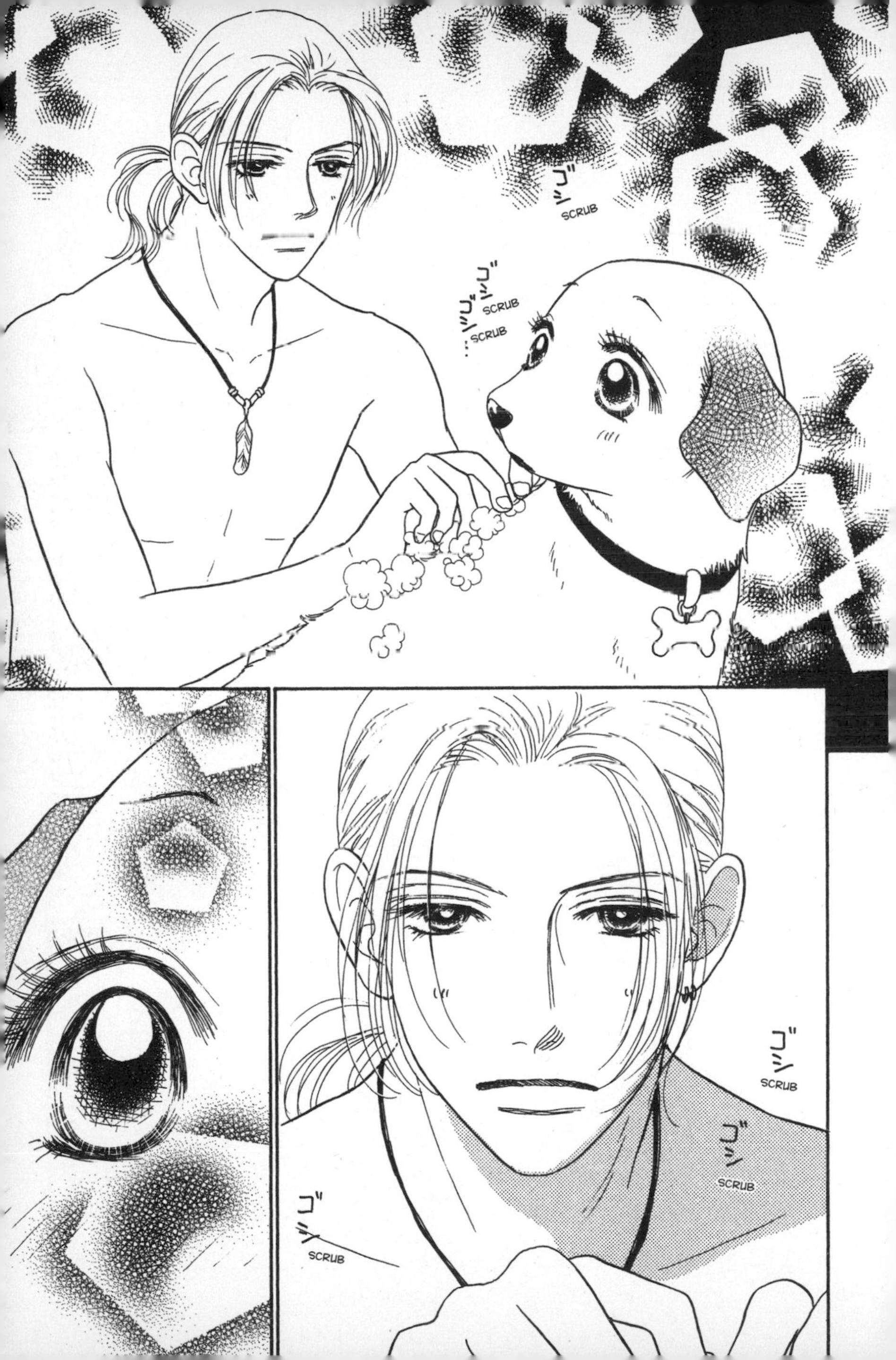
ゴシ SCRUB
ゴシ SCRUB
ゴシ… SCRUB
ゴシ SCRUB
ゴシ SCRUB
ゴシ SCRUB

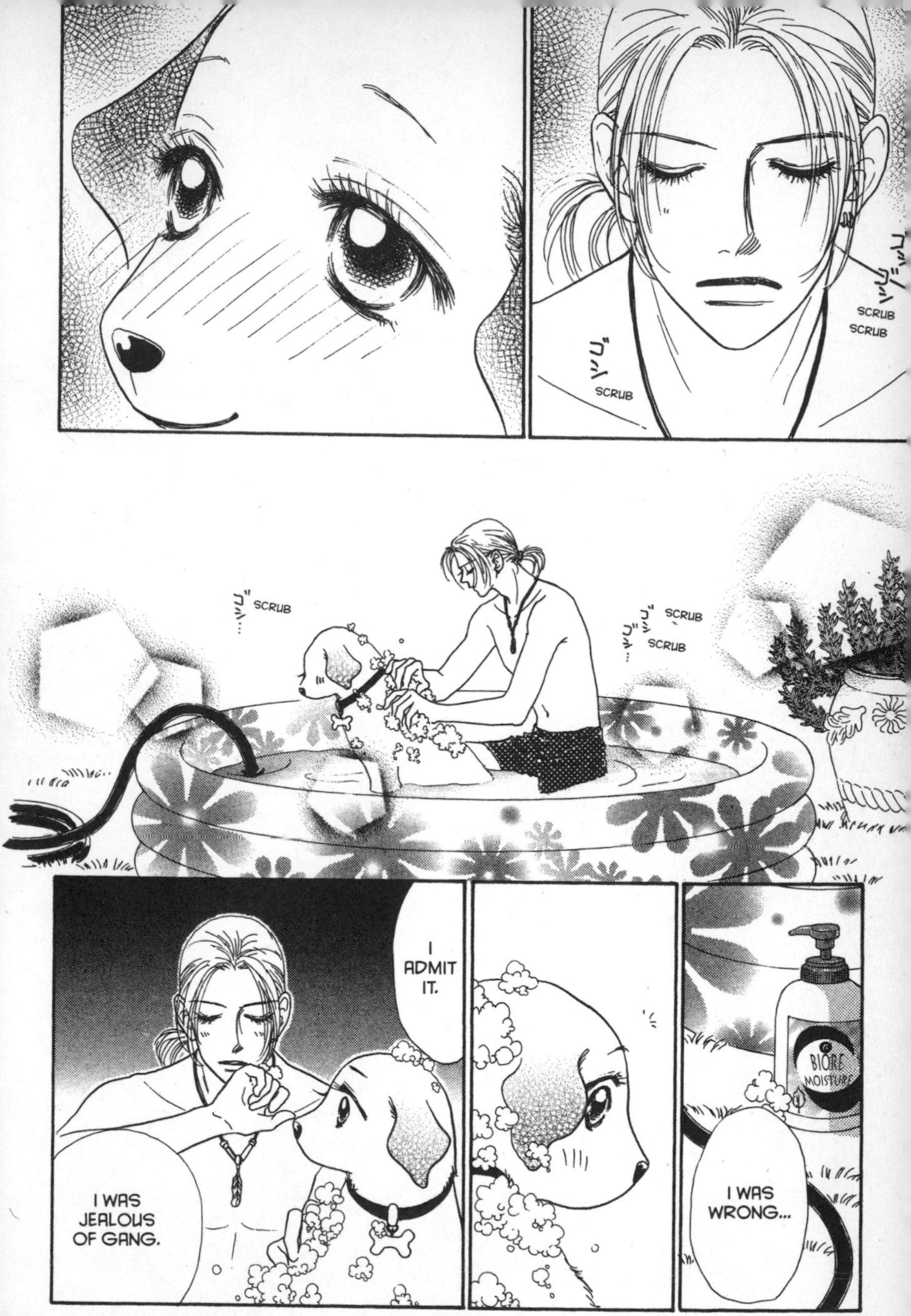
SCRUB
SCRUB
SCRUB
SCRUB
SCRUB
SCRUB
BIORE MOISTURE
I WAS WRONG...
I ADMIT IT.
I WAS JEALOUS OF GANG.

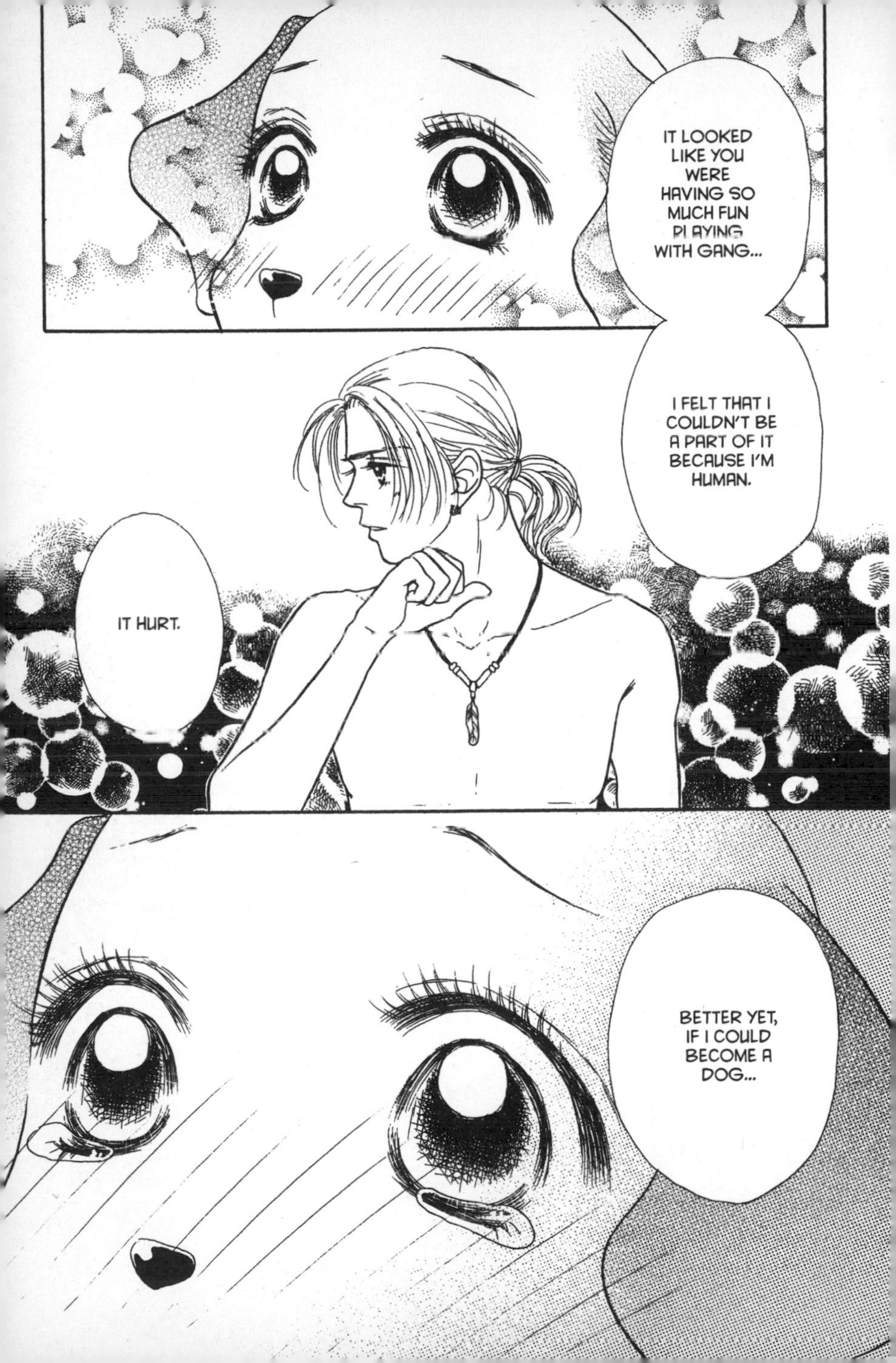
IT LOOKED LIKE YOU WERE HAVING SO MUCH FUN PLAYING WITH GANG...
I FELT THAT I COULDN'T BE A PART OF IT BECAUSE I'M HUMAN.
IT HURT.
BETTER YET, IF I COULD BECOME A DOG...

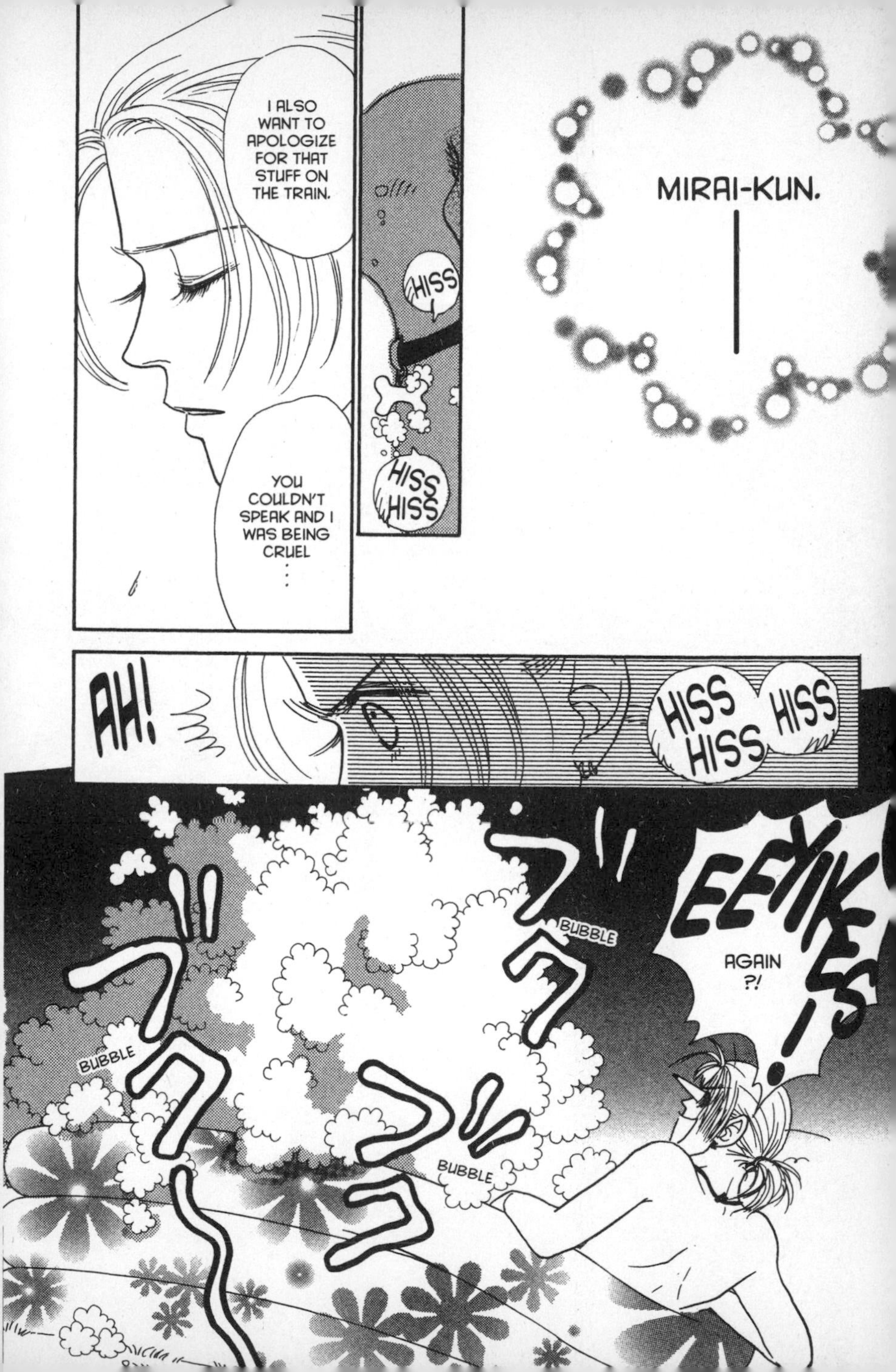
MIRAI-KUN.
HISS
HISS HISS
I ALSO WANT TO APOLOGIZE FOR THAT STUFF ON THE TRAIN.
YOU COULDN'T SPEAK AND I WAS BEING CRUEL ...
HISS
HISS HISS
AH!
EEYIKES!
AGAIN ?!
BUBBLE
BUBBLE
BUBBLE

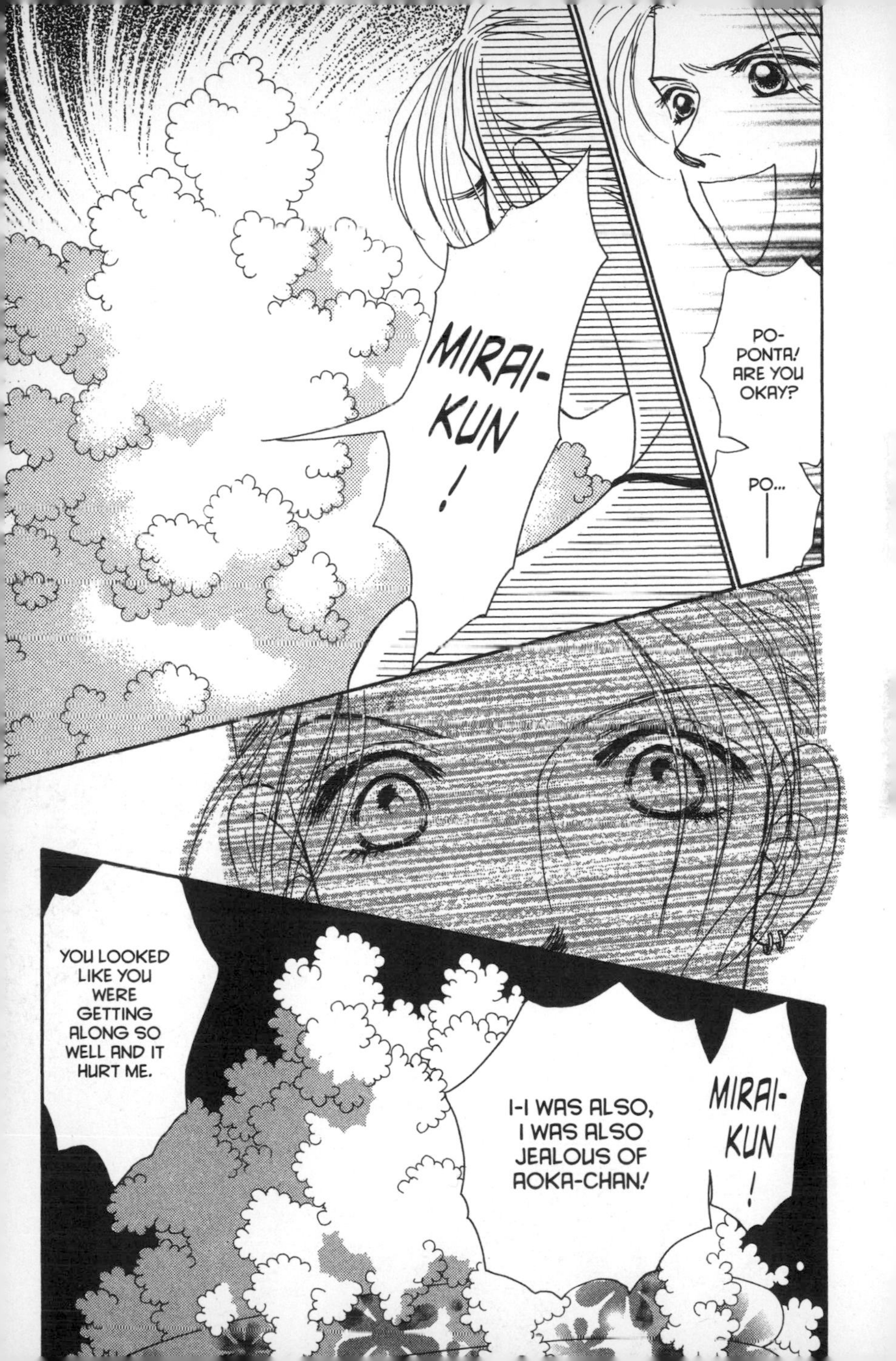
PO-PONTA! ARE YOU OKAY?
PO...
MIRAI-KUN!
MIRAI-KUN!
I-I WAS ALSO, I WAS ALSO JEALOUS OF AOKA-CHAN!
YOU LOOKED LIKE YOU WERE GETTING ALONG SO WELL AND IT HURT ME.

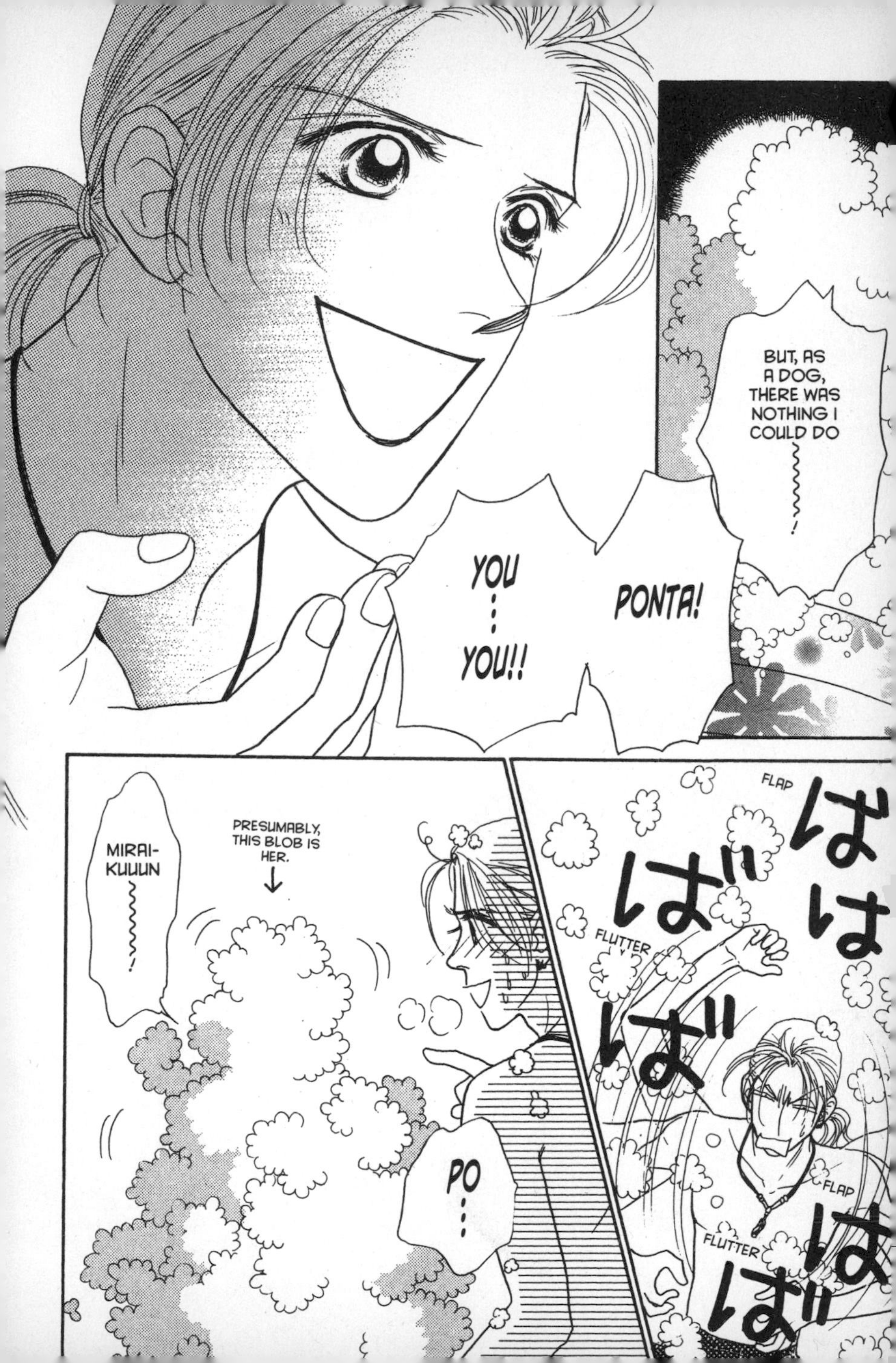
BUT, AS A DOG, THERE WAS NOTHING I COULD DO ~~~!
PONTA!
YOU... YOU!!
FLAP
ぱは
ばば
FLUTTER
FLAP
FLUTTER
はば
はば
PO...
PRESUMABLY, THIS BLOB IS HER.
MIRAI-KUUUN ~~~!

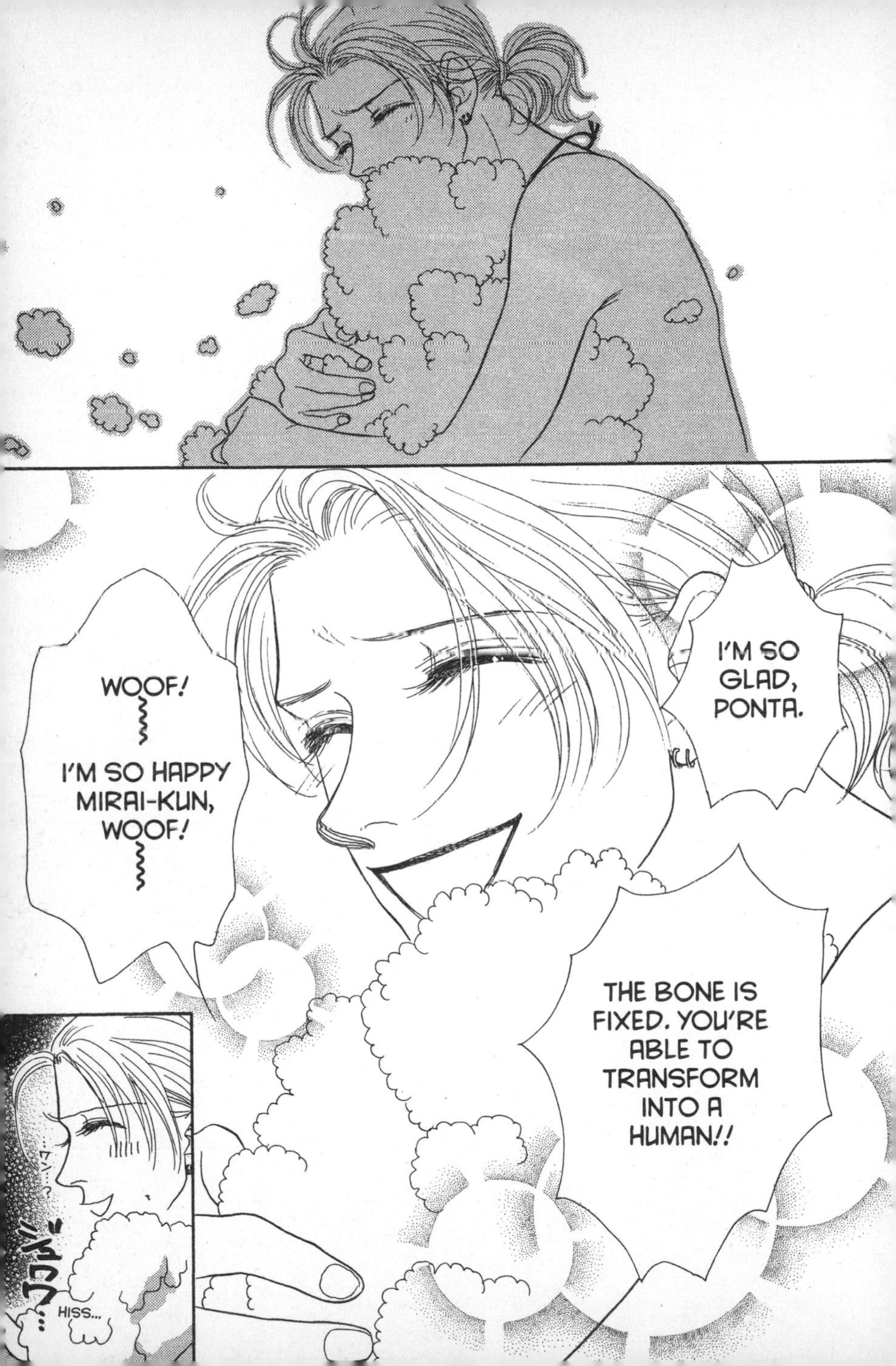
I'M SO GLAD, PONTA.
WOOF! I'M SO HAPPY MIRAI-KUN, WOOF!
THE BONE IS FIXED. YOU'RE ABLE TO TRANSFORM INTO A HUMAN!!
HISS...

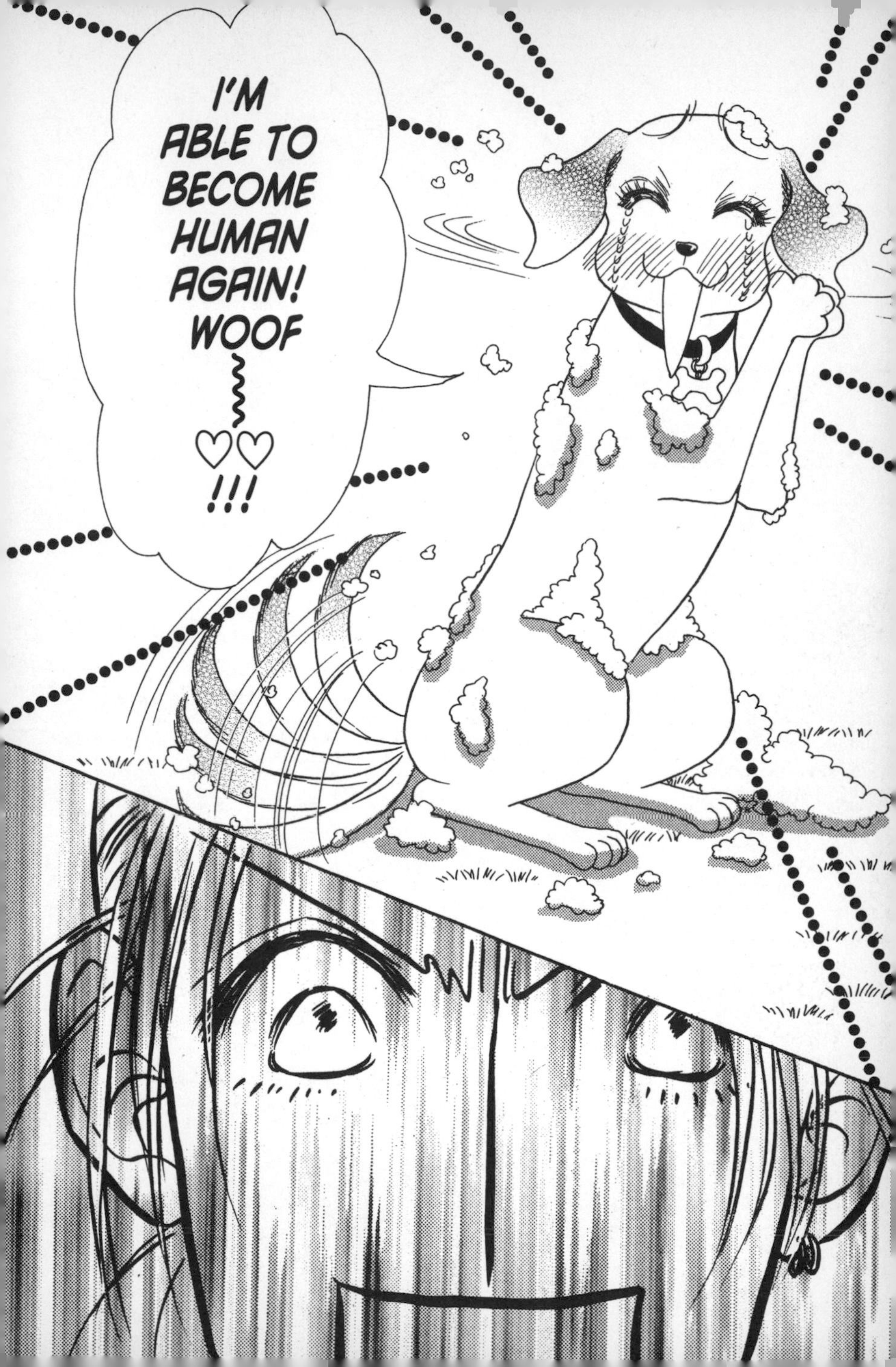
I'M ABLE TO BECOME HUMAN AGAIN! WOOF ♡♡ !!!

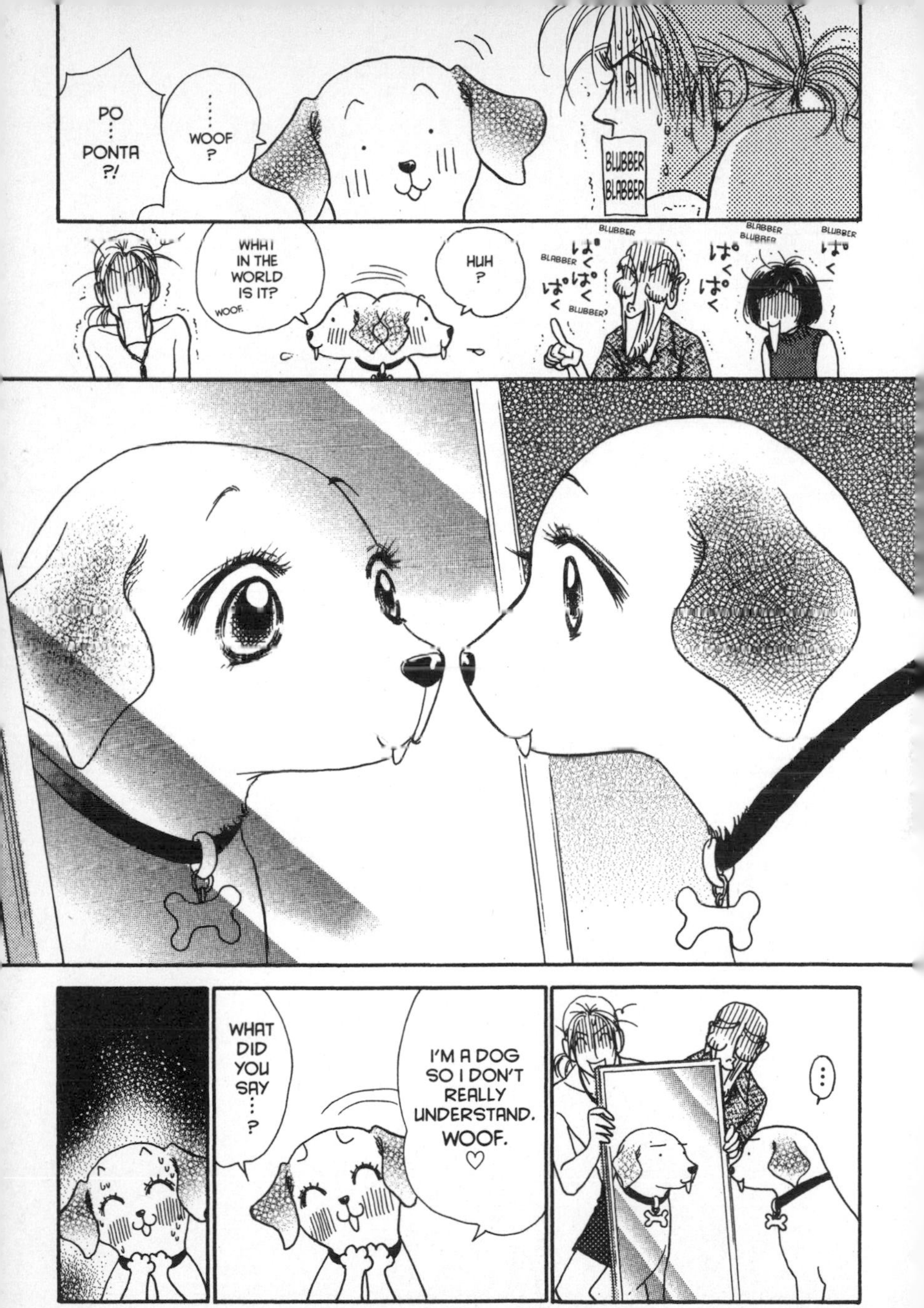
BLUBBER BLABBER
WOOF ?
PO... PONTA ?!
BLUBBER
ぱく
BLABBER
BLUBBER
ぱくぱく
BLUBBER
ぱくぱくぱく
BLABBER
BLUBBER
HUH ?
WHAT IN THE WORLD IS IT?
WOOF.
...
I'M A DOG SO I DON'T REALLY UNDERSTAND. WOOF. ♡
WHAT DID YOU SAY...?

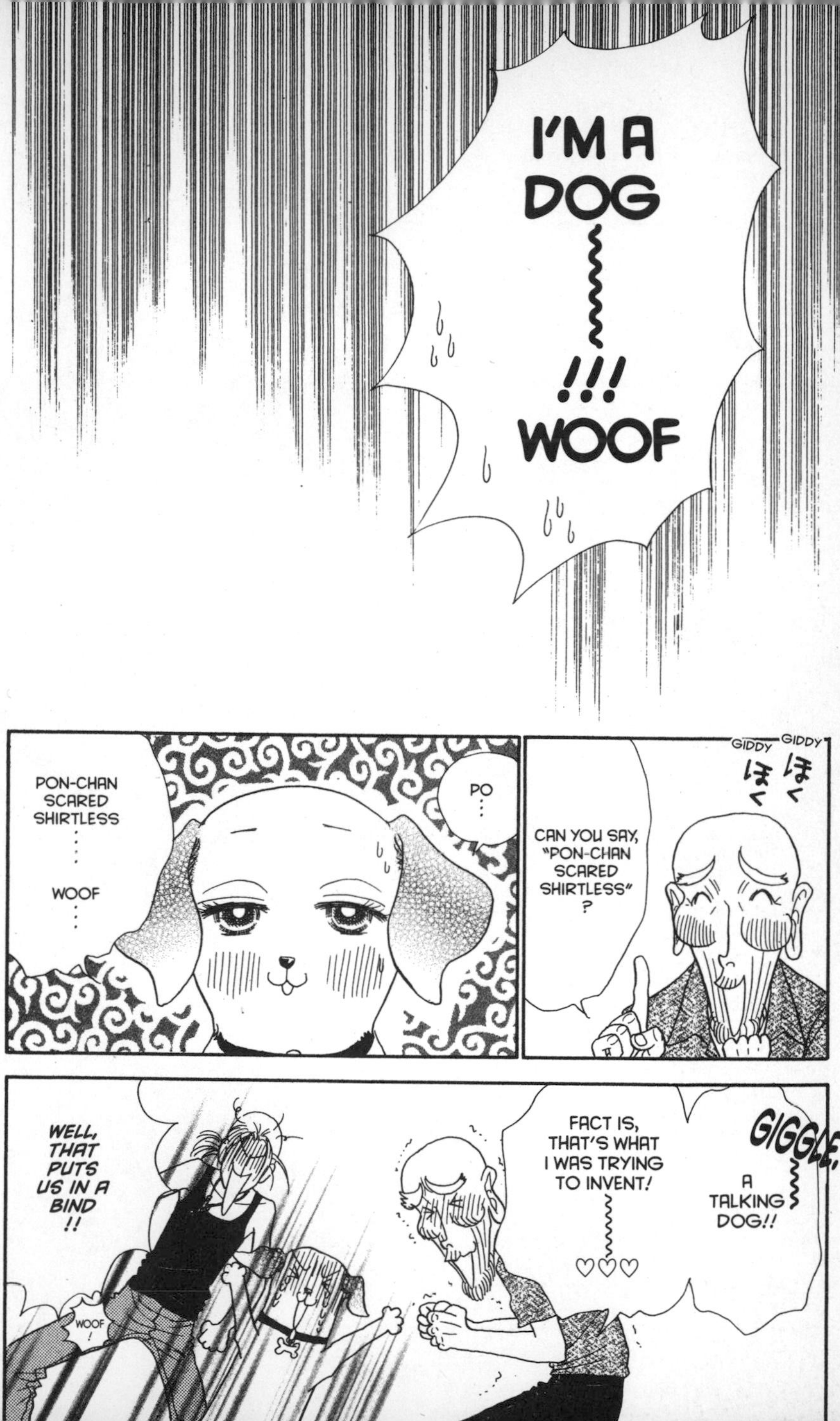
I'M A DOG~~~!!! WOOF
GIDDY ほく
GIDDY ほく
CAN YOU SAY, "PON-CHAN SCARED SHIRTLESS"?
PO...
PON-CHAN SCARED SHIRTLESS... WOOF...
GIGGLE,
A TALKING DOG!!
FACT IS, THAT'S WHAT I WAS TRYING TO INVENT!~ ♡♡♡
WOOF!
WELL, THAT PUTS US IN A BIND!!

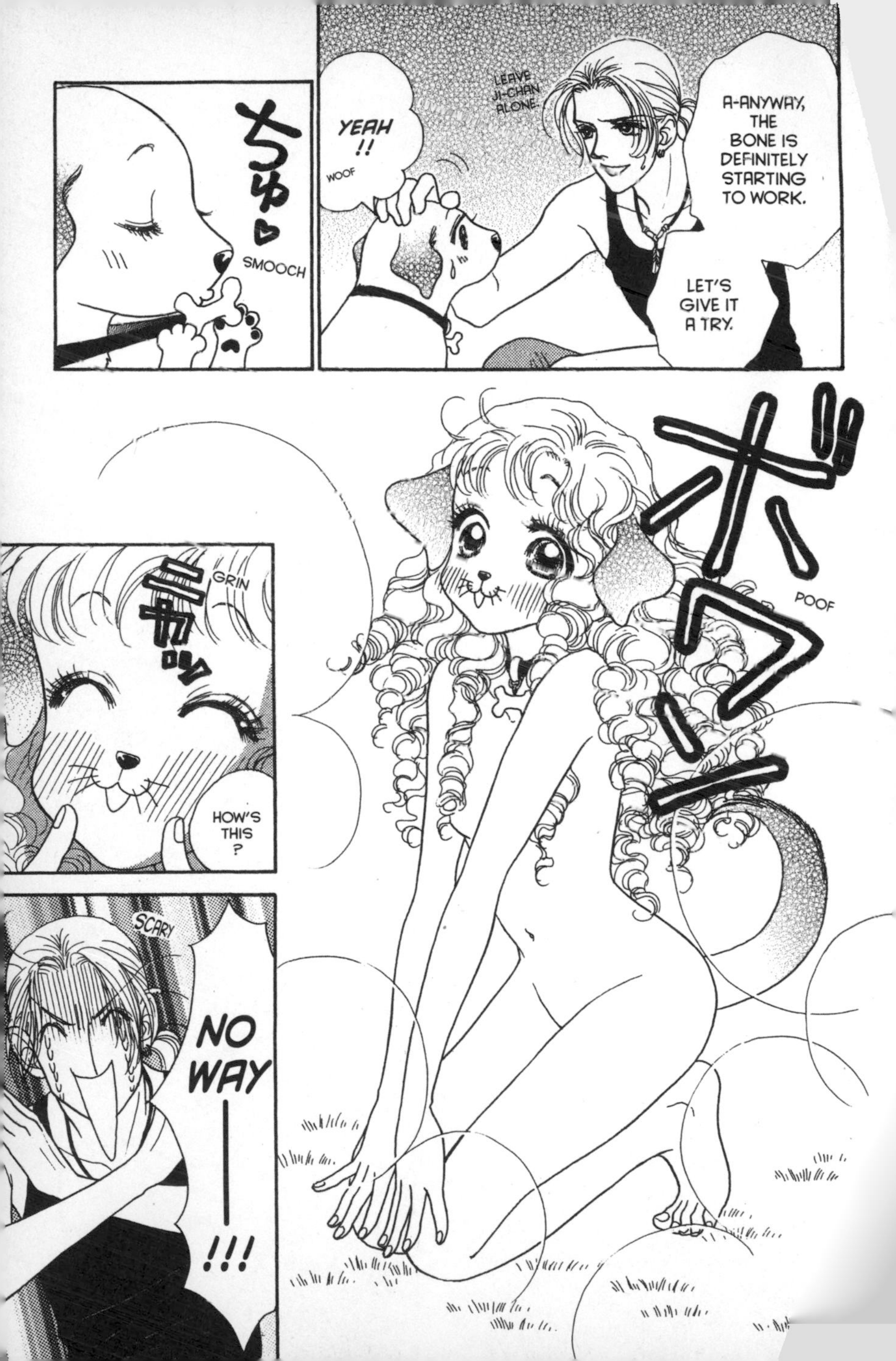
A-ANYWAY, THE BONE IS DEFINITELY STARTING TO WORK.
LEAVE JI-CHAN ALONE.
YEAH !!
WOOF
LET'S GIVE IT A TRY.
ちゅ♥
SMOOCH
ボワン
POOF
ニカッ
GRIN
HOW'S THIS ?
SCARY
NO WAY —!!!

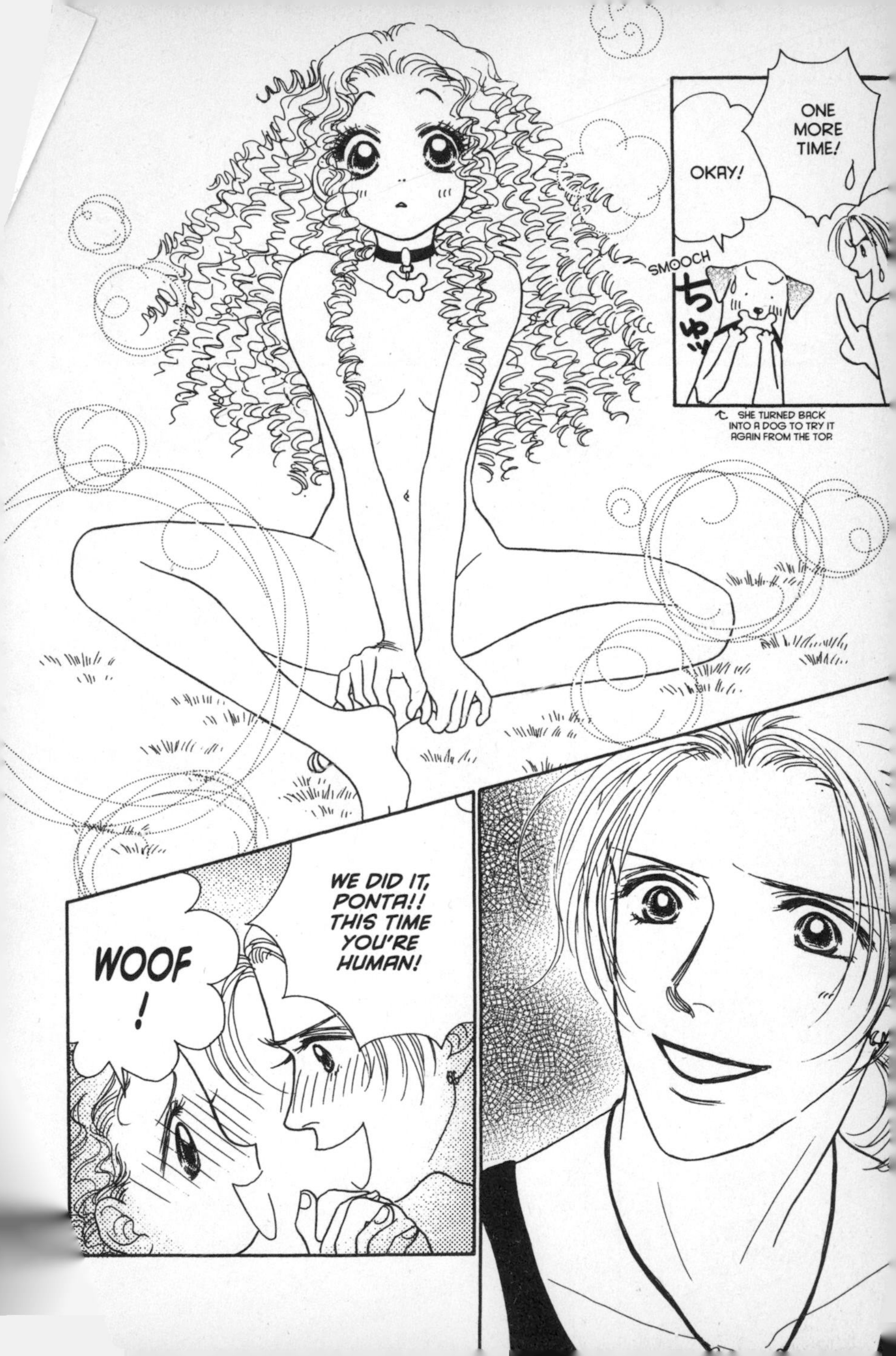
ONE MORE TIME!
OKAY!
SMOOCH
ちゅッ
SHE TURNED BACK INTO A DOG TO TRY IT AGAIN FROM THE TOP
WE DID IT, PONTA!! THIS TIME YOU'RE HUMAN!
WOOF!

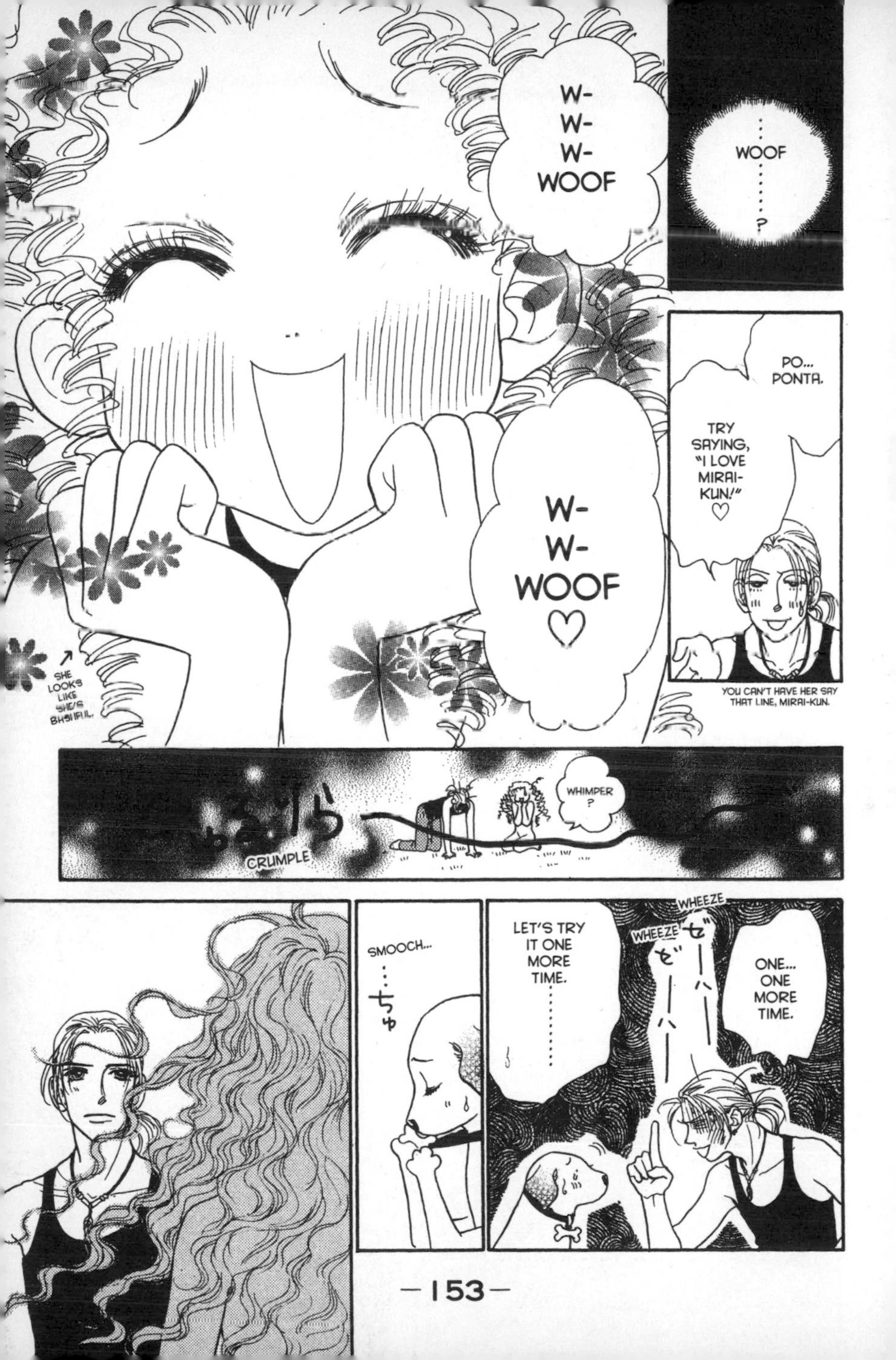

...WOOF.....?
PO... PONTA.
TRY SAYING, "I LOVE MIRAI-KUN!" ♡
YOU CAN'T HAVE HER SAY THAT LINE, MIRAI-KUN.
W-W-W-WOOF
W-W-WOOF ♡
SHE LOOKS LIKE SHE'S BASHFUL.
WHIMPER?
CRUMPLE
ONE... ONE MORE TIME.
WHEEZE
WHEEZE
LET'S TRY IT ONE MORE TIME.......
SMOOCH...

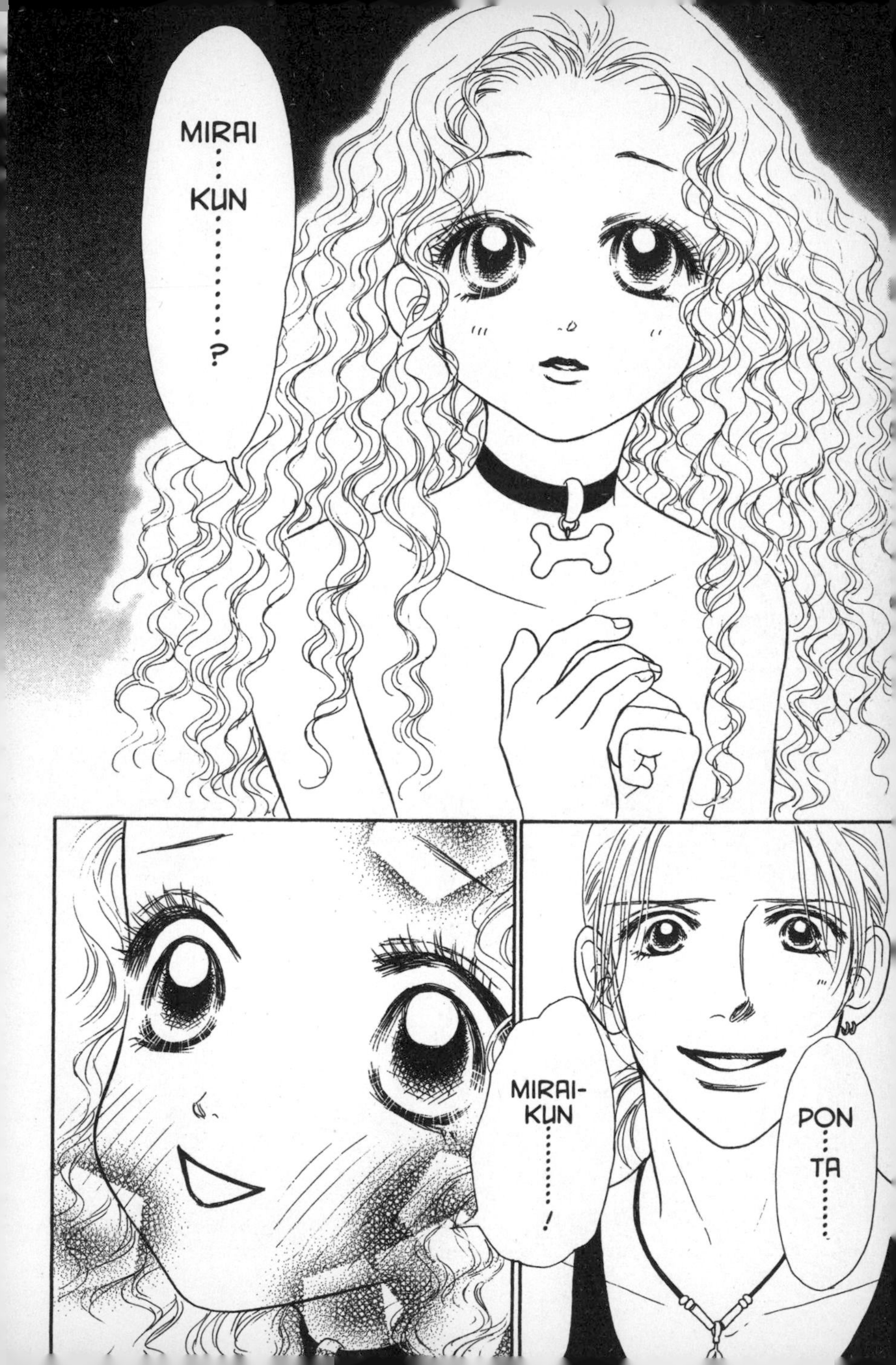
MIRAI...KUN.........?
PON...TA......
MIRAI-KUN........!

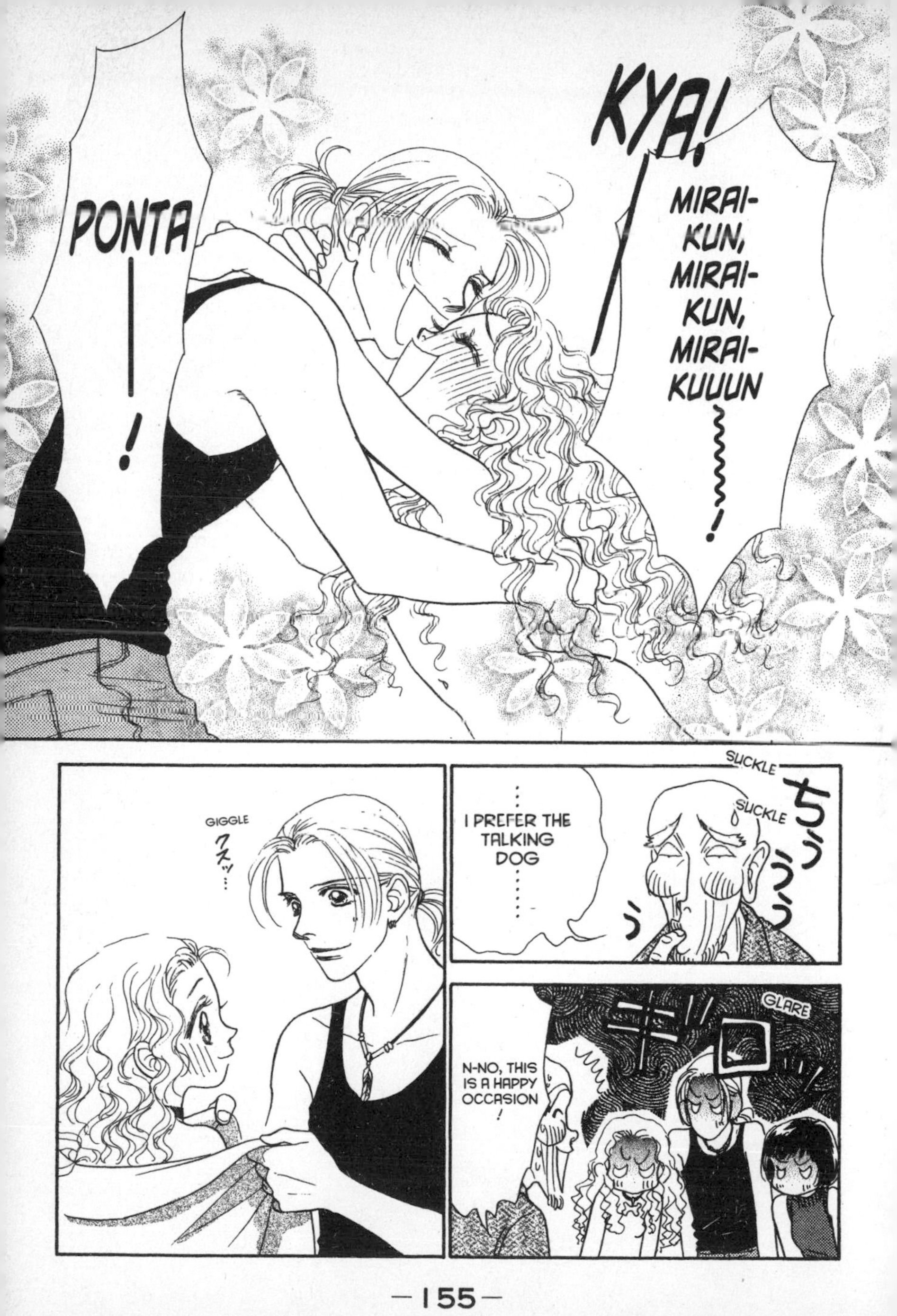
KYA!
MIRAI-KUN, MIRAI-KUN, MIRAI-KUN, MIRAI-KUUUN~!
PONTA—!
SUCKLE
ちううう
SUCKLE
... I PREFER THE TALKING DOG ......
GLARE
ギロッ
N-NO, THIS IS A HAPPY OCCASION!
GIGGLE
クスッ...

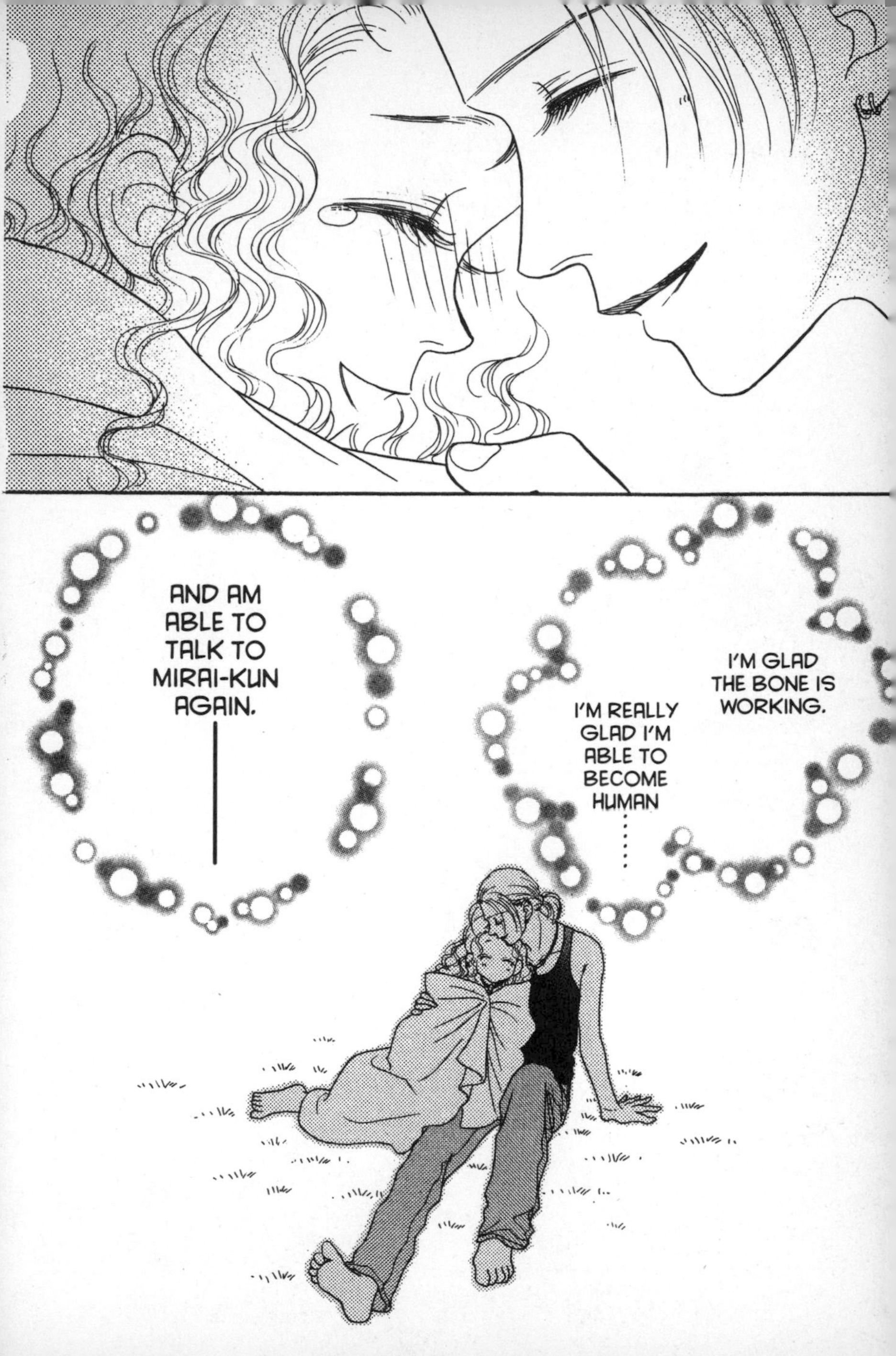
I'M GLAD THE BONE IS WORKING.
I'M REALLY GLAD I'M ABLE TO BECOME HUMAN ......
AND AM ABLE TO TALK TO MIRAI-KUN AGAIN. —

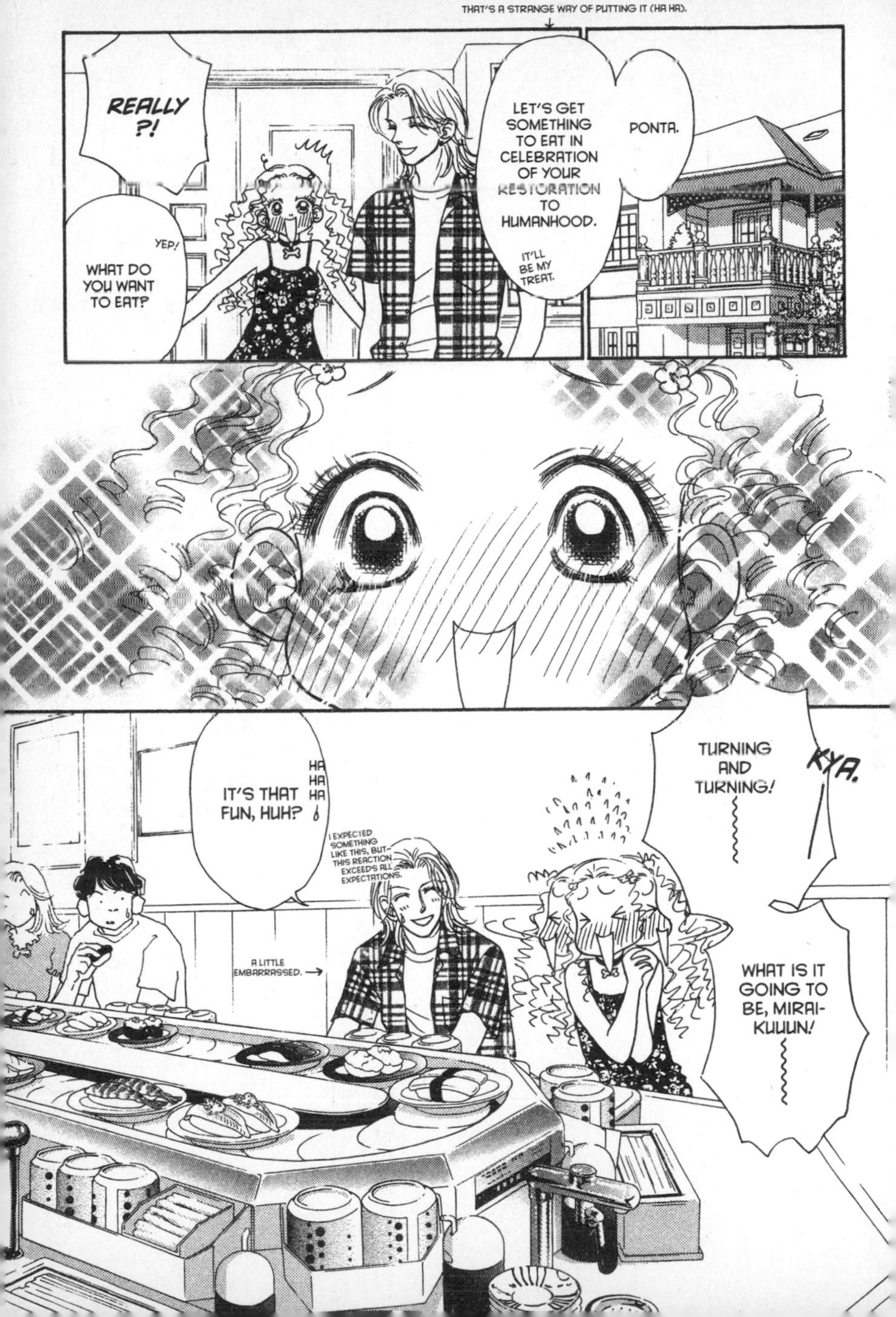
THAT'S A STRANGE WAY OF PUTTING IT (HA HA).
PONTA.
LET'S GET SOMETHING TO EAT IN CELEBRATION OF YOUR RESTORATION TO HUMANHOOD.
IT'LL BE MY TREAT.
REALLY ?!
YEP!
WHAT DO YOU WANT TO EAT?
KYA.
TURNING AND TURNING!
WHAT IS IT GOING TO BE, MIRAI-KUUUN!
IT'S THAT FUN, HUH?
HA HA HA
I EXPECTED SOMETHING LIKE THIS, BUT THIS REACTION EXCEED'S ALL EXPECTATIONS.
A LITTLE EMBARRASSED.

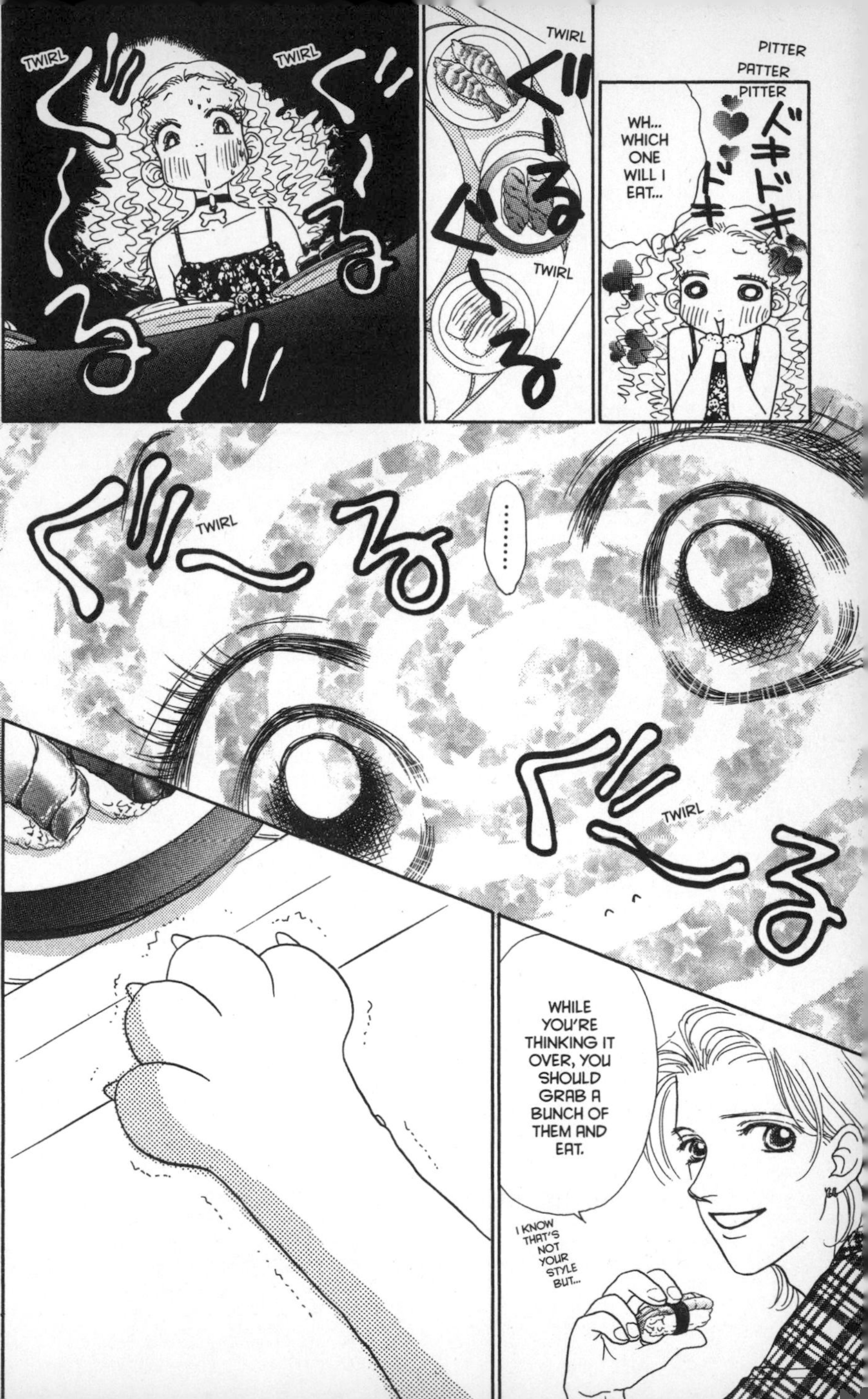
PITTER
PATTER
PITTER
ドキドキ
WH... WHICH ONE WILL I EAT...
TWIRL
ぐーるぐーる
TWIRL
TWIRL
TWIRL
ぐ〜る
TWIRL
......
ぐ〜る
TWIRL
WHILE YOU'RE THINKING IT OVER, YOU SHOULD GRAB A BUNCH OF THEM AND EAT.
I KNOW THAT'S NOT YOUR STYLE BUT...

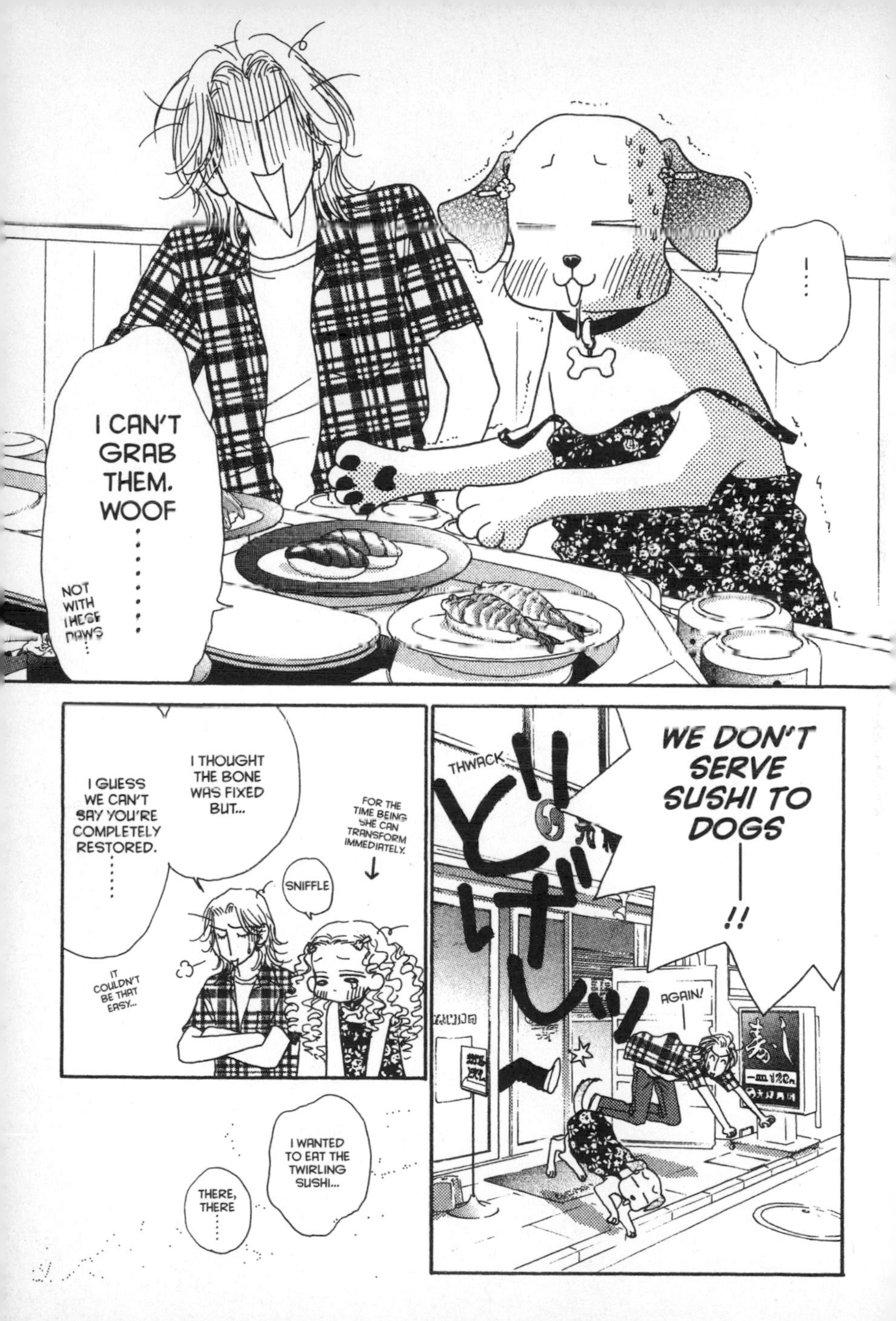

…
I CAN'T GRAB THEM. WOOF ……
NOT WITH THESE PAWS…
WE DON'T SERVE SUSHI TO DOGS —!!
THWACK
AGAIN!
FOR THE TIME BEING SHE CAN TRANSFORM IMMEDIATELY.
I THOUGHT THE BONE WAS FIXED BUT…
I GUESS WE CAN'T SAY YOU'RE COMPLETELY RESTORED. …
SNIFFLE
IT COULDN'T BE THAT EASY…
I WANTED TO EAT THE TWIRLING SUSHI…
THERE, THERE …

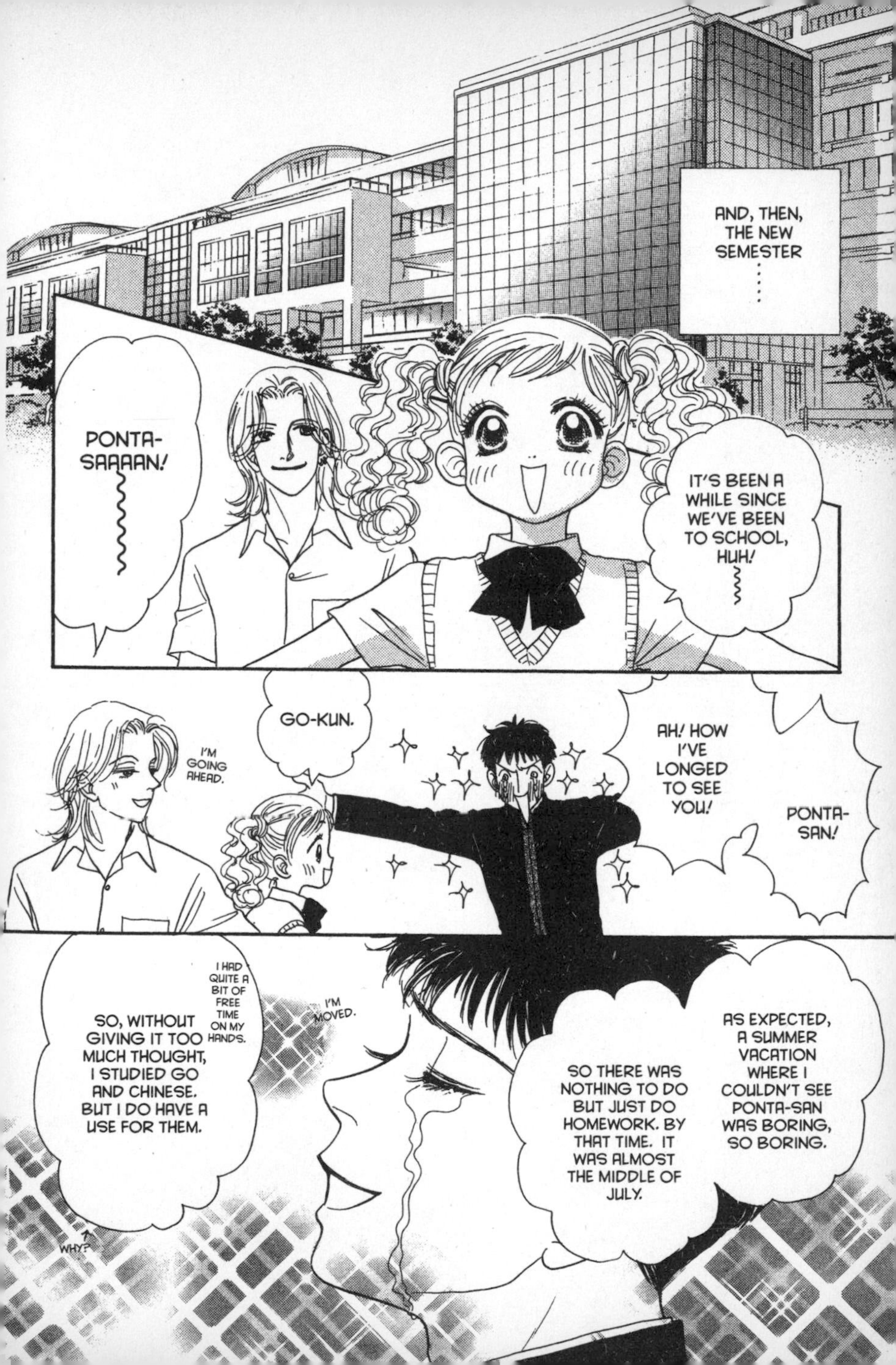
AND, THEN, THE NEW SEMESTER ....
IT'S BEEN A WHILE SINCE WE'VE BEEN TO SCHOOL, HUH!
PONTA-SAAAAN!
PONTA-SAN!
AH! HOW I'VE LONGED TO SEE YOU!
GO-KUN.
I'M GOING AHEAD.
AS EXPECTED, A SUMMER VACATION WHERE I COULDN'T SEE PONTA-SAN WAS BORING, SO BORING.
SO THERE WAS NOTHING TO DO BUT JUST DO HOMEWORK. BY THAT TIME. IT WAS ALMOST THE MIDDLE OF JULY.
I'M MOVED.
I HAD QUITE A BIT OF FREE TIME ON MY HANDS.
SO, WITHOUT GIVING IT TOO MUCH THOUGHT, I STUDIED GO AND CHINESE. BUT I DO HAVE A USE FOR THEM.
WHY?

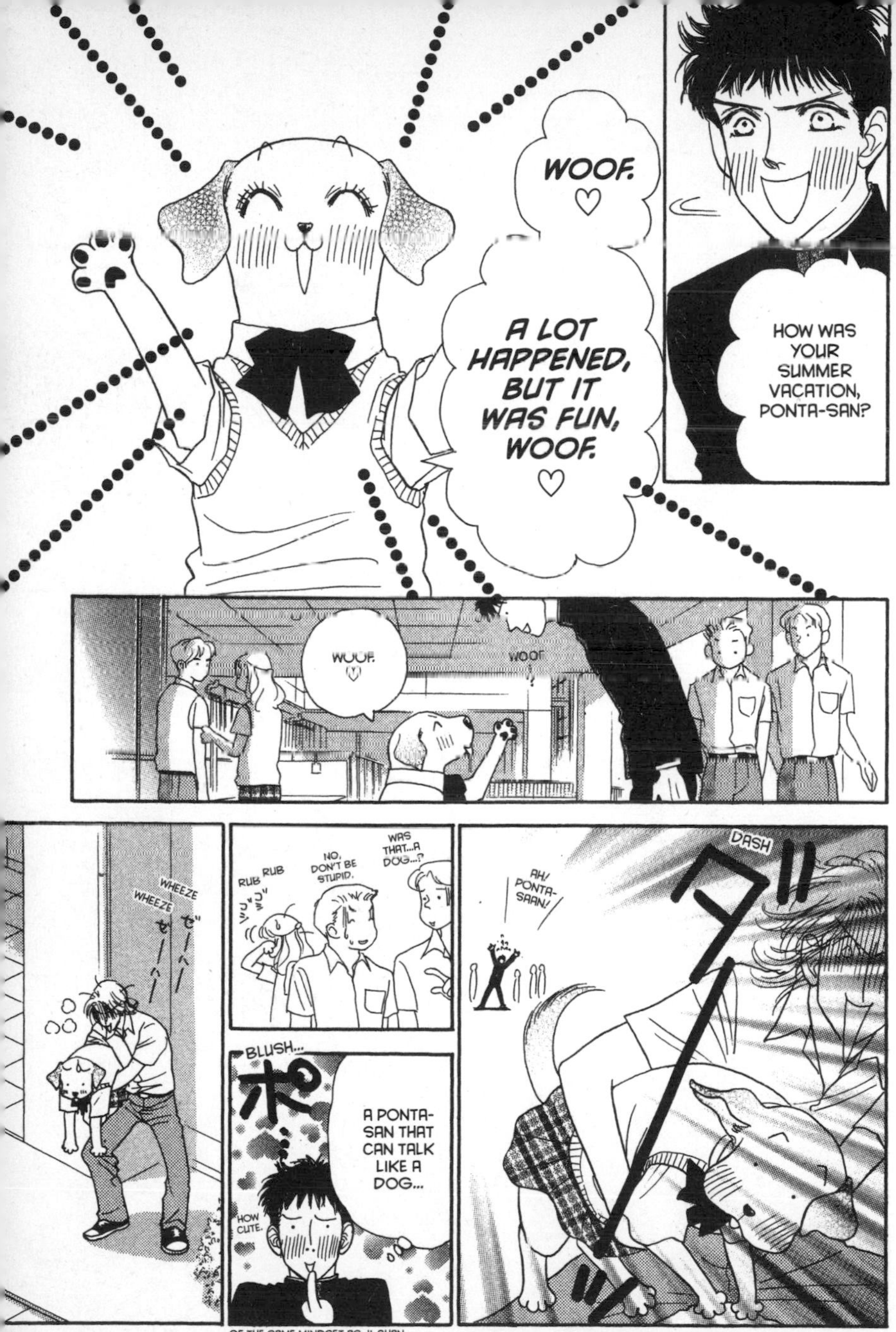
HOW WAS YOUR SUMMER VACATION, PONTA-SAN?
WOOF. ♡
A LOT HAPPENED, BUT IT WAS FUN, WOOF. ♡
WOOF ?
WOOF. ♡
DASH
AH! PONTA-SAAN!
WAS THAT...A DOG...?
NO, DON'T BE STUPID.
RUB RUB
BLUSH...
A PONTA-SAN THAT CAN TALK LIKE A DOG...
HOW CUTE.
WHEEZE WHEEZE

OF THE SAME MINDSET AS JI-CHAN.

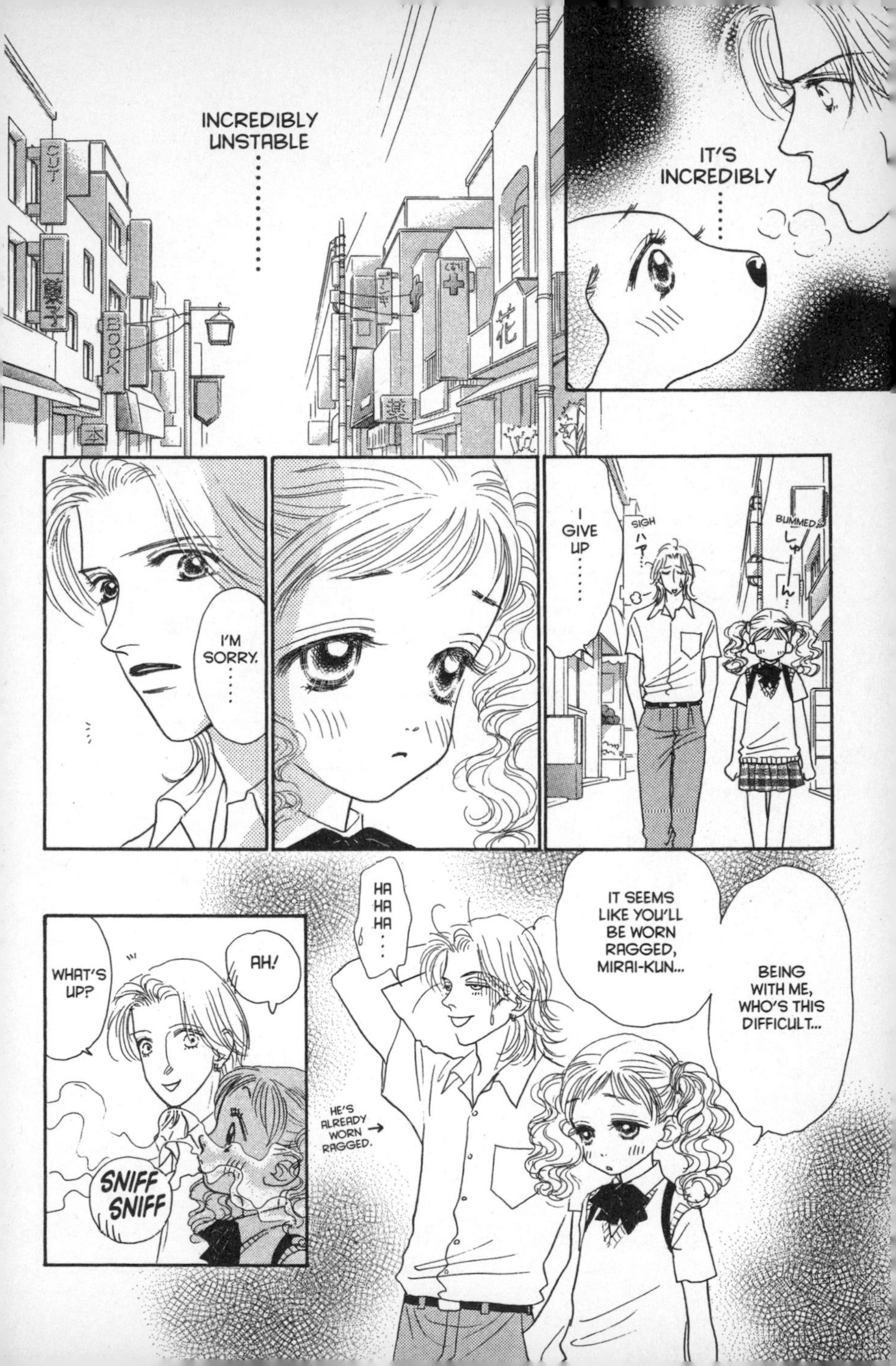

IT'S INCREDIBLY ...
INCREDIBLY UNSTABLE ...
CUT
菓子
BOOK
花
I GIVE UP ......
SIGH
ハァ
BUMMED
しゅーん
I'M SORRY. ...
IT SEEMS LIKE YOU'LL BE WORN RAGGED, MIRAI-KUN...
BEING WITH ME, WHO'S THIS DIFFICULT...
HA HA HA ...
HE'S ALREADY WORN RAGGED.
AH!
WHAT'S UP?
SNIFF SNIFF

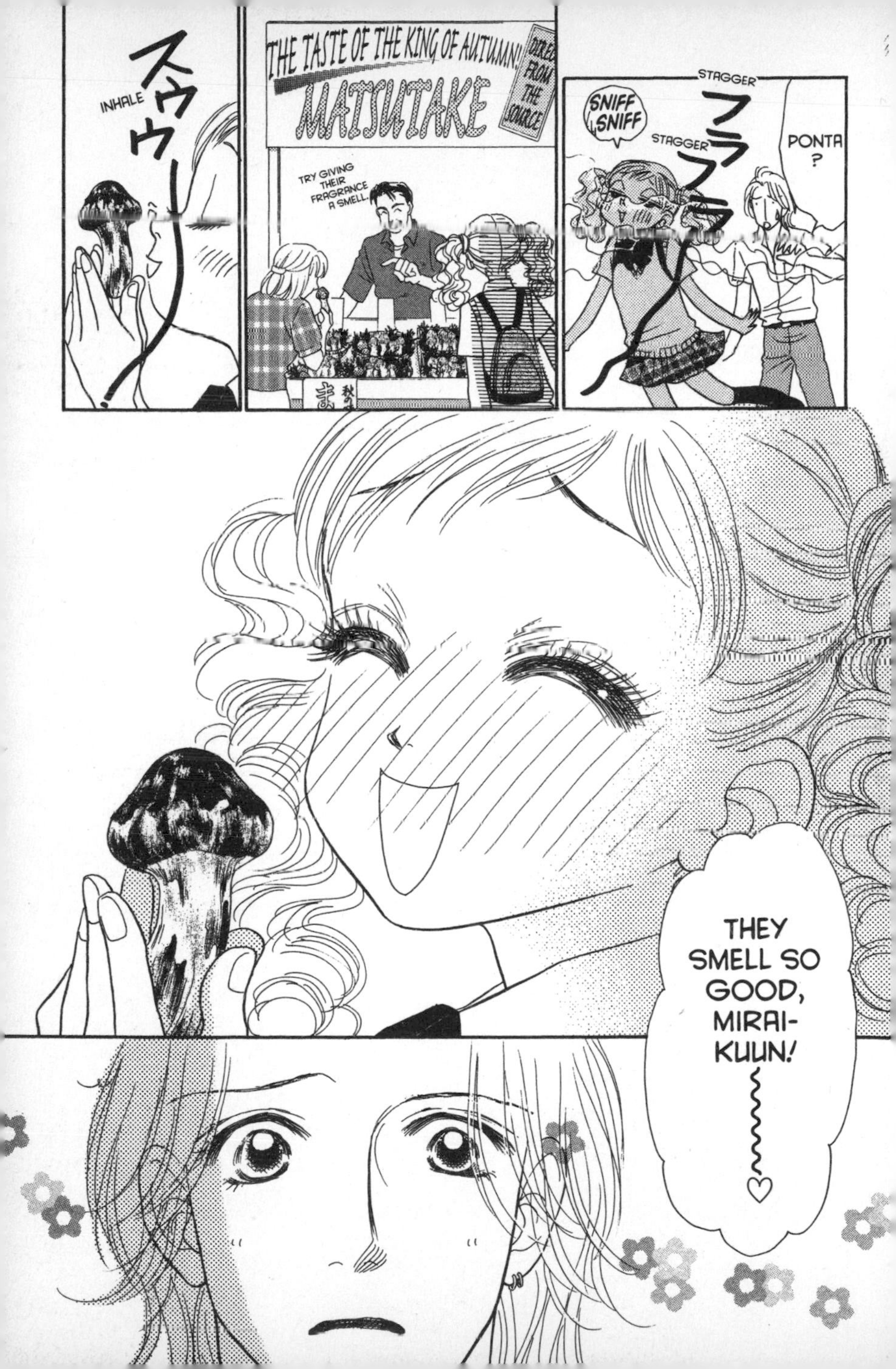
PONTA?
STAGGER
フラ
STAGGER
フラ
SNIFF SNIFF
DIREC FROM THE SOURCE
THE TASTE OF THE KING OF AUTUMN!
MATSUTAKE
TRY GIVING THEIR FRAGRANCE A SMELL.
スウー
INHALE
THEY SMELL SO GOOD, MIRAI-KUUN! ♡

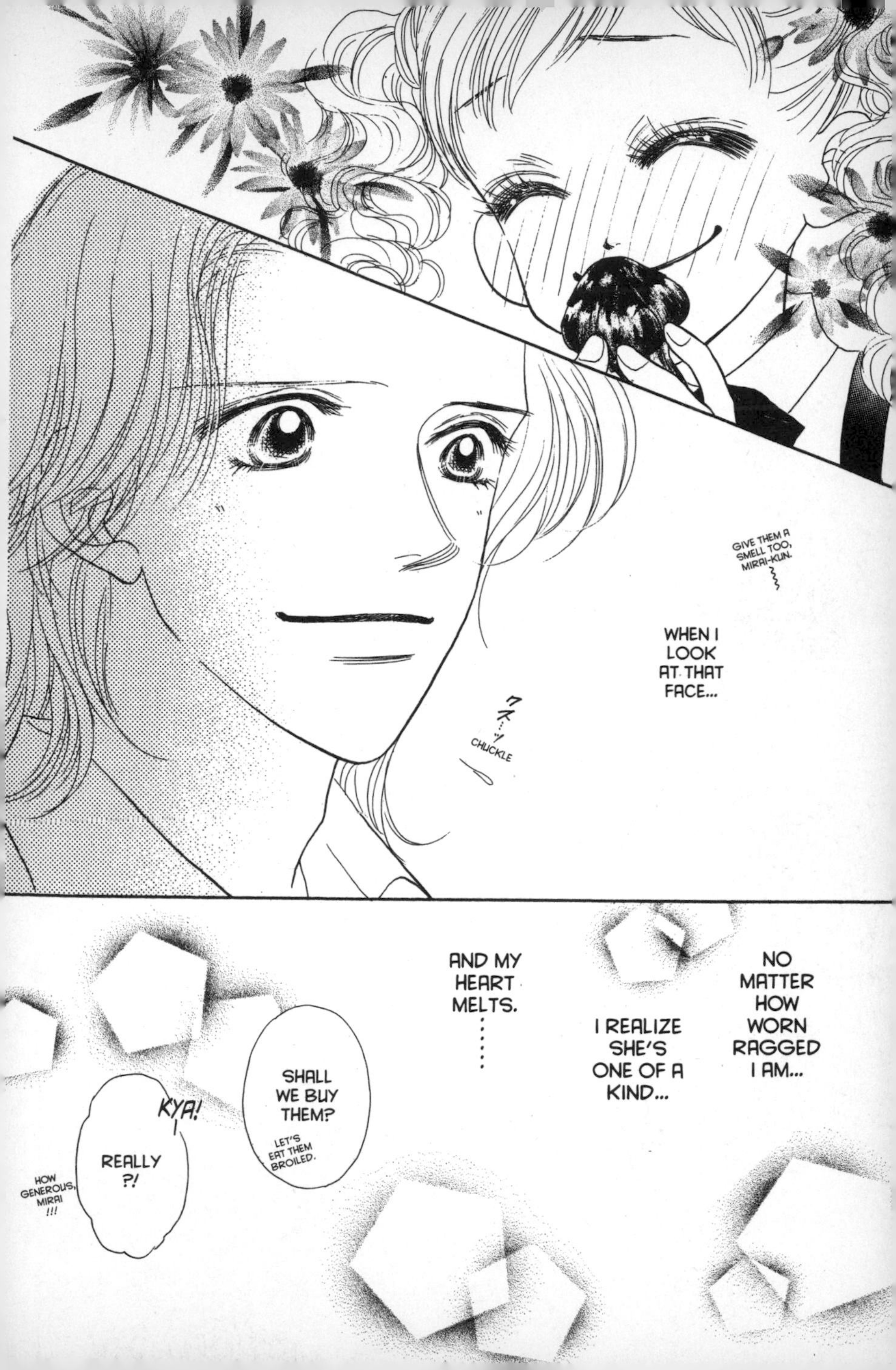
GIVE THEM A SMELL TOO, MIRAI-KUN.
WHEN I LOOK AT THAT FACE...
クスッ
CHUCKLE
NO MATTER HOW WORN RAGGED I AM...
I REALIZE SHE'S ONE OF A KIND...
AND MY HEART MELTS. ......
SHALL WE BUY THEM?
LET'S EAT THEM BROILED.
KYA!
REALLY ?!
HOW GENEROUS, MIRAI !!!

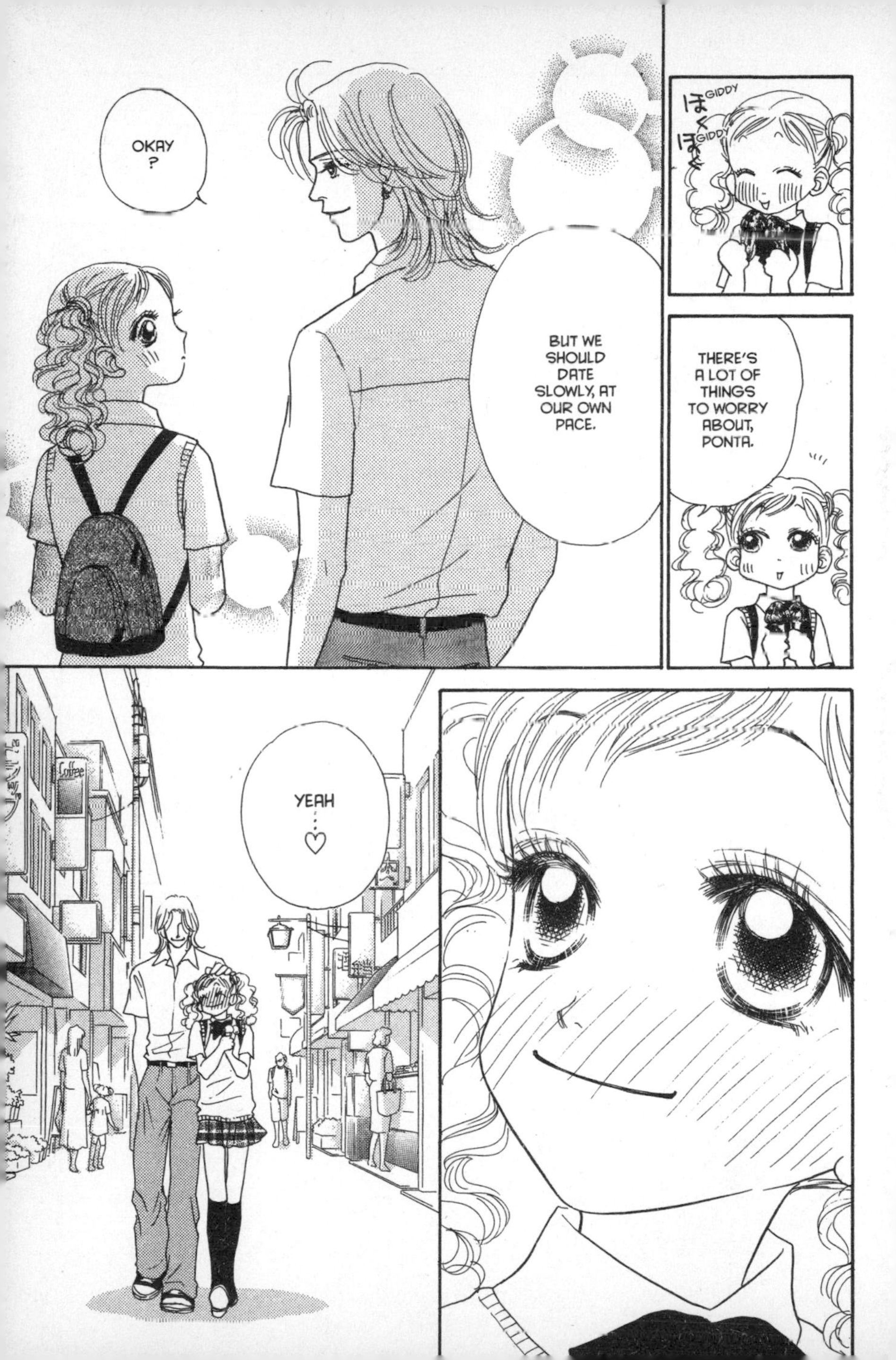
ほくほく GIDDY GIDDY
THERE'S A LOT OF THINGS TO WORRY ABOUT, PONTA.
BUT WE SHOULD DATE SLOWLY, AT OUR OWN PACE.
OKAY?
YEAH... ♡

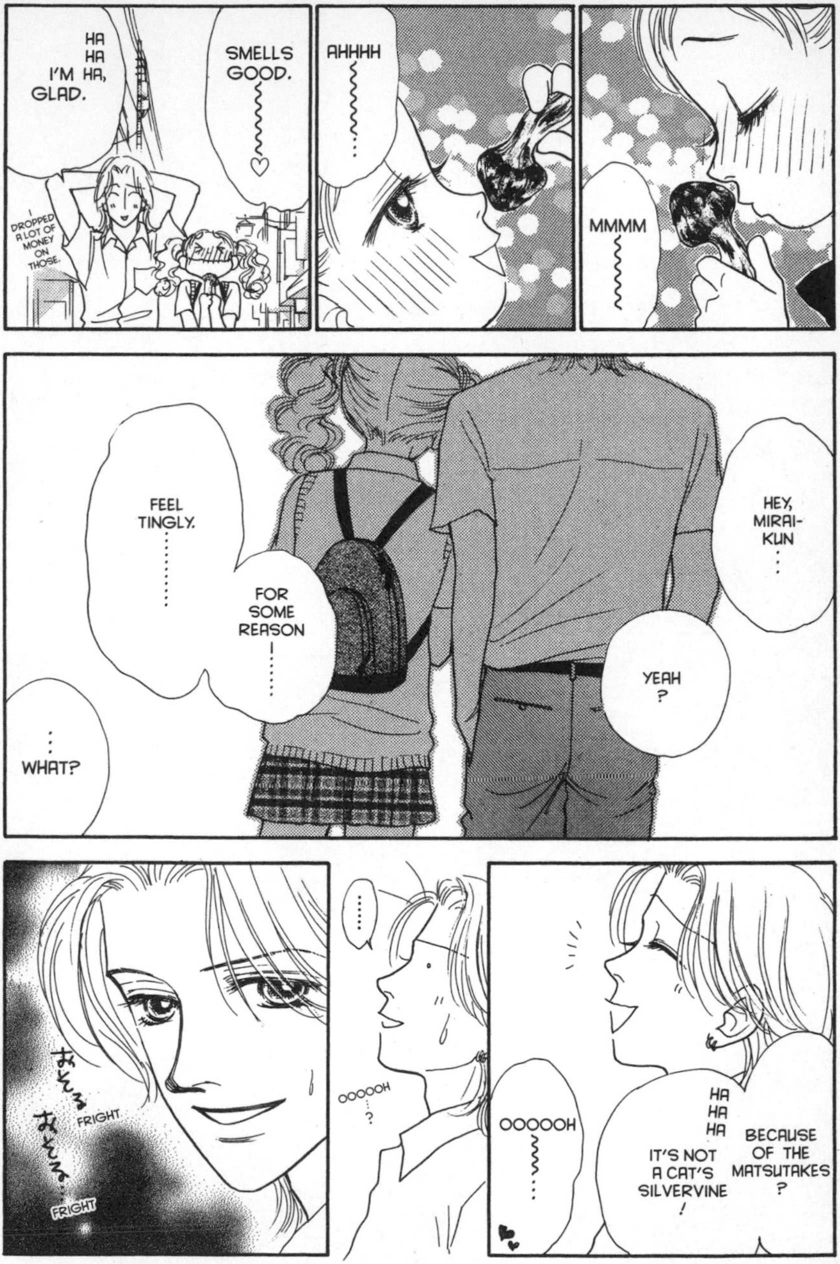
MMMM
AHHHH
SMELLS GOOD.
HA HA HA, I'M GLAD.
I DROPPED A LOT OF MONEY ON THOSE.
HEY, MIRAI-KUN...
YEAH?
FOR SOME REASON I......
FEEL TINGLY.......
...WHAT?
BECAUSE OF THE MATSUTAKES?
HA HA HA
IT'S NOT A CAT'S SILVERVINE!
OOOOOH~...
......
OOOOOH...?
おそる FRIGHT
おそる... FRIGHT

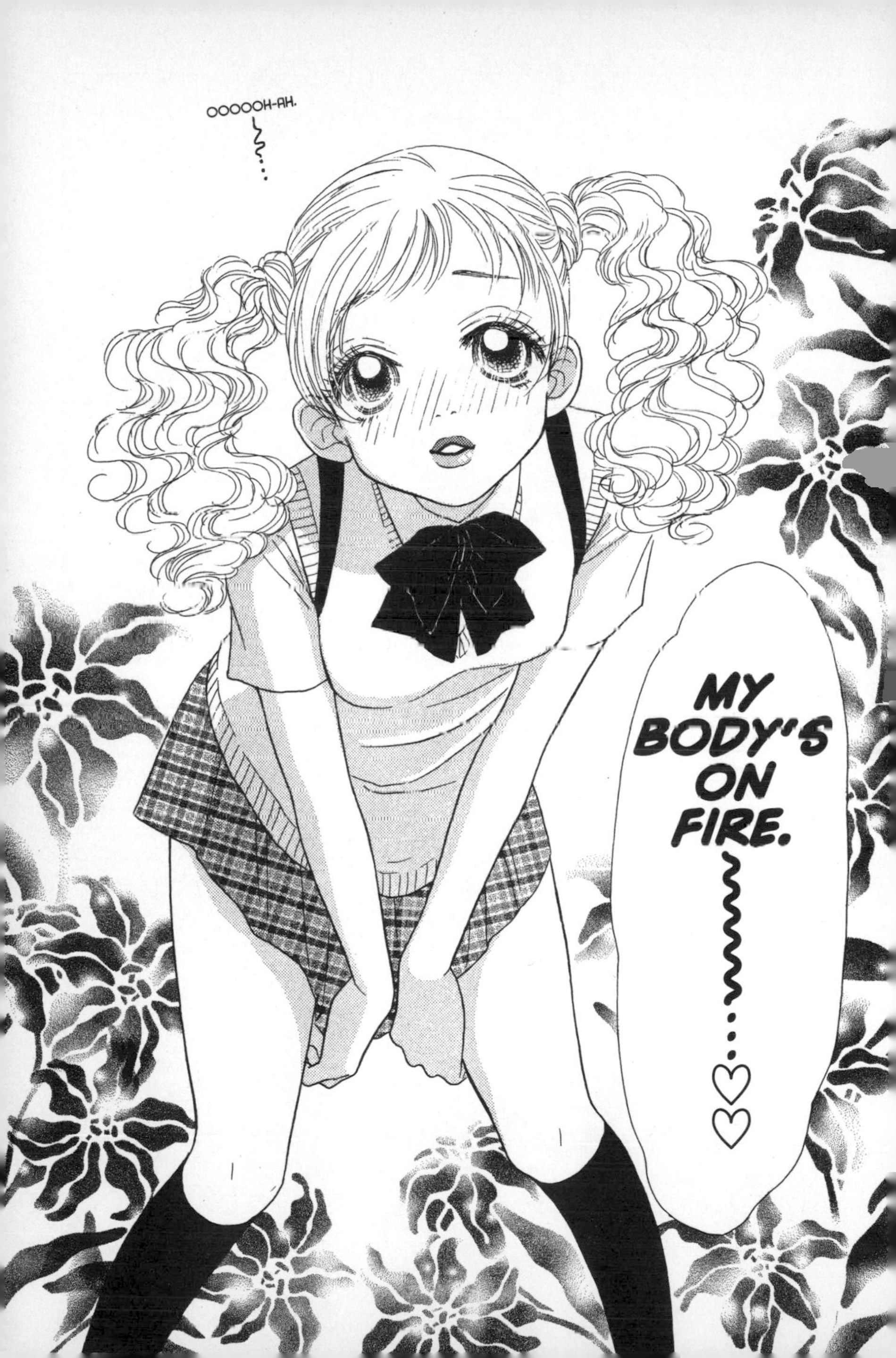
OOOOOH-AH.
MY BODY'S ON FIRE.

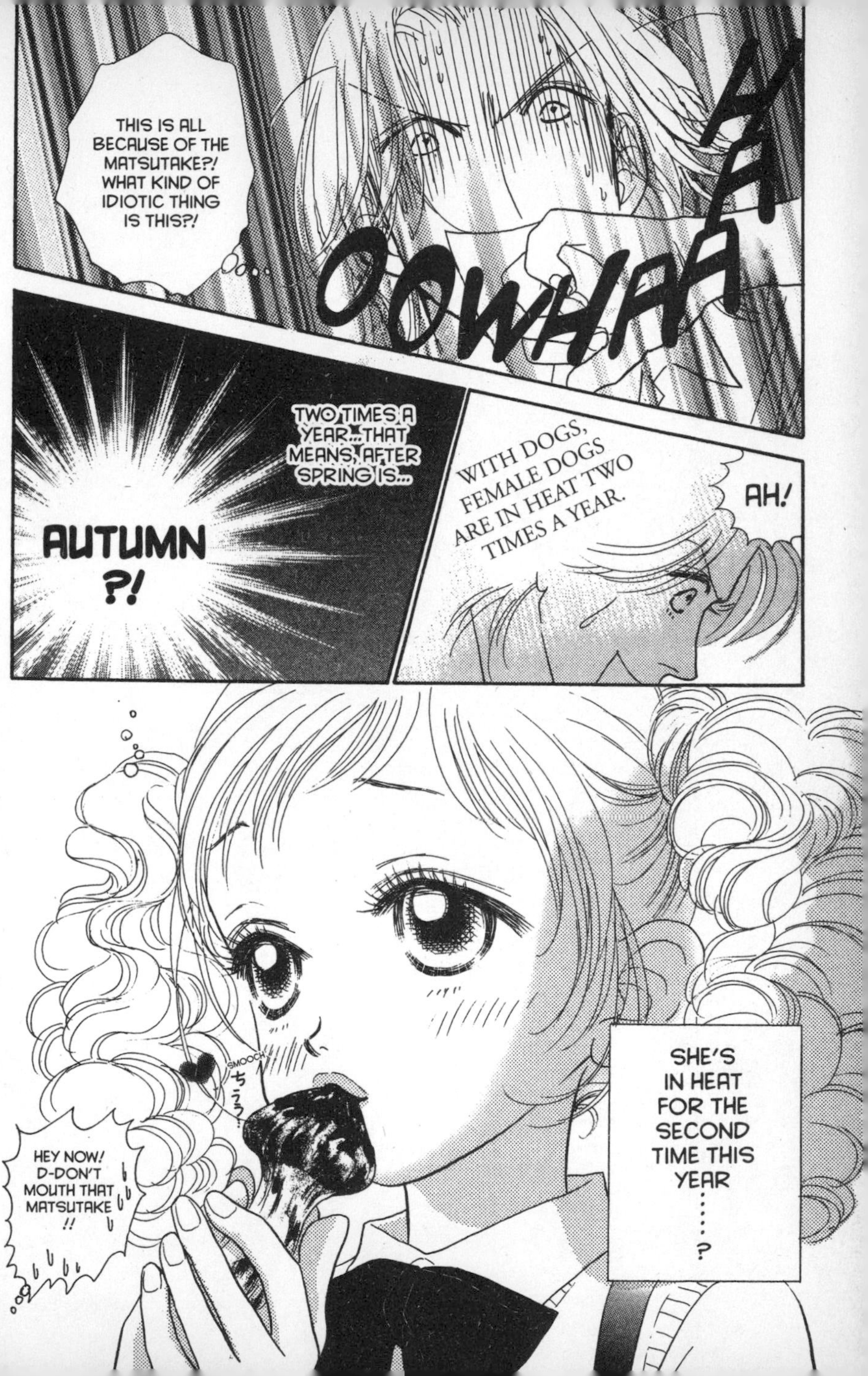

THIS IS ALL BECAUSE OF THE MATSUTAKE?! WHAT KIND OF IDIOTIC THING IS THIS?!
AAA
OOWHAA
AH!
WITH DOGS, FEMALE DOGS ARE IN HEAT TWO TIMES A YEAR.
TWO TIMES A YEAR...THAT MEANS, AFTER SPRING IS...
AUTUMN ?!
SHE'S IN HEAT FOR THE SECOND TIME THIS YEAR .....?
SMOOCH
HEY NOW! D-DON'T MOUTH THAT MATSUTAKE !!

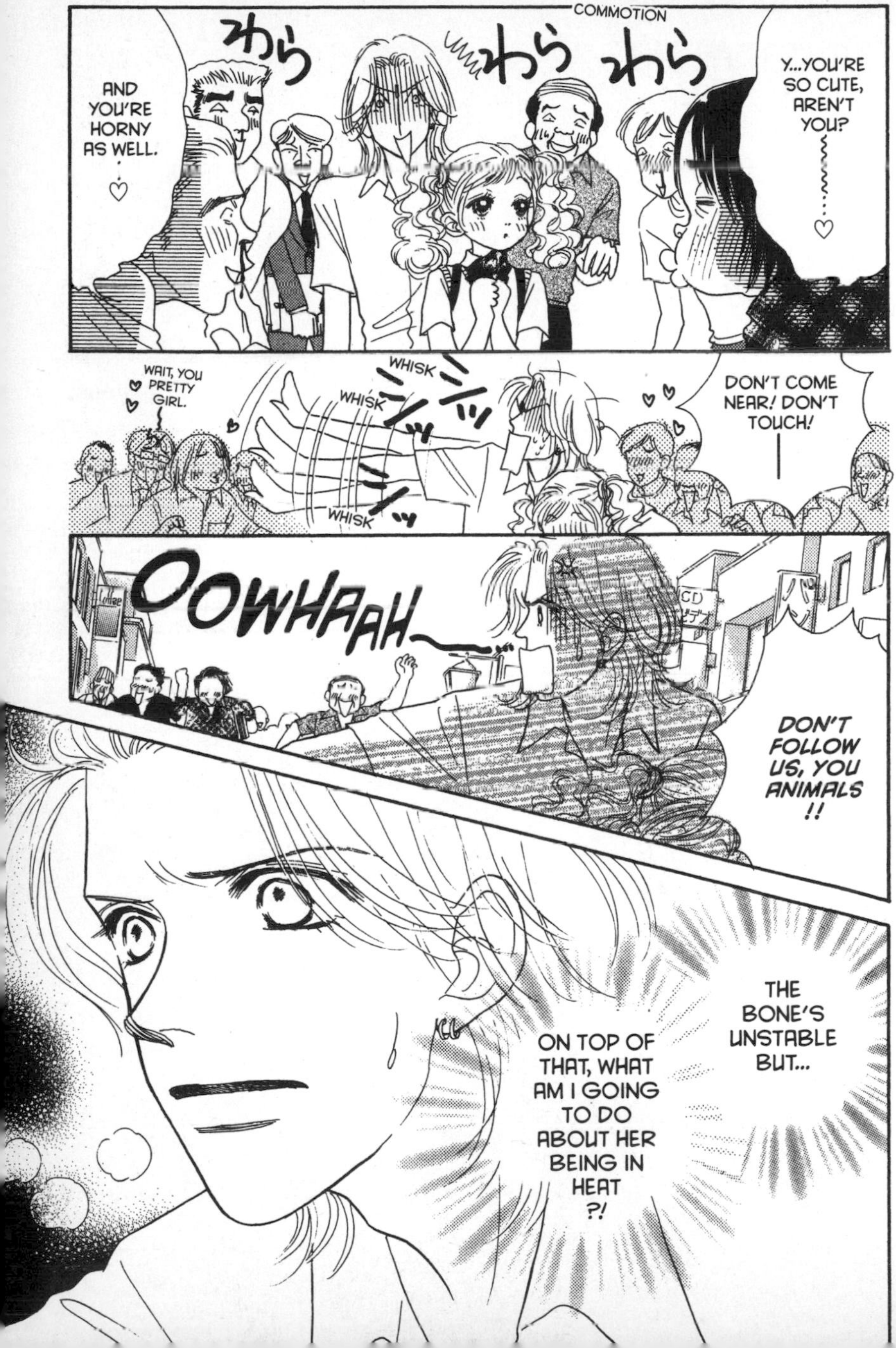
Y...YOU'RE SO CUTE, AREN'T YOU? ♡
COMMOTION
わら わら わら
AND YOU'RE HORNY AS WELL. ♡
DON'T COME NEAR! DON'T TOUCH!
WHISK
WHISK
WHISK
WAIT, YOU PRETTY GIRL.
DON'T FOLLOW US, YOU ANIMALS!!
OOWHAAH~
THE BONE'S UNSTABLE BUT...
ON TOP OF THAT, WHAT AM I GOING TO DO ABOUT HER BEING IN HEAT?!

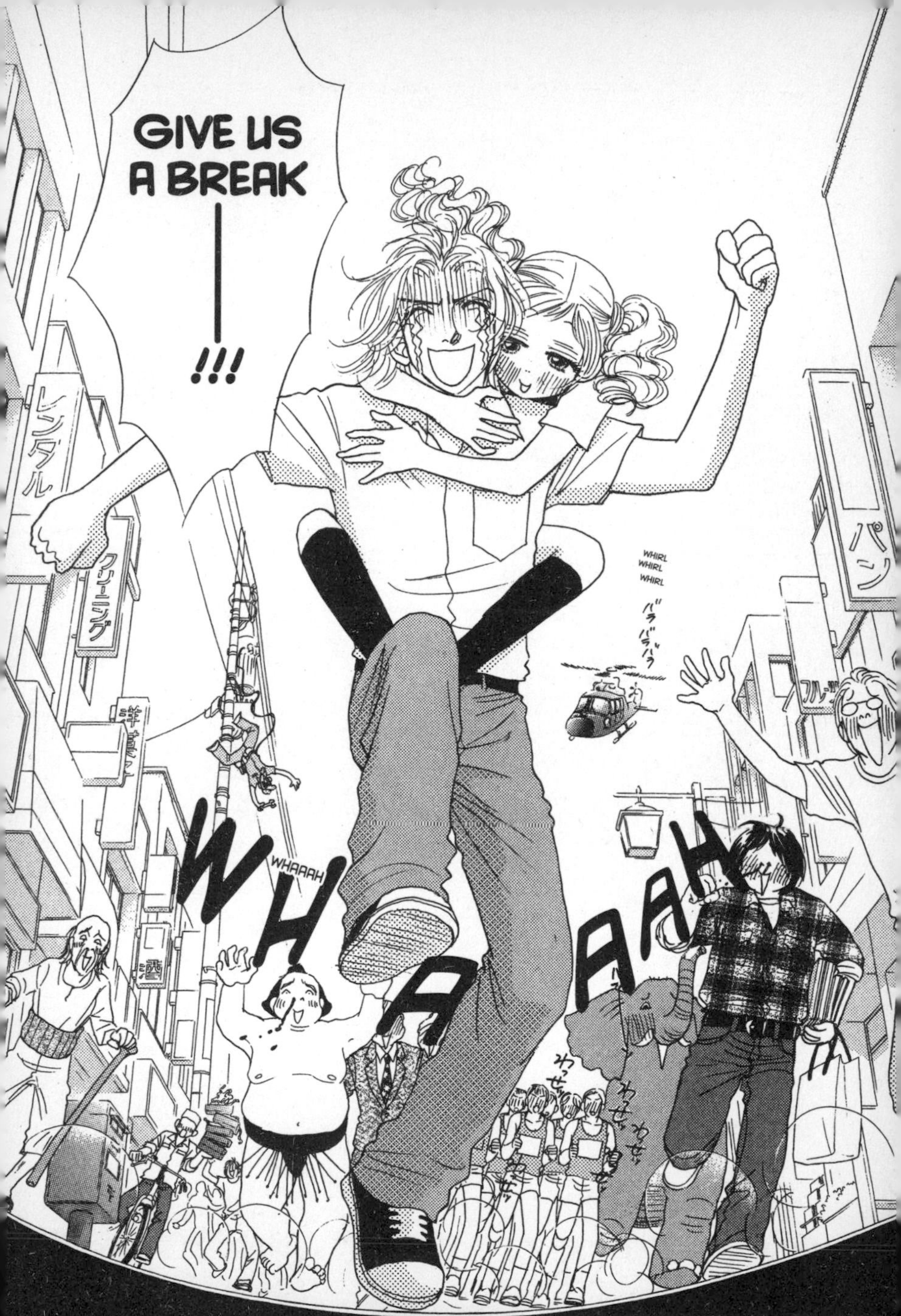
GIVE US A BREAK—!!!
WHIRL WHIRL WHIRL
バラバラバラ
パン
レンタル
クリーニング
WHAAAAH
WHAAAH
CONTINUED IN GURU GURU PON-CHAN 7

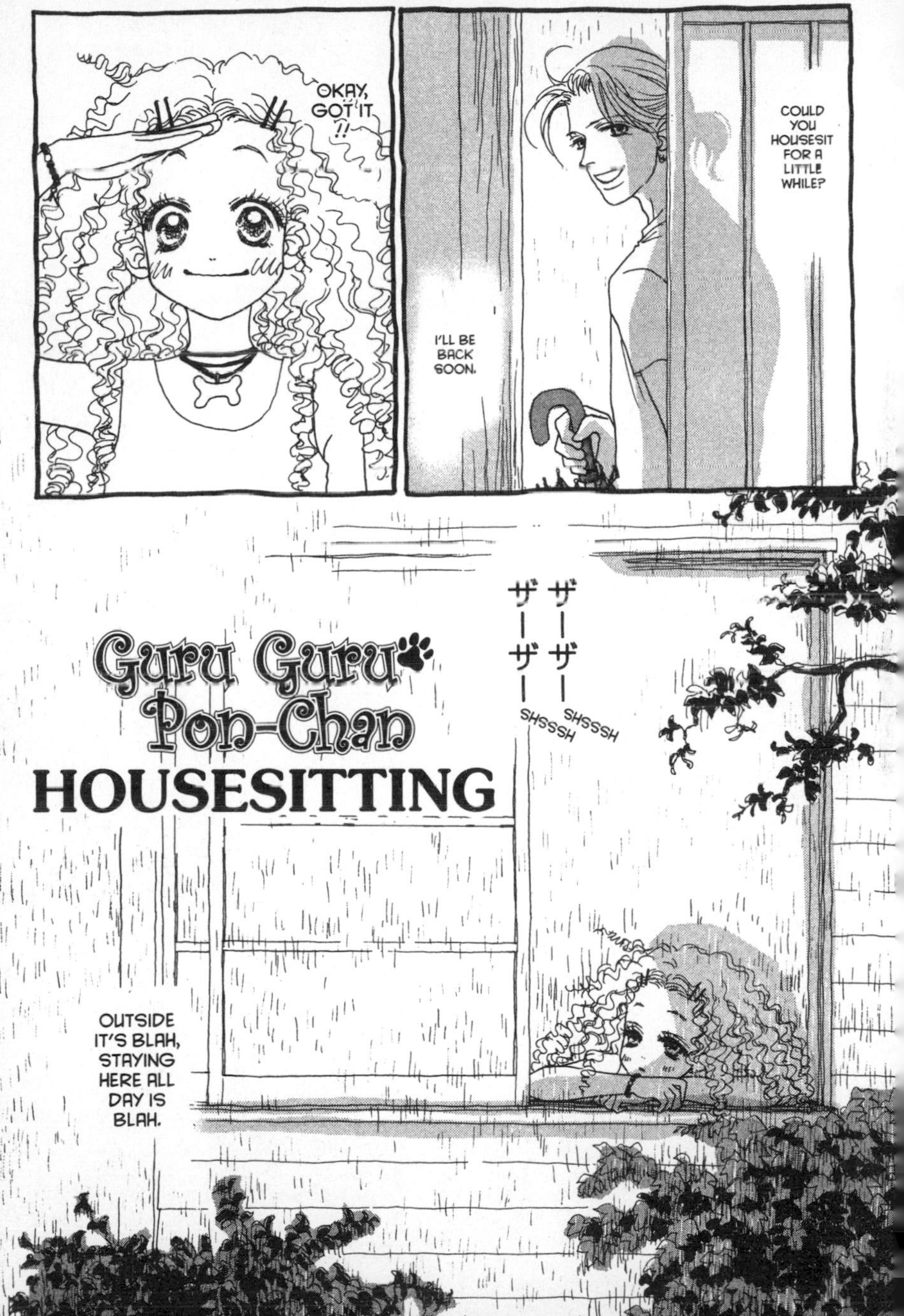
COULD YOU HOUSESIT FOR A LITTLE WHILE?
I'LL BE BACK SOON.
OKAY, GOT IT!!
ザーザー
ザーザー
SHSSSH
SHSSSH
Guru Guru Pon-Chan
HOUSESITTING
OUTSIDE IT'S BLAH, STAYING HERE ALL DAY IS BLAH.

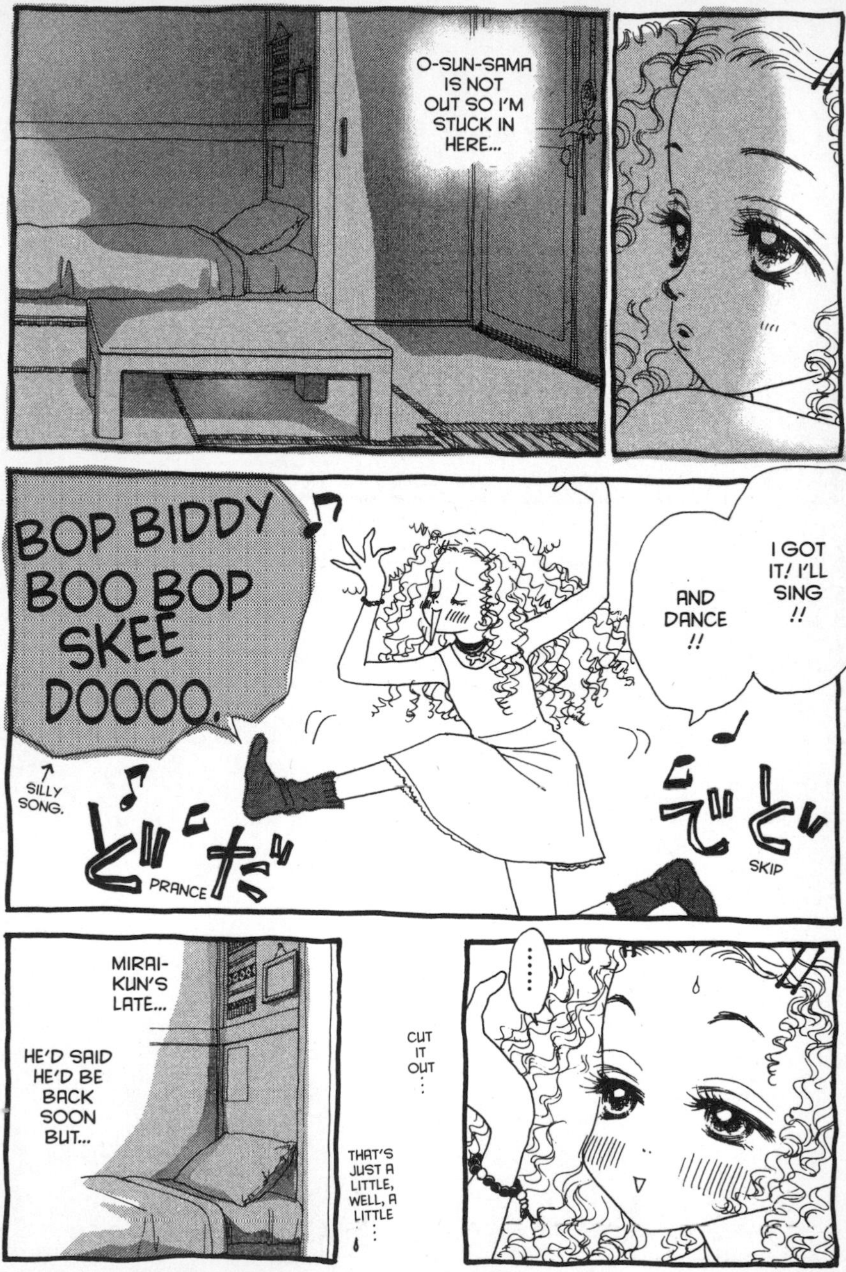
O-SUN-SAMA IS NOT OUT SO I'M STUCK IN HERE...
I GOT IT! I'LL SING !!
AND DANCE !!
SKIP
BOP BIDDY BOO BOP SKEE DOOOO.
SILLY SONG.
PRANCE
......
CUT IT OUT...
THAT'S JUST A LITTLE, WELL, A LITTLE ...
MIRAI-KUN'S LATE...
HE'D SAID HE'D BE BACK SOON BUT...

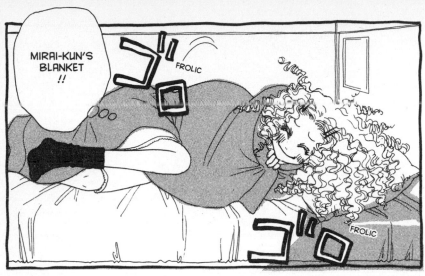

MIRAI-KUN'S BLANKET !!
ゴロ
FROLIC
ゴロ
FROLIC
くふ
GIGGLE
IT SMELLS LIKE MIRAI-KUN'S. ♡
IT'S LIKE BEING HUGGED BY MIRAI-KUN. ♡ ♡
ぎゅむむ
SQUEEZE
I CAN IMAGINE IT. ♡
I'LL IMAGINE MORE. ♡ ♡
ちゅううう
SMOOCH

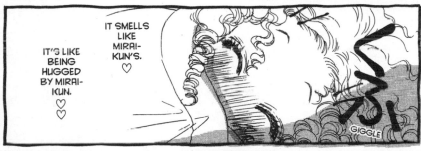

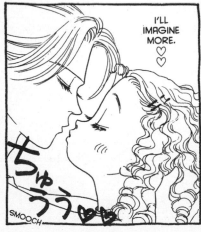

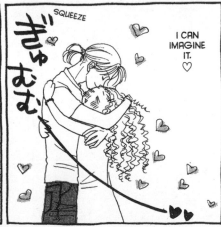

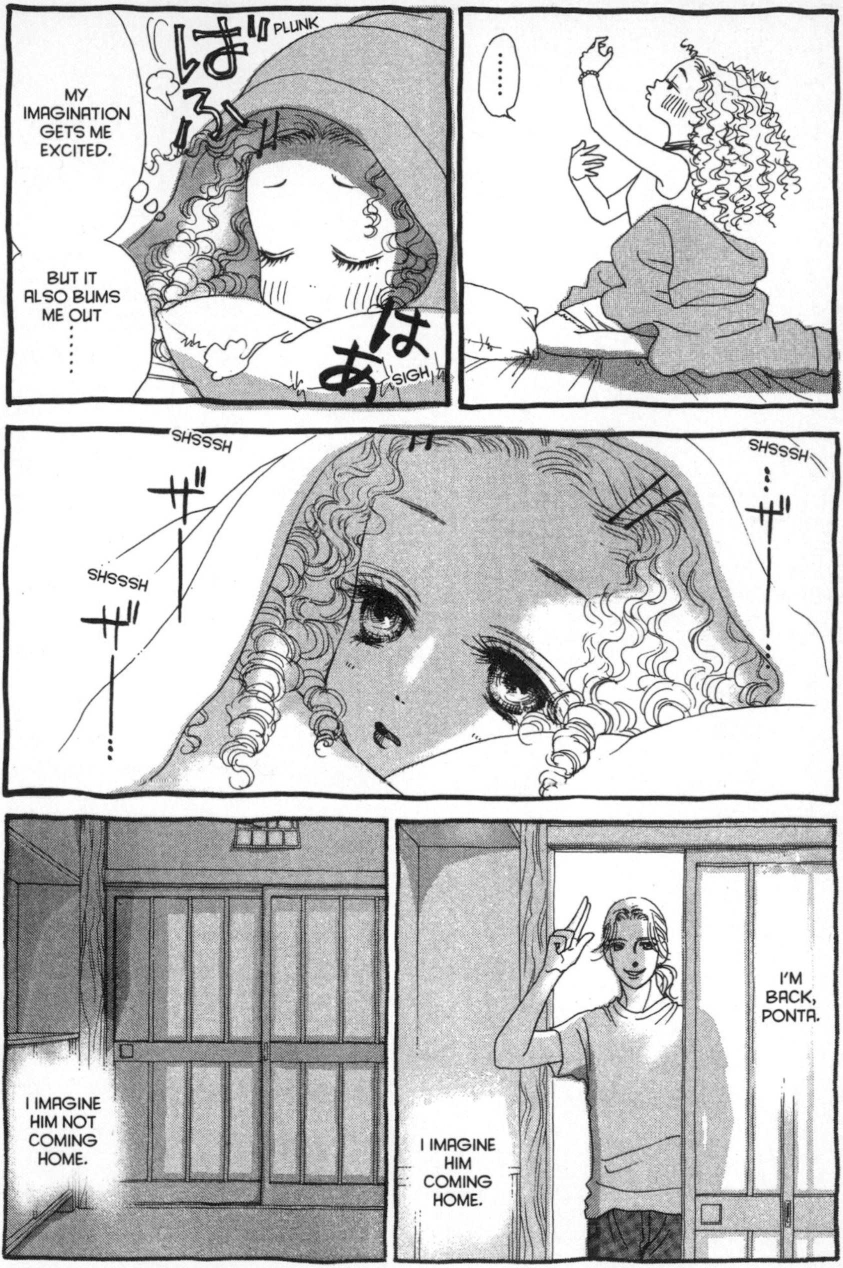
......
PLUNK
MY IMAGINATION GETS ME EXCITED.
BUT IT ALSO BUMS ME OUT......
はあ
SIGH
SHSSSH
ザー
SHSSSH
ザー......
SHSSSH
ザー......
I'M BACK, PONTA.
I IMAGINE HIM COMING HOME.
I IMAGINE HIM NOT COMING HOME.

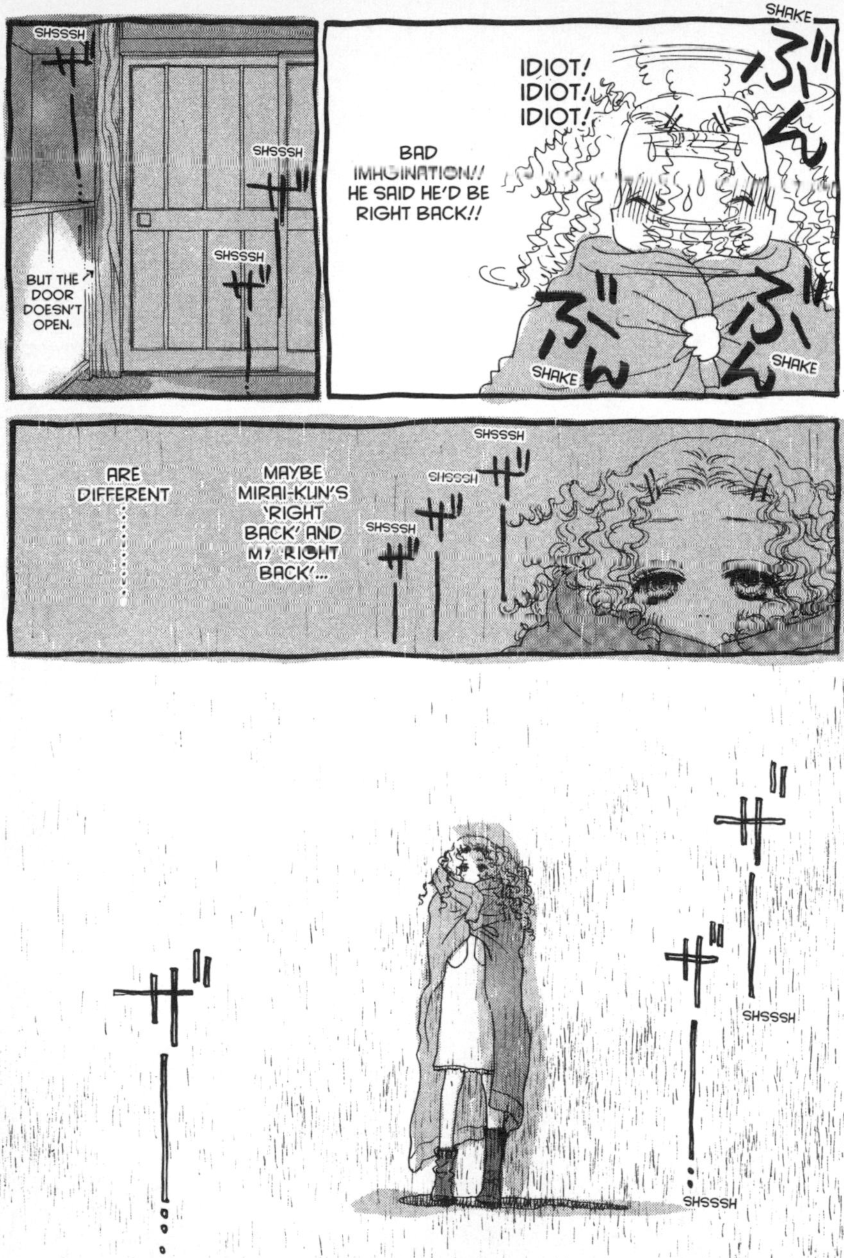
SHAKE
IDIOT! IDIOT! IDIOT!
BAD IMAGINATION!! HE SAID HE'D BE RIGHT BACK!!
SHAKE
SHAKE
SHSSSH
SHSSSH
SHSSSH
BUT THE DOOR DOESN'T OPEN.
SHSSSH
SHSSSH
SHSSSH
MAYBE MIRAI-KUN'S 'RIGHT BACK' AND MY 'RIGHT BACK'...
ARE DIFFERENT ....
SHSSSH
SHSSSH
SHSSSH

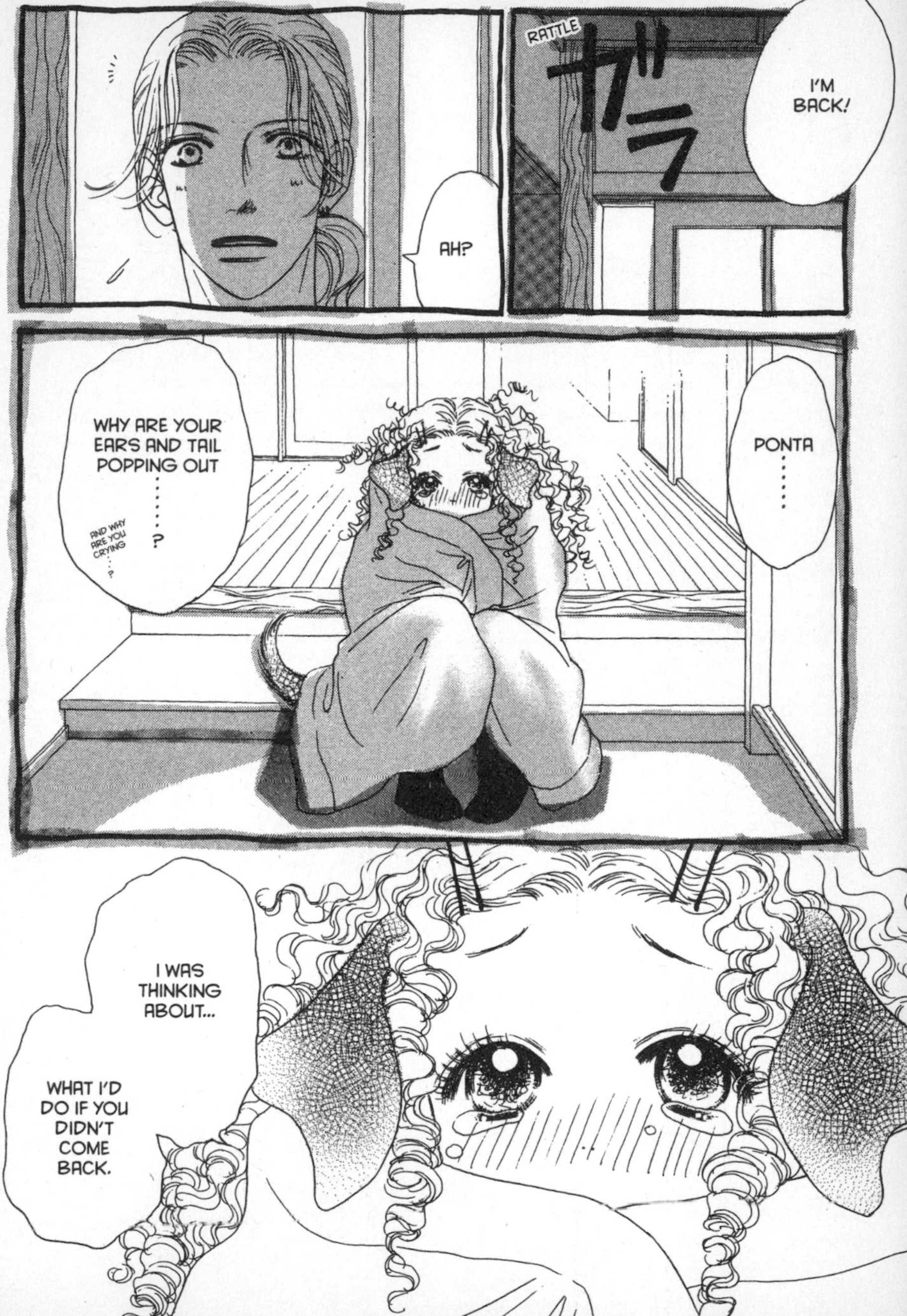
RATTLE
I'M BACK!
AH?
PONTA......
WHY ARE YOUR EARS AND TAIL POPPING OUT......?
AND WHY ARE YOU CRYING...?
I WAS THINKING ABOUT...
WHAT I'D DO IF YOU DIDN'T COME BACK.

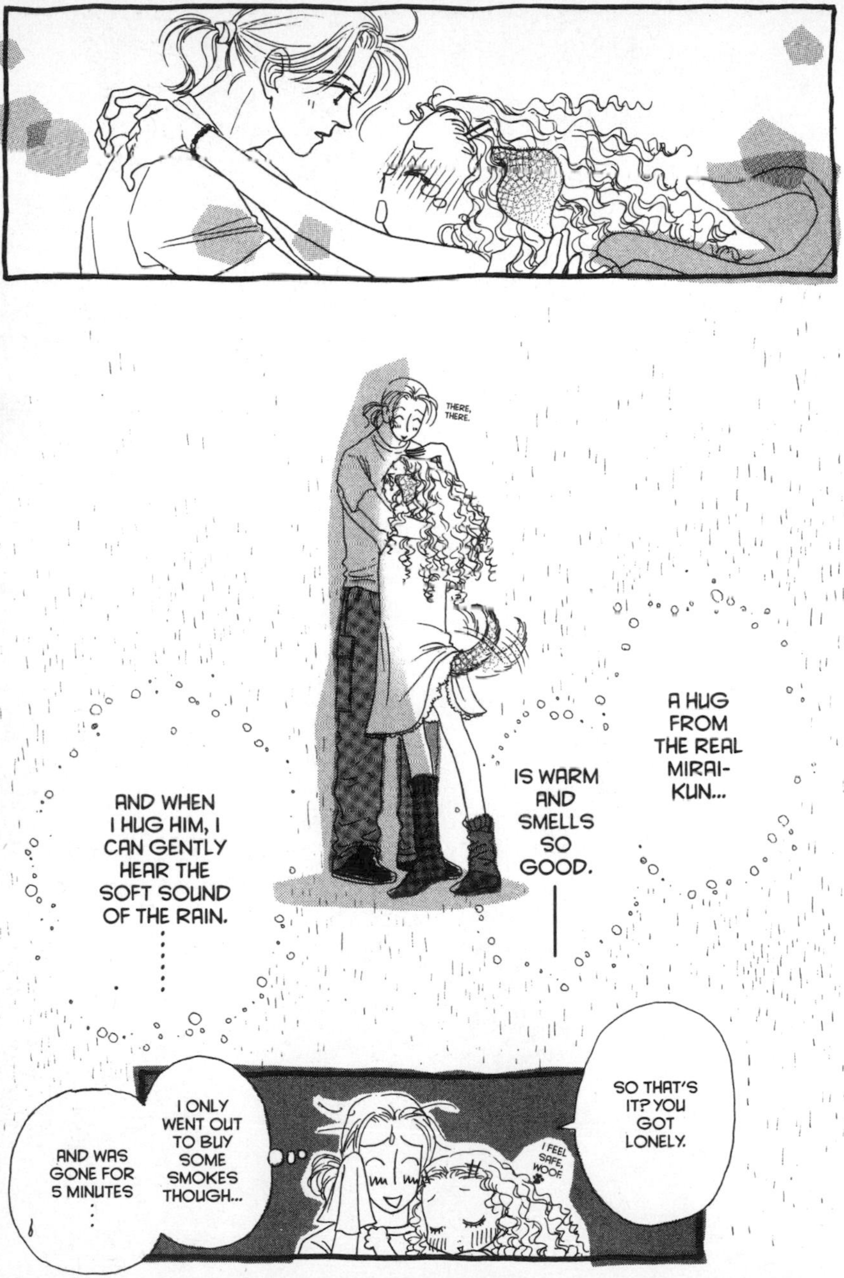
THERE, THERE.
A HUG FROM THE REAL MIRAI-KUN...
IS WARM AND SMELLS SO GOOD. —
AND WHEN I HUG HIM, I CAN GENTLY HEAR THE SOFT SOUND OF THE RAIN. ...
SO THAT'S IT? YOU GOT LONELY.
I FEEL SAFE, WOOF.
I ONLY WENT OUT TO BUY SOME SMOKES THOUGH...
AND WAS GONE FOR 5 MINUTES ...

THE END

About the Author

Satomi Ikezawa, a prolific manga-ka, finished *Guru Guru Pon-Chan* in 2000. She recently completed *Othello*, which is being serialized in the Kodansha weekly manga magazine, *Bessatsu Friend*.

Ikezawa won the 24th Kodansha Manga Prize in 2000 for *Guru Guru Pon-Chan*.

She has two Labradors, named Guts and Ponta. Both are male, despite the Ponta of *Guru Guru Pon-Chan* being a girl.

Translation Notes

Japanese is a tricky language for most Westerners, and translation is often more art than science. For your edification and reading pleasure, here are notes on some of the places where we could have gone in a different direction in our translation of the work, or where a Japanese cultural reference is used.

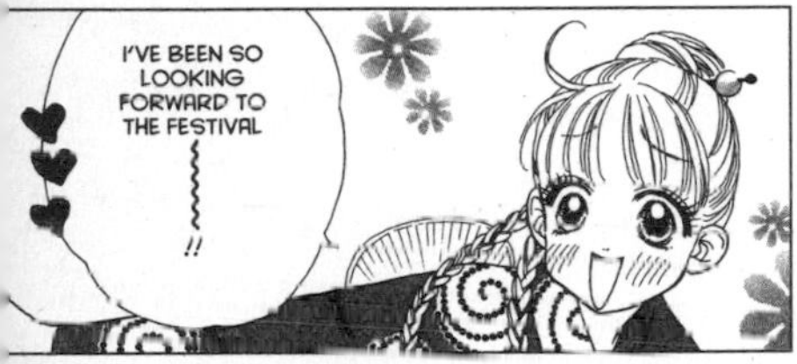
I'VE BEEN SO LOOKING FORWARD TO THE FESTIVAL !!

The festival, page 9

In Japan, festivals, or *matsuri*, are held year round, but especially in the summer. These festivals are often—but not always—associated with a shrine or temple. In the summer, people dress up in their *yukata*, or summer kimonos, and enjoy the numerous food stalls, carnival-type games, and impressive fireworks displays held all over the country—much like American 4th of July celebrations. No wonder Ponta is so excited!

Tortoiseshell candy, page 11

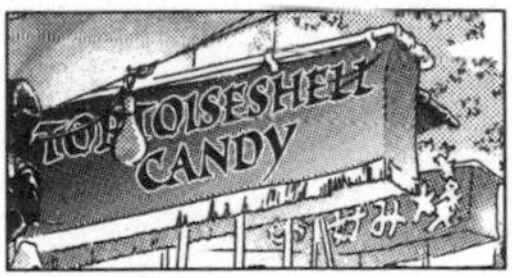
TORTOISESHELL CANDY

Tortoiseshell candy, or *bekkouame*, is a slightly crispy candy made of hot, melted sugar poured into a mold. It's called tortoiseshell candy because the color is similar to that of a tortoiseshell.

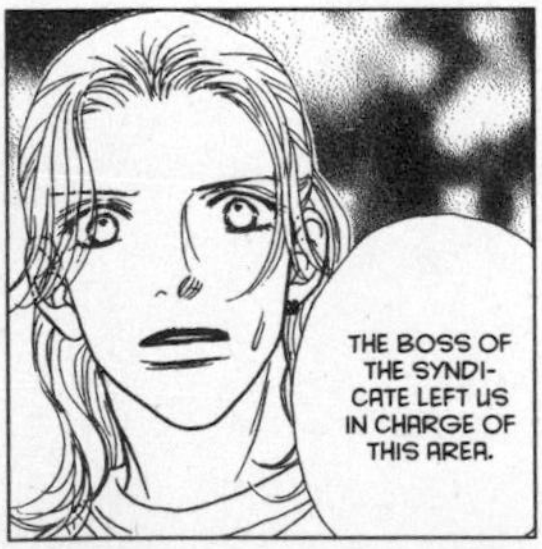
THE BOSS OF THE SYNDI-CATE LEFT US IN CHARGE OF THIS AREA.

The syndicate, page 30

Apparently, these guys are low-level *yakuza*, or Japanese mafia. Like organized crime here, they're involved in various criminal activities and can often be distinguished by a missing pinky, which is the sign of a "made man."

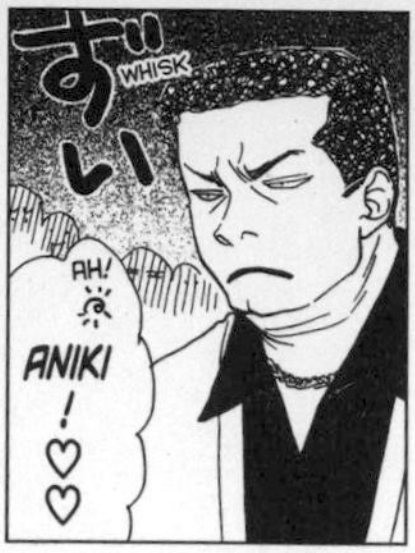
WHISK
AH!
ANIKI!

Aniki, page 41

Aniki is a term of respect and devotion usually reserved for an older brother or peer.

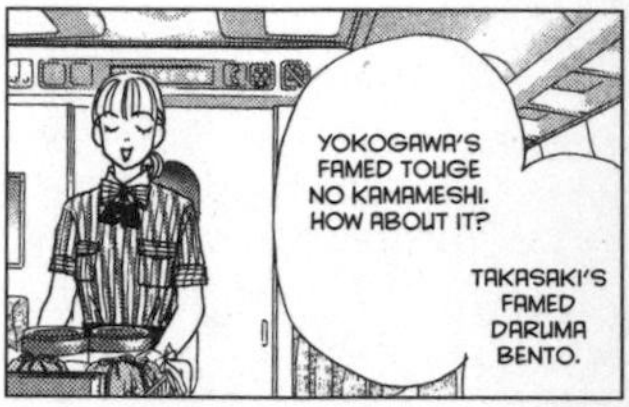
YOKOGAWA'S FAMED TOUGE NO KAMAMESHI. HOW ABOUT IT?
TAKASAKI'S FAMED DARUMA BENTO.

Daruma bento and *Touge no kamameshi*, page 66

A *daruma* is a doll that depicts Bodhidharma, a monk who brought Zen Buddhism to Japan from India. It is believed he lost his arms and legs meditating in a cave for nine years. The dolls have come to represent positive images of hope and perseverance as their round shape enables them to stand up when knocked over. One eye of the doll is usually painted black before a task is undertaken, and the other eye after it is accomplished. The *daruma bento* is sasanishiki rice, stewed mushrooms, ginko nuts, and other mountain veggies in a hollowed out *daruma* doll. *Touge no kamameshi* is rice flavored with soy sauce, topped with chicken and shiitake mushrooms and served in an earthenware pot.

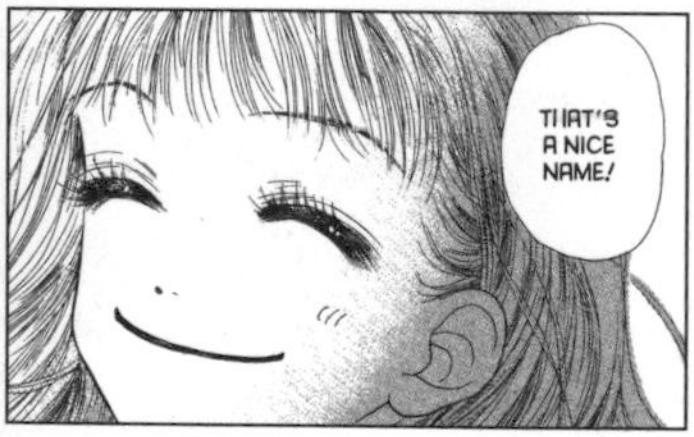
THAT'S A NICE NAME!

Mirai, page 77

Remember that *mirai*, besides being our hero's name, also means "future." Now that is a nice name!

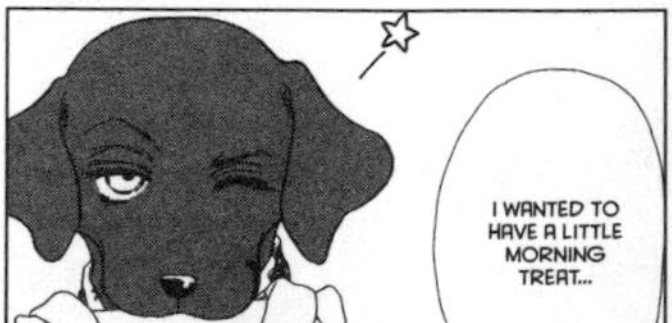
I WANTED TO HAVE A LITTLE MORNING TREAT...

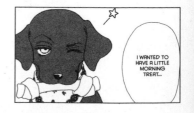

A little morning treat, page 94

The treat Gang offers Ponta is *honneko*, a popular dog treat in Japan. Gang asks Ponta to share *yoake no kohi*, which literally means "daybreak coffee" or "coffee at dawn" and is often used to suggest having morning coffee together after a night of lovemaking. So it's also often used as a sort of pick-up line, along the lines of "*Yoake no kohi ha issho ni nomimasenka?*" or "How about drinking morning coffee together?"

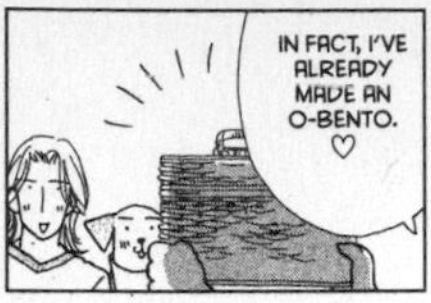
IN FACT, I'VE ALREADY MADE AN O-BENTO. ♡

O-bento, page 103

An *O-bento* is a lunch box filled with neatly arranged food items. The *O-bento* is an art form and there are many books on how to prepare them creatively—a good *O-bento* can be a source of pride for a housewife with a hungry family.

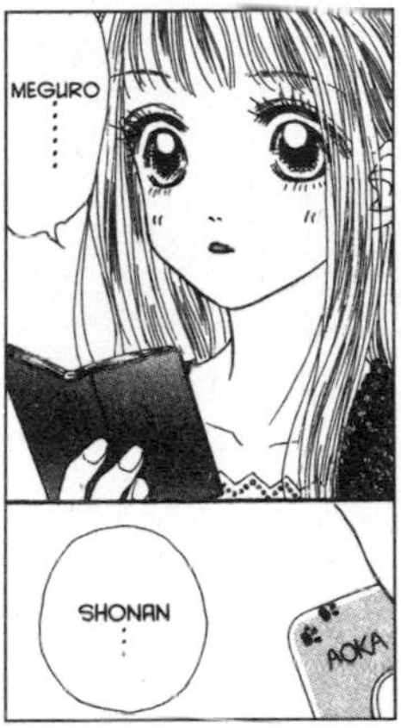
MEGURO
SHONAN
AOKA

Meguro* and *Shonan, page 118

Meguro is one of Tokyo City's 23 ku, or wards. *Shonan* is the southern coastal region of Kanagawa Prefecture.

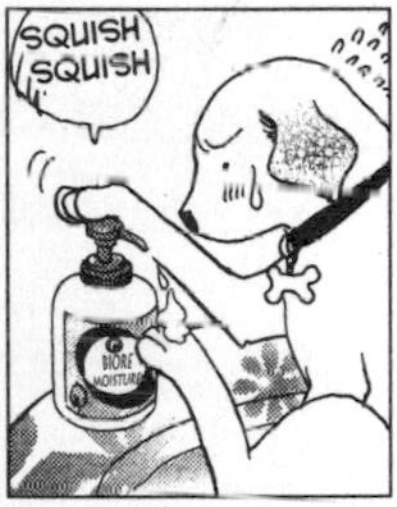
SQUISH SQUISH

Biore, page 140

Biore is a line of hygiene and beauty products in Japan.

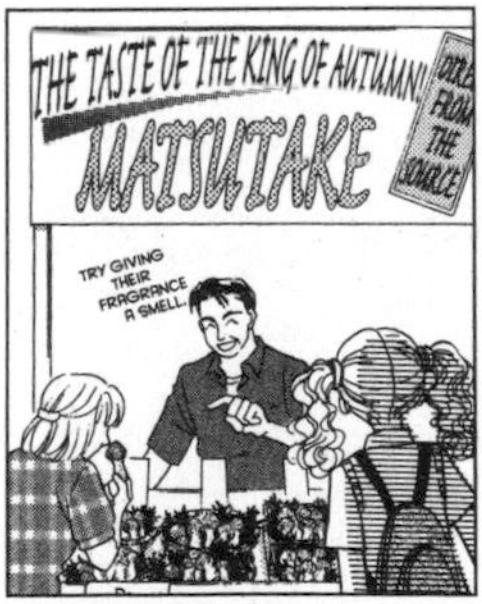
THE TASTE OF THE KING OF AUTUMN!
MATSUTAKE
FROM THE SOURCE!
TRY GIVING THEIR FRAGRANCE A SMELL.

Matsutake, page 163

Matsutake are mushrooms that grow on the roots of the Japanese red pine in autumn. They are highly prized for their rich flavor and strong fragrance. They are extremely expensive and can sell for hundreds of dollars.

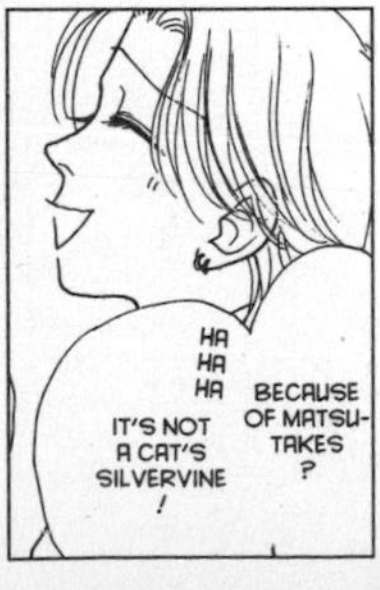
BECAUSE OF MATSUTAKES?
HA HA HA
IT'S NOT A CAT'S SILVERVINE!

Silvervine, page 166

Neko no matatabi means "cat's silvervine" or "silvervine for cats." *Matatabi*, or silvervine, is a plant similar to the kiwi vine and is found in the highlands of Honshu. It's similar to but more powerful than catnip. It is also used in traditional medicine, and its edible berries were once used to make wine.

Preview of Volume 7

We're pleased to present you with a preview from Volume 7. This volume will be available in English soon, but for now you'll have to make do with Japanese!

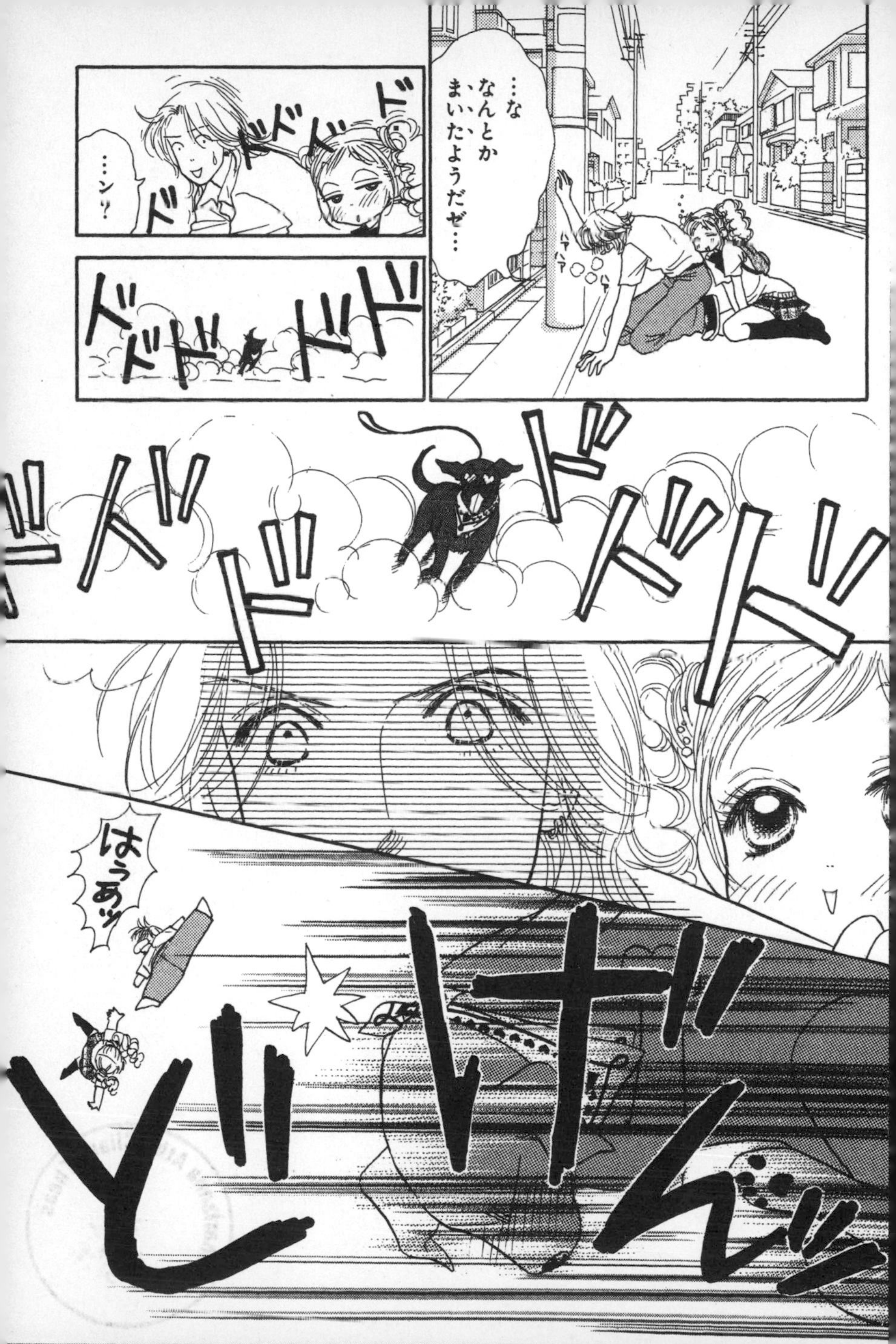
…な
なんとか
まいたようだぜ…
ハァ ハァ ハァ
…
…ン？
ドドドドドド
ドドドドドド
ドドドドドドドッ
はうあッ
どげんッ

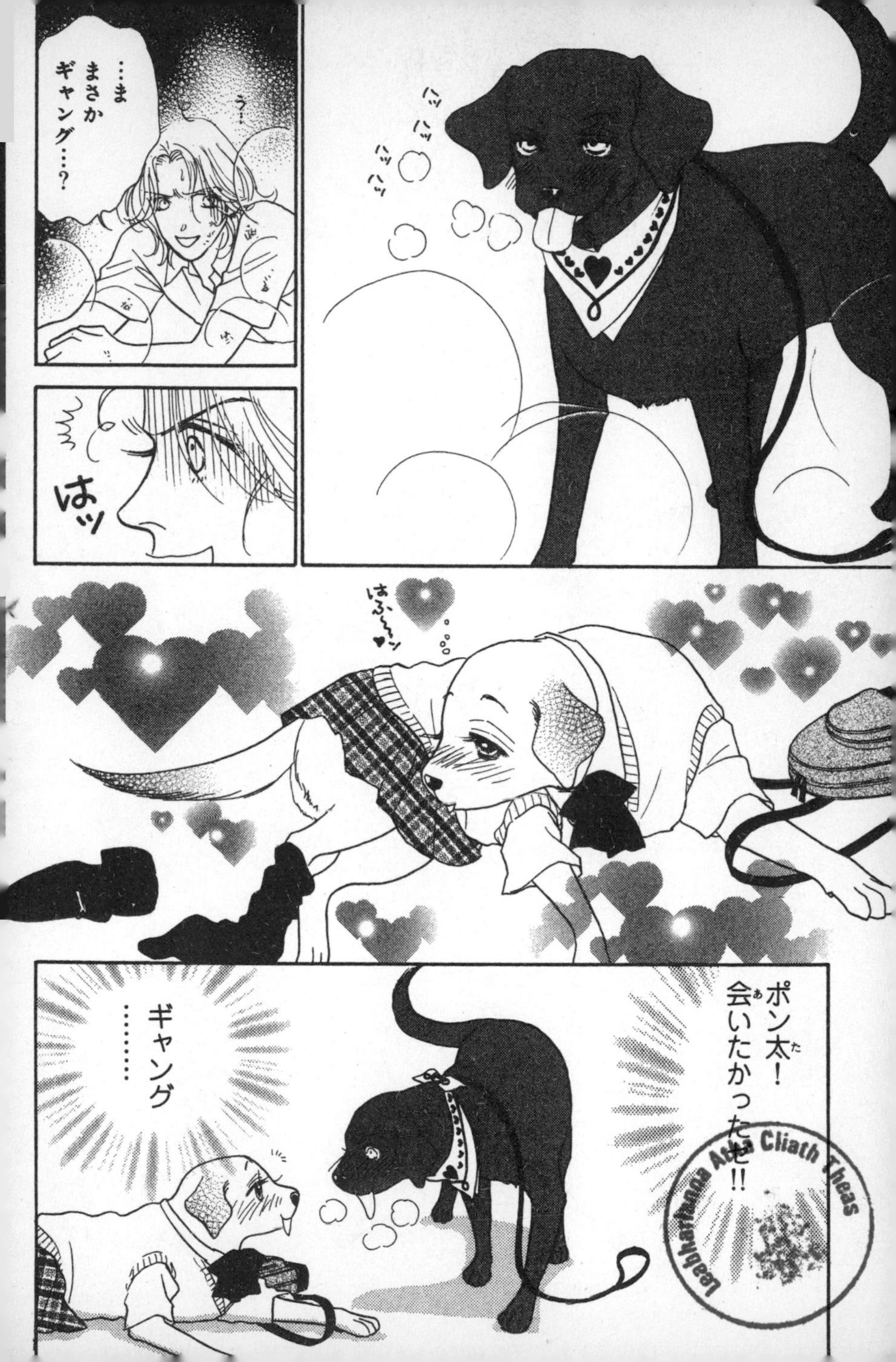

ハッハッ
ハッハッ
…まさかギャング…?
う…
はッ
はふ〜〜ン♥
ポン太!
会いたかったぜ!!
ギャング……

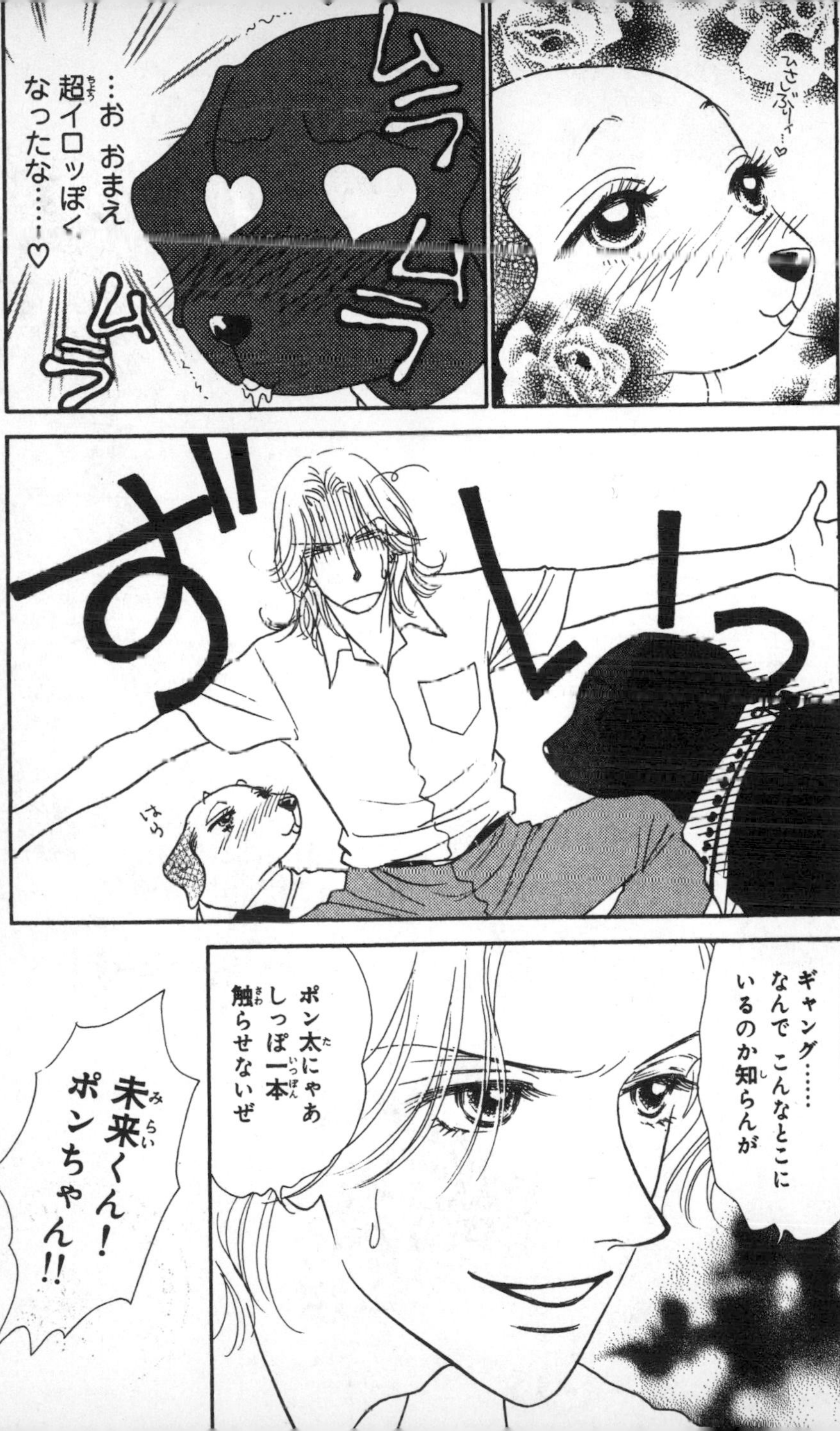
ひさしぶりィ…♡
ムラムラ
…お おまえ 超イロッぽく なったな……♡
ムラ
ずしーっ
ギャング…… なんで こんなとこに いるのか知らんが
ポン太にゃあ しっぽ一本 触らせないぜ
未来くん！ ポンちゃん!!

TOMARE!

STOP!!

YOU'RE GOING THE WRONG WAY!

MANGA IS A COMPLETELY DIFFERENT TYPE OF READING EXPERIENCE.

TO START AT THE BEGINNING, GO TO THE END!

THAT'S RIGHT! AUTHENTIC MANGA IS READ THE TRADITIONAL JAPANESE WAY—FROM RIGHT TO LEFT. EXACTLY THE OPPOSITE OF HOW ENGLISH BOOKS ARE READ. IT'S EASY TO FOLLOW: JUST GO TO THE OTHER END OF THE BOOK, AND READ EACH PAGE—AND EACH PANEL—FROM THE RIGHT SIDE TO THE LEFT SIDE, STARTING AT THE TOP RIGHT. NOW YOU'RE EXPERIENCING MANGA AS IT WAS MEANT TO BE.

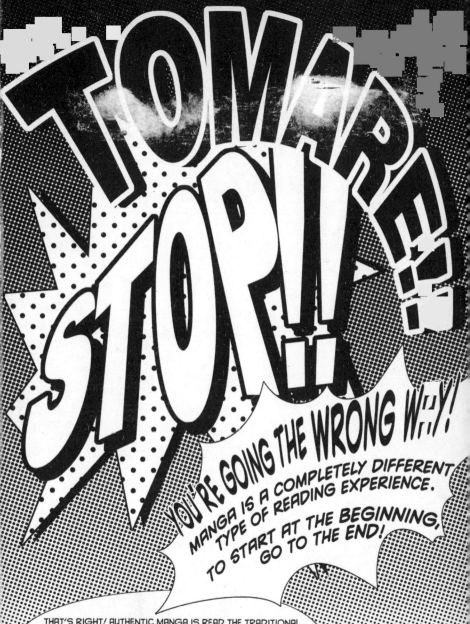